THE DANCER

Other books by Leland Cooley

FICTION

The Run for Home
God's High Table
The Richest Poor Folks
The Trouble With Heaven
Condition Pink
California
The Art Colony

NONFICTION (WITH LEE MORRISON COOLEY)

The Simple Truth About Western Land Investment
The Retirement Trap
How to Avoid the Retirement Trap
Pre-medicated Murder

THE DANCER

LELAND COOLEY

STEIN AND DAY/*Publishers*/New York

The Dancer is for my own nonfictional "Leya," who accepted my bouquet from the stage of the Adelphi Theater lo, those many performances ago.

L.C.
June 1977

First published in 1978

Designed by Tere LoPrete

PRINTED IN THE UNITED STATES OF AMERICA

Stein and Day/*Publishers*/Scarborough House,
Briarcliff Manor, N.Y. 10510

Library of Congress Cataloging in Publication Data

Cooley, Leland Frederick.
The dancer.

I. Title.
PZ4.C774Dan [PS3553.O564] 813'.5'4 77-81040
ISBN 0-8128-2319-2

The Dancer is also intended as a tribute to that enormously talented, disciplined, good-natured, and energetic band of "gypsies" who worked with this one-time television musical producer.

That my wife (then my choreographer) recognized exceptional talent is attested to by the extraordinary number of dancers who have graduated from the chorus line to distinguish themselves on both sides of the cameras and the footlights.

They numbered nearly one hundred on the Chesterfield Perry Como Show alone. They are acknowledged with affection and admiration in the following roster. Any omissions are entirely inadvertent and, quite probably, are the result of time's erosion of both records and recollections.

Dick Beard
Anna Baldwin
Margie Beddow
Lynn Bernay
Jeanna Belkin
Pat Birch
Jack Blair
Bill Bradley
Mark Breaux
Hank Brunjes
Jean Caples
Anna Collins
Lynn Connor
Lyn Connorty
Dean Crane
Peter Dane
Linda Danson
Harry Day
Doug Dean
Marlene Dell
Imelda De Martin
Michael Dominico
Ray Dorian
Sandra Devlin
Helene Ellis
Bettina Edwards
Don Farsworth
Shellie Farrell
Ronnie Field
Gary Fleming
Glenn Forbes
Cyprienne Gabol
Paul Gannon
Luanna Gardner
Trudi Gasparinetti
Janet Gaylord
Peter Gennaro
Peter Gladke
Irma Grant
Tommy Hansen
Jean Harris
Suanne Hartman
Gretchen Hauser
Chris Karner
Pat Karlis
Anna Konstance
Roy Kreiser
Alicia Krug

Joan Kruger
Ray Kyle
Grebb Laber
Hugh Lambert
Al Lanti
Kenneth Lawrence
Jackie Laughery
John Laverty
Joe Layton
David Lober
Linda Lombard
Joan Lowe
Loyce Lozano
Ray Malone
Remi Martel
Ethel Martin
Frank Marasco
Rudy Mattiace
Matt Mattox
Marian McPerson
Patricia Metcalf
Bill Miller
Buzz Miller
Meri Miller
Jean Mingin
Nancy Newton
Frank Pagliaro
Janet Perry
Ingred Secretan
Jet Sharon
Buff Shurr
Schwanee Smith
Marla Stevens
Rita Tanno
Mary Ellen Terry
Nick Vanoff
Wendy Waldron
Toni Wheelis
Joe Wiley
David Winters
Joan Wynne
Carolyn Wynn

"When lovely woman stoops to folly
And finds too late that men betray.
What charm can sooth her melancholy?
What art can wash her guilt away?"

OLIVER GOLDSMITH

CHAPTER 1

"*One*—two—three—four— *That's* right—three—four— *Watch* Leya—three—four— *Very* good—three—four—"

Each time she heard Mrs. Zuckerman admonish the other seven girls to follow her example as they rehearsed for the fifth-grade dance recital, eleven-year-old Leya Marks glanced across the hall at her father.

Harry Marks, his merry blue eyes glistening, nodded his approval. *My God,* he thought—and how many times had he thought since Anya had died in childbirth—*how lucky I am to have such a good home for my daughter to be raised in as the Brooklyn Hebrew Orphan Asylum!* Mrs. Zuckerman's hand continued to set the tempo as the other girls struck dainty poses, and Leya stepped downstage for her solo.

When she finished with a pirouette in fourth position, Leya felt her face flush as her father's applause echoed through the big indoor playroom. Mrs. Zuckerman smiled and applauded, too. "Clap your hands for Leya, girls," she said. "And Mr. Marks and I are going to applaud for all of you because you have done very well."

Harry Marks led a second round of applause. Mrs. Zuckerman ordered all of the girls to curtsy; then she dismissed Leya to go to her father. An instant later she was in his arms, unaware that the teacher was urging the others not to linger.

Harry released his bear hug and held his daughter away to look at her.

"Papa, did you see how I dance?" she asked, reaching out to touch the tight curls of dark-brown hair at his temples.

"Of course I saw you dance, baby! How could I not see the greatest dancer in the whole world when she is my daughter?" He slipped an arm beneath Leya and lifted her onto his lap. "*Bubeleh,*" he said, "someday the world will watch how you dance—and they'll pay good money, too." He pulled her close again and snuggled his cheek against the silky cushion of thick braids coiled atop her head.

"Go wash your face now, and get your coat. We're going to Cousin Minnie's."

Harry watched his daughter skip across the cement floor. *So much like Anya,* he thought again. *The same fine features—the hair thick, the color of burnished copper. And her face, too—heart-shaped, with Anya's uptilted, gold-flecked brown eyes.*

Leya was just beginning to show signs of developing. She would be slenderer than Anya, but Harry knew her graceful little body would be strong like his own. Beauty, his daughter had already—and intelligence, too. Even at three and four her questions could confound him! Also, from the very beginning, didn't she show a love for music?

He recalled the little Swiss music box with the dainty ballerina atop it that whirled to the tinkling of the "Sugar Plum Fairy" melody. The music box had been his most extravagant present when he was courting Anya. They had laughed together when she had tried to imitate the mechanical pirouettes, and he, with comic courtliness, had pretended to be "de grreat Rawshun dancer, Igor Marksky!"

Harry had wept the first time he had played the music box for his infant daughter. Later, he had managed to laugh, too, when Leya gurgled and tried to move her tiny body—still in diapers—in rhythm. Could he—and his darling Anya, if she had lived—give their child any greater gifts than a good body, an inquisitive mind, and a love of music? Unaccountably, he recalled a fragment of an old Hebrew prayer:

The Dancer

Blessed are Thou, O Lord our God, King of the Universe, who dealest kindly even with the unworthy, for unto me Thou has shown great favor . . .

Things would be good now even if Wall Street was having *tsouris.* He would be able to do for Leya. Five years a mechanic at Studebaker's Brooklyn Service Center on Dean Street. Forty dollars a week. Not so much as he had made working for Salvatore Di Romano's bootlegging operation, but not such nervous work, either. *Oy veh is mir!* What a father wouldn't do for his kid!

For a moment Harry Marks did not see Shirley Zuckerman of the Women's Auxiliary standing in front of him.

"You know, Mr. Marks, Leya is a very gifted child."

Rising from the chair, Harry extended his hand. "Thank you, Mrs. Zuckerman. What could a father hear to make him happier?"

"You're welcome, Mr. Marks." Lowering her eyes modestly, she added, "Would you believe—once I was going to be a great dancer?"

"I believe, Mrs. Zuckerman," Harry lied gallantly.

"If you didn't, I wouldn't blame you," she responded, flattening her palms atop her ample bosom. "It was all in here, Mr. Marks, but it wouldn't come out here," she said as she extended a foot with bovine grace from beneath her long wool skirt. "But your Leya has it in her heart—and in her arms, in her legs, in her feet, in her head. Everywhere! When the time is right, we should speak of private lessons, and maybe even a scholarship."

"We'll speak!" Harry Marks replied. "You tell me when is the time. I'll work two shifts to get the money. Also, you'll tell me how much."

Shirley Zuckerman frowned. "For a good teacher? For twelve lessons? Ten dollars. No more."

"Ten dollars? For ten dollars we can start right away!"

Mrs. Zuckerman shook her head. "You won't rush, Mr. Marks," she urged, "until we find out how strong Leya's ankles and knees will be. It's very bad to start with toe dancing too soon."

On the way to Minnie Tabotchnik's flat, Harry stole glances at his elegant little daughter, walking so proudly beside him.

"My daughter, the toe dancer," he said. "Roses I'll throw to you over the footlights someday—in Carnegie Hall, even!"

"Oh, papa." Leya looked up at him smiling. "That would be so much fun. But Mrs. Zuckerman told us that I will not know for a year if I can be a real ballet dancer. She said it is very hard work. And . . ."

"And what?"

"And very expensive, she said."

"So? To make you a dancer, *bubeleh,* I'll get the money."

They walked in silence for a time. *Mostly with papa, money seems to be the problem,* Leya thought. Except that for some things money was not a problem. How could that be? If money was no problem now, why couldn't papa hire somebody to stay with her after school until he got home from work? Then she could live with him in her own home, sleep in her own bed, as she did every Saturday night, knowing that he was close and that she could run to him and kiss him in the morning—and again at night—and share all the things that had happened during the day. Leya wondered about Cousin Minnie. She was papa's second cousin, and she cared about papa—and about her, too. Cousin Minnie had told her once that she could not live at home with papa until she was older because the Children's Aid Society made the rules for kids from "motherless" homes—and besides, it was better in these uncertain times for her to be brought up properly, to have a good place to live and a school to go to, and to have other good people who really cared about her, too. Something called Black Thursday had scared everybody, and papa should be saving money—not spending—especially for anything unnecessary.

At dinner that night, when Harry spoke about the dance lessons, Leya noticed that Cousin Minnie did not look at her.

"You'll do what you want, Harry. But I don't like what I'm

hearing—on the street, at the factory." She shook her head. "You should put away money."

Leya found herself feeling resentful. The lessons were papa's business, she thought. It gave him pleasure to see her dance. Was it wrong for her to want to please him by learning to dance well? Except for letting her live at home, papa did everything for her.

When Minnie persisted with her dire predictions, Harry shook a finger at her. "So you hear at the factory, and you hear on the street! Did you hear what the president says?" he challenged.

"I heard," Minnie said, "and from Herbert Hoover I don't believe anything. What does he know about us?"

"He knows about business! He says our country is still on a sound basis." Harry thumped his chest. "And what about my job? A hundred thousand automobiles a year, Studebaker is selling! This is not a sound basis?"

"If business is so good, then why is the president of your company committing suicide?" Minnie asked.

Harry shrugged. "Who knows? Maybe he's got trouble at home. You can always hear bad news. But for good news you've got to listen," he warned. "So why don't you listen to that bright young professor at Yale? Irving Fisher says the economy has reached permanently a high plateau. And tell me, cousin dear, what could be smarter than an Irving Fisher at Yale?"

It was the first unhappy dinner that Leya could remember. Papa and Cousin Minnie argued all through the meal and were still going over things when Leya and Harry left to go back to their flat. On the walk home, Leya asked her father what was the matter.

He squeezed her hand. "The matter," he said, "is that your cousin is afraid she's going to be an old maid!"

It didn't make sense to Leya, but she did not press for an explanation. For the time, it was enough to know that among the girls at the home she was special because she had people—a father and a cousin.

Lying on the sofa in her father's little railroad flat, Leya remembered the time in the first grade when Penny Feitelson, who slept on the cot next to hers in the dormitory, had whispered, "What's it like to have a father?" The question had puzzled her. Her only answer had been, "It's nice." But then Penny had asked another troublesome question. "If you have a real father, Leya, how come you have to stay here with us?" Leya could not come up with an answer to that one.

Since then, she had asked herself the same question on a hundred other Sunday nights after papa had returned her to the home, and she was in bed, and the floor monitor had put out the lights. But it was not a question she would ever ask aloud. She could tell papa didn't want to talk about it.

Papa worked. So did Cousin Minnie. She understood that. But other kids in papa's neighborhood had mothers and fathers who worked, and they lived at home. Cousin Minnie said they were older. They could take care of themselves after school. Well, one day she would be older, too. In the meantime, the most important thing in the world, after her father, was to learn to dance.

In January, the Studebaker Corporation's Service Center management stuffed termination notices in the pay envelopes of more than a hundred men. Harry Marks found one in his.

Suddenly the bread lines and the mission soup kitchens in New York took on a frightening reality. Harry went straight to Hymie Solomon's Saloon on Pitkin Avenue. Good friend Hymie had helped him before by introducing him to Salvatore Di Romano. He'd still be a maintenance man for Sal if it hadn't been for the trouble with the Volpes. But if the Di Romanos were again operating their stills somewhere, he was sure they'd take him back on. All he had to do was locate Sal.

In the back of Hymie's place, out of earshot of customers scattered along the old saloon bar that had been converted to a delicatessen-restaurant, Harry questioned his old friend.

"Can I tell you the truth, Harry? I haven't seen Sal for some years," Hymie said. "I have another connection now. Believe me, as your friend, I wouldn't introduce you. God forbid, if I stopped doing business with them, the police would find me full of holes. So don't ask, Harry. Look around in Jersey. Maybe you'll find someone to tell you where Sal is."

After fruitless questions that were met with blank stares, Harry returned to Brooklyn and went to the Hebrew Orphan Asylum. "About myself I'm not worried," he said to Emma Goldman, the girls' supervisor. "But what will happen to my little Leya now? Until I get work, I can't pay. For years I've paid every week. But now—" He closed his eyes and wagged his head. "Who knows?"

Mrs. Goldman looked at the small-statured man she had come to admire. Of two hundred children, orphaned or abandoned, Leya was the only one whose father came to visit regularly.

"Mr. Marks," she said, "you won't worry for now. Leya will not be asked to leave here. When you find work, you'll give what you can." She reached over and patted his arm. "You shouldn't worry about Leya's dancing lessons, either. Boys with musical talent get lessons so they can become members of our band. A Hebrew Orphan Asylum ballet company we can't afford, but also we can't let an exceptional gift go untrained. Things will work out. Who knows better than our people, Mr. Marks, that the difference between bad luck and good luck is faith?"

Faith, sorely tried, can become fragile. Harry Marks understood that. He also knew that if his own faith had been wanting, he would have been defeated on that day eleven years earlier when the Lord had seen fit to trade one precious life for another.

The year of Leya's birth was numbered A.D. 1919 on the Gregorian calendar. On the Hebrew calendar in Harry Marks's cold water railroad flat in Brooklyn's Brownsville district, it was noted as the Year 5680.

By either reckoning, it was not a year of good omens for the world in general or for Harry Marks in particular. True, towns across the nation were welcoming with parades and oratory the victorious doughboys who had fought in the AEF to make the world safe for democracy. But the postwar slump had begun. A lot of good men were out of work now that "the war effort" was ended, and Harry Marks was one of them.

When he was told by the doctor that his wife Anya, who had been ailing for most of her pregnancy, must go to the hospital immediately after a difficult birth, attended only by a neighborhood *hebam*, Harry concealed his fear. He rode in the old Reo ambulance, saw his young wife carried to the charity ward, then walked to Hymie's saloon and dug out a quarter for a shot of slivovitz. When Hymie Solomon heard the news, he stood Harry a second drink and offered a short prayer.

When a half-dozen friends gathered to sit *shiva* for Anya Rosen Marks, those who had survived enough persecution in the old country and disillusionment in the Promised Land to know that death can be a blessing, comforted Harry and ate sparingly of the food they had brought.

Some days later, birth certificate number 47599 was placed on file in the Bureau of Records and Statistics at the Department of Health of the City of New York. On the line "Name of Child," only the surname was entered. Where the given name should have appeared, an apathetic clerk had scrawled the word "Female."

The infant did not come by a first name until she was ten weeks old. On her dead mother's birthday, Harry and his only living relative in America, a second cousin, Minerva Tabotchnik, recited an ancient Hebrew prayer:

> May the Lord remember the soul of Anya, daughter of Mendel, who has departed this life to her eternal abode. May her soul attain everlasting life together with the souls of Abraham, Isaac, Jacob, Sarah, Rebecca, Rachel and Leah, and with the other righteous men and women who are in Paradise; and let us say Amen.

Minnie lifted her head and looked at the baby, nestled in a packing crate beside the coal stove that supplied the flat's only heat. "You didn't tell me, Harry. What name do you call her?"

The question seemed to startle him. For a long moment he stared blankly at his cousin, a *zoftik* woman in her early thirties with blue eyes, an "Irisher" pug nose, fine pink skin, and thick reddish blonde hair. Milt Mendelbaum, at the undergarment factory where she was head seamstress, called her his "strawberry sundae" and threatened to eat her with a spoon someday, a joke that produced brays from the male cutters and clucking from the women bent over the sewing machines.

Harry rose to look down at his daughter.

"Do you know something?" He turned to Minnie. "I didn't give it a name yet."

Minnie moved beside him. Bending over the infant to resettle the blankets, she said, "It's not an 'it,' it's a she, and God forbid you should give her a name like Minerva!"

"God forbid!" Harry murmured. "For her I want a good Jewish name."

"So call her Leah," Minnie said. "Every time good Jews pray for their dead, they'll mention her name." She poked at the blanket again. "Believe me, you won't find a woman to love her like her own. She'll be needing all the prayers she can get."

Harry grunted. "Such a common name. Already I know ten Leahs."

"So change the spelling. Spell it with a y. L—e—y—a." She repeated the spelling several times. "*Leya Marks.* It's got style."

Harry capitulated and thanked God for Leya. He was only a little less grateful for his second cousin, Minnie, and her willingness to help as she had been able. A good woman! Still not married! At odd moments, he would wonder why. But when Hymie Solomon had suggested that Minnie's interest in him was something more than charitable concern, the possibility had shocked Harry.

"*Meshugener!*" He shouted. "You're a crazy one, Hymie! She's my cousin."

The saloonkeeper had smiled. "So, where does it stand written that from sleeping with a second cousin you get *hoyber?* I can tell you, Harry, give her half a chance, she'll pull the rabbi out from under the bed. Use your head. From sewing she makes twenty-two dollars a week. Since a month now you make *bupkes*. Nothing! Things won't be better!"

Hymie was correct. On January 16, 1920, the United States officially went dry. Crowds of men who had worked in distilleries and breweries joined the thousands already on the street. The Brooklyn Navy Yard, where Harry Marks had worked for three years, cut down to a skeleton civilian staff. He was among the first to be laid off.

Two heavy snowstorms brought temporary work at twenty-five cents an hour as an emergency employee of the Department of Sanitation. Those dollars and more of Minnie's went for medicine when wet feet and a chill brought Harry close to pneumonia.

Minnie called it a "ten-chicken sickness," as she cut up the last kosher-killed hen for soup and wondered that Harry's wiry, dead-white, five-foot-six body had not wasted away in the sea of perspiration she had sponged when the fever broke. He was tough and well made, she noted—short, but very much a man.

During Harry's illness Leya made her first trip to a foster home, recommended by the Women's Auxiliary of the Brooklyn Hebrew Orphan Asylum. After six weeks, Harry brought his daughter back to the cold-water flat. She had been there for a short time when a woman and a young intern from the Children's Aid Society came and took her away at the crack of dawn. They had been called by the neighbor who was caring for Leya, in addition to her own three children, while Harry worked nights as a dock watchman in Greenpoint.

Leya's scalp lesion was diagnosed as ringworm, and the infant was ordered to the contagious diseases ward at Kings County Hospital.

At seven o'clock that morning, distraught and half ill from lack of sleep, Harry Marks was told that he was not permitted to see his daughter.

The senior nurse was sympathetic. "Ringworm is infectious but not serious. She'll be here a week, maybe longer. We'll call you when she is well, but you'll have to get a clearance from the health department before you can take her."

Harry dragged himself into Hymie's Place. Gone was the designation "Saloon" and all of the familiar trappings. The once-genial Hyman Solomon had been transformed into an angry martyr. When Harry entered, there were only two people at the lunch bar, Hymie and a strongly built, swarthy-skinned man with wavy black hair. As Harry approached, the men broke off talking.

Halfway along the bar, Hymie met him with a gruff "So—why don't you sleep?" Harry leaned heavily against one of the new stools.

"With the trouble I got, Hymie, only the dead could sleep."

"So, what now?"

"The kid's in the hospital. Some kind of worm. It makes on the head and on the skin."

Hymie uttered a sound of disgust. "*Drek* from those kids she's been sleeping with. You're lucky it's not serious."

Harry Marks wagged his head. "So I'm lucky."

Hymie glanced down the counter at the man he'd been talking with. "You still working?"

"Friday it's finished."

"You got other prospects?"

"Nothing."

Hymie nodded in the direction of the ornate Old World samovar that had long dominated the center of the back bar. "Make a glass of tea, Harry. Later, we'll talk."

Harry snugged his calloused palms around the metal glass holder and let the heat soak in. Without making a conscious effort to eavesdrop, he knew that Hymie was talking to the stranger about him. As he was about to refill the glass, Hymie summoned him.

"Harry, this is Sal Di Romano. He's boss stevedore on the Columbia Street docks."

Harry made no effort to greet the big Italian—dark like a Sicilian but bigger, more like the men of Calabria, and mean looking. There was no friendliness in the dark eyes that seemed to be studying him muscle by muscle. Harry returned Di Romano's gaze.

"A little guy, huh? Ever worked on the docks?" The voice was deep and heavily accented.

Harry shook his head. "I'm a mechanic. Also a pipe fitter."

"Hymie says you got bad luck."

Harry glanced around the converted saloon. "With me it's not exclusive."

Sal Di Romano studied the little Jew for a long moment, then eased off the stool. "Monday morning, five o'clock, you come to the shapeup—Pier Twenty-one. If you get picked, you get a day—four bits an hour. Ten cents an hour back to me. Give the money to him." He indicated Hymie.

Harry wanted to thank the big Italian, but words didn't come. He edged away and almost overturned a stool as Di Romano brushed past him on his way to the door.

Hymie stood silently until his visitor had gone. Then he turned to Harry.

"You'll work. He understands. He's got a little kid, too." The saloonkeeper walked to the front door, opened it, and looked up and down the avenue. Satisfied that nobody was coming in, he took two coffee mugs, opened a cupboard beneath the bar, and removed an unlabeled bottle from which he poured two stiff drinks.

"It's from a friend. Try it," Hymie said as he pushed the cup across the bar.

Harry looked at the clear fluid and sniffed it.

"It's gin," Hymie said. "It wouldn't hurt you." Lifting his own cup, he glanced once more toward the door.

"Mr. Volstead, *Du kenst kush mir in tukus!*"

"He can kiss mine, too!" Harry added. "*L'Chaim.*"

CHAPTER 2

Huddled on the dock with the other hopefuls, overpowered by the rust-streaked bow of the freighter *Louis A. Luckenbach,* home port San Francisco, Harry Marks shivered in the predawn chill. Most of the men around him were Italian, Irish, and Polish—*bullvanters,* peasant offspring whose bodies were bred to hard labor. He was, so far as he could tell, the only Jew.

Of the hundred or so men who had shown up, only three gangs were hired. Just as he was about to give in to gut-deep anxiety, Harry heard his name called—next to the last. As he pushed through the men, huddled together for protection from the icy wind coming off Lower Bay, he was jostled by those who, once again, had come to the shapeup only to be turned away.

Sal Di Romano assigned the other men to gang bosses. When he descended from the stack of pallets that had been his podium, he turned to confront Harry.

"Hey, Marks, can you read?"

"I can read English, Polish, Hebrew."

"Can you count?"

"I'm a mechanic. I can count," he replied.

Di Romano regarded him skeptically. "An empty belly says it can do anything!" Holding up both heavily gloved hands with the fingers spread apart, he demanded, "What comes after this?" At first Harry did not understand. Then he realized the big Italian wanted to be reassured.

"After ten comes eleven. After eleven comes twelve. After twelve—"

"Okay! Come with me."

Ten minutes later, Harry began keeping the tally sheet for the gangs working numbers one and two holds. When the steam winches retrieved the empty pallets and swung them upward and inboard to drop them into the holds, he would duck inside the pier shed, gather his worn overcoat around him, and blow on his hands. It was cold, rotten work; but it was forty cents an hour net to him. Harry wondered if Hymie Solomon was getting any of the rakeoff for Di Romano. That wouldn't be like Hymie, but then it wasn't like Hymie to make business with a man like Di Romano.

On the second morning, when the men gathered for the five o'clock shapeup, a grimy stevedore confronted Harry and struck him on the chest with the back of a gloved hand. "Hey, kike, you got your day," the man growled. "Get the hell outta here!"

Harry backed off a step and looked up at the fellow. "So who's telling?"

"I'm telling!" the stevedore snarled. "For those guys, too!" He jerked a thumb toward the shivering men gathered around the stack of pallets that Salvatore Di Romano would mount like a demigod to dispense the few jobs that would pay for a meager meal a man could eat with self-respect.

"So maybe you work for Mr. Di Romano—and he told you to tell me?" Harry asked.

"*I'm* telling you! Don't sneak in and take somebody's job. You kikes always try for the soft jobs—counting, handling the money. I can count, too, you little bastard, and if you're not around the corner of the pier shed when I count ten, they're gonna carry you away. Un'nerstand?"

Harry continued to gaze up at the stevedore. For some reason the man, bundled in his dirty mackinaw and a ratty fur cap, reminded him of the evil-faced Genghis Khan he had seen in a book.

"I'm here because Mr. Di Romano tells me to be here,"

Harry replied. "I stay until he tells me."

As he started to move on, the man stuck out a foot and tripped him. Harry went down on the frozen cement surface of the pier. As he tried to scramble to his feet, the stevedore aimed a vicious kick at his head. The sole of the heavy work shoe grazed Harry's cheek. Cursing because he had missed, the man kicked again and caught his victim in the middle of the back. The blow brought an involuntary howl that made heads turn.

"Get up, you little prick!" the man shouted.

Harry rose and tried to circle toward the safety of the open pier-shed door. "What a big brave *shtarker!*" he yelled, aiming a finger at his tormentor. "*Grobber! Shtick fetts!* Keep your hands!"

Ignoring the laughter of the gathering crowd, Harry continued to back away. The stevedore, wearing a menacing smile, advanced.

Harry felt a pair of hands at the middle of his back. A voice shouted, "Go get him, Jew boy!" A powerful shove propelled him into the arms of the stevedore.

Harry struck wildly at the arms that were trying to pin him. Behind him he heard mounting laughter, the kind he had heard as a child back home in Poland. He kicked and cursed as he found himself being lifted bodily from the pier and carried toward the dark opening between the dock side and the towering topside plates of the freighter.

"I'm gonna cool you off, little job stealer," the stevedore purred. "You're gettin' too hot for yer own good!"

Terrified now, and certain that the man seriously meant to throw him into the freezing water, Harry cried out. Abruptly, the laughter cut off, and he heard another voice, deep, coarse, and menacing.

"Put him down!"

Harry felt his assailant's grip loosen. As his feet touched the dock, he scrambled free just as Sal Di Romano's fist smashed into the stevedore's face. Spurting blood from a split lip and smashed nose, the man staggered back. Di Romano grabbed his filthy mackinaw in time to keep the stevedore from stumbling over the side.

"Get off the dock, you stupid son of a bitch! I say who

works and who don't. Now beat it! Don't show up here again."

Ignoring Harry's thanks, Salvatore Di Romano watched as the troublemaker stumbled away. After a moment, he turned and mounted the stack of pallets.

Again Harry's name was among the last called, and he was assigned as a cargo checker. At the end of the third day, Di Romano pulled him aside.

"You know why you got this job, Marks?"

"Hymie Solomon spoke for me—no?"

"You got this job so I could watch you."

Harry nodded. "You watched. So?"

"You work okay. You keep your mouth shut."

Harry spread his hands. "I work. I don't talk."

"Okay. You're gonna work for me. Keep machinery running. You start at fifty dollars a week. No kickback."

Fifty dollars a week! It was a fortune! More than he had made with overtime at the shipyard. Now he could take care of Leya!

Then, as quickly as the elation had come, suspicion replaced it.

"What kind of machinery?"

For a moment it seemed Di Romano would not answer. Finally, he said, "Pumps—a boiler—pipes."

Relieved, Harry nodded. "So, when should I come?"

The big Italian took the clipboard from him, scribbled an address on the bottom of a mimeographed form, and tore it off. It was a place in Greenpoint, across the East River from lower Manhattan . . . a café called the Reggio.

The three-story Industrial Pipe Supply Company was as plausible a front for a high-capacity alcohol still as was ever devised during the Prohibition era. So was the Island Feed and Grain Company that adjoined it and supplied the cereal grains. Both were owned by the Di Romano family. The grain company occupied a one-story brick warehouse fronting on a narrow, unpaved street that paralleled Newtown Creek just above the point where it emptied into the East River. Both buildings backed up to rickety docks, usable only at high tide.

The still, bought from a defunct plant in New Jersey, was operated by a German named Hans Volkman. Two flatbed trucks, bearing the pipe company's sign, loaded and unloaded lengths of pipe of various sizes in what appeared to be a normal receiving and delivering operation. In fact, each length of pipe above six inches in diameter was a container filled with ninety percent pure grain alcohol. The Industrial Pipe Supply Company trucks, driven by members of the Di Romano family, ranged across Manhattan and the Hudson to Union City, Jersey City, and Hoboken, where the alcohol was delivered to controlled fronts. There it was blended, bottled, and distributed.

The Greenpoint still was one of five operated by the Di Romanos. Harry Marks's job was to keep it maintained during a seven-to-seven shift, six days a week. Every Saturday night, he clutched the reassuring wad of bills in his pants pocket and tried not to think about the consequences of a raid. When he mentioned it, Sal Di Romano laughed.

"That's the trouble with you Jews. You're always looking over your shoulder. Relax. Everybody's greased."

Harry did his work well. He talked so little that Di Romano's men accused him of not speaking English. Hans Volkman, a pudgy, broad-faced man in his early fifties who prized meticulous work, defended the quiet little Jew he had come to admire.

Leya Marks was kept in the contagious diseases section of Kings County Hospital for three weeks. Harry visited her each Sunday afternoon. On the fourth Sunday he brought a release order from the health department and a confirmation from the Children's Aid Society. Within the hour his tiny daughter was sleeping contentedly in the living room of the new flat he had rented.

Harry leaned down to kiss her. They had shaved her hair off, but her little head had healed. The hair would grow again—long this time and pretty. "*Mein shaifeleh,*" he whispered, "for you I promise to God a better life than I could give your darling mother!"

CHAPTER 3

As the Di Romano bootleg empire prospered, so did Harry Marks. Salvatore Di Romano's "genuine bonded ten-year-old whiskey" sold as fast as he could distill the alcohol, cut it to eighty proof, and bottle it. Twenty dollars a quart was the going price, and people paid it eagerly.

Strikes and race riots, soaring inflation, exorbitant rents, bombings and street crime headlined the nation's newspapers. Cynics laughed when the press revealed that President Warren Harding scrupulously upheld the Constitution of the United States on the first floor of the White House, but on the second floor he and his cronies violated the Eighteenth Amendment and most of the Ten Commandments.

When Minnie challenged Harry to leave the Di Romanos, he called her a "*kvetch*" and echoed the rationalizations of all the bootleggers who made "good stuff."

"People are going to buy booze from somebody," he argued. "Better they get it from Di Romano. Ten years old, it's not. Ten days, maybe! But it's honest alcohol. It wouldn't kill you."

Minnie murmured, "*Auf 'em gonov brennde dem hittel!*" If, in fact, Harry did suffer the burning guilt of a thief, it caused him less discomfort than the memory of poverty.

Two-year-old Leya was his delight. "A *shayna maydl,* the

prettiest baby in Brooklyn," he called her. She was alert and easily amused, especially when she imitated the movement of the whirling ballerina atop the music box. It was a diversion that absorbed her until, dizzy from turning, she would lose her balance and sit down unexpectedly. When Harry would laugh and clap his hands, little Leya would laugh, too, push herself upright, and beg to have the music box wound again.

"The child has to have somebody full time now, Harry. No more neighbors!" Minnie warned.

Harry nodded and clasped his forehead. "Oy! No more neighbors!"

A classified advertisement in the *Brooklyn Eagle* produced a response from a widow in her late thirties who did custom knitting for a shop on Fulton Street. She would be happy to work at Mr. Marks's flat and look after his little daughter for ten dollars a week and food. The arrangement seemed ideal.

Myra Sachs was a brunette. Her most charitable friends would not have called her pretty, but most of them—particularly the men—conceded that she possessed a very womanly figure and that dressing modishly, as she did, made the most of it. Harry found it increasingly agreeable when Myra, long past grieving for her departed husband, who had been twenty years her senior, prepared and shared an occasional evening meal.

One afternoon toward the end of summer, neighbors, eager to enjoy the excitement of a scandal, confided to Minnie that Mrs. Sachs's activities were positively no longer confined to the nursery and the kitchen. That evening Minnie decided to "look in."

"You'll excuse me, Harry," she said, ignoring his consternation, "but I just happened to be in the neighborhood."

Harry had scarcely managed to get himself together to answer the door. He stalled for time now to give Myra a chance to get back into the dress she had been removing when the knock came.

"So how's the baby?" Minnie asked innocently.

"Asleep," he answered bluntly.

"That's nice," Minnie murmured. "And so how is Mrs. Sachs? She's gone already?"

"She's going," Harry replied.

The bedroom door opened, and Myra Sachs appeared, flushed and overly animated.

"Would you believe it, Mrs. Tabotchnik—" she began.

"Miss!" Minnie corrected.

Myra Sachs indicated her large knitting bag. "Mr. Marks and I got to playing with the baby." Her eyes rolled. "Such a doll! With her, time gets away. I didn't even finish my knitting for the shop."

When Myra left, Minnie invited herself in for a glass of tea. Later, as she walked home through the humid summer night, it became clear to her that the solution to the problem was not in hiring a succession of women but in removing the need for them.

At eight o'clock the next morning, convinced she was motivated only by concern for the child's welfare, she went to the operations office at the end of the loft floor and made an anonymous call to the Children's Aid Society.

At seven that evening, Harry arrived at the brownstone, eager to wash up, play with Leya, and join Myra at the table. As he mounted the front stairs, he caught sight of expectant faces peering from behind the coarse cotton-lace curtains and sensed something was wrong.

At his door, Myra greeted him hysterically and told him Leya was gone. She thrust the removal order at him.

"How could anybody know, Harry? Maybe you talked! Men brag about such things. I *know!*"

The document charged Harry Marks with being an "unfit father" and directed that the child be taken to the Brooklyn Hebrew Orphan Asylum's preschool nursery as a full-time ward. The money the father had been paying to the day nurse henceforth would be paid to the asylum toward the child's keep.

Stunned, Harry called Minnie. When she met him at the Ralph Avenue entrance of the turreted, three-story, fortresslike building that, along with playgrounds, pavilions, and outbuildings, occupied four square blocks, he was in tears. It was the first time she had seen a man cry. Sudden remorse brought tears to her own eyes. Harry mistook them for manifestations of sympathy. Weeping together, they went to the second-floor administration office, only to be told that Leya could not be seen after hours. Nobody with authority would be available until morning.

Minnie's flat was closer to the asylum than Harry's, so he walked his cousin home. While they had tea and homemade honey cake, self-reproach drove Minnie close to offering herself as the solution. But the possibility that he might suspect her complicity stayed her tongue.

"Believe me, Harry, I couldn't tell you how sorry I am. Even if I knew the details, I wouldn't want to hear them!"

Harry rested his elbows on the table and braced his head on his palms.

"Details—*schmeetails!* What father could love more? So tell me, from making a good living, from hiring a good woman to look after her, am I unfit? Did I steal? Did I beat? Did I murder? Since when do I don't love my daughter?"

Minnie wanted to take his head in her hands and comfort him, but she knew better than to try. Harry would survive. To survive was the ageless philosophy of their people.

Two years would pass before the first hint that the Di Romano bootleg empire was in for troubled times. On a snowy night in February of 1923, along a lonely stretch of Amboy Street just south of Rahway, New Jersey, two Torre Vecchio Olive Oil Company trucks were hijacked. Each truck carried one hundred and fifty cases of new "ten-year-old bourbon."

The drivers and swampers on both trucks were found face down, bound hand and foot. All had been executed with forty-five-caliber slugs through the back of the skull.

When the news came, Sal Di Romano did two things; he armed his drivers, and he began asking discreet questions about his old friend Vito Volpe. On several occasions during Di Romano family vacations in Atlantic City, Volpe had hinted that he would like to be cut in for a piece of the action, preferably as distributor for Torre Vecchio products in south Jersey. Each time, when he had been told that the time was not right yet, Vito had smiled and said, "*Capisco, gumba. Tutto va bene.* I can wait."

Di Romano did one other thing; he sent two of his family down to Camden to make some connections with speak-easies. If they were able to buy his Golden Anniversary bourbon whiskey there, he would have all the proof he needed to substantiate his suspicions.

Within the week his men were back with the evidence. Di Romano went to a public telephone. Several minutes later Vito Volpe heard his cordial greeting.

"*Come va,* Vito? *Come va?*"

"*Non che male, grazie. E lei?*"

"*Benessimo, gumba, grazie.*"

"*E la famiglia?*"

"*Bene, anche. Bene, grazie.*"

"*Buono! Che cosa fa?* What goes?"

Di Romano took his time responding. He felt certain that the thin, dapper Volpe—the name meant "fox"—knew what the call was about.

"You remember what I said when you asked for a piece of the action?"

"Sure. You told me to wait. So I'm waiting."

Di Romano paused again. "The time is right now."

Volpe's delight sounded genuine. "Hey, *gumba!* That's good! Let's talk!"

"We're going to talk, Vito, my friend. We take dinner tonight. Taverna Ulpia. Okay?"

"Sure. *A che ora?*"

"*Alle otto.* Only you and me, huh?"

"*Si. Solo.* You and me." Volpe's voice turned warmer still. "Hey, Sal! You make me very happy, *gumba!*"

"Me, too, Vito. *A rivederci.*"

Shortly after ten o'clock the two men slipped the checkered napkins from their belts and lit up Salvatore Di Romano's handmade Havana *claros.* Both men wore the satisfied expressions of old friends comfortable with each other.

Vito had listened carefully and congratulated himself on the success of his duplicity during the two hours that Sal had spent revealing every aspect of the business. To Volpe, wary at first, the details bespoke the *confidenza* that exists between men who enjoy unquestioned mutual trust. He knew that Sal Di Romano had built a strong family organization, but he could not have imagined how complex and efficient it had become. Vito had absorbed every detail, for he planned to pattern his own organization after Di Romano's.

At ten-thirty, Di Romano flipped open the case of his heavy gold pocket watch.

"*Andiamo*, Vito. We go look at the stills. It's the same we're going to put for you in Camden."

As they left the restaurant, Di Romano rested his arm on Volpe's shoulder. "I'm very happy tonight, Vito. It always makes me happy to keep a promise."

Twenty minutes later, a black Packard limousine pulled away from the Industrial Pipe Supply Company's warehouse. There were three men in it, but only Salvatore Di Romano and his enforcer, young Tony Spacco, were visible. Vito Volpe, bound, gagged, and unconscious from a blow on the head, sprawled on the floor in the rear.

The following morning two youngsters, bound for exploration along the tidal flats at the foot of Pennsylvania Avenue, discovered a trussed-up body lying face down in a backwash. They froze long enough to see the back of the victim's head had been blown off. Terrified, they fled to report their find.

Huddled on the back seat of the bus, Harry Marks consulted the soiled piece of paper on which Hans Volkman had penciled several minor repairs the still needed before the next startup. A block before his stop, he returned the paper to his overcoat pocket and got up to wait by the door.

Predawn darkness enveloped the ramshackle buildings along the tidewater slough as Harry made his way toward the Industrial Pipe Supply plant. When he was a block from the buildings, a black sedan pulled out of the service yard and roared toward him, forcing him into a doorway. Puzzled, Harry stared after the car until it careened around the far corner and headed east.

He resumed walking, keeping close to the buildings. As he

turned into the pipe storage yard in front of the large building that housed the stills, the two-story structure seemed to erupt. A blinding flash and explosion shattered the early-morning silence, and Harry was struck by a shock wave that propelled him into the street. He lay for a moment, unable to hear and only dimly aware of the flames leaping from the crumbling building.

Then he felt someone tugging at his overcoat collar. "Harry! Harry! Are you all right?"

It was Hans Volkman. "*Mein Gott!*" the big German cried as he pulled him to his feet. "If I hadn't missed my bus, inside I would have been!"

Aware now of distant shouts and figures running toward them, Harry allowed Volkman to half drag him across the street. Concealed in the dark, narrow space between the café and a boarded-up brick building, both men watched in disbelief as the flames spread to the adjoining grain storage building.

"What happened, Hans?" Harry said. "Did the still blow?"

"Some son of a bitch blew it up!" Volkman answered. "Everything was shut down to work on."

In the distance they heard a siren. The shouts were closer now. When Harry started for the street at the rear of the buildings, Volkman stopped him.

"Stay here! We don't want to be seen running. Let's wait for the crowd and mix in for a while. Then we can walk away."

After a dozen or so curious men had gathered, the pair moved unobtrusively to join them as two police cars and a fire engine careened into view at the end of the street.

Harry and Volkman watched as three more engine companies arrived and trained their hoses on the spreading fire. Within minutes, water began turning to icy stalactites around the fringes of the devastation.

Harry shook his head. "*Gornisht helfin,*" he muttered.

Hans Volkman nodded. Nothing could help either of them now.

The two were still standing with the crowd when the federal men drove up. Volkman nudged Harry.

"Let's go," he said quietly. "We don't need any questions." They sidled around the onlookers and entered the all-night café. Seconds later, on the pretext of going to the toilet, they slipped out the back way and headed for the corner.

Volkman stuck out his hand. "I wish you luck, Harry. You're a good man."

"Believe me, I wish you the same, Mr. Volkman," Harry responded. It was the last time they were to see one another.

CHAPTER 4

Times were a little better by the mid-1920s. The rampant inflation of the war years eased. Some types of jobs were not as scarce, and Harry Marks found part-time work in an auto-repair shop. In the fall, when the peak motoring season tapered off, he was fired. An acquaintance told him about a new service center the Studebaker Corporation of America was planning in Brooklyn. He made an application and was told that the employment office would keep him in mind.

The only bright spots for Harry and Leya during those months of uncertainty were his weekly visits at the "home." He could never bring himself to think of the place as "the asylum."

Leya, five years old now, was called "the little charmer" by the volunteers of the Women's Auxiliary, who conducted fund-raising drives for scholarships and improvements at the Brooklyn Hebrew Orphan Asylum and gave generously of their time to instruct the girls in nonacademic activities—music, drawing, and dance. Leya couldn't wait for the weekends to show her father the new dance steps she had learned.

For Harry Marks the New Year, 1925, dawned auspiciously. In February, Studebaker kept its promise. He was hired at forty dollars a week as a mechanic. On forty dollars a man could keep his pride intact, his stomach reasonably full, and his bills paid!

When her father brought Leya a large Whitman Sampler, she knew he was working full time again. One prayer had been answered. Now maybe God would answer the one about going home with papa for keeps.

When Leya talked about living at home with him, Harry would assure her that when she was older, she would understand. How could he tell his little girl that the Children's Aid Society would settle for no more live-in ladies unless a union was solemnized? The last time the condition had been spelled out, he had gone into the little bedroom, absently wound the music box, and listened to the tinkle of the Tchaikovsky melody. When the music wound down to the final metalic "plink," he had muttered, "A wife . . . I couldn't do it—yet."

By 1926, with Calvin Coolidge well into his second term, the country was forgetting the depression, and HCL, the familiar abbreviation for high cost of living, was less often seen on the front pages. People were more concerned with the phenomenal achievements of Coach Knute Rockne at Notre Dame and with the feats of the Wheaton Iceman, Harold E. "Red" Grange, who played football for the University of Illinois until the Chicago Bears lured him to professional football at the highest figure ever paid a gridiron star. Babe Ruth and Lou Gehrig of the New York Yankees inherited Ty Cobb's mantle, and Little Poker Face, Helen Wills, and a tall aristocrat named William Tilden elevated tennis to a major-league amateur sport.

If most women seemed less than preoccupied with outdoor sports, they managed to distract men with a promise of "indoor sport" by embracing the latest fashion. Hemlines rose above the knees. "On some women, skirts above the street should be against the law!" Harry Marks complained. Like most of his contemporaries, he was delighted by the minimal attire worn by the more daring girls—"flappers," the magazines were calling them—particularly when they revealed rolled silk stockings and fancy garters that were obviously designed to be admired. As skirts rose, waistlines fell until they were midway down the hips.

"Can I tell you," Harry said to Minnie, "the garment industry is getting rich from putting in the dresses only half the goods at twice the price!"

If Harry's criticism of the new fashions in clothing was not entirely sincere, it was not so with the new hairstyle called the shingle bob.

"If I ever caught a woman of mine doing that to her hair," he said, "I'd lock her up until it grew out again!"

The following week, when he visited his daughter at the orphan's home, his wounded cry echoed through the building.

"Who did it? Tell me! Who said you could?" He looked around wildly. "Did anybody ask me if my daughter could cut off her hair?"

Mrs. Goldman and Miss Weil, Leya's floor monitor, hurried to him.

"Please, Mr. Marks," Mrs. Goldman soothed. "Don't get yourself aggravated!" She put an arm around Leya, who stood trembling at the spectacle of her father's rage. "Leya did nothing wrong! The barber across the street, Mr. Russo, offered to cut the girls' hair in the latest style as a contribution. He cut the boys' hair for free, too. He is very generous." Mrs. Goldman pulled Leya back against her skirt. "I think your daughter looks beautiful," she said.

"And besides," Miss Weil added, "it is a very practical haircut for the girls. Even in a place as clean as the home, the children occasionally get lice."

"Lice, schmice!" Harry shouted. "Lice drown from long hair, too! All you got to do is wash!"

Unaware that tears had come to his daughter's eyes, he shook his finger in the woman's face. "Russo should have his hair cut!" he shouted, running his index finger along his Adam's apple. "Down to here yet!"

"Mr. Marks! Calm yourself!" Mrs. Goldman said. She released the child to Miss Weil and drew Harry aside. In a low voice she went on. "We do everything we can to remind our children that they are not different because they live in the asylum. But it's difficult for them to build confidence when they get used to us making all the decisions for them. So about some things we ask them. Leya *wanted* her hair cut."

Harry aimed a finger at Leya's shingle-bobbed hair. "So show me a ballet dancer with–with–" Words failed him.

Mrs. Goldman hushed him sternly. "Leya is very sensitive, Mr. Marks. Try to have more understanding–please!"

"I'm trying," Harry replied. "But I can't understand why you would let that barber make her look like something from a freak show!"

Her father's words struck Leya like blows, and she pressed closer against Miss Weil. The floor monitor leaned down and whispered, "He's only angry at the barber, darling."

Leya pressed her face against the woman's skirt. "But they asked me, and I said yes."

"Your father knows why you said that. He doesn't blame you."

"He does!" Leya managed between sobs.

"You are being cruel, Mr. Marks!" Mrs. Goldman said sharply. "Don't you understand? She thinks she is even more beautiful now because she is in the latest style. All week she's been talking about how her papa will love her haircut because it shows off her lovely neck, like Mr. Russo said."

Taking Harry by the arm, she led him back to Leya and Miss Weil. "Now that you understand, Mr. Marks, Leya is going to dance for you, aren't you, darling?"

Leya could manage only a tentative nod.

"Good!" Mrs. Goldman put a motherly arm around Harry. "We'll go to the girls' indoor playroom," she said, guiding him to the door. Mrs. Zuckerman greeted them and put on a recording of Roy Turk's newest hit, "I'm Gonna Charleston Back to Charleston."

Leya stood staring at her father in confusion. Harry found his voice was tight and unnaturally high.

"So, dance, *bubeleh.* Dance for papa."

Mrs. Zuckerman took Leya's hand, and side by side they picked up the basic steps of the newest dance rage. The Charleston had begun in a Harlem revue and worked its way downtown to the fashionable speakeasies and cabarets.

Harry watched with a set smile as Leya struggled to get into the spirit of the dance. *Oy veh,* he thought. *This is dancing?* Halfway through the record, in spite of himself, Harry Marks found his smile broadening. His foot started to tap.

"Stop the music!" Mrs. Goldman called. "I have an idea!"

She led Harry to the middle of the floor. "Do you know, Leya, it would be very good if you taught your father the steps? He is a very handsome man, and you get your talent from him. I know because he taps his foot to music just like you do."

She took Leya's hand and put it in Harry's. "Start the music again."

From early youth, Harry had been one of the most enthusiastic dancers at bar mitzvahs and at weddings. After several bars of watching, he began to imitate Leya. Mrs. Zuckerman moved back to join Mrs. Goldman. When the recording ended, they applauded vigorously. Harry led his daughter forward.

"So take a bow, *bubeleh,*" he said. Smiling for the first time since her father's outburst, Leya curtsied, and Harry joined in the applause.

"Your father will take a bow also for being such a good student," Mrs. Goldman said.

Leya reached for her father's hand. Harry allowed himself to be led forward for an exaggerated vaudeville bow. Then he stepped back and regarded his daughter. When he saw her apprehension return, he kneeled and opened his arms.

"Come here. Papa wants to speak to you." Placing a finger beneath her chin, he turned her head from side to side to examine the shingled hair. Inwardly he groaned. Such an elegant little head and neck she'd had, with her hair braided and coiled on top. Now her head looked like a tin lizzie off the assembly line. Even as he acknowledged the Italian barber's generosity, Harry damned the man for his lack of taste.

"You know something?" Harry said. "When I first saw your hair, I thought you had been ruined, I admit. But now I think for practicing dancing it is very good. Only when you are a real ballet dancer will you need long hair again. There's time to let it grow." He pulled her close and snuggled his chin atop the short gleaming crown. "Yes. I like it. I *like* it!"

By the time Harry had reached the bottom of the Ralph Avenue steps, Leya was upstairs at the dormitory window. Each time he came to visit, Leya watched until he stopped at the corner, waved, then disappeared from view. Each time she felt that strange, empty feeling that started in her throat and went all the way down inside her middle. She had learned that if she gave in to it, she would cry—as she used to in bed late at night, after a Sunday outing with papa and Cousin Minnie. There were lots of beds in the dormitory—all the same kind—side by side, with aisles in between. Sometimes, after some of the other girls had been invited out to family homes, she could hear them trying to stifle sobs under the blankets. If Miss Weil, who had her own little room in the corner of the dormitory, heard them, she would come in and kneel by the bed and whisper until things were quiet again.

Leya had never allowed herself to be heard, not even by the girls in the beds on either side of her. She knew that if she could make herself think of other things, after a while the empty feeling would go away. But you had to think hard—about safe things. You couldn't think about how good papa's arms felt when he squeezed you and called you his little sack of sweet potatoes and how it felt when he made a lump in his cheek and rubbed the scratchy stubble against yours until you pulled away, laughing. You couldn't let yourself think about things like that or the other feeling would come back.

Leya turned from the window and threaded her way between the beds to the washroom. Standing before the mirror over the troughlike basin that accommodated a dozen girls at a time, she fussed with her hair, spread the bangs evenly along her forehead, and pulled the points on the sides into place over her cheekbones. Her shingle looked better than most because her hair was thick. And it felt good when she was dancing, especially when she whipped around in the pirouettes. Somehow it seemed that she could turn faster.

A few minutes later, kneeling beside her bed in the darkness, she rested her forehead on her folded hands. Leya had learned that it wasn't wise to let people know you wanted something too much because then it might not happen. But it was all right to confide to God because He could make things happen—like Mrs. Zuckerman told her once—if you did your share to help Him.

When she finished the prayer in Hebrew that all the kids said, she added the private prayer she had said faithfully for years. "And please, God, bless papa and let him earn money—and let me hurry up and grow older so I can live with him—and let me be a good dancer so papa will be proud of me. And please, God, bless my mother and my Cousin Minnie, too—because she is good to papa—and—and— Amen."

Leya snuggled into the blankets and buried her face in the pillow to shut out the dim ray of night light that shone through the washroom door. She pressed her eyes tightly shut and thought of the little music box. She was the lovely ballerina in the tutu and tiara, showing papa the new steps she had learned, and he was smiling and applauding, and the terrifying sound of his voice when he had seen her hair and shouted at Mrs. Goldman and Miss Weil had not happened. All that was real was papa smiling and touching her hair—and putting his arms around her and saying, "I like it. I *like* it!"

Leya, now sixteen, pulled her hair forward over her left shoulder, brushed out the burnished copper ponytail, and caught it close to the back of her head with a heavy barrette. Across the hall in her father's room, she caught sight of her mother's little ballerina poised on point in the midst of a *piqué* turn. Smiling to herself, she went to it, wound the music box, and did a series of pirouettes on demi-point. As she turned, her hair switched across her face. How much more manageable it was when it was braided and coiled in a ballet bun!

She stopped, tossed her hair back in place, and remembered that day nine years earlier when papa had discovered her shingle bob. What a scene he had made! And what unhappiness they had both endured while she let her hair grow out. For a time she had worn a babushka that Cousin Minnie had bought for her on Pitkin Avenue. In class she had disguised her hair with a bandeau during its awkward length. That had been a difficult time! The growing-out process had taken forever. And so, she thought, had the growing-up process!

She sat on the covered box stool with her back to the mirror, absently studying the new Selva ballet slippers she had bought. They were seconds—only one dollar and eighty-eight cents—because the stitching over the instep was irregular. They were a full size smaller than her street shoes because they had to fit like skin. She leaned down and massaged the new leather over the protruding joint of her big toe. In time, after years on point, it would protrude more. Ballet dancers should not hope for beautiful feet except in slippers and toe shoes. It was one of the penalties of their endless pursuit of perfection.

At the home, some of her classmates regarded her single-minded dedication to the dance as "strange." That had become a penalty, too, particularly when she worked, as Mrs. Zuckerman had told her to, in front of the long mirror on the back of the washroom door. Because of classroom schedules it was difficult for her to find private time to criticize her posture and line in the mirror. When she was discovered, she braced herself for the derision of her classmates.

"Look at Leya! She loves Leya! Leya doesn't love boys, she loves Leya!" Once, at the end of her endurance, Leya had charged into them with a screaming fury that had sent them scurrying. That episode had reduced the taunting but had reinforced the impression that, in fact, the Marks girl was "different."

"Don't worry about it, dear," Mrs. Goldman had told her. "To be an artist is to be different. The children in the home who have gone on to distinguish themselves have all been different from the ones who use up their energy with hanky-panky. Be a nonconformist, Leya! They may laugh behind your back now, but later they'll brag about knowing you."

The childhood fantasy world in which she had danced like

the little ballerina on her mother's music box was slowly transforming into a real world. The grueling discipline of dance lessons after school five days a week and the additional hours of barre on her own, usually with her leg propped on the edge of the dresser, were commitments made to herself to try to do still better as part of her obligation to her father, now that she was living at home with him. There were moments of deep despair, times when fatigue, accentuated by the changes in her body, made it seem impossible to persevere. But she drove herself to keep to the regimen. She had come home to live and help papa during the most difficult time of the Depression. Every gain had been made through struggle, and even with the help of the scholarship, the struggle was not over.

CHAPTER 5

Madame Alexandra Baronova, mistress of the Metropolitan Opera Ballet Company, inspected the young girl in front of her and removed the pince-nez glasses from her bladelike aquiline nose. Her long, angular face and her intense dark eyes betrayed nothing.

To Leya, standing before her in sweat-sogged black leotards and homemade leg warmers, improvised from the sleeves of an old wool sweater, these next few minutes would be crucial. In the three years since she had left the home, both she and her father had made grinding sacrifices for this audition.

"Who trained you?" Madame Baronova demanded as she tugged on the pince-nez chain until it reeled itself into the round jeweled case pinned to the lace collar of her long black dress. "Obviously you've had training of a sort—no?"

Leya pressed away the perspiration from her upper lip with the side of her index finger. "I began my studies in the Brooklyn Hebrew Orphan Asylum, madame—with Mrs. Zuckerman."

"Mrs. Zuckerman? This is not one of the great names in ballet. What did she teach you?"

"She taught us a lot of steps, but mostly how to move in time to the music—"

"Well, you seem to do that," Madame Baronova conceded, "and you seem to have some knowledge of basic ballet positions. Who taught you that?"

"I studied at Carnegie Hall, madame."

"Carnegie Hall is filled with people who pretend to teach ballet. With whom?"

"Eddie Caton, madame," Leya replied

The older woman sniffed. "How long with Caton?"

"Six years, madame."

"Only ballet?"

"I took one year of tap, also—with Billy Ray, when I was fourteen."

Madame Baronova waved a long, knobby hand. "And ruined your chances to amount to anything as a serious dancer, no doubt! Why did you waste such important time?"

Leya smoothed a strand of hair from her temple. "I didn't waste time, madame. I really wanted to be a ballerina. But if I was not good enough, then I wanted to be a dancer in musical comedy. It did not hurt me. I worked very hard at my ballet classes. They were more important."

"*Most* important!" the old ballet mistress corrected sharply. "Nothing else—father, mother, relatives—nothing but God is more important!"

Madame Baronova thought she detected a trace of defiance in the girl's face. That could be both good and bad. Spirit was important but not rebellion.

"Why did you come to this school?"

"Because I was told it was the best."

"It is, of course, but who told you that?"

"Mrs. Goldman, the head of the girls' school at the home. She is the one who arranged for my scholarship."

"Very well," the ballet mistress said. "They were correct about this school. Whether or not they were correct in assuming you are promising enough to be a student here is something else."

The ballet mistress knew Leya had just completed an exceptional audition. Her elevations and extensions were remarkable. She seemed always to be just a bit "above the floor"—all the more unusual because of her short stature.

Five feet four—perhaps five—a bit full in the bust for a dancer but a good figure. Small waist, twenty-two inches at the most. Strong hips and thighs. Upper legs a bit too short for perfection of line but good lower legs, ankles, and feet. The girl's hands were good, too. Not as good as her own long hands had once been but acceptable, as were the arms. And a good neck, with head elegantly held. High Slavic cheekbones and large, uptilted topaz eyes—the girl would be lovely on stage. She had a look about her more earthy than ethereal.

"So you wish to be a prima ballerina—a *première danseuse?*"

"If I can, madame."

"You are still on a scholarship from the Brooklyn Hebrew Orphan Asylum. Yes?"

"From the Hebrew Benevolent Society, madame."

"Do not correct me!" the older woman snapped. "Do you have any family?"

"A father."

"Do you see him?"

"I live with him now."

"And he wants you to be a dancer?"

"Ever since I was a little girl."

"So you want to be a dancer only to please papa. Yes?"

"That is not true," Leya replied instantly. "I want to be a dancer because that is all I have ever wanted to be!"

Madame Baronova nodded. "*Bien!* So, Leya Marks, we will try you. We will see!"

The girl's obvious joy carried Alexandra Baronova back forty-seven years to that day in Paris when her own father had taken her to audition for the great Michel Fokine on the stage of l'Opéra. My God! How easy she was being on *this* girl! Fokine had drilled her to exhaustion before accepting her with an imperious order to join the fortunate ones. Had the years of work, the discipline, the sacrifice been worth it? Of course! A *première danseuse* would not question that. Pavlova, Nijinsky and Nijinska, Karsavina, Massine, Mordkin, Lifar—What memories! Innovative ballets, so daring! *Scheherazade, Firebird, Afternoon of a Faun, Rites of Spring,* music composed by young rebels, exciting, controversial scores by Stravinsky, Debussey, Ravel, Dukas—yes, and even the great Richard Strauss. How outraged the critics had been! And how delighted were the younger balletomanes to be able to laugh at the old classicists. In all the theater there was nothing to compare to those times.

Three months after Leya was accepted as a member of the chorus of the Balanchine Company, itself the de facto corps de ballet of the Metropolitan Opera Company, the class went into rehearsal as dancing "spear carriers" in Edward Johnson's production of *Aida* with Elizabeth Rethberg and Giovanni Martinelli.

Those who were chosen greeted the news with squeals of delight. Leya restrained herself when she saw the ballet mistress's expression of disapproval. Later, in the dressing room, she gave vent to her joy in a series of abandoned pirouettes.

That night her father caught her beneath the arms and swung her recklessly. "*Bubeleh,* you'll be a star!" he said, ignoring her laughing protests.

At six-thirty on opening night, when Leya came through the stage door with the others to get ready for makeup and costumes, the opera house had been transformed into a magic castle. Even Madame Baronova's constant reprimands could not dim the enchantment Leya shared with her classmates as they made their way through the dingy corridors, cluttered with scenery and racks of costumes that, under the lights, would be transformed into the bejeweled panoply of fairy-tale royalty. "In the theater, reality begins as a dream," Madame Baronova had said. How right she had been! Leya thought.

Just before the curtain rose on Act One, she managed a quick search through the peephole for Harry and Minnie. "I'll find them," she had assured her friend Heather O'Brien, "because I'll be able to see the dark place in the lines of white shirts. Papa wouldn't get one. He calls them 'monkey suits'!" But Heather was right. Leya couldn't make out either of them.

Harry kept his promise to be in the theater, but because of

his precarious financial situation he and Minnie sat well to the back of the main floor. Minnie had insisted on buying her own ticket. Even so, Harry skimped for two weeks to accumulate the admission price, plus a modest amount for a treat after the performance. He brushed aside Minnie's suggestion that they should sit in the balcony because he didn't have formal clothing.

"Where is it written that my good suit isn't enough?" he replied.

"Your good suit is your only suit," Minnie reminded him, "and confidentially, Harry, it's not too good."

He and Minnie were waiting when the main doors opened. When the usher pointed to the checkroom, Harry said, "I'll keep on my overcoat 'til the lady gets to her seat."

Harry strained forward each time the entire company came on stage. "Do you see her? Which one is she?" he whispered a dozen times as Minnie tried vainly to hush him.

Later, as they walked up Broadway on their way to Longchamps Restaurant to celebrate, Harry held Leya's arm closely and glowed with pride.

"You know why we're going to such a ritzy place?" he asked.

Leya rested her cheek against the sleeve of his overcoat—it still smelled of naphtha where Minnie had spotted it—and smiled up at him. "Because you are an extravagant man, papa. We should go to the Automat."

Harry looked aghast at Minnie. "What kind of dancing star do we have here?" he demanded. "She wants to eat with peasants!"

"I want you to save your money, papa, she said. "You know this is the last year of my scholarship. When I finish with Madame Baronova, I'll have to pay for my lessons. I have to go on, papa. A dancer can never stop working."

"So, you'll go on, *bubeleh*. We'll find the money."

"But that's why we should go to the Automat. You're wasting money. Save, papa. Please!"

Minnie nodded to herself. The girl has sense! Now if she could only have sense enough to make a career of something that paid, someplace where she could meet a nice young

Jewish man—a doctor, a lawyer, even a manufacturer. Not only does dancing not pay, except maybe for a few stars, but also, what kind of young men use makeup and go around in tights with their arrangements sticking out in front making ipsy-pipsy on their toes? Only a *fageleh* could do it!

Leya stopped her father outside the entrance to Longchamps. "Papa, you've got to promise me. We'll go in just this once. Next time it's the Automat, and you and Minnie sit in the balcony. Promise?"

"Okay. I'll also promise you wouldn't have to worry about not having a scholarship."

When they were seated, Leya was tempted to tell her father and Minnie about Madame Baronova's promise that those in the advanced class who worked hard and showed real progress would get to dance in the Flamenco chorus in the next production of *Carmen.* She would surely be seen then—if she was chosen. Caution made her keep the news to herself. Silence was safest because in the theater it was bad luck to talk in front.

CHAPTER 6

Illness in the Metropolitan Opera's regular corps de ballet forced Balanchine to call on Madame Baronova sooner than she had expected. Leya and her two closest friends from the class, Heather O'Brien and Celine Cervier, were chosen to dance the seductive bits as Carmen's flirtatious friends from the cigarette factory.

After the performance, Harry and Minnie were pleased when Leya insisted that her two friends join them at the Automat.

"We are going 'dutch,' papa. It is always understood, and no argument!" she warned.

Over hot chocolate, Harry and Minnie listened as the three girls relived the muscle-torturing qualification lessons that Madame Baronova had put them through, the excitement of being fitted for costumes and being made up properly, and the thrill of performing downstage with the star.

Of Leya's two friends, Heather O'Brien, the Boston "black Irish" girl with the full figure, the creamy complexion, and the deep-blue eyes, seemed the most ambitious, the most worldly. It was obvious that her real goal was Broadway. More exciting for her than the performance at the Metropolitan Opera was the prospect of being part of a new musical that George Balanchine was going to choreograph.

The chorus call was for the following Monday. "Don't say anything!" Heather warned, "Madame will skin me alive. But I'm skipping class. Broadway's where the money is—and the fun, too."

Harry liked better the "little Frenchie," Celine Cervier. The slender ash-blonde girl with the serious gray eyes had dignity, like his Leya.

On Monday, Heather was absent from class and missed the conditional accolades accorded the trio by Madame Baronova. Members of the regular cast had commented favorably on the Balanchine students who had filled in at the last minute. Leya, in particular, had earned praise for the controlled sensuousness of her performance as Carmen's special friend.

On Tuesday, Heather entered the dressing room, elated. "They picked me!" she said. "I'm going to try out for the chorus. My father and mother are so excited, they want me to come to Boston tomorrow and tell them everything."

"You may go to Boston today, young lady. And you may not return to this class!"

Madame Baronova's voice filled the room.

"Don't bother to change. I will not have your body here and your mind elsewhere." She turned to the others and rapped her long malacca staff for emphasis. "The rest of you will be at the barre in exactly two minutes."

Here and there a girl murmured, "Yes, madame." The ballet mistress stood glowering for a moment, then left.

"The old bitch!" Heather's jaw was thrust forward. "She had no right to do that! She works for Mr. Balanchine, too. I'm going to tell him. She's cruel! She's ten times worse than the sisters at school!"

While Heather emptied her locker, most of the girls whispered their congratulations. A sharp tattoo of raps brought them scurrying back to the studio, still occupied with last-minute adjustments to their leotards.

As the eleven girls and eight boys took their positions at the barre, Madame Baronova moved to the center of the floor and again rapped her stick for attention. "How many of you envy the O'Brien girl?" she asked as she studied each of them in turn.

Anxious glances were exchanged, but no hands were raised.

"I don't believe you!" the ballet mistress snapped. "Mr. Balanchine was a superb dancer. He is a superb choreographer. But he can be misleading in his desire to explore new ways. It is my opinion that he may have impaired Tamara Geva for serious ballet. Do you know why? Because two years ago he and Richard Rodgers and Lorenz Hart paid her a fortune to come to Broadway to dance the lead in *On Your Toes.* A popular musical!" She leaned forward, bracing her hands on the head of the long staff. "Next it will be Vera Zorina, the *danseuse étoile* of Colonel W. DeBasil's Ballet Russe de Monte Carlo, the best company since the Maryinski." Straightening, she nodded. "One by one they go. All of the discipline, all of the perfection, wasted!" She broke off, then lapsed into Russian and signaled the rehearsal pianist impatiently.

For twenty minutes of barre warmup and over an hour of ballet variations, Alexandra Baronova worked the young students unmercifully. When the class was over, she ordered the dancers to stand as they were, exhausted, dripping sweat. "I am hard on you. Yes? Well, if you did not have promise, you would not be here. I see perhaps six of you who have"—she pantomimed the turning of a switch—"a spark." She paused, deliberately refusing to single out any of them.

"You think I don't know how you feel? I was one of you once, an eternity ago. And I begged God to strike down Leon Bakst and Marius Petipa and Bronislava Nijinska—and as many a *régisseur!* And later, when I was chosen to dance Odile in *Swan Lake,* my heart burst with love for them, for I understood at last." Her gaze moved across the line of sweat-beaded faces. "You do not believe that now. But you will—someday—unless you give in to temptation!" Her eyes questioned them briefly. "All right. Now you are dismissed."

In the empty studio, she sat down on the bench beside the rehearsal pianist, a Juilliard music major working to supplement his tuition.

"Oh my God, but I grow weary." She closed her eyes. "It is hell, perfection. You understand that. Do you not?"

"I do, madame," the accompanist replied without lifting his head.

The ballet mistress knew she was not being entirely fair. Tamara Geva had made a great hit in *On Your Toes.* Balanchine's ballet, *Slaughter on Tenth Avenue,* had become an instant classic. She could return to the Ballet Russe a greater star than ever as a result of her triumph on Broadway. If, in fact, Balanchine had managed to persuade Vera Zorina to leave the Ballet Russe for a starring role in the new Rodgers and Hart musical, she had no doubt that history would repeat itself. But it was true, what she had told these eager young ones. They could not expect greatness unless they were willing to do the groundwork.

Heather O'Brien's place in the chorus of the new Rodgers and Hart musical, *I Married an Angel,* was secure. The show, starring Vera Zorina, together with Dennis King, Vivienne Segal, and Walter Slezak, opened at the Shubert Theater on May eleventh. The reviews were excellent. Several days after the opening in New York, Heather came by the rehearsal hall with a pair of house seats for Leya and Celine. It was the first time any of them had treated the others.

A few minutes past eleven that night, the two classmates left the theater in Shubert Alley and met Heather at the stage door. She hugged them carefully to keep from spoiling her makeup.

"Did you like it?" she asked.

Of course they had! Everything about it! And Heather had stood out among all the other girls in the chorus.

"I wish I could introduce you to Miss Zorina," she said apologetically, "but her dressing room is mobbed after every performance." Sensing their disappointment, she took each by an arm. "Come on. Seven-layer cake at Little Lindy's, my treat."

As they fell in beside one another, Heather's tone turned confidential. "Do you know what our stage manager told us? Sol Hurok is going to pay Miss Zorina two thousand dollars a week in concerts—after our show closes. And old Baronova says doing a show is the ruination of a ballet dancer!"

"I'd like to be ruined like that for two thousand a week," Celine murmured.

"I can't even think of that much money," Leya said.

Heather laughed. "I can!" She stopped for a moment, then steered them out of the way a few doors so they could pass Sardi's.

"Someday," she said grandly, "I'll make a stunning entrance. Vincent Sardi will greet me and take my mink—full-length, naturally—and he'll say, 'Your corner table is ready, Miss O'Brien.' I'll thank him sweetly and plead with him to keep the autograph hounds away while I'm having my steak tartare and Clicquot thirty-three." The three of them laughed and headed uptown.

Over cake and tea, Heather answered their questions about backstage life with a musical show. "It's scads of fun, compared to that horrible grind with Baronova. You work, of course, but it's all so informal. Half the kids call Mr. Balanchine 'George.' And also I've met some of the backers—one especially." She rolled her eyes. "What a heart throb! And I think he likes me."

Heather was disappointed when neither Leya nor Celine questioned her about her new love interest, but she volunteered nothing more. By midnight they were saying their good nights.

On the subway to Brooklyn, Celine gazed up at the car cards thoughtfully. One of them read, "START AN EXCITING NEW CAREER AS AN EXECUTIVE SECRETARY AT $25 A WEEK!"

"I still think Heather did the right thing," she mused, "even if she does have help from her family. It must be nice to have help like that."

Leya nodded. Her scholarship would be ending soon. Even with such help it had been difficult to scrape together enough to buy leotards and ballet slippers. Threadbare toe shoes could be patched only so often, and even leg warmers improvised from the sleeves of one of her father's cast-off sweaters would wear out. Leya remembered her father's futile protest when she had taken a baby-sitting job at London Terrace. She had walked to the job from class to save carfare. A young assistant professor at N.Y.U., whose wife was working on a master's thesis, paid her twenty-five cents an hour to sit three evenings a week. The three dollars she brought home bought soup bones, lentils, tired vegetables, and two-day-old bread.

When they could not afford coal, she and her father had taken the skuttle and a lard pail and followed the delivery trucks, scavenging the dropped pieces for the kitchen stove. For twenty cents they could get a gallon of Pearl Oil for the kerosene heater in the front room. With care they could make it last a week.

If the weather turned very cold, her father would close off the bedroom, move her cot into the kitchen, and he would bundle up in blankets and a topcoat on the sofa.

Celine startled Leya with a question about her father's work.

"Papa's been working for two months now," she replied. "He's a mechanic for a motorcycle dealer. Papa's a master mechanic, but it was all he could find."

"At least he's working at something he knows. My father is a barman now. His father was a cordon bleu chef, and father was studying to be a chef, too, when he got drafted. He worked for a while in the kitchen at the St. Regis until men with seniority came back. Then he bussed for a year before they broke him in at the service bar at the Vanderbilt. If he finally gets work at the main bar, his tips will make it easier for him." Celine lowered her head. "I really feel guilty about not working to help my father pay for my lessons and my dance things. That's all my parents have ever dreamed for me—being a classical dancer."

Leya realized that her friend was echoing her own feelings. The small difference in her own case? Her dance lessons were still being paid for through the generosity of an anonymous donor at the home. But when the scholarship ran out, things would be much more difficult.

* * *

It was twenty after one when Leya let herself into the upstairs flat on New Jersey Avenue. She was certain her father would be asleep. Instead, she found him sitting at the kitchen table, his head in his hands.

"Papa, are you all right?"

Harry Marks looked up.

"If unemployed is good, then I'm all right."

Leya dropped onto the chair opposite him. "What happened?"

"A new shop boss. He's got *mishpocha* to take care of."

"But papa—you were his best mechanic. How could he do it?"

Harry smiled bitterly. "The Irisher *momser* did it easy. He said, 'Marks, I like it better working with my own kind.' " He straightened, and his eyes challenged his daughter. "Do you know what I said? 'Murphy, are your kind human beings?' He said, 'Okay, wise guy, don't give me your lip.' I said, 'I'm a human being, too, Murphy, with mouths to feed. I do good work. I do it fast. So what's wrong with that?' "

Leya rose and came around to stand behind him. "Papa, look," she said, resting her hands on his shoulders, "it was only an in-between job, anyway."

Harry nodded. "Sure, but in between jobs an in-between job is the best kind!"

"We'll make out, papa. I'll find a temporary job."

"You'll dance!" Harry said emphatically.

"I'm not a child now," Leya protested. "I know how much you want me to be a dancer. But even with the scholarship, you've gone without to buy me leotards and ballet slippers and toe shoes and to give me carfare and lunch money—everything!"

"*Bubeleh.*" He reached for his daughter's hand. "In all of your life, ever since I wound up your mother's little music box and let you watch the little dancer go around, what have you always wanted to be?"

Leya smiled. "Your daughter, papa."

"Don't joke!"

"It would only be temporary, papa."

Harry Marks studied his daughter.

"Leya," he said quietly, "to let something go out of your heart is not a temporary thing. Believe me, your father knows!"

CHAPTER 7

The following Monday morning, Harry Marks went to the employment office at the New York World's Fair grounds. He took a job digging trenches for the forms that would contain the asphalt walkways.

"Now I'm a ditch digger," he said to himself, "but it pays sixty cents an hour. So I'll dig!"

The fair opened on the thirtieth of April, 1939, a month after Adolf Hitler marched into Austria. One of Harry's co-workers, a World War I veteran, predicted the United States would stay out this time.

"Hitler just wants to make the Versailles Treaty fair," the man insisted. "Germans are decent. Give them a chance."

"From putting innocent people in prison you don't get to be decent!" Harry countered.

A week later the job ended. By early June there was no money left. Minnie Tabotchnik tried to give Leya twenty dollars to take home to her father. "Tell him you earned it," she urged. "You'll give it back to me when you get a job."

"But I can't, Cousin Minnie," Leya protested. "I've got to find work! I can sew. Maybe you can speak to Mr. Meyers about a job at Super Figure?"

Minnie glanced at her. The last thing she wanted for

Harry's girl was the need to follow in her own footsteps. She had been pretty once, too. So at forty-five what could a girl like Leya look forward to? A line supervisor like herself? God forbid!

Minnie studied Leya's figure. Few in this world could be better, she thought. A money-making proposition dancing wasn't, but if dancing helped make bodies like this girl's, Super Figure could put its entire line out in a one-page catalogue!

Suddenly a self-evident truth dawned on Minnie Tabotchnik. "My God!" she breathed.

Leya frowned. "What is it, Cousin Minnie? What's the matter?"

"Six months ago you could have been making good money." She clasped a palm to her forehead. "I should drop dead from stupidness!"

When Leya protested, Minnie silenced her. "Last year I supervised the garments for pictures in two catalogues. Believe me, Leya, a model you could be." She paused to give the girl another close inspection. "I forget you are growing up. A woman now. Next week, when the samples are finished, a photographer is going to take pictures for the new catalogue. I'll speak to my boss." A smile warmed her full, smooth face. "Believe me, if Mr. Zimbalist recommends you, the photographer will be happy to pay you, anyway, ten dollars an hour, maybe even twenty."

"But Cousin Minnie," Leya said, "I have never modeled. Even if they take me, how could they pay me like a professional?"

"You ask for it!"

"What if they want to know about my experience?"

"Darling, you have turned down a hundred modeling jobs because you are a professional dancer. You are only taking this job to please Mr. Zimbalist."

"But I'm such a bad liar. I don't even know Mr. Zimbalist!"

"Never mind," Minnie said, dismissing her objections. "Mr. Zimbalist will know you. He'll see your picture."

Leya shook her head. "I don't have any pictures."

"I have a snapshot, of you in your bathing suit at Coney Island last summer. Believe me, it will be enough. I'll have to reach to get it back!"

When Leya expressed her concern about missing dance lessons, Minnie waggled an admonishing finger.

"Two or three lessons you can skip. Better you miss dancing than eating!"

Leya smiled. "I'm very grateful, Cousin Minnie. I know I should do it. I was only worried about the scholarship."

"Maybe you won't need it anymore. Who knows? And one more thing. A girl who is old enough to dance in the opera and model for Super Figure is old enough now not to call her cousin 'cousin' anymore. So you'll do me a favor, darling, and just call me Minnie?"

At three o'clock the following afternoon, Leya Marks got off the bus at the corner of Fifth Avenue and Fifty-seventh Street and walked west to number 40. The city had been sweltering for more than a week. She had put on a demure yellow cotton short-sleeve, full-skirted dress trimmed with a white piqué collar and cuffs. Her hair was up in a braided "ballet bun" that poked prettily through the matching yellow cotton crescent hat. Later, when Christopher Morley's best-selling novel was made into an Academy Award-winning film with Ginger Rogers, Leya would refer to it as her "*Kitty Foyle* outfit."

John Wales's photo studio was on the fourth floor. Two models, carrying the badges of their profession—a round patent leather hat box and a large book of photographs—were waiting in the lobby. As they got into the small elevator, the taller of the two girls examined her coldly. The shorter one, a kitten-eyed blonde, smiled and pointed to the door. "Squeeze into the cattle car, honey!"

In the sweltering reception room, Leya's heart sank. The only chairs were occupied by four stunning girls. She recognized one of them from a recent *Vogue* cover. A half-dozen other girls were lounging against the walls, blotting away perspiration or repairing their makeup. Leya eased her way to the unattended desk and stood uncertainly.

"Sign the register, honey." She turned to find the blonde girl standing behind her.

"Oh? Thanks," Leya said, and reached for the pencil. She put her name below the others but hesitated when she came to the column marked AGENCY.

"You've got to put your office down, too," the girl said. "Otherwise, they won't know where to reach you—or send the check."

Embarrassed, Leya said, "I don't have an office. I'm not a model."

The tall brunette rolled her eyes. "Oh, great! There goes another job to an amateur!"

Several of the girls laughed, and Leya could feel the blood draining from her face.

"I'm no amateur," she said. "I'm a dancer. I came here because I was told to."

The blonde, who had signed in as "Dulcy Devine," slipped an arm around Leya's shoulders. "Don't pay any attention to this stone-faced klutz."

She turned Leya back to the desk again and pointed to the right-hand column.

"Put down your home phone—if you have one."

"I live with my dad," Leya explained. "We don't have a phone, but I guess I could put down my cousin's."

"Put it down. If you're planning to do some modeling to fill in, I know at least two agencies that will be glad to list you. You're a good type, honey. Hey—my name is Dulcy. What's yours?"

"Leya Marks."

The high-fashion model murmured, "Oh, Christ! Another relative!"

Dulcy Devine turned to face Leya's antagonist. "Listen, you stupid bone bag, one more crack out of you and I'm going to shove this box right up yours! Now lay off the kid!"

"Why can't these goddamned dancers stick to their own work!" the brunette retorted.

"Moving gracefully *is* their work!" She turned back to Leya. "Did they ask you to come for the Super Figure catalogue job?"

"Yes."

"That's what I'm here for, too." She gave Leya a quick appraisal. "With your body, you've got a chance." She aimed a thumb over her shoulder. "If they ever saw that flat-chested cartoon in the buff, they'd call the coroner!"

The burst of laughter in the tiny reception room was interrupted when the studio door opened. A smart, businesslike woman in her midthirties signaled the waiting models, "Okay, kids. Come in."

To Leya, the photographer's studio was not unlike the backstage area in the theater. The large room was cluttered with spotlights on stands, cables, tripods, and great rolls of photo background paper leaning against the walls. One wall was almost entirely concealed by a blown-up photomural of billowy cumulus clouds. Nearby were several huge photo cutouts of Manhattan skyscrapers. Overhead, the high ceiling was crisscrossed with a pipe grid. Clamped to it were clusters of spots and fill lights. In one corner was a pile of furniture and other props that could be used to dress the backgrounds.

The woman who had summoned them was interviewing the high-fashion models. Dulcy identified her as Dorothy Simpson. "She's Jon Wales's stylist. Stay on the good side of her and you'll get a lot of calls. Don't get too cozy, though. The rumor is that she prefers girls to boys."

Several minutes later the high-fashion girls were dismissed. Miss Simpson called the others together.

"How many of you are dancers?" Dulcy Devine, Leya Marks, and three other girls raised their hands. The two remaining girls hesitated and then raised theirs. The stylist regarded them with an amused smile. "What shows have you danced in?"

The girl who had been the least hesitant said, "Well, we didn't mean we were professional. But we're both good dancers—the Charleston, the Big Apple, the Jitterbug, stuff like that."

"Stuff like that is fun," Miss Simpson said. "In fact, I wish I knew how. But that's not what I mean. Let me see both of you do a pirouette."

The girls stared at her blankly. Miss Simpson turned to the Devine girl.

"Show them what I mean, Dulcy,"

"On this floor?" Dulcy pointed at the cement with exaggerated alarm.

"Do the best you can, dear."

Dulcy stepped out, crossed herself comically, made a small preparation, and executed a smooth turn.

Miss Simpson nodded in approval and turned back to the two girls. "That's what I meant. If you can do that the way Dulcy does it, you've got the job."

The two girls exchanged hopeless glances. One of them said, "We don't know how to do that stuff. But we could learn."

The stylist moved between them to steer them to the door. "By the time you learned, you'd be too old for this job. But thank you. And come back again."

"All right." She turned to the others. "You five will do." She looked closely at Leya. "But I'm afraid I don't know you."

"I'm Leya Marks."

"Oh, the dancer Mr. Zimbalist wanted us to see. I suppose it would be impertinent of me to ask you to do a pirouette?"

Leya moved out on the floor and pushed some bits of paper aside with her foot. Then, after the briefest preparation, she did an effortless double outside pirouette to the right and finished in the fourth position.

Dorothy Simpson was impressed. "My word! How long did it take you to perfect that? Or was it just a lucky one?"

"It wasn't luck," Leya said. "It happens by practice."

"I can believe that!" The stylist scrutinized the new girl again. "Well! You'll do just fine, I'm sure."

Turning to the others, she added, "All of you. But, of course, Jon's got to have the final approval. He'll be out in a minute."

She gave Leya another brief smile, then crossed the studio to the darkroom.

The other girls broke into relieved chatter. Dulcy Devine came over. "I'll say there was no luck in what you did, just hours of sweat."

"But I did have luck when you stood up for me out there," Leya replied.

The remaining three girls were conjecturing about how long the catalogue job would take.

"Last year it took five three-hour sessions," Dulcy said. "We got fifty bucks a session, not counting preparation and clean-up time. Two-fifty for the week."

"Two hundred and fifty *dollars?*" The blurted query was involuntary. Leya felt like a fool.

"Two hundred and fifty big ones," Dulcy replied. "And I got about fifty of it. My old lady and my old man drank up the rest, celebrating my good luck!"

"Do you think we'll get that much for this job?"

"Sure. Unless they've cut their line in half, that's how long it's going to take. And you want to know something? Working in underwear in this kind of weather is the best modeling job in town! Last year I did bathing suits in January, and they had to put on extra help to retouch the goosebumps!"

Leya laughed with the others. "How long have you been modeling, Dulcy?" she asked.

"It's been off and on. I was on the road with a show for over a year, and I danced in club choruses for a while." She thought a moment. "About six years."

"You must have started doing preteen clothes," Leya said.

"Preteen? Holy mother! How old do you think I am?"

"I don't know. My age, I guess. Nineteen?"

Dulcy Devine smiled sadly. "I was nineteen once. In fact, I've been nineteen six times already. And if you're smart, you will be, too!"

CHAPTER 8

Slender, blond, and balding, Jon Wales (he had been born Jacob Wallenstein) was a versatile photographer with a talent for discovering models who had what he called—with charming apology for the pun—"*je ne sais qualité.*" He could also meet unrealistic deadlines with no apparent sacrifice in the excellence of his work.

The girls he had chosen for the Super Figure job would do justice to his reputation. He could not claim to have discovered the new girl, Leya Marks, but he would be able to take credit for presenting an exciting new model who, if she wished to, could go on to jobs far more important than displaying the armorlike Super Figure foundations designed to preserve some vestige of youthful line in more than ample middle-aged figures.

In addition to her remarkable body and her lustrous copper hair, the Marks girl possessed one hell of an interesting face. Her complexion was smooth, and his practiced eye told him that her high cheekbones and the subtle almond uptilt of her wide-set eyes would all but preclude the possibility of an unflattering shot. Moreover, that the girl was connected in some way with the client made her a double asset. Another good year of Super Figure bread-and-butter catalogue work would more than pay the overhead.

Turning on his most charming smile, he addressed the girls. "We're going to have a week of hot work here, but on this job you ladies may be cooler than we are. I'll see you Monday at nine—in makeup. Thank you for coming."

The heat wave broke late Sunday night with great flashes of lightning, followed by thunderclaps that made Leya bury her head beneath the sheet. By morning the temperature had dropped thirty degrees, and the city seemed freshly scrubbed.

At twenty minutes of nine, she entered the elevator and was about to press the button when she heard a voice call, "Up, please! Hold it!"

Dulcy Devine hurried into the little cage. "Oh, hi, Leya! Missed my damned bus. I meant to be here at eight-thirty." She put her hatbox down and made a stab at settling her hair. Then she gave Leya a critical once-over. "Honey, you look great!"

At nine-thirty, Dorothy Simpson called the five girls out on the floor. Dulcy slipped a light cotton robe over the first set of bra and panties she would model and turned to Leya.

"Okay, dear heart, today you are a model. Come on out and give the little boys a thrill."

Leya hesitated.

"Hey! You don't have a wrapper, do you?"

"No. I didn't think to bring one."

Without a word, Dulcy Devine removed hers and put it around Leya's shoulders. "Take this one. We don't really need the damned things. It's just a habit."

Before Leya could protest, she found herself propelled into the studio where Miss Simpson was waiting.

"All right, girls. Leya, you're in the bedroom. Dulcy, you're in the bathroom," she said, indicating the two adjacent sets.

Dulcy clenched her fist against her forehead and made a tragic face. "Shot in the can? That is the story of my life!" She started for the set.

When Leya didn't move, Dulcy stopped and looked back. "You okay?"

"I don't know. All of a sudden I'm nervous."

"I was, too, the first time. And when I get nervous, I have

to pee. For a while the photographer thought he'd have to shoot the whole date in the loo!"

"When I get nervous, I freeze!" Leya replied.

"That's normal. But Jon'll thaw you out. He's easy to work with. Come on. Just visualize a couple of crisp, green C-notes dangling in front of your eyes and everything'll be peachy dandy."

By the end of the day, Leya felt more at ease than she would have imagined. Because of the slow shutter speeds, it was necessary for the models to hold absolutely still. Her ballet training helped. The principal problem was holding the smiles that Jon Wales wanted. They tended to freeze, and her eyes would grow glassy. Again Dulcy was helpful. In the dressing room, when they were changing after the first shots, she said, "Don't worry. The first time I modeled, my face turned to cement, too. Here, rub this olive oil on your teeth. Then your lips won't stick to them—and try to think of something funny."

By the third day, Leya felt that she had been modeling for years. During a lunch break in the sandwich shop down the street, Dulcy confessed that she had married at seventeen to get away from an unhappy home in Manhattan's Yorkville section.

"He was a musician in the club I was hoofing in," she explained. "I slept with him a couple of times. I thought I loved him." She smiled and looked off reflectively. "Love? He was nothing but a nonstop screwing machine. I was never off my back, for God's sake! In two months I was pregnant. He kept right on banging away, no matter how I felt—up against the red flag—any old time!" Dulcy shrugged. "So—what else? I miscarried."

Leya saw the anguish in the girl's eyes.

"God! I'll never forget that day! I was alone in the room with six bucks in my purse—and no friends. The son of a bitch had gone on an out-of-town gig the night before."

Leya shuddered. "What did you do?"

"I damned near bled to death."

"Couldn't you call somebody?"

"All I could do was sit on the can and scream bloody

murder. I thought my guts were falling out. Thank God the door was unlocked. There was a model who lived across the hall. She figured I was in trouble, so she knocked, and I screamed at whoever it was to come in."

Dulcy closed her eyes. "She took one look, and I thought she was going to pass out, too. Then she ran to her place and called a doctor who lived across the street." Dulcy looked up, suddenly contrite, "I'm sorry. I don't know why I dribbled all over you—and at lunch, too." She shrugged. "I guess—because of the thing I've got going now—I have to say it out loud once in a while to remind me not to be a horse's ass again." She cocked her head. "And maybe it's not so bad for you to hear some of this. With your looks you could have your problems, too—except maybe you've got more brains than I had—going in." She brightened. "Anyway, it wasn't all bad. The girl who helped me got me into modeling, and things have been going right ever since."

"I'm really glad," Leya said.

Dulcy gave her a grateful grin. "Just call me Hard-Way Hortense! Only from then on, if a guy wants in, two things have got to happen. I've got to like him a lot, so I don't have to do it with my eyes closed, and he's got to be real generous. I mean, *real* generous! You come up to my apartment sometime, dear heart, and Aunt Dulcy will show you what she means."

On Friday, the last day of shooting, Arthur Lieberman, the young merchandising manager for the Super Figure line, came to the studio with the proofs of the previous four days' work. When Dulcy saw him, she edged closer to Leya.

"His old man owns the company. But he's one of the nicest guys you're ever going to meet in this goofy business. Attractive, isn't he?"

"Yes," Leya answered. "He really is."

She studied the young executive as he stood talking with Jon Wales. She would have called him less handsome than nice looking. His features were regular. His sandy hair was wavy—like her father's—except that it was neatly trimmed and somewhat shorter. He was tall—almost six feet, she guessed—straight, and well set up. His conservatively cut gray suit fit easily.

"I really like the guy," Dulcy said. "I mean, just as a person. His mother used to be one of the top fashion illustrators back in the twenties. She paints now. Serious art. I met the Liebermans at the trade show I did for them last year. They're really great."

Leya continued to watch as Arthur Lieberman and the photographer appraised the black and white proofs.

"He's not thirty yet," Dulcy added, "but they say he's one of the comers in the industry. He's a real catch." She pretended a sad expression. "He never messes with the kids who work for him, though—worse luck!"

Dorothy Simpson hurried up to them and glanced at her watch. "I'm going to let the other girls go at five. Can you two stay for a couple of more hours? Overtime, of course."

"For double time," Dulcy said, "I'll skin in and out of these things all night. You just bring on the empty bras, honey. We'll fill 'em."

The stylist turned to Leya.

"How about you?"

"I'll be all right if I can use the phone."

"Use the one on the front desk. Mr. Lieberman wants us to reshoot four of the garments, and he wants you two to model them."

Dulcy did a couple of exaggerated tap turns and finished by blowing kisses to an imaginary audience. "We're stahs, dolling! We're stahs!"

Dorothy Simpson clucked. "You're incorrigible, Devine! I'll call you when they're ready. We should be finished by seven."

When Leya and Dulcy returned to the set, Arthur Lieberman came over to them. "I want to thank you both for staying. I was glad to see you on the date again, Miss Devine," he said. "The more we see of you in our catalogues, the better we like it."

Leya saw the twinkle in her friend's eyes.

"If you see any more of me," Dulcy said, "City Hall will censor us."

Consternation clouded young Lieberman's blue-gray eyes. Suddenly, he broke into helpless laughter. "I asked for that, didn't I? Let's put it this way. You're one of our favorite models. And now, you, too, Miss Marks," he added.

Dulcy patted his cheek and replied, "And you're one of our favorite clients!"

The shooting ran until a quarter to eight. When the girls were finally dismissed, Arthur came to the dressing booth and called through the curtain.

"Miss Devine—Miss Marks—Because your staying late is my fault, will you let me take you both to dinner?"

Leya paused with one leg in her skirt and whispered, "I thought you said—"

Dulcy shushed her. "So I was wrong!" she whispered. Parting the upper half of the curtain, she called out, "You mean overtime and food, too?"

"That's right. To be honest, I get heartburn when I eat alone, so I'm bribing you."

"I'm bribable," Dulcy called, "but I don't know about Miss B Cups here."

"You've both got to go," Arthur explained. "Otherwise, I can't take you off as a business deduction."

Dulcy pushed through the curtain, still buttoning her blouse. "I get it. Two girls for dinner is a deduction. One girl is a seduction. Is that it?"

Unable to cope with the Devine girl's fast gagging, he raised his arms in surrender. "What can I tell you?" he pleaded. "I don't have a date, and I hate to eat alone."

Dulcy pursed her lips. "That's not exactly the greatest compliment us kids have ever heard, but we understand." Ignoring Dorothy Simpson's scandalized stare, she continued, "But I'll tell you what—if you promise to take us to a real ritzy place like the Paper Cup Room at Nedicks, you've got a date." As she spoke, she linked her arm through Leya's and gave it a squeeze.

"It's too late to get a good stool at Nedicks," Arthur said. "I'm not known there. But if you girls don't mind, how about slumming at the St. Moritz?"

"We can tolerate it—just this once," Dulcy said archly.

Leya knew that she really should go home, fix an eggnog, and do the forty-five minutes of barre that she promised she would complete faithfully to keep in condition. But Dulcy's peremptory manner and the prospect of getting to know Arthur Lieberman weakened her resolution.

The dinner was a novel experience for Leya. Long Island duckling a l'orange, a vegetable new to her called "broccoli," served with sauce Hollandaise, scalloped potatoes, Bibb lettuce with Stilton cheese dressing, and cherries jubilee. When the ceremonious dessert was made in the chafing dish at the table, and the tongues of blue-green flame flared suddenly and enveloped the captain's hand, Dulcy looked up at him raptly. "How cozy!" She breathed. "There's nothing like warming your hands over an open fire in the middle of summer, is there?"

The man smiled. "When I was learning at La Chaumière near Versailles many years ago, m'amoiselle," he said, "another beautiful young lady distracted me, and I set my sleeve on fire!"

"And it burned all the way up to your heart, and you married the girl, didn't you?" Dulcy asked.

The captain recovered quickly. "But of course! How did you know, m'amoiselle?"

Fixing him with a sultry look, Dulcy replied, "Because, monsoor, I know zee Fraaanch!"

Leya laughed with Arthur Lieberman and wished that she had Dulcy's talent for clowning. All during the meal she had silently damned herself for the reticence that masked her self-consciousness. Every time her eyes met Arthur's, what she saw in them made her flush.

Dulcy, aware of the obvious chemistry, excused herself to go to the powder room.

Arthur Lieberman smiled across at Leya. "I want to tell you again how happy we are that you could give up your dancing long enough to do this job for us. I think you five girls are the most attractive we have ever used. I really hope you can arrange your schedule to do our new spring catalogue, too."

Leya felt herself flush again. "I'd like to work—I'd like to pose for the catalogues again, Mr. Lieberman."

"If your career permits?"

Leya hesitated. From the moment she had seen Arthur Lieberman, she had felt an undeniable attraction. She wished she were more experienced so she could tell if it had been—or was—mutual. He seemed eager to make himself agreeable. Was he just being very polite? Dulcy said he never messed with the kids who worked for him. But he was a very sophisticated man. Maybe this was all just part of a smooth line. Suddenly it was important to know.

"I like working for—" Leya broke off. "Posing is fun with Mr. Wales—and Super Figure. If you wanted me, I would try to work it out with the lessons."

Arthur Lieberman appeared relieved.

Shortly before eleven o'clock, he asked for the check, signed it, and received profuse thanks from the captain and the *sommelier.*

"My car's in the garage over on Broadway. Will you girls let me drive you home?"

Dulcy pointed south to Fifty-seventh Street. "By the time we walk over there, Mr. Lieberman, I can be halfway across town. But thanks a million."

He turned to Leya. "How about you, Miss Marks? It's no trouble, really."

"I live in Brooklyn," Leya replied. "It's silly to drive all the way over there when the subway runs just a block from my house."

"I don't mind at all," Arthur said.

Leya hesitated. "Gee, I really thank you, Mr. Lieberman, but I think I'd better take the train." She grew more flustered. "I mean—it's easier—and anyway—I really enjoyed the dinner and everything. It was wonderful. And thank you for saying I—we—did all right."

"You did more than all right, Leya." It was the first time he had used her given name. "If you're not a famous ballerina by then, we'll count on you to do our next catalogue—both of you, of course," he added, turning to Dulcy. "Come on," he said, moving between them and offering his arms. "Let's walk

Dulcy to her bus, and then I'll see you to the subway."

Excited though she was, Leya sensed that the evening had better end like this. Things had gone well up to now. In high school, she had met a boy who had kept her in a romantic flutter for a time. But Arthur Lieberman was no boy. And she was no longer a schoolgirl! She wanted very much to see him again, but she felt instinctively that he would be more eager if she did not appear to be.

"If you're sure you won't change your mind, Leya, I guess I'll have to let you go. By the way, does Miss Simpson know where we can reach you quickly—in case there is more to do?"

"Yes, Mr. Lieberman. I left my cousin's phone."

"Good!" Placing his left hand over hers, he said, "I hope I have a chance to see a lot more of you." Suddenly, the stricken expression was there again, and they both burst into laughter. "Damn it!" he groaned, still holding her hand. "Why does it always come out wrong?"

Some minutes later, relaxed on the single seat at the end of the subway car that she deliberately chose to avoid unwanted companions, Leya Marks thought over the past five days. Sometime on Monday, Arthur Lieberman had promised, there would be a check for three hundred and ten dollars waiting for her at Jon Wales's studio. My God! Enough money to last them for three months. Leya found herself drawn into a strange new fantasy, one in which she was transformed from an anxious teenager scavenging coal in the gutter to a glamorous photographer's model whose face and figure attracted men, all of whom resembled Arthur Lieberman. Suddenly, she was guilt-stricken. This was the first time since the lessons had begun in earnest in fifth grade that she had ever dreamed of being anything other than a prima ballerina.

She forced her thoughts back to practical necessities. Of course—except for this one night—she had done her barre work at home. But if there was to be more modeling work, and that seemed certain now, it was going to be far from easy to accept those dates and keep up with her classes. And still, she thought, until papa found steady work again, she could not refuse such an easy solution to their money problems, such an easy way to pull her share of the load after all those years.

A moment later, with a stab of conscience, Leya realized that, in all the excitement, she had not sent word to Madame Baronova that she would miss classes for several days. Those days would add up to a week now, a week without lessons to ensure that she would be able to continue them. The irony of it produced a mirthless little laugh.

CHAPTER 9

At one-thirty on Monday, Leya got off the subway at Columbus Circle and walked east on Fifty-ninth Street to Fifth Avenue. The weather had turned warm again, but the humidity was down. It was the sort of day that made you grateful for the good fortune that had made you a New Yorker. Part of the elation Leya felt was directly related to the pay check waiting for her at Jon Wales's studio. Another, more subtle part of the welcome sensation had been building since the previous Friday and the unexpected dinner date with Arthur Lieberman.

Dorothy Simpson had the check waiting—three hundred and ten dollars—PAY TO THE ORDER OF LEYA MARKS! The check was on the Chase National Bank, and the stylist, correctly assuming that the Marks girl would not have identification, phoned to expedite the cashing.

A half hour later, Leya left the bank with two hundred and sixty dollars in cash and a passbook for the new savings account she had opened with an initial fifty-dollar deposit. Also, on the plus side, was confirmation from Miss Simpson that there would be more Super Figure jobs later and perhaps some for other clients much sooner. Suddenly, Leya felt her world had turned right side up.

As she entered the dance studio, she found Celine had

arrived early, too. "I came to work out a sore tendon in my left ankle," she said. Her gray eyes turned grave. "Madame is very angry with you!" In another instant, her mood changed again. "I have something wonderful to tell you, Leya! Later!"

Alexandra Baronova was at the piano going over music with the accompanist. She turned as Leya came up and made the required *révérence.*

"I'm sorry I missed class, madame. I should have called, but we had some trouble at home. I had to help out."

The ballet mistress unreeled the glasses from the case pinned to her collar and held them to her nose. "What trouble can keep a serious ballet student from class for one week?" she demanded. "You had no death, did you?"

"No," Leya replied.

"Well? Tell me!"

"My father lost his job. I had to get temporary work."

"Tap dancing, I presume?"

"No, madame. I got a week's work as a model."

"I see. So your father lost his position, and you used that as an excuse to earn some easy money for easy work. Is that it?"

Before Leya could respond, Madame Baronova aimed a bony finger at her. "Let me tell you something, Marks. Short of death or serious illness, there is no excuse on this earth that can keep a dedicated ballet dancer from practice. Class! Every day! Sick or well! That is the heartbeat of ballet! If your heart stops, you die. If you stop dancing, you die!"

"I did what I had to do," Leya replied, and there was no mistaking the defiance in her tone.

Alexandra Baronova did her best to maintain the authoritarian façade that was so necessary to dance discipline. It was not always easy. Leya Marks was one of three or four students who were exceptional. In fact, she had hoped to show her off to Mr. Balanchine in a class concert soon.

"All right. We have a few minutes before class starts. Let us see what absence from class has done to you. Change immediately and come back to me."

Ten minutes later, Madame Baronova rapped the floor with the metal tip of her staff. "That will not do at all! You cannot miss a week of class and hope to come back in proper condition." The ballet mistress tapped the barre. "Stop clutching at it like a drowning person. Must I tell you that the barre is there only for the slightest assistance in keeping balance?" She glared at Leya. "Now, then. While I count, I want you to do four of each—no six of each—through the fifth position *grand plié* again. Ready? And one—and two—and three—and four—"

Leya was stiff, but she continued doggedly until the double exercise was finished.

"Terrible!" Madame Baronova scolded. "You are as tight as a fiddle string, and you have no stamina. That is why I say, if you girls and boys cannot keep up your lessons faithfully, you have no business taking up my time—or Mr. Balanchine's!"

Leya was unable to conceal her annoyance. "I told you, madame, I had no choice. I have been doing barre at home every night. If I were not serious about ballet, I would not be here."

"If you were in condition, you would not be so uncoordinated."

Leya felt tears of anger threatening. She turned and leaned against the barre.

Madame Baronova studied her for a time. "All right," she said in a gentler voice. "Rest a bit and wipe that makeup off your face. You look like Petrouchka! Then do the *port de bras, battement tendu simple,* and *jeté* and the *grand battement jeté.*" She glanced at the clock. "After that do them *sur la pointe, en avant, à la seconde,* and *en arrière.*"

The ballet mistress started to move away, then paused. "And do them very well. It is a poor time for any of my students to be sloppy. Mikail Khazar is coming by to watch class today. Of course, you know who he is?"

"No, madame," Leya replied.

"If you had studied the tradition of the ballet, you would know his name like you know—" She flapped her hands. "—Fred Astaire's!"

"I'm sorry, madame."

"The world will know him as an impresario here very soon, as they once knew him as a great star in Paris when I danced with him. He is here to choose dancers for the corps of his new Ballet International. If you impress him, in two or three years you might aspire to join him—if Balanchine continues to be entranced by Broadway and pictures." Disapproval dripped from the words. "Go on! Remember—finish *à la seconde*—and *en arrière!*"

My God, Leya thought, still leaning with her moist forehead almost touching the mirrored wall, *I'll have to do all of this again with the class! It's not fair!* Straightening, she rotated her head to free the trapezius muscles and the splenius muscles in her neck. They were the ones that always tightened under tension. Then, trying to ignore her aching muscles, she went through the exercises as madame had ordered.

By the time she had changed back from her toe shoes into her ballet slippers, the class was ready. Leya hurried to the water fountain in the hall. It was against the rules to drink, but she felt she had to. When she raised her head, Madame Baronova was standing in the doorway.

Behind her was a man who appeared to be her contemporary. Instantly, Leya knew it was Mikail Khazar. His bearing and dress were typical Old World. The supercilious gaze, directed down his thin straight nose, differed little from madame's gaze when she was registering disapproval.

"So, Miss Marks, you do have a penchant for disobeying, do you not?"

"My mouth is very dry, madame. I did not swallow much, but I had to have just a little."

"Very well," the ballet mistress replied. "We shall see what other tolls your infractions have taken."

By the time Leya had taken her place at the barre, she was seething. "Damn her!" she exploded. On her right, Celine Cervier shot her a warning glance and made a shushing sound. On her left, Kent Kendall, a strongly built young man with a sensitive face and expressive blue eyes, whispered, "Bravo!"

At twenty-four, Kent was the oldest and the most accomplished male dancer in the class. He had studied in Paris at the Ecole Royale and in Florence as the protégé and companion of an effete Italian count. Leya knew that Kent's family was reported to be wealthy. They had a home at Southampton on Long Island—an estate, really. And Kent had spoken of his own summer cottage at a place called Cherry Grove on Fire Island off Long Island's south shore.

In the upcoming student recital for Mr. Balanchine, Kent Kendall would dance the coveted male solo in the *Les Sylphides pas de deux.* It was generally conceded that the female soloist would be Leya or Celine. In making her plans, Madame Baronova knew that Marks and Kendall would be the more attractive couple. In contrast to Kendall's muscular, golden blond beauty, the exotic earthiness of the copper-haired, full-figured Marks girl would be stunning. Even so, the ash-blonde French girl seemed to typify best the ethereal old-school ballerina. The ballet mistress conceded privately that as dancers there was little to choose between Marks and Cervier.

Underlying Madame Baronova's harshness with Leya was a deep concern that the girl would not be "up" for the performance because of outside distractions. If George Balanchine—already impressed by Kent Kendall—found that Leya Marks was as promising, both students might very well receive featured roles in the upcoming opera productions. Madame Baronova had little to comfort her in her late years other than the precious few students who fulfilled their promise under her tutelage.

By the time the customary twenty-minute barre exercises were completed, Leya's muscles were screaming, but there was to be no relief. Madame Baronova called the class to the center of the floor.

"Marks—Cervier—Nestler—to the right first—and then to the left—*glissade, tour jeté, glissade, arabesque.* Ready?" The ballet mistress nodded to the pianist, who struck the preparatory chord.

In threes, the class executed the first combination without comment from Madame Baronova.

"All right. In the same order again—*brisé, brisé—assemblé—* also to the right and to the left. Ready?"

Again the class went through the combination.

"No, no! Miss Marks, please step out!"

Puzzled, Leya glanced at her classmates and moved out front.

"When an *assemblé* is left, it is necessary to do what?"

The way the question was phrased confused Leya. "I'm afraid I do not understand, madame," she replied, trying to suppress her shortness of breath.

"Miss Marks! The question is simple, and so is the execution. When an *assemblé* is left or right, it must be preceded by a definite preparation. Is that not correct?"

"Yes, madame."

"Then why did you not do it?"

Leya stood mutely. Of course she had made the preparation. It was physically impossible to do the transition from a *brisé* to an *assemblé* without a *demi-plié.*

"Why do you not answer me, Miss Marks?"

"But madame, I did the *plié—*" Automatically, Leya's body moved to demonstrate.

"Ah, yes! Now you do it with style and expression. Then why did you do that childish little—"Madame Baronova fluttered her hands in annoyance—"hopscotch, or whatever it was? Perhaps you were combining tap dancing with ballet?"

Snickers from several of the younger girls were silenced by a warning look. When Madame Baronova turned back, Leya made no attempt to conceal her feelings. "I am sorry, madame." Her voice was edged with anger.

The older woman turned back to the class.

"All of you were sloppy! Now, once again—*brisé, brisé, brisé, assemblé* left—and do not make the *plié* preparation a little hippety hop. Make it smooth and fluid. All right? Again please."

Still angry, Leya made a supreme effort to do the exercises flawlessly. When they reached the end of the sequence, Kent leaned close to her. "You're a tough little thoroughbred!" he whispered. "If she can keep you angry enough, she'll make you a star!"

"Much better," Madame Baronova said, avoiding Leya's eyes. "Now then, one more combination. We have worked on this before, and we will continue until you can do it as second nature." She paused and allowed her eyes to move to each of the perspiring students in turn. "Do you know the secret of a virtuoso performance? Practice! Practice! Eternal practice! You must know every possible combination so thoroughly that you need to give it no more time than an answer to the question how much is two plus two? Paderewski does not wonder where the chords are. Heifetz does not grope for double stops. To a virtuoso, a perfect performance is as natural as breathing. And so it must be with dancers! When you have reached that state of perfection, you will know freedom." She lifted a warning finger. "But you will never be free!"

She paused again for emphasis.

"Now then, we will do four times *brisé volé,* a *glissade jeté,* a *relevé arabesque,* closed fifth *failli* to the fourth-position preparation, and six *fouettes,* and finish cleanly. Clean!"

The combinations continued for an hour before the class was allowed a break. At the barre, where Leya had hung her towel, Kent Kendall flexed his legs to keep his muscles warm and spoke to her in a quiet voice. "You were not sloppy, you know. I led off the group right behind you, and you did it perfectly. it was very unfair."

"It sure was! I'm dead serious about dancing, Kent! I'm not like some of these kids from Park Avenue who take lessons because it's something rich young ladies do."

Kent laughed. "I'm glad you didn't include rich young men! My parents live on Park Avenue, through no fault of mine."

"I didn't mean you, Kent," Leya replied with a touch of contriteness. "You're the best dancer in this group. Everybody says you're ready to go with Balanchine now."

"Not with Balanchine, dear girl. I have some other ideas about where our generation of dancers should go." He glanced toward Madame Baronova, who was talking with Mikail Khazar in the far corner of the studio. "I'll be more definite later."

Madame Baronova saw Mikail Khazar to the door and rapped the class to order. The second hour was devoted to variations, movements strung together in a fluid series. Each member of the class was required to submit to Madame Baronova's scrutiny. Few of them passed without correction.

Leya received more than her share. "Weak, Miss Marks,

very weak! At this late date, do you remember why the emphasis on turnout? It must become a part of your subconscious. If your turnout is maximum, you have complete freedom to move in any direction. All afternoon you have been restricting yourself. Your turnout is far less than ninety degrees. By your absence you have lost technique!"

If she brings that up once more, Leya thought, *I'm going to scream.* She knew that during directional changes she had been cheating a bit, skidding on the ball of her slipper on demi-point, but there was a reason for it. Her hip joints ached, and the menstrual cramps that were threatening made her lower stomach tender.

After what seemed to be time interminable, Madame Baronova called them all together at the barre. "You know that on the fifteenth of September we have our invitational recital in Mr. Balanchine's honor. Yes? This year," Madame Baronova continued, "we will choose our program from Michel Fokine's examination performances for the Imperial Russian Ballet School. We will take excerpts from the second version of his *Chopiniana.* It is known now by a more familiar name. Will you tell it to me, please?"

A dozen voices responded, "*Les Sylphides.*"

"Yes, a classic that will make sufficient demands on you students to permit Mr. Balanchine a fair judgment of your progress and your potential."

Madame Baronova cupped her clawlike fingers over the ornamental silver head of her staff and gazed at the line of perspiring faces before her. Deliberately, she let the anticipation build, then singled out four girls and four boys and asked them to stand apart.

"You will be used . . ." Her gaze returned to the others, and Leya was aware, as were Kent and Celine, that she was purposely ignoring them. Kent nudged her.

"If she's going to do variations from *Sylphides,* the entire class must be used," he whispered. "The old dame is playing games!"

The ballet mistress called out two boys and four girls. "Please stand with the others," she directed. Drawing in a deep breath, she resettled her hands on the head of the staff and gazed at Kent Kendall.

"The choice for *premier danseur* seems obvious, does it not?" The question was addressed to herself. "So, Mr. Kendall, you shall do the Nijinsky role in the second *Mazurka.* Also the *pas de deux* in the second *valse.*" She paused.

"We have two roles remaining, *première danseuse* to dance the first *valse*—the Karsavina role, Opus seventy, number one—and a *danseuse étoile* to dance the first Mazurka—the Pavlova role, Opus thirty-three, number three." She paused again, looking above their heads.

"Good God, how she loves to prolong the agony!" Leya whispered to Kent.

"So," the ballet mistress said with maddening deliberateness, "let us choose for the *première danseuse* a lady whose industry has earned her a principal role perhaps a bit sooner than is wise." She turned to a young blonde standing a bit apart. "You, Kyra, shall have a chance to show Mr. Balanchine what you have learned."

Kyra Koslov, a sturdy sixteen-year-old girl whose long blonde hair obviously required "regular maintenance," as Kent put it, gasped audibly. The choice was less a happy one than a surprise. Instantly, all attention was focused on Leya and Celine. Kent Kendall, standing between them, reached down and took each girl by a hand. Leya's was trembling.

"So now," Madame Baronova was saying, "we must choose between two of our most promising young ladies for the *danseuse étoile* role. Yes?" She paused with pursed lips, lifted her head, and looked down her nose at the two girls.

"This is a most difficult choice. In reaching it, it has become necessary to make a decision based not alone on talent—which is equal in this case—but also on what I must assume will be the condition of the dancers six weeks hence."

She looked directly at Celine. "A very difficult decision, and a deep disappointment for one of you, but I have judged that the role must go to Miss Cervier."

Kent Kendall felt Leya's body go rigid. An instant later, she jerked her hand free, moved forward as though to challenge the decision, then whirled and fled from the studio.

A charged silence fell over the class. Madame Baronova continued to look at Celine.

"In the sense that it demands faultless execution, purest sense of line and timing, and the most perceptive understanding of the story, *Les Sylphides* is one of the most difficult ballets. When Fokine conceived it after listening to Chopin's suite and eventually revised it to make it a classic romantic ballet, he did so to put the students to a rigorous test at the annual Imperial Ballet recital. Nothing choreographed since that time makes a more subtle demand." She paused and looked around at those who had not been singled out. As she was about to speak, Celine raised her hand.

"Madame–"

"Yes?"

"I am very happy to have been chosen, but–" She broke off uncertainly. "Well, I intended to speak to you before class, but there was no opportunity." As she groped for words, Celine knew that she was not keeping to the truth. She had been certain that she and Leya would end up in the two leading roles. Which one she got made little difference to her. The important thing was to have her right to perform a leading role confirmed in the presence of the entire class.

"What did you intend to speak to me about?" the ballet mistress demanded.

"I will not be here to dance in the recital, madame."

"Indeed? And just where will you be, if I do not presume?"

"I have been offered a position with a professional company, beginning immediately."

An excited whisper ran through the class. Madame Baronova pounded her staff, pistonlike, on the floor.

"Silence!" Slowly, she went on. "And may I ask just what professional company finds it necessary to offer contracts to babies? Of course, you will start as a *première danseuse* at the very least?" she added with chilled sarcasm.

"I will start as a member of the *corps de ballet* at Music Hall, madame," Celine replied.

"So, you have waited for this most propitious moment to advise me that all of my consideration is for nothing. That is very thoughtful of you, Miss Cervier, particularly since you must have known of this great opportunity some days or weeks ago. No?"

"I did not learn of it until yesterday afternoon, and I have not given my word yet, but I intend to at five o'clock, as I promised."

Madame Baronova rapped her staff viciously. "All right! The class is dismissed!" When the students began to scamper toward the dressing room, Alexandra Baronova confronted Celine.

"You have left me in an impossible position. You realize that, do you not?"

"I do now," Celine confessed. "But I thought Leya and I would dance those principal roles. Kyra could have taken my place, and one of the other girls, Nestler or Newman, could have done the Karsavina role."

The ballet mistress smiled humorlessly. "You also presume to make my choices for me, do you? Well, it happens I do not agree with you."

"I am sorry," Celine replied, "but I can't help it. I need to earn money. Besides, why can't Leya dance the part? She is one of the best in the school."

"The right of judgment is mine!" the older woman snapped. "Miss Marks is out of condition."

"But there are six weeks, madame." Celine said. "That is plenty of time."

"Perhaps, but most likely not!" The ballet mistress glared at Celine. "So. You are dismissed now! I am not required to have such discussions with students!"

Celine retrieved her towel from the barre and walked to the dressing area. She expected to find her friend in tears. Instead, she found Leya seated on the long wooden bench, stripping off her sweat-soaked leotards. Her face was hard set with frustration and anger. Celine dropped down beside her.

"I was going to tell you first that I got a job. I'm leaving to join the *corps de ballet* with Leonidoff. But after that horrible thing she did to you, I told her in there." Celine reached out and rested a hand on Leya's forearm. "That was terrible, to do that to you in front of the class."

When Leya did not respond, Celine peered at her anxiously.

"You are not mad at me, are you?"

Leya lifted her bottom from the bench to slip the leotards from beneath her and skinned them down her legs.

"Don't be silly."

"I wouldn't blame you for being sore, Leya. If I had told her I was leaving when I first came in, she probably would have chosen you for the Pavlova part."

"No, she wouldn't."

"But there's nobody else, Leya. Kyra is a year from ready. Besides, she's not right for the part. She is too heavy." Celine paused. "How do you know she wouldn't have given the role to you?"

"Because she wants to make an example of me for missing a week of class."

"That's silly!" Celine said. "There's six weeks to get up again. And besides, I watched you. You looked tired, but gee—a double dose of barre—I'm surprised you could even stand up." She glanced toward the entrance. "I think you're wrong. I'll bet she thinks you're not serious about ballet anymore because of the modeling."

Madame Baronova had been standing in the dressing-room entrance for some seconds before the two dancers were aware that an unusual silence had fallen over the room. When Leya, now clad only in her cotton panties, turned from her locker, the ballet mistress addressed her.

"When you have dressed, Miss Marks, I would like to speak to you." She nodded toward the studio. "Out there, if you please."

The anger that she had been trying to control rose in Leya's throat.

"If you want me to dance Celine's role now, no, thank you!" she blurted.

"You will not be in the recital," the ballet mistress replied in a firm voice. "But I want you to understand why. Whether or not you choose to believe me, it is for your own good." As she turned away, Leya called after her.

"Whether or not you believe it, for my own good, I'm leaving your class!"

CHAPTER 10

On Tuesday morning, in his office at Seventh Avenue and Thirty-fifth Street, Arthur Lieberman answered the buzz that told him Jon Wales was returning his call.

"You're going to like the latest proofs, Arthur," Wales said. "Do you want me to send them down by Red Arrow?"

"Don't bother, Jon. Hold them there. I want to talk to you about a promotion tie-in on our Circe negligees and Night-in-Gale nightgowns. We don't have much time on it. If we can get the effect we want, we'll put the promo in the works now with Arnold Constable here and Marshall Field in Chicago—and probably the Broadway in L.A."

"What sort of effect do you want, Arthur?"

"Do you remember those flying-through-the-night shots you showed me some time back?"

"Very well. They were low-angle strobe shots. The kid who wore the Hattie Carnegie gown was a dancer. I don't remember her name."

"That's not important. If we go ahead, I'd like to use Miss Marks, anyway. But what I want is not a leaping effect. I want more of a suspended-in-space dream effect—very graceful and filmy."

Jon Wales made a musing sound. "Leaps generally come out looking like leaps, Arthur, but I've been toying with another idea. Let me think about it. One way or another I'm sure I can get the effect you want. How soon would you like to try some test shots?"

Arthur Lieberman glanced at his desk clock. It was nine-fifteen. "The sooner we find out if it will work, the better. This would be a pre-Christmas promo."

"How about midafternoon tomorrow? I'm going to be clear after twelve."

"Fine—if I can reach Miss Marks. I'll get back to you."

Jon Wales was about to volunteer to assume the task and thought better of it. Normally, he would contact the models and ask them to come in for client approval. But not in this case. He smiled to himself. It had been obvious ever since the catalogue date that where Leya Marks and young Lieberman were concerned, standard operational practice would not hold.

Seconds after the pair finished their conversation, Dorothy Simpson called United Theatrical Supplies and ordered an eight-foot trampoline sent over by truck.

Arrangements were not so simple for Arthur Lieberman. After frustrated efforts to reach Leya, he remembered the obvious and had his secretary call Minnie Tabotchnik to his office. That evening, unable to conceal her satisfaction, Minnie gave Leya the message to call Arthur first thing in the morning.

"Never mind the ballet dancing now, darling—for a while. If Arthur is calling you for another job, it means what I am hearing is correct."

Leya felt a stir of excitement. "And just what are you hearing?"

"That Mr. Arthur and his father and Mr. Zimbalist are thanking me for speaking for you. You have made a very good impression. You won't be sorry you told the old Russian to drop dead."

"I'm not sorry about that, Minnie, but I'm not stopping my lessons, either. I'm going to study with Eddie Caton again."

The older woman threw up her hands. "Make money modeling, spend it dancing." She leveled a finger at Leya.

"Believe me, it's better you should make money modeling and *save* it!"

At eight-thirty the following morning, Leya called from the public phone in the pharmacy down the block. She was put through to Arthur immediately.

"Thank you, Leya. I didn't mean to make it sound quite so urgent, but something has come up—a new promotion for some department stores—and if you are able, Jon Wales and I would like to have you model for us. Could you possibly do it this afternoon—for a couple of hours?"

"Yes. I'm sure I can, Mr. Lieberman." She hoped she hadn't sounded too eager.

"Great! I'm not sure just when Jon will be ready for us. Could you call him and ask, and arrange to be there?"

"Yes."

"I'll call him after my meeting and confirm the time. I want to try for a very special effect. One that needs a dancer. I can't imagine anyone better for it than you—if you like the idea."

"Thank you, Mr. Lieberman. I'm sure I will. I mean, I—we—enjoyed working with you very much."

Arthur laughed. "As my father used to say before mother broke him of it, 'likewise!' "

Jon Wales was securing the top batten of the large photomural cloud drop to the overhead pipe grid when Leya entered the studio. He greeted her with a surprised smile.

"You're earlier than I expected! A commendable trait in a model."

Dorothy Simpson entered the studio carrying a small package. "Hello, there!" she said. "Obviously somebody got the message through." She indicated the package. "Wait until you see the gorgeous jewelry I borrowed. All genuine imitations from Ciro. And wait until you see the gossamer dreamies you're going to wear."

Jon Wales cursed under his breath as he skinned a knuckle on a wing nut holding a fill light. Turning, he addressed his stylist.

"Take Leya to the dressing room and show her the things Arthur wants to photograph."

When Dorothy held up the first of the sheer creations, Leya's eyes widened. "My God!" she gasped. "You can see right through them!"

"But of course, darling," Dorothy replied. "That's what these little flimsies are all about—transparent seduction!"

Leya held the tissue-thin silk up to herself. "I guess with panties and a bra it won't be so bad."

Dorothy tried to suppress her amusement. "I don't believe you, Leya Marks! You can't model sexy garments like these with your underthings on. If we see anything but you under them, the whole illusion will be spoiled."

Leya slipped her hand beneath the sheer full skirt of the negligee and held it to the light. "But you *can* see everything!"

"Of course, dear, if you pull the material tight against your skin. But these things have twelve yards of silk in the skirts. They're so full from the waist down that you'll barely see the outline of your body. Just a suggestion is what we want."

When Leya began examining the other things in the large, flat cardboard garment box, the stylist excused herself and hurried across the studio.

"Jon," she called in a low voice, "I need to see you for a minute."

"What's the matter?" he asked as he tightened a knob on a multiple flash tripod.

"We're having a bad case of modesty in there."

"Okay. I'll be there in a minute. So see what you can do with her hair."

Wales finished positioning the last of the multiple flash stands that would illuminate Leya as he tried to catch her in midleap. He understood her problem. Leya as a new model had not been self-conscious for long in the serviceable foundation garments and bras she had worn for the catalogue shots. Actually, they were less revealing than the bathing suits the girls were wearing. The expensive filmy garments Arthur had sent would pose no problem for a Dulcy Devine or for a dozen other veteran models, most of whom suffered no compunction about posing for so-called "artistic nudes." But there were ways to reassure a modest newcomer!

He paused outside the dressing cubicle. "Are you decent in there?"

"Come in, Jon. We're fooling with hair," the stylist answered. He entered to find Leya, still dressed in her blouse and skirt, seated before the dressing-table mirror.

"Your hair looks beautiful," he said. "Let's have it brushed out and caught loosely with a ribbon for now."

Leya looked up at his reflection in the mirror, and he saw her uneasiness. To Dorothy Simpson, he said, "Get me the Sally Bain bath oil shots."

The stylist returned in a matter of seconds with an envelope file. Wales removed several black-and-white prints and handed them to Leya.

"I want to show you these because they've won some awards."

While Leya studied the shots, the photographer spoke. "As a dancer, you are asked to interpret many roles. As a model, you'll be asked to do the same thing. It's a part of your professional obligation—a part of your job—and that's just what it is—a job. Nothing more." Leya continued to look through the proofs but made no sign she had heard.

Slightly annoyed, Jon Wales continued. "With that dancer's body of yours, Leya, it's inevitable that you're going to be asked to pose in the nude. Whether or not you do will depend on who does the asking, what the photos are intended for, and how cleverly you are posed." He pointed to one print in particular. "This is all the same model. Do you recognize her?"

The model's face, partially in shadow, was turned a bit away from the camera. The leg nearest the lens, bent at the knee, was embraced by the girl's arms. The swell of her breast was visible but the nipple was concealed behind the arm. The effect was sculptural and lovely.

"You still don't recognize her?" Wales asked. "You call the girl your friend now."

Suddenly, Leya knew. "It's Dulcy, isn't it?"

"It's Dulcy all right, and the reason I wanted you to see these is to prove that an unself-conscious model with a beautiful body—and a photographer who is serious—can collaborate to make a genuine work of art. I took these last year. They won first prize at the Annual Fashion Photographers' Exhibition."

Wales returned the prints to the envelope and handed them to the stylist. Resting a reassuring hand on Leya's shoulder, he said, "The shots I'm going to take of you this afternoon and this evening will be beautiful, too, Leya, and just as impersonal. In your model's book, they'll get you a lot of high-class, high-paying work." He patted her paternally. "The last thing in the world I want is to have you uncomfortable in front of the camera. Do you understand that?"

"Of course," Leya replied with less conviction than she felt.

"Good. Now, come on out to the studio. I want to show you how I plan to get these shots. I'd like you to do some mild acrobatics for me, and let me add that if you were not a beautifully coordinated dancer, I would not even suggest this. Do you know what a trampoline is?"

"Yes," Leya replied. "I've never been on one, but they look like fun."

He led her across the studio to the area where the large sky cyclorama had been rigged. Six feet or so in front of it the trampoline had been positioned so that Leya, propelled upward by the springs, could be snapped in midflight against the sky.

"Take off your shoes," he instructed, "and let me help you up on the thing. I want to show you what I have in mind. If you know what effect I'm trying to get, you'll feel more at ease."

As he steadied her, he added. "There is something else you should know. I'm going to be shooting in virtual darkness except for a flash that lasts about one five-hundredth of a second. In those full negligees and nightgowns, Leya, your figure is going to be in silhouette. The light will bounce off the material—and some off your face and neck and arms. The finished shots will be as subtle, and in as good taste, as those I took of Dulcy."

When he saw Leya begin to relax a bit, his manner lightened. "Okay? Now, why don't you try to get the feel of this thing for a moment? If you have any misgivings, then it's out. We'll try something else."

Leya took a few uncertain steps on the elastic canvas. The springs around the edge of the trampoline snapped her leg up the instant she unweighted her feet. After a minute or so, she got used to the fast reaction and compensated for it.

"It's like walking on a rubber floor," she said, smiling at the photographer. "It's sort of fun."

"Good!" Jon Wales said. "You're just what I thought you'd be—a natural." He moved back and picked up one of the reflex cameras. "Now just stand in the middle of the thing for a second and let me see something."

He squatted down with the twin lenses angled upward until the trampoline was out of the shot. "Do you want to try a couple of trial bounces? Just little ones, so I can see how high I can pan without going off the top of the cyc."

Gingerly, Leya bounced without letting the springs lift her completely clear of the canvas. After a few trials the fun of the thing overcame her timidity. At Coney Island, all the kids from the home would have rushed to give their coupons for a try at it! While Wales checked the field he would have to work with, Leya continued bouncing until her feet were well clear of the canvas.

"Don't get reckless, girl!" Dorothy Simpson warned. Then she added, "How wonderful your hair looks flying free!"

"Keep on bouncing until you get used to it," Jon Wales said without looking up from the reflex finder. "It looks just great!"

After a half-dozen more springs, each a bit higher, Leya landed, laughing and out of breath. "I've got to stop for a minute," she said. "This is harder than class!"

As Wales looked up, Leya lost her balance and sat down unexpectedly. After an instant of surprise, she joined in the burst of laughter.

Wales was excited. "Do you think after a little more

practice you could move your arms and legs into some balletlike positions?"

Leya leaned against the device's pipeframe, still breathing heavily. "I can try, I guess."

"Good. Let's try it a little later. Why don't you and Dorothy go to the dressing room now and change and put on some makeup? This sort of shooting requires some special makeup, so take your time. We won't do anything, really, until Arthur gets here." He moved to the edge of the trampoline and helped Leya down. Instead of following the stylist, she stood, frowning.

"I still don't see why I can't wear my underthings. They won't show, and I'll feel a lot easier, especially if . . ."

"Others are watching?" The photographer finished the thought for her.

"Yes."

Wales managed a good-natured laugh. "Leya, have you any idea how many times I've heard that from would-be models? Act like a pro, not some little pretty face hoping for a career. Unless you think I'm both an amateur and a liar, you have nothing at all to be embarrassed about. Do I have to assure you still again?"

When Leya did not react, he removed his handkerchief and patted a cluster of perspiration beads from her temple. Gently, he said, "Now go get made up."

The stylist returned to Leya and took her hand. "She'll be just fine, Jon," she said, smiling, "after I show her some of the tricks."

CHAPTER 11

In the dressing cubicle, Leya applied her makeup. Dorothy Simpson suggested light powder on the lower eyelid, darker on the upper eyelid, and a dot of cream on the lower lip for a more sultry look. Later, Leya allowed the stylist to brush out her hair and catch it at the nape of her neck with a short piece of faille ribbon. The soft, coppery fall cascaded in gentle waves almost to the middle of her back.

"If you're irresistible in that homemade outfit, God knows what you'll do to us in those!" Dorothy indicated the filmy boudoir garments. "Come on. Slip out of your things now. We're going to use some body makeup for these shots. I'll help you put it on."

She opened the drawer of the dressing table and took out a dried, encrusted sponge. "Ugh!" she said. "This one's for the 'verschloppen bucket,' as Jon calls it! I'll be back in a minute."

Leya was down to her panties and bra when the stylist returned. For a long moment, Dorothy stood stock still, and her impersonal façade appeared to crumble. Then, seeming to regain control of herself, she reached for the first of the negligees.

"Slip out of your underthings, my dear, and let's see how this one looks."

At the home and at the ballet classes, Leya had never felt any embarrassment at stripping. Now, in the presence of the stylist, she was strangely uncomfortable. She turned away to unhook her brassiere. Dorothy draped the garment over her arm and smoothed her palms across Leya's back.

"We'll have to touch out those strap marks," she said. "Turn around. Let me see how bad they are in front."

Leya obeyed reluctantly, half covering her breasts with upraised arms.

"For goodness' sake," Dorothy laughed, "let me see them, girl!"

Leya lowered her arms, well aware that there would be reddish crescents in the smooth white flesh beneath her bosom. There always were.

Dorothy laid aside the negligee and patted the fresh sponge on the cake of body makeup.

"Let's just cover these a little," she said, indicating Leya's nipples. "I don't think they'll show, but let's be sure. Thank God they're not those large brown splotchy ones that some of the girls have." She cocked her head. "Yours are absolutely pink and delicious! "

Leya reached out abruptly and took the sponge from her. "Let me do it, please."

Surprised and then amused, the stylist stepped back. "Of course, dear. Don't dab on too much."

Acutely self-conscious, Leya lifted each breast and blurred out the nipple with moist, flesh-colored powder while Dorothy watched.

"All right, dear, I'll do your back. I'm not sure Jon will shoot it, but let's do it, anyway." Leya wondered why the stylist's voice had gone strangely husky. "Good. Slip out of your panties now."

"I want to put on the negligee first," Leya said. The stylist made no effort to conceal her amusement as she held the garment open. When Leya slipped into it, she pulled the long hair free of the collar and led the tie around her waist from behind. Leya secured it and backed away from the mirror. After a brief glance, she groaned and gathered the loose folds to the front. "I can't go bounding around out there like this!"

Dorothy Simpson turned her around gently. "Now slip out of those panties, darling, and I'll show you a trick."

When Leya hesitated, the young woman gestured impatiently. "Dear Miss Marks, you're behaving like a rank amateur! Now do as I say—please!"

Reluctantly, Leya opened the front of the negligee, slipped the underwear down to her ankles, and stepped free. When she closed the garment and turned to the mirror again, the dark triangle of pubic hair was plainly visible.

"Don't worry," Dorothy said as she reached for the pancake makeup. "Turn around and face me. Jon doesn't want that in the photos any more than you do. This will save retouching."

Before Leya could protest, the stylist dropped to one knee and opened the folds. "Hold them away so I don't smear them," she said, smiling up at Leya.

Dorothy Simpson's left hand moved inside the garment to Leya's waist, paused lightly for an instant, then came to rest atop the curve of her hip. The movement raised goosebumps on the smooth flesh. Leya understood that the gesture was more than an attempt to reassure her. The sensation it caused in her was all the more frightening because it was strangely pleasant. As the young woman's hand moved inside the garment to explore her other hip, Leya shuddered. In the mirror she could see Dorothy looking up at her, but she could not force herself to look down.

Then the husky voice again. "Dear little Leya, can you imagine how exciting it is to work with one so lovely as you?"

Dorothy was openly caressing her now. Her right hand slipped around until its palm rested just below Leya's navel. Her fingers made feather-like kneading movements as they worked toward the edge of the pubic hair.

Leya felt her throat go dry. She was aware that Dorothy's voice had grown urgent. The words were unintelligible, but the whispering itself was a caress, and Leya felt herself tremble. Again she reached for the sponge. "I don't like to be touched," she managed to say. "I'd rather take care of it myself."

Suddenly, Dorothy Simpson rose. Her hands slipped up

beneath Leya's breasts. For the briefest moment, her thumbs moved on the erect, sensitized nipples. Then her arms slipped around Leya to urge her closer.

Terrified by her own emotional turmoil, Leya felt Dorothy Simpson's quickened breath as the stylist's lips attempted to press against hers. Leya uttered a wordless cry, wrenched herself free, flung the curtain aside, and burst into the studio. Jon Wales looked down at her curiously from atop a nearby stepladder.

Realizing that the entire front of her body was exposed, she darted back into the dressing cubicle and tore at the negligee.

"I don't want this job!" she gasped. "I'm leaving!"

Dorothy Simpson glanced frantically toward the studio. "You're not going anywhere!" she rasped. "You've got to do this job!" Stooping, she picked up the sponge she had dropped minutes earlier and thrust it into Leya's hand. "You have completely misunderstood my interest in you. Now, take the sponge and lighten yourself. I'll tell you how much."

Before Leya could respond, Wales came to the curtain.

"Are you two okay in there?"

"Fine, Jon," the stylist answered. "Are you ready for us?"

"Not quite. I want to see you first in the darkroom—right now, if you don't mind."

Dorothy shot a worried look toward the curtain. "I'll be right there, Jon." Turning to Leya, she pointed to the container of makeup. "Pat it on. Not too much. I'll be back in a minute—and for heaven's sake, Leya, don't do anything silly."

Confused and close to tears, Leya dressed hastily and hurried through the studio to the outer door. As she reached for the knob, it was pulled from her grasp by Arthur Lieberman, who was about to enter from the reception room.

Leya gasped when she saw him.

"Miss Marks—Leya!" He glanced at her curiously. "Don't tell me Jon's taken the shots already?"

"N-no," she stammered, trying to edge past him, "he's not ready yet. I was just going out."

Arthur caught her arm gently. "To get some coffee? Don't

bother. I'm having some sent up. I need some, too, after the day I've had." He smiled at her. "And besides, I have some ideas about dinner after we finish."

When she did not respond, Arthur looked at her closely. "Is something wrong?"

Leya brushed a hand across her eyes. "I—uh—" She shook her head. "I'm all right—thank you, Mr. Lieberman. I just need to get outside for a while—please?"

"Certainly." He studied her eyes. "If you don't feel well, why don't we postpone this session until tomorrow?"

"I feel all right, thank you. I just—" Before she could find a plausible excuse, Jon Wales peered from the darkroom door across the studio and waved. "Hi, Arthur! Be with you in a few seconds. I've got something to finish up in here."

Arthur returned the greeting. "Take your time, Jon. I'll visit with Miss Marks."

When he turned back, Leya was hurrying through the outer door. He thought of following her, then decided not to. Leya Marks was a dancer. Like actresses, they could be more temperamental than other women. He smiled to himself. Let her have a few minutes alone, he thought as he sauntered over to the set.

In the darkroom, Jon Wales studied his stylist. "Simpson," he said, fixing her with a severe look, "I thought you and I understood the playground rules around here."

"We do, Jon," the stylist answered with a trace of defensiveness. "The girl is as green as a gourd but worth taking a lot of trouble with. I simply wanted to put pancake on her patch, but you'd have thought I was trying to—" She broke off and wagged her head.

"Well, were you?" Wales asked.

"I was not! The girl's modesty is ridiculous! I could hardly adjust the garments on her, she's so jumpy."

"Look, Simpson," Wales said, deliberately prolonging her discomfort, "you and I have both been in this business long enough to make reasonable judgments about intended bed-mates. And we've been in it long enough to know which clients have personal plans for which girls." He sighed wearily. "So let it be understood right now, Marks is ripe and delicious, and we could both eat her with our favorite spoons. But where she is concerned, you and I are on a strict diet! If I can practice self-control where she is concerned, so can you. Can't you?"

Dorothy Simpson looked indignant. "My God, Jon, but you jump to conclusions!"

"Okay, Simpson, so I jumped. But don't you!" He affected a sorrowful demeanor. "I'd really hate to lose you—but not as much as I'd hate to lose the Super Figure account. Do I make myself clear?"

Dorothy tried to match his gaze. Finally, she averted her eyes.

"You make yourself brutally clear, Mr. Wales," she replied.

"Good." His look turned thoughtful. "You know, Simpson, it has just occurred to me—if the first man who tried to lay you had known what to do with you, he'd have had a purring tigress to comfort him, and things would have been a lot less nerve-racking for me."

Dorothy gasped. "That's the only stupid, cruel thing I've ever heard you say, Jon Wales!" She whirled and pulled open the inner door. "Goddamn you for it!" She left the darkroom.

A moment later, Jon Wales appeared, smiling blandly.

"Sorry. I had to put something in the stop bath," he said, glancing at Dorothy, who was walking toward the dressing cubicle. "Where's Miss Marks?"

"She's gone downstairs, I guess," Lieberman replied. "She seemed upset about something."

Dorothy stopped in midstride. Wales, concealing his own alarm, tried not to hurry to the outer door. "I know where she went," he called. "I'll be back in a moment."

Instead of taking the elevator, Wales ran down the fire stairs two at a time. On Fifty-seventh Street, he peered to the west. The sidewalk was crowded with office workers and late shoppers making their way home. Breaking into a trot, he made his way through them toward Sixth Avenue. At the corner, he found Leya waiting for the light.

"Look," he pleaded, "I know you're upset. But wait. I

must talk to you." He urged her out of the mainstream of hurrying pedestrians.

"Please don't jump to conclusions," he said. "I suspect that Simpson upset you with her—her attentions, didn't she?"

Leya's face was still set with anger.

"Yes, she did! I don't like strangers being personal with me. Not like that!"

Wales closed his eyes and nodded wearily. "I know, Leya, I know. But I also know Dorothy. She's one of the best stylists in the business. From the very beginning she took a shine to you, just like we all did. I guess you could say her affection sometimes goes overboard." He nodded, seeing the agreement on Leya's face. "But it won't happen again. I promise. Dorothy feels terrible. I had to beg her to keep her from quitting. It was very embarrassing with Arthur there."

When he saw her begin to waver, he pressed on. "This is a very important job, Leya—for all of us. I guess that's why we are all wound up a bit too tightly." He reached out and took her hands. "Please come back, Leya. You know Arthur picked you, especially. If you don't do this for him"—he broke off and shrugged—"I suppose he'll chuck the whole dream-girl idea."

Leya looked up at him uncertainly. She did not want to be the cause of a breach between Jon Wales and Arthur Lieberman. Moreover, she was anxious to see the young executive again.

Jon began to ease her back toward the studio. "Let's pretend nothing happened—because nothing did, really. Did it?"

Leya hesitated. "Except for her just being too—"

"Attentive? Well, we understand that now, don't we? So let's get back to the studio and see if we can't take some shots that will make us all famous." He smiled reassuringly. "And rich, of course!"

When Leya re-entered the studio with Jon Wales, they found Arthur Lieberman, coatless and shoeless, bouncing on the trampoline. Grinning like an overgrown kid, he absorbed the final bounce expertly with both knees and hopped to the floor.

"I haven't been on one of these things for years." He braced his hands against his stomach. "I'd forgotten how rough they are on your innards!"

"I know," Leya said. "I tried it a little while ago."

Arthur turned to Jon Wales. "After getting on this thing, I'm beginning to wonder if my idea is wise."

The photographer glanced at the setup, which had required several hours of meticulous planning.

"So far as I could tell, Leya handled herself very well on it, considering—"

"Considering that the girl's a dancer, not an acrobat!"

Dorothy Simpson's gratuitous comment made both men turn. She held up the negligee Leya had removed so hastily. "Somehow this one got torn under the right arm. I can fix it so it won't show, but I need a little time."

"Take all you need," Arthur replied amiably. Then he turned to Leya. "How long did you bounce on this thing?"

"Just a little."

Wales picked up one of the Rolleis and squatted in the position he had marked on the floor with blue grease pencil. "We didn't try it with the garments, but in her street things she got up high enough to lose the tramp." He peered into the ground-glass finder. "You could have gone higher, couldn't you, Leya?"

"I think so."

Arthur looked concerned. "If I hadn't gotten up there myself just now, I probably wouldn't be giving it much thought. But it's not as easy as I'd remembered it, and I used to be able to do back flips and layouts when I was a kid." He turned to the photographer. "Is this the only way we can get the midair effect, Jon?"

"No. But I think it's the most effective way. If I catch her at the top of the bounce, the material should be clouding around her. Back lit, it can be beautiful—stunning!"

"What's the alternative?" Arthur asked.

Wales looked up from the finder hood. "Get rid of the trampoline, pull down a big, neutral space cyc so the background and foreground blend, and ask Leya to try some of those running leaps ballet dancers do." He glanced at Leya. "*Grands jetés?*"

She nodded. "Yes—or *grand jeté dessus en tournant* if you want to see the face better."

"But," Jon Wales continued, "if we go that way, we'll get the usual running-in-the-wind effect."

Leya moved to the trampoline. For the moment, the problem of the all-but-transparent negligee was forgotten.

"Maybe a *brisé* would be better—with arms in an *arabesque* third. Let me try it." She slipped out of her shoes.

"Let me help," Arthur said, steadying her as she stepped up to the trampoline.

Moving with more assurance now, Leya positioned herself in the center of the canvas. She looked down uncertainly at her full cotton skirt. "I don't know if I can do a good *brisé*, but let me bounce a couple of times and see."

Still on his knees so he could shoot up for a low-angle composition, Wales bent over the finder again.

"Try a couple, Leya, but be careful. Don't overdo it, okay?"

Leya began a series of small bounces, increasing them until her feet were leaving the canvas. As she cleared the trampoline by a foot, then a foot and a half and two feet, Jon Wales kept muttering his approval.

Using her arms to help propel herself upward, Leya cleared the canvas by more than two feet. The sensation was exhilarating. For some reason, she found herself recalling an incident Madame Baronova had related about a critic who asked the great Nijinski how he managed to seem to float at the top of his spectacular leaping entrance in *Spectre de la Rose*. "You have but to pause for a moment at the top," he had replied. For the first time, Leya thought she understood what he had meant, for she did seem to pause momentarily at the apex of the leap.

"You'd better rest now," Jon Wales called to her. "Don't overdo it!"

Leya, remembering how Arthur had stopped the momentum instantly by absorbing the final bounce with flexed knees, timed the move perfectly and came to a rest.

"You did that like a pro!" Arthur said. "The next thing you'll be doing is a roundoff to the floor."

While Leya sat catching her breath, the photographer came to the edge of the trampoline.

"Do you think, at the top of the leap, you might be able to do something with your arms—like holding your skirt with your left hand? Can you pull it forward so the material will be between your body and the camera?"

Leya expelled a big breath and nodded. "This skirt's not all that full, but I'll try."

"What about your legs? Can you get them into position and arch your back?"

"I think so," Leya replied. "If I can get high enough."

"Try it whenever you're ready," the photographer called as he repositioned the camera. "Real easy at first, right?"

Leya drew in several more long breaths, then positioned herself in the center of the canvas with her body in profile to the camera. Holding the hem of her skirt in her left hand, she pulled it forward slightly as she began the preparatory bounces. As she went higher, Jon Wales's voice grew more excited.

"Wonderful, Leya!" he called. "When you feel ready, position the legs."

Arthur moved back and crouched beside the photographer to get an approximation of the effect.

Leya tried a little backward arc at the apex of the leap, then brought her feet together again for the next bounce.

"Great!" Jon Wales called out. "Can you do a couple more without tiring?"

"I think so," Leya gasped as she drove her feet still harder into the elastic surface in an attempt to gain more height. The extra effort sent her up higher than she had gone before. At the top, she elevated her chin unconsciously as she would have in class. Her arms moved forward in a full third position, her back arched, and her legs extended behind her far more than they had.

You have but to pause for a moment at the top, she thought, and she tried to, holding the position a split second too long. Suddenly, she was coming down too fast. Her right foot struck the trampoline slightly behind her, and she felt her body being propelled forward out of control. As she tried desperately to regain her balance, her left foot struck the canvas at the welted edge, where the material was secured to the springs by metal grommets. It seemed to hold there for a second, and then the canvas rolled down. Her ankle and lower leg plunged between the springs, and her knee wedged between the canvas and the pipeframe. An instant later, with nothing to grasp, her body twisted backward off the edge.

CHAPTER 12

As the big Checker cab lumbered up Fifth Avenue toward Mt. Sinai Hospital, Arthur Lieberman tapped the driver's shoulder.

"Go straight to the emergency entrance," he ordered.

He turned back to Leya, who was propped in the corner with her left leg stretched out along the seat. Her face was dead white, beads of perspiration were forming on her forehead and upper lip. Arthur, riding backward on the jump seat, did what he could to comfort her.

Waiting for them in the emergency room was Arthur's doctor, Max Lewin, a stocky man with a broad, well-seamed face and a shock of curly, iron-gray hair. After examining her knee, he gave her a sedative and sent her to the x-ray room.

It was almost eight o'clock by the time the tests were completed and Leya was wheeled to a private room overlooking Fifth Avenue. Dr. Lewin came in, accompanied by Arthur. As drowsy as she was, she could see the concern on Arthur's face.

Dr. Lewin reached for her hand.

"Well, young lady, I must say that an x-ray does not take the most flattering picture of you. But it does tell us some things that we need to know."

He reached behind him and pulled a chair up.

"It is not as bad as it might have been. Two ligaments appear to have been pulled but not torn. Still, it's not the simple sprain I hoped it was."

He paused, still holding her hand.

"You chipped off a little piece of cartilage. It's floating around in there now with no place to go. So—tomorrow morning we'll just wheel you down the hall to the shop where we repair dancers and other athletes and remove it."

Leya's eyes began to fill.

"It's a very simple procedure. Dr. Wald, who specializes in arranging short naps, will give you something, and before you know it, you'll be back in the room wondering who the flowers are from."

Leya looked up at Arthur, then rolled her head back toward the physician.

"Doctor—" The pain suppressant made it an effort to speak. "Will I be able to . . ."

"Will you be able to dance again?" he asked. "We'll think about that, young lady. We'll immobilize the knee for a little while. In three or four weeks you can begin to exercise it. We'll know more then."

Leya stared at him and struggled to keep back tears. Three or four weeks—exercise—a month, two months without class—without work of any kind! She rolled her head away, closed her eyes, and struggled against an overwhelming sense of hopelessness.

Doctor Lewin motioned to Arthur to join him in the hall.

"It's a natural reaction," he said. "An operation always seems like the end of everything to an active person."

Arthur compressed his lips. "What a goddamned idiot I was! The whole thing is my fault, wanting to set the retail world on fire with a new kind of fancy ad!" He shook his head. "I don't know how in hell I'm going to explain this to her family. Her cousin is one of our best supervisors."

Dr. Lewin rested a hand on Arthur's arm. "Look, son, it could have happened a dozen ways—getting on a subway, off a bus, stepping from a curb—you mustn't blame yourself."

"I have to blame myself for rotten judgment. They'll blame me for it, too, and they should!"

"So it happened." Max Lewin looked at the younger man closely. He had known Arthur ever since he and Martin Lieberman had become good friends at the club, ever since the boy was bar mitzvahed fifteen years earlier, in 1924. "I'll do what I can to reassure Miss Marks," he said. He tapped his temple. "After we've done the mechanical things we can do, there's where the rest of the healing is accomplished. I'll call you after surgery."

Arthur said good-by to Dr. Lewin and returned to Leya's room to peer in. She was lying quietly, apparently on the edge of sleep. She did not open her eyes when he tiptoed to the bed. Looking down at her, Arthur had never felt such remorse. Neither had he ever felt such an urge to take a girl in his arms, hold her close and safe, and try to find adequate words for a thousand things that he had never before felt, much less wanted to say.

When he touched her hair gently, her eyes opened for an instant and then closed again, but she did not turn her head. The burnished copper ponytail, still held in place by the orchid ribbon, trailed down her cheek and over her shoulder. Her head had rested against his cheek when he carried her to the elevator and into the cab that Jon Wales had somehow commandeered during the rush hour. He was about to lean over and kiss Leya's forehead when the door opened and the night nurse came in carrying a paper cup of medication. Embarrassed, he straightened quickly.

"I'm just going," he whispered.

Harry Marks paced Minnie's small front parlor.

"I'll sue! I'll call a lawyer! What kind of underwear pictures do you take jumping in the air?"

The tirade had been going on for ten minutes, ever since Arthur Lieberman had called from the hospital.

"So it happened," Minnie said, unconsciously echoing Dr. Lewin. "She's going to be all right! The doctor says so."

Harry lowered his head and closed his eyes. "This I heard before," he moaned, "when Anya got sick. If they cut her leg open, who says she will dance again? Who knows?"

"It wouldn't happen, Harry," Minnie said with more

confidence than she felt. "But even if it does—only for a while—it could be a blessing. I know from the shop that our Leya also has a career as a model."

Minnie left the kitchen doorway and went to him.

"This is not chopped liver, Harry," she said, resting a hand on his arm. "Dancing is all right. But modeling is also a good career—and it pays better, too!"

"So it pays better," he replied, "but from dancing she didn't get an operation."

Minnie shrugged and returned to the kitchen and her tidying up. From the very first dance recital, when Leya was in the fifth grade at the home, she had been as proud as Harry of his daughter's talent. Dancing had been something nice for the child to do. For an adult it was not so practical. "To be a serious ballet dancer," she had warned Harry more than once, "is to work like a horse—to waste your youth—for *bupkes!* Does this make sense? To encourage Leya to scrimp all of her life for hand clapping and maybe bouquets?"

But Harry had been as adamant as his daughter. Neither would change. Except, maybe, now . . .

Some minutes later, when Minnie finished and turned out the kitchen light, she found Harry sitting disconsolately on the sofa. His head was propped in his hands.

"Go home to bed now, Harry," she urged. "Arthur will tell me how she is first thing in the morning. You'll call me on your break, and I'll tell you. Young Arthur is *haymish*—an *edeler mensch*, Harry. Believe me, he wouldn't lie."

CHAPTER 13

Leya rolled her head and tried to clear her blurred vision. Dr. Lewin came to the bedside. "Well, how's my pretty lady with the cement knee?"

Leya moistened her parched lips.

"Okay, I guess," she whispered.

"You were a good soldier, Leya." He laughed softly. "Do you know what the anesthesiologist said? He said, 'It's a shame to put a mask over a face like this.' " The doctor paused, his eyes twinkling. "Do you know what I said? I said, 'Doctor, if the young lady were awake, it would be a crime *not* to put a mask over a face like yours!' "

Dr. Lewin laughed at his own joke as he pulled the covers away to look at Leya's knee. "Your scar won't be worth bragging about. It follows the inside of your kneecap. In two months you'll hardly see it."

"I'm glad about that," Leya said. She regarded him with a steady gaze. "The only thing is—will I be able to dance again—I mean, seriously? All of the barre work and the hard combinations?"

The surgeon pursed his lips. Early in his practice he learned that equivocation can be more cruel than the truth.

"Leya, you have a superb physical machine. It has been well trained. With rest, with determination, if you are not foolish and try to rush it, I think you'll be able to dance again. But I can't say when or even *if* you'll be able to stand up under professional training. We'll have to wait and see."

He patted her reassuringly. "In the meantime, rest, good food, optimism, and the therapy I'm prescribing will give you the best chances. Promise me you'll give yourself those breaks?"

Leya closed her eyes and nodded.

As Dr. Lewin turned, he saw the blue silk bed jacket, trimmed with white lace and hand-crocheted rosettes, draped over the visitor's chair. He pointed to it. "You're going to do a lot for that! Wear it when I come in next time!"

After the night nurse had given her the medication and propped a pillow under her knee to relieve some of the tension, Leya rolled her head toward the window. As she looked down on the dark tracery of limbs on the trees bordering Fifth Avenue and beyond to the lights in the apartments on the west side of Central Park, she allowed her thoughts to turn to the grim irony of the accident, that it had happened on a job she had taken so she could continue dancing. Instead of easing the financial situation, she was making it worse with this expensive hospital stay. How would they ever pay for it?

Leya wondered what the doctor had said privately to her father and to Minnie. They had said he had called—to reassure them, too? Or to tell them the truth and advise them not to discourage her—yet? Her father had been as grim as a man sitting *shiva!* And Minnie had brought the expensive bed jacket. Were those little signs that things were more serious than she was being told?

Actually, Minnie had resisted pretending the bed jacket was her gift. She had become Arthur's accomplice in the conspiracy only after he promised to confess later, when such a personal gift from him would not seem presumptuous.

"It's nothing," Minnie had said, dimissing an extravagance that should have moved her to a jeremiad on the virtues of thrift.

Leya remembered the sprains and broken bones some of the kids had sustained during play at the home. It had taken all of them a long time to come back. The tears that threatened were those of frustration, not of self-pity. She blamed herself for the accident, not Arthur or Jon—or, for that matter, Dorothy Simpson, whose advances had unsettled her. She could have assessed the risk and refused. God! If only she had!

By noon the third day the hospital room was bright with flowers and plants, and Leya's spirits were noticeably higher. In the morning, Kent dropped by with an enormous bouquet and the latest gossip from the class. Everyone sent regrets, even little Kyra, who had profited most by Leya's decision to leave.

At two o'clock, Celine appeared with an old-fashioned nosegay and an amusing card. "I have rehearsal at three-thirty, but I wanted to see you. Did you hear? Kent's family has promised him the financing for his own dance concert group. He is very excited. He wants me to join him. Isn't it great?"

Leya's spirits flagged visibly. Kent had said nothing to her about it. He was deliberately remaining silent, and for perfectly obvious reasons!

Celine took Leya's diminished enthusiasm for fatigue and cut the visit short with a promise to look in again in a few days.

Shortly after Celine's departure, the nurse brought an envelope bearing a return address on East Fifty-second Street. Leya opened it and felt a stab of anxiety.

"Leya, dear," it read, "I am absolutely distraught over my behavior. Somehow I can't rid myself of the feeling that I'm partially to blame. Get well soon, Leya, and come back to work. I promise you that you will never have a more devoted friend." The word "friend" was underlined three times. "Sincerely, Dorothy Simpson."

Leya read the note a second time and laid it aside. If someone had asked her how she might react to such a message, she would have responded "with disgust." Instead, quite unexpectedly, she found herself feeling sorry for the stylist.

The depression caused by Celine's news was lessened by a short visit from Dulcy.

"How long are you going to be in Mount Cyanide?" she asked, surveying the far-from-spartan surroundings.

"It depends on how fast I heal, I guess," Leya replied.

Dulcy lifted the covers and looked at the cast. "Jon Wales should be wearing this on his *schmeckle!* Why in hell didn't they hire one of those sour-armpit trapeze broads from Barnum and Bailey to do that kind of work?"

Her friend's graphic description made Leya laugh.

"It was my fault, too, you know. I could have said no."

Dulcy gave her a skeptical look. "Not to Arthur Lieberman, you couldn't!"

When the nurse came in with some late-afternoon medication, Dulcy kissed Leya lightly and left.

At seven-thirty that evening, Arthur rapped on the door and opened it a crack. "Can I come in?"

Leya brushed at a wisp of hair and settled the silk bed jacket to hide the hospital gown.

"Come in, Arthur," she called, "and excuse me if I don't get up to greet you."

For a moment he stood in the doorway, his face a study in wonderment. The dozen American Beauty roses, whose long stems protruded from a cornucopia of green waxed paper and a cloud of maidenhair fern, seemed forgotten.

"You know something?" he asked. "If it weren't such a grim joke, I'd say you've never looked lovelier."

"Oh, Arthur," Leya moaned, pointing to the mound of bedspread bulging over her left knee, "you wouldn't say that if you could see what a horrible-looking mess I am."

The memory of Leya lying in his arms as he carried her downstairs to the cab had all but obsessed him since the accident. Dr. Lewin would have permitted him to visit the evening before, but when the surgeon pointed out that she would be under heavy sedation and would probably resent it when she found out later, he decided to wait.

When the flowers were taken care of, Arthur pulled a chair close to the bed.

"Leya, I can bring you bouquets and make jokes to cheer

you up, but I can guess at what is going on in that head of yours." His eyes questioned her. "Two things. Will you dance again, and how will all this get paid for. Right?"

Leya studied her folded hands. "Yes. Dulcy told me this is a very expensive hospital."

"It is. It's also one of the best in the country. That's why I brought you here. If you're worried about the bills, you can stop. Our lawyers are certain that it will be called a work-related injury, and our insurance will cover it. If it doesn't, then I'll see that it's taken care of in other ways. After all, it was my fault."

"But it was my fault, too, for saying I'd try it."

"No more of that!" he said. "So now all we have to worry about is whether your knee will be as good as before."

Leya nodded unhappily. "That's the biggest worry."

"Of course it is. I've talked with Max Lewin. Personally, I think he's very optimistic, but he doesn't want to mislead you."

"I don't want to be misled. But if I can't dance—then . . ." Leya closed her eyes and shook her head viciously, a denial of threatening tears.

"I know," he said gently. "Max did a little surgery on me once. I went clomping around on crutches for three weeks after a football injury. It seems like it takes forever." He leaned closer. "It's going to take time for you to get back in shape again. You know that. But even if you can't dance professionally, you can still be active and earn your keep—if that's the way to put it. I talked to Harry Conover at the Powers Agency today. He was very encouraging about the jobs he can get for you. Good jobs for important clients." In an earnest voice, he added, "I hope you don't think I'm meddling?"

Leya reached out for his hand. "I don't know what to say, Arthur. I appreciate it. Very much." With his hand over hers, Leya found herself responding again to the good feel of him—his concern, his strength, his tenderness, all those things that she had somehow been aware of in the midst of her pain as he carried her downstairs and comforted her on the ride to the hospital.

"I really feel terrible having everybody worry about me so much," she said.

"Don't," he said quietly. "If it makes you any easier, I've got a confession. This is the first time I've worried about anybody like this." Arthur seemed startled by his own words. He rose, stood looking down at her for a moment, murmured, "Good night," and abruptly left the room.

Seconds after the door swung closed, tears relieved the ache in the base of Leya Marks's throat.

CHAPTER 14

Four weeks after the operation, Dr. Max Lewin removed the cast. Leya looked at the knee and grimaced. "It looks dead!"

"Take it from an old knee man," the doctor countered, "it looks very much alive. You can use a cane for a week or so now. Don't rush things. A month of therapy and it should be almost as good as new."

Leya wished the doctor had not qualified his prediction. Almost as good as new would not be good enough. But she found herself feeling more optimistic than she had expected. Arthur had been wonderfully supportive. So had Dulcy. The Powers Agency, she said, had begun to regard her as a minor celebrity. Harry Conover referred to her as the beautiful model on the flying trapeze and seemed anxious to send her out on calls. Jon Wales had come by twice, each time mentioning accounts that wanted her. So far as her earning capacity was concerned, Leya knew she had reason to be hopeful. The overriding question remained: Would she be able to dance again? The answer from the doctor was always the same: patience and time.

Two weeks of hydrotherapy with supervised exercise, and Leya discarded her cane. Arthur had promised a celebration at a dinner dance club, most likely Sherman Billingsley's Stork Club. The date had finally arrived.

Leya checked her calendar. Two morning interviews for modeling jobs had gone well, and now the afternoon was free. There was nothing to keep her from a long-delayed visit with Dulcy before she went home to change and wait for Arthur to pick her up. The prospect of her first real date with him since the accident so excited her that she welcomed the chance to pass the time with Dulcy.

It had been ten days since Arthur's last visit, ten days that had seemed like ten times ten! His father had not been well. Additional responsibility had fallen on Arthur. Now both men were returning from visits to Southern textile mills that had developed a new elastic material that Super Figure was interested in using. They were due in LaGuardia Field on the late-afternoon plane from Charlotte.

Leya took the subway to Fifty-second Street and walked south, window shopping, pleasantly aware of the admiring looks that her beige-and-brown Ceil Chapman linen dress with the white organdie trim earned her. She was grateful that the full skirt hid the ugly knee support.

At Forty-seventh Street, she saw the entrance marked "Buchanan Apartments." Several minutes later, Dulcy, wearing a light kimono, greeted her at the elevators.

"Welcome to the House of Devine Assignations! And just how do you manage to look so cool on a sweltering Turkish bath day like this?"

"I'm not cool," Leya admitted, "and I'm dying for a long cold drink."

"Which, coming from you, means water, of course," Dulcy added. "Or can I tempt you with something stronger, like a genuine imported ginger ale?"

"I'd love one," Leya replied.

"Come in, park your ailing member on the sofa. Tonight's the big night, isn't it?"

"If I can stay on my feet!" Leya sighed.

"If you can't stay on your feet, it could turn out to be a bigger night." Dulcy turned from the little Pullman sink with a contrite smile. "Me and my fast lines. Sorry!"

Leya settled in the corner of the sofa and let her leg rest along the cushions. "Oh, that's good!" she said as she worked her shoe off with the other foot and bent forward to remove the elastic support bandage. The skin beneath it looked normal now except for the coarse weave of the bandage impressed in the flesh.

Dulcy put the drink beside Leya and leaned over to trace her forefinger along the nearly invisible crescent of the incision. "Does it still hurt much?"

"No, not really. I still feel a little stiffness at the back of my knee in the morning, but it's okay after I've worked it loose."

"Great!" Dulcy dropped into the overstuffed chair at the end of the coffee table and waved a hand at the room. "Pretty good for a furnished pad, huh?"

"Furnished? This?" Leya asked incredulously as she indicated the really fine things in the room.

"The landlord furnished the basics—the sofa bed, the chairs, and some crappy linen and stuff—and the rest of the things have been furnished by an admirer, William Granville Vandercort, the Fourth, otherwise known as my devoted little 'Willie Four.' "

Leya's eyes roved again over the collection: a pair of exquisitely made Louis chairs, a small gilded marble-topped occasional table, a half-dozen vases, two of them cut from intricately carved lavender jade, and several expensively framed prints that seemed to be more striking than beautiful.

"All you need to fix up a place like this," Dulcy said, "is a rich friend and a certain liberal attitude toward reciprocity." She picked a ring from the side table. "This was the first little trinket I got from Willie Four, who is convinced that I have perfect hands for jewelry and everything else. It's a peridot. Ever seen one?"

Leya held the rich green cabochon, surrounded by diamonds, to catch the overhead light. "No, I haven't. It's beautiful."

Dulcy slipped it on and displayed it with comic elegance. "It's only a trifling ten carats, daaahling, but it's not one of those inferior domestic stones. He bought this in the Virgin Islands. Under the circumstances, I expected it to shatter when I first slipped it on!" She gave Leya an impish smile.

"He's insured all my nice little gifts. Isn't that sweet? Willie's a love, but he's getting to be a bit of a problem, too. I helped him to stop playing with himself and got him started playing with little girls instead." She rolled her eyes. "There's so little we poor but honest folks can do for the idle rich. I felt it was my Christian duty."

Leya gasped, then burst into delighted laughter. She indicated the valuable things scattered around the spacious room. "It doesn't look like such a terrible problem to me."

"He's a problem, sweetie. You see, the dear boy thinks he's in love with me." Dulcy frowned. "Maybe he is, but under the circumstances, I've got good reason to look at the whole love scene with beady eyes."

"Do you think you could love him?" Leya asked.

"I don't know. I'm very fond of him. For thirty million bucks I'd be a fool not to try." Suddenly she broke into a giggle. "Can't you see Willie Four taking me home to mother, roaring up the half-mile driveway at Seafair House on their 'Long Guyland' estate in his baby-blue Packard roadster? And can't you see me gawking and falling on my ass on the marble staircase, offering to shake hands with the butler, spilling the tea, and then finding *Harper's Bazaar* on the coffee table, opened to a double spread of me modeling Super Figure girdles?" Her shoulders bounced with laughter. "Holy mother! I could get poor Willie disinherited!"

The mental picture set Leya to giggling. "How long have you known him?"

"About a year. I modeled at a snooty charity fashion show his mother sponsored last year. Poor little Willie sat at the ringside with her. His mouth was open so wide that everytime I passed by on the runway, I could look all the way down his throat and see his pecker lighting up. The next day I got a call inviting me to lunch."

"Did you go?"

"Of course! What mercenary little blonde from the wrong side of the tracks wouldn't want to meet the scion of the Vandercort billions?" Dulcy gave Leya a speculative look. "Know something, kiddo? I've developed a real fondness for you. And out of the best motives in the world, that could lead me to annoy the crap out of you with a lot of nosey personal questions . . . like, for instance, if you understand musician talk, do you really dig Arthur Lieberman?"

Leya met Dulcy's gaze for a few seconds, then lowered her eyes and smiled.

"Yes. I think he's wonderful."

Dulcy expelled a huge sigh of relief. "Good! I was hoping it wasn't just gratitude for his generosity—et cetera." She frowned thoughtfully. "Okay. Are you ready for the next one?"

Leya shrugged. "I guess."

"Tell me, dear heart—" She broke off and held up a finger. "And before I ask, let me say this. You can tell me to screw off, and I will, but are you still a virgin?"

For a moment Leya sat perfectly still. Then her body seemed to sag into the corner of the sofa. In a small voice she asked, "Is—is that bad?"

Dulcy frowned and gazed across the room. After a time her eyes returned to the younger girl.

"Sweetie, on the calendar I'm only five years older than you. But on the record, I'm a hundred and five." She paused. "Even so, what in God's name can I tell you, really? Is it bad to be a virgin? Hell, no, honey! But in our work it's damned near impossible. The married guys are the worst. Most of them will be figuring angles to get you alone so they can tell you what a pity it is that their dull little wives in Pound Ridge, Larchmont, White Plains, Cos Cob, Westport, and points east don't understand them."

Dulcy reached for a cigarette on the end table. Holding it unlit between her fingers, she waved it to punctuate her words. "When you told me before the accident that you got a call from Wales to do Arthur's negligees, I figured it had happened sooner than I thought. You really grabbed him. You know that, don't you?"

"I didn't really notice—then," Leya answered.

"Well, everybody else did," Dulcy said. "Wales didn't go on the make for you because he didn't want to louse up with Artie Lieberman. I don't really know Arthur all that well. The longest I ever spent with him was our night at the St.

Moritz. I think he's keen." She smiled bitterly. "But that's what I thought about the son of a bitch who stuck it into me the first time! So, who knows what a guy on the make really is? As far as I'm concerned, if you're smitten, all of this bullshit about women's intuition is—bullshit." She repeated the word brightly as though the effect pleased her. "Anyway, dear heart, date Arthur again and watch yourself at all times. He's the kind of a guy a girl could get loopy about. In fact, if he had a twin brother who dug *shiksas,* I'd trip him and beat him to the floor myself."

Dulcy let her fingers trail across the jade mandarin figure on the end table.

"On the other hand, I really should be ashamed. My darling little Willie Four is really a love, too." She shot Leya an innocent look. "Do I sound like a mercenary bitch?"

Leya shrugged. "I don't think so, after what you've told me about—about . . ."

"About my lurid love life?"

"I guess."

"Well," Dulcy said, extending her well-shaped legs out from the kimono. "Maybe old Sigmund Freud would say that the miscarriage trauma left me with a 'get even with men' complex. But I don't think so. I was young and friendly and dumb. And in this modeling business, where beauty and—let's face it—sex appeal are our stock in trade, who can really tell whether some joker's intentions are honorable or not? If you let a guy take you in his arms, and he lights you up and you know you light him up, then you can't really blame him if he wants to sample your goodies."

Leya shifted her leg to ease the pull on the tendons.

"With my dancing and the problems at home, sex just hasn't seemed all that important—for now at least."

Dulcy held up both hands in a hallelujah gesture. "Great, sweetie! Point is you're going to make a good model. You're going to meet a lot of new guys. You're going to have your pretty puss spread all over creation, you're going to make more money than you've ever made before, and you're going to have a lot of free time, too. Add that whole combination up and it can spell trouble unless you get smart and stay that way." Dulcy grinned apologetically. "End of lecture!"

Leya was silent for a time. "I know what you're telling me is right," she said slowly, "but I'm not giving up dancing. I'm going on with ballet. I've been exercising my body and my arms to keep limber. I plan to start class with Eddie Caton again just as soon as my knee can take it. And if that's okay, then I'm going on with modern and jazz, too."

Dulcy smiled. "If easy-money modeling doesn't change your mind, you mean?"

"No. I'm definitely going to try to go on with my dancing. It's all that's really important. I like the modeling jobs, and I need them. But only to pay for class and help out at home."

"You are unreal, Marks. I'm not sure I understand you, but I sure do admire you!" She got up to replenish her drink and glanced at the alarm clock on her dressing table. "Quarter to three. What time do you have to meet Arthur?"

"He said he'd leave word at the office. I have to call there and find out."

Dulcy pointed to the phone on the hall table. "Go ahead, sweetie. Why don't you call now? Better still, why don't you stay put and I'll call for you?"

A few moments later, Dulcy turned from the phone and motioned to Leya to come over.

"Arthur wants to talk to you."

Leya got up so quickly a sharp pain in her knee made her grimace.

"Hello—Arthur?"

"Leya! I've left word everywhere for you. I don't know why I didn't think of trying there." He paused. "Leya—look—I'm sick about it, but I've got a problem tonight. My father's gall bladder is kicking up again. I brought him home on the early plane, and I've got to cover for him tonight with a buyer from Consolidated Stores. He and my mother were going to entertain her. But I've got to do it now." He paused. "I'm sorry, Leya—really—but I have no choice."

Dulcy saw her friend's face fall.

"It's all right, Arthur. I understand," Leya said.

"It's not all right, Leya. I've been planning this for weeks now. I'm going to be stuck with this lady for at least two days because Consolidated has our line in thirty of their stores, and that's a real bread-and-butter account for us. They all but kept us alive during the Depression."

"When will I see you, then?" Leya asked.

"The minute I put the dear lady on the Broadway Limited for Chicago. Probably Friday night. This is a buyer who really loves to be entertained—damn it!"

Arthur Lieberman questioned Leya about herself and her work for several more minutes, inventing queries to keep them on the phone. When Leya hung up, Dulcy pouted sympathetically. "Whatever it is, it's a damned shame. I hope he's not ill?"

"No. His father is, though, and he's got to entertain some buyer."

"I know those freeloading buyers, dear heart. You can take that as the gospel truth!" She brightened. "Hey! I just got an inspired idea! I've got a date with Willie tonight, and I just don't feel like coming back here later to play house. He's such a juicy rascal! If you'll stay over with me, the three of us will have dinner, and you'll get a chance to meet him." Dulcy started for the phone. "I'll call him and let him know in my own inimitable way that he's got two dates tonight—for some elegant place like Nino's."

Leya fingered her simple daytime dress. "I can't go anywhere like this."

"You don't have to," Dulcy replied. "We're the same size—except in the buzooms. I've got a closet full of things."

While they were going through expensive dresses, the house phone rang.

Dulcy frowned, walked to the entrance hall, and removed the intercom receiver.

"Yes?"

The doorman's rich Irish brogue came through the earpiece. "There's a gentleman to see you, Miss Devine. It's Mister Vandercort."

Dulcy slammed her palm over the little speaker grill. "Oh God!" she called. "It's Willie Four. I told the little bastard never to come barging in!" She uncovered the receiver. "Put him on, will you please, Tim?"

In the lobby, William Granville Vandercort, IV, handed a large gift-wrapped box to the doorman. "Would you hold this for me? Hello, Dulcy?"

"What on earth are you doing here, Willie? There's no matinee today."

Willie Four grinned sheepishly. "I just happened to be in the neighborhood, and I saw something I thought you would like. May I bring it up?"

"That depends on where you were and what you saw. If it was in the men's room, Willie, forget it. Today I'm not even holding hands!"

Willie Four glanced nervously at the old doorman. "It's a surprise, Dulcy. I have it with me. Can I bring it up?"

"Hold on," Dulcy said, covering the mouthpiece again.

"Willie's bringing me the Kohinoor diamond or something. He wants to come up. Do you mind?"

"Whatever you want," Leya said.

"What I want is for him to quit dropping in whenever he 'just happens to be in the neighborhood,' " she said, turning back to the house phone.

"Talk to Tim for five minutes, Willie. And I mean *five* minutes, not four and a half. I don't exactly sit around in my Sophie gown waiting for you to drop in, you know."

"I'm sorry, Dulcy, honestly. I really did just happen to be in the neighborhood. We've been at the Grand Central Gallery."

"My God!" Dulcy gasped. "You didn't buy me a Rembrandt, did you, Willie? You know it won't match my wallpaper!"

Dulcy's offbeat, sometimes not so gentle, sense of humor confused young William Vandercort more often than it amused him.

"I'll talk with Tim," he said. "And I'll wait five minutes. G'by."

Dulcy returned the earpiece to the brass hook.

"If I didn't have all the insecurities of the native-born poor, I'd never let him get away with this!" Undoing her hair, she went to the wardrobe, removed a beautifully cut deep-brown silk voile dress with a low square-cut neckline, and handed it to Leya.

"You can wear this, sweetie. It'll go with the pumps you're wearing." She indicated the bathroom. "Hang it on the shower curtain for now."

Leya straightened her hair and checked her minimal makeup in the bathroom mirror while Dulcy finished dressing. In five minutes to the dot, the door buzzer sounded.

"Brace yourself," Dulcy whispered as she squirmed her foot into a shoe. "I didn't tell him I had company."

Leya did not quite know what to expect. Multimillioned aristocrats and socialites peopled a world that she was dimly aware of but one that she gave little thought to. She assumed that Kent Kendall came from such a world, but he was a tall, handsome god who came down from some distant Olympus to dance and sweat and swear and become one of the mortals for a few hours of class. Occasionally, Leya had tried to envision him in a lush but undelineated storybook environment; but with nothing in her own experience to relate to, she had simply accepted the fact that Kent lived in two worlds.

When Dulcy greeted William Vandercort, IV, at the door with a peck on the cheek and led him into the room, Leya tried to conceal her disappointment. Willie Four looked not one bit different from scores of other young, neatly barbered, narrow-shouldered, seersuckered, buttoned-down old-school-tie types that crowded Manhattan's midtown avenues at noon. He was another five foot ten, one hundred and forty pound picket in a fence, and at the moment his mouth was slightly opened as he stared at her across the top of a foot-square box tied in ribbon.

"Willie, I want you to meet my dearest friend, Leya Marks. She's in town shopping today. She gave me such a pleasant surprise when she called to ask if she could stop by for tea."

William Vandercort glanced from Leya to Dulcy and back again, then ducked his head. "It's a pleasure, Miss Marks." He turned to Dulcy and offered the present. "You should have said you had company; then I would have just sent this up. I really didn't mean to barge in."

Dulcy took the box and blew him a kiss. "Stop worrying, Willie! If I'd told you I had company, you'd of imagined the worst, and I'm too fond of you to do that."

She shook the box gently. "What's in it?"

"Open it," he said. "I hope you like it, because I can't exchange it."

Dulcy put the box on the coffee table. "Willie, I've warned you never to bring me something I can't exchange—or pawn." She clucked. "You know us mercenary chorus girls!"

Willie grinned and sat down beside Leya. "I never know when she's joking," he confessed.

"I'm never joking—when I'm joking," Dulcy retorted. As she pulled ribbons apart carefully and loosened the stickers on the outer wrapping, Leya had a chance to study Willie Four. On closer inspection, she found the heir to the Vandercort millions pleasant looking. His head was well shaped, and his features were regular. His thick brown hair, cut moderately short, was parted on the left side and combed slightly forward. If his mouth seemed a bit soft, certainly his jawline and chin were not. His hands, in repose on his knees as he leaned forward watching Dulcy, were clean lined and strong, and his nails were professionally manicured. Leya could understand why Dulcy returned his favors, and she wondered if some of her friend's oblique disparagement was intended to obscure a deeper interest.

"Mark Cross!" Dulcy exclaimed, looking at the embossed box lid. "What on earth have you bought?"

A moment later she lifted out a beautifully designed alligator handbag. On a gold tab beneath the clasp the initials "D. D." were engraved.

"My lord, Willie!" Dulcy breathed as she handled it like a treasure. "It's—it's—too much!" Suddenly, she fixed him with an accusing stare. "Do you know what you've just done, Willie Four?"

"What did I do wrong?" he asked.

"What you've done is cost me a fortune!" She placed her hands lovingly on the gleaming sides of the bag. "Do you realize that I'm going to have to buy a whole new outfit—dress, belt, shoes, the works—to go with this?"

Dulcy leaned over and gave him an enormous wet smack full on the lips. Then, with a sweet look, she kneeled in front of him and held his hands. "Thank you, Willie darling!"

William Vandercort, IV, looked at Dulcy with frank adoration. When they were together, what he experienced with her was worth even the cataclysmic complications that would result when he pursued their relationship to its illogical end. Sooner or later, he would have to bring Dulcy to the family. At that point . . .? Willie tried to cope with the eventualities by refusing to think.

He watched Dulcy's antic posturing as she pretended to model the bag in front of the full-length mirror on the closet door. Then he turned to Leya.

"You're a model, too, aren't you, Miss Marks?"

"I've done a little. Really I'm a ballet dancer. But at the moment, I'm sort of bent up"—she pointed to her knee and the elastic support that she had put aside—"from an accident."

"I remember now," Willie Four said. "Dulcy told me about it. Since you've been modeling, do you suppose I've seen your photos in the magazines?"

Before Leya could answer, Dulcy turned from the mirror.

"So far she's done only a few *very* exclusive things, darling, for a limited-edition publication."

Willie Four looked pleased. "I imagine I would know the publication," he said confidently.

"Not unless you dig underwear catalogues," Dulcy replied as she returned to the sofa. Willie laughed nervously and glanced at his wafer-thin wristwatch. Rising, he said, "Well, I've got to run along now."

"Darling," Dulcy said, "I was going to do a horrible thing. Call you and beg off tonight. This is the first chance Leya and I have had to really dish the dirt. I'll fix something here, and you're welcome to join us. But I really want to be selfish and visit."

"Oh?" Willie Four was nonplussed. "I was going uptown to change—"

"I'm sorry," Dulcy said as she slipped her arms around his neck. "Forgive me?"

"Of course! Only—why bother with anything here? Why don't the three of us go out?" He looked at Leya and brightened. "I'd like that very much! You girls could visit at dinner, and then we could come back here for coffee or something."

Dulcy released him and frowned uncertainly. "Gee, Willie, that sounds fine—only—" She broke off to give him another chance to protest.

"Then it's settled." He edged around Dulcy. "I'd like very much to have you join us, Leya. You two can 'dish the dirt,' and I'll listen and complete my education."

"Sweet Willie," Dulcy said, "where women like us are concerned, you're still in prep school!"

Leya found herself feeling a bit sorry for William Vandercort, IV.

At the door Dulcy gave Willie a quick farewell peck. "Eight? Eight fifteen?" she asked.

"Fine," he agreed. "Any particular place?"

She pretended to consider. "Why not Nino's?"

"Good. I'll call. See you at eight."

Dulcy waved as Willie got into the elevator, then came back and settled on the arm of the sofa.

"Well, what do you think of my little gold-plated playmate?"

Leya inclined her head. "He seems very nice, but I really don't know. He's the first millionaire I've ever met."

"Correction!" Dulcy said, holding up two fingers. "He's the second one. With a small loan from papa, Arthur could probably slip in under the wire." She got up. "And speaking of assets, let's spend a little time making the most of ours."

CHAPTER 15

When the buzzer sounded, and the doorman announced, "Mr. Vandercort," Dulcy gave her short, naturally curly, golden-blonde hair one last poke and cocked a critical eye at Leya.

The deep-brown silk voile dress with the low, square-cut neckline, fit perfectly. The single-strand pearl necklace, the matching earrings, the baroque pearl dinner ring, and the thick, gleaming auburn hair pulled back tightly across the ears and caught in a large bun at the nape of the neck created a stunning effect.

"My God," she breathed, "I'm not sure I want my Willie to see you all turned out like this!"

When William Vandercort, IV, saw Leya, his eyes and mouth opened simultaneously. "Hi—" he breathed. Then he broke into a boyish smile and said, "Holy tomato! You look absolutely super!"

At 10 East Fifty-second Street, Nino, the handsome, silver-haired owner, greeted them and saw them seated near the front room so they could listen to Rudy Timfield at the piano. Dulcy was amused at the effect Leya was having on the men nearby. "Sweetie," she whispered, "I'll never get into the dress again without wishing I could do for it what you're doing! In fact, I may never get into it again. I may just give it to you!"

When the check came, Willie sent a gratuity to the pianist, who came to the table to say his courtly Viennese thanks.

Outside, Willie glanced at his watch. "We can't go home yet! It's only ten o'clock!"

Dulcy gave him a mischievous look and turned to Leya. "He sounds just like one of us peasants! Work in the factory all week, then take a bath and stay out all night. Imagine!"

"Well, it is early," Willie insisted. "Besides, I half promised that we'd stop at the Stork. One of my old classmates from Groton is in town on leave. He's an Annapolis grad. He's been on duty in the Mediterranean, but his ship's in the Brooklyn Navy Yard now."

"Why didn't you ask him along tonight?" Dulcy asked.

"I did," Willie replied. "He had to dine with his parents. Let's just go over for a little while. Do you mind—really?"

"If you've seen one sailor, you've seen them all," Dulcy said, "but it's okay with me. How about you?" she asked, turning to Leya.

"Whatever you all want to do." In truth, she would have preferred to go back to the apartment. The Stork Club would be a new experience. It was one she wanted to share with Arthur. It had been his choice as the place to celebrate their first dinner-dance date.

As the Stork Club's doorman assisted Leya from the taxi, she heard a delighted squeal, followed by her name being called. Suddenly, Heather emerged from the knot of people around the door towing a well-turned-out dark-haired man by the hand.

"Leya! For God's sake, how are you? I couldn't be happier to see you!" She pulled her escort close. "Darling, this is my dear friend, Leya Marks. We were ballerinas together. Leya, this is my friend, Carlo Romano." She linked her arm through his.

Carlo Romano waited for Leya to offer her hand. When she didn't, he offered his. "I'm happy to meet you, Miss Marks," he said in a smooth, rich voice that betrayed a suggestion of an Italian cadence. "Heather's been talking about you," he said, still holding her hand. "What a good dancer you are, and how you got hurt. I hope you are better now. Yes?"

"I'm fine," Leya said. The feel of Carlo Romano's hand around hers was disturbing. There was a sense of great power deliberately restrained. His eyes were brown, but the pupils gleamed like polished obsidian. His face was square, and Leya saw that the coarse black, precisely barbered hair was brushed with premature gray at the temples.

After Leya managed the introductions, Heather looked from one to the other. "Gee, I wish we'd run into you before we went in. We could have made a little party and gotten caught up."

"So, we'll fix that another time," Carlo said.

The obsequious doorman coughed. "Your car's ready, Mr. Romano."

Ignoring the man, Carlo turned to Dulcy and Willie. "I'm glad to meet you." As he spoke, his dark eyes appraised the young millionaire.

When they parted, Dulcy turned to Leya. "I don't trust those slick wopolas who only smile with their teeth!"

The after-theater crowd had not yet arrived, but the club was packed and sweltering. As they stood waiting for the maître d'hôtel, Leya looked through the foyer to the main room. The small dance floor was crowded with couples who seemed preoccupied with everything but the music, which was bouncing along in a businesslike, metronomic beat. She did not find the ultra-chic supper club a particularly appealing place.

Just then, an attractive, deeply tanned navy lieutenant in dress whites pushed through the crowd waiting at the bar.

"Willie!" he called. "I'm glad you could make it. I've got to be back aboard ship at midnight, but I wanted to see you."

The one-time prep school classmates greeted one another, and Willie turned to the girls.

"Dulcy Devine and Leya Marks, may I present Gardner Sutton—" Willie squinted at the black shoulder boards that bore the gold stripe and a half of the young officer's rank. "—who is now a something-or-other lieutenant."

"J. G.," Gardner smiled, "which means 'junior grade' or

'just getting there.'" He bowed formally to each girl. "I'm very happy to know you." His eyes lingered on Leya.

"Shall we go in? I took the precaution of holding a table for ten-thirty."

When they were seated, Gardner rebuked his friend. "If you had given me even an inkling that you were convoying two special beauties tonight, I would have telephoned the family and made up some implausible lie so I could have joined you for dinner. That's not a very patriotic thing to do to the brave men in middies who are defending the outposts of freedom in cafés from Barcelona to Beirut!"

"He's not to blame, lieutenant," Dulcy said. "It was all very last-minute."

"In that case, we won't waste time on recriminations." Turning to Leya, Gardner said, "Would you care to dance?"

Leya hesitated. "If you don't mind carrying me off the floor if my knee collapses," she replied. "I've only had it out of a cast for a little while."

"Car accident?"

"If you want to know the truth, lieutenant," Dulcy put in, "in the circus Leya is known as Tillie the Beautiful Trampoline Artist."

"Don't listen to her," Leya laughed. "I hurt my leg doing a modeling job. It had to be operated on."

After a few tentative moves, Leya felt encouraged. Gardner Sutton proved to be a skillful partner, easy and assured. It felt good to be moving to music again.

Gardner was taller than Arthur. Somehow he reminded Leya of Kent Kendall, but harder appearing, more masculine. Certainly he was more adept at small talk than poor Willie—every bit as facile as Dulcy, if not quite as blunt and earthy.

When they returned to the cramped table, he amused her with accounts of night life in the ports the fleet had visited on its good-will tours.

"Good will, in diplomatic language," he explained, "means 'be good or we'll blow you to hell.'" He had served aboard the heavy cruiser *Tuscaloosa* for a year, but he told her that he felt promotions would come faster if he transferred to destroyers.

"There's a lot of inside poop that our vessels will be doing convoy duty before long. I'm not too keen about destroyer duty in the North Atlantic, especially in winter, but they'll be promoting line officers fast."

Dulcy and Willie rejoined them, and the talk turned to the prospects of the United States becoming directly involved. "It might take another *Lusitania*," Gardner observed. "If Roosevelt makes a run for a third term, I think the navy will get the money Admiral Stark wants. German U-boats followed us all the way back from Gibraltar. One of them, the U-Forty-Five, surfaced alongside of us off the Azores and ran with us for an hour. The German skipper spoke perfect English with an Oxonian accent. He said he was happy to see us going home where we belonged because he didn't want to see any of his American friends get wet."

"What did you say to him?" Leya asked.

"Our captain told him not to worry, that we were going home to get our foul-weather gear and that we'd be back. The German skipper laughed and saluted and said, 'We'll be waiting!' "

"Arrogant bastard!" Dulcy breathed.

"Precisely what our skipper said!" Gardner looked off thoughtfully. "I'm betting we will be back. The British merchantmen are taking a horrible beating. It can't keep on like that much longer, or Hitler's going to starve England into surrender."

When the orchestra began a new set, Willie looked at Leya. "This talk is making me gloomy. Come on. I've never danced with a real-live ballerina."

"It's very pleasant duty, Willie," Gardner said as he rose and turned a questioning look to Dulcy.

"This may be a comedown, lieutenant," she said. "I was only a lowly chorus girl."

Gardner laughed. "Willie's not noted for bravery under fire, and he seems to have survived all right. Incidentally," he added, "your friend is a smash. How come she's on the loose?"

"She's not—except for tonight," Dulcy said, easing into his arms at the edge of the floor. "In fact, the hopeful are lined up, hoping."

"If I were around, I'd crash the head of the line," he replied.

After a few bars, Dulcy stiffened and gasped. Gardner Sutton leaned away and looked down at her. "Don't tell me I wounded you?"

"Oh, God, no!" she whispered. "I just saw somebody come in."

Resisting his lead gently to keep him from turning, she watched as Arthur Lieberman and a conspicuous brunette in her early thirties followed the captain to a ringside table at the opposite end of the dance floor.

"Is something wrong?" Gardner said.

"Not with me," Dulcy murmured, "but I may have made a heck of a problem for Leya." She craned to see over Gardner's shoulder. Willie and Leya were still on the far side of the dance floor.

"That fellow who just came in is a special friend of Leya's. They were supposed to have a date tonight, but something came up, and he couldn't make it." She nodded toward Arthur and his date. "If that's the something, then we may have loused her up good by coming here."

"I hope you did louse things up," Gardner said. "Maybe I'll have a chance."

"Damn it!" Dulcy murmured. "I'm really worried about—" She broke off with an annoyed shake of her head. "Just take my word for it. Things didn't work out."

"For me they did," Gardner chuckled, "except that I've got to run like the devil and bribe a cab to fly me to Brooklyn right after this set."

"Gardner, please, could we dance around by the band and go back to the table?" From Willie's concerned expression as he led Leya from the floor, Dulcy knew that Leya had seen Arthur. Her face was a mask.

At the table again, Dulcy leaned close to her. "You might as well smile, sweetie. Be nonchalant. Light a Murad!"

"I'd like to go now, please?" Leya said.

"We are—right this minute," Dulcy replied. "Gardner's got to get back to his ship."

As Gardner was trying to persuade Willie to let him have the check, Arthur and his date, who was elegantly turned out in a pink Italian ribbon knit, danced to the edge of the floor by the table and paused, moving in place.

"I'm happy to see you, Leya," he said with convincing surprise. "Congratulations on being out among us again—so soon."

Before Leya could find her voice, he disappeared in the moving crowd.

Willie Four looked up from the check. "Who was that?"

"A business friend of ours," Dulcy said flatly. "Come on. Make your mark, Willie, and let's go before we get the handsome lieutenant fired from the navy."

On the Fifty-third Street sidewalk, Gardner Sutton held Leya's hand. "Thank you for being here tonight. Whether or not you know it, you've just become an official sailor's sweetheart. Can I see you again?"

"Thank you," Leya replied. "That would be nice—sometime."

Dulcy slipped an arm around Leya's waist. "Anchors Aweigh, sailor! You'll miss the boat!" She deliberately emphasized the double entendre.

Gardner released Leya's hand and ducked into the waiting cab.

A few minutes later, after Dulcy had frustrated Willie's attempts to be asked up for a nightcap, she closed her apartment door and leaned back against it.

"Well, shall we try to figure it all out now or wait until we get into bed?"

Leya slipped out of the borrowed dress and unhooked the strand of pearls. "I know he was there on business," she said, "but I wish it hadn't happened."

Dulcy set the night chain on the door. "I've seen a lot of buyers, sweetie. But that dame looked more like a seller. Anyway, it was the best thing that could have happened. I don't care if his excuse was kosher. Seeing you there with dreamy Gardie was a fortuitous happenstance, to say the least."

Leya was uncertain. "Maybe. But I'm not very good at playing games."

CHAPTER 16

Monday morning Leya called the Powers Agency and was asked to go to an interview at an advertising agency on Madison Avenue. When she arrived, she found Dulcy there.

"Hey, Leya, I was going to call! I've got a T. L. for you. Willie called me Saturday and said that Gardner had called him from the Navy Yard. You really lit his lamps. What did you do over the weekend? Did Arthur call?"

Leya shook her head. "No, I spent the weekend with my father and cousin."

"That's okay. He'll call, dear heart. Bet on it!"

After receiving the account executive's approval, the two of them were sent downtown to the offices of Revel Cosmetics.

"This could be a good job. I've worked for Gordon Revelsky," Dulcy said as they made their way toward the Empire State Building. "He's tough, but he pays well. He started the company with a chemist who invented a new lipstick. *'He'll revel in your kisses if you're a Revel girl!'* Remember that ad? They're branching out now—makeup, hair dye, nail polish, the works."

When the girls went in—four had been sent on the call—Gordon Revelsky was lunching at his desk. He was a slightly built man with graying curly hair, penetrating brown eyes, and a tight, thin-lipped mouth. As he slumped in his green Florentine leather executive chair, the food on the tray was almost level with his chin. He was coatless, and a large linen napkin was tucked into his monogrammed shirt collar. He gestured impatiently for the girls to come closer.

"Look at me! At my face," he ordered. "Never mind my office. I want to see your eyes and your mouths." The four girls stood obediently while he studied each in turn. He finished a mouthful of macaroni salad.

"Okay," he said, dismissing them with an impatient wave. The waiting secretary motioned them to the door.

"Your date is nine o'clock tomorrow morning at the Peter Basch studio." She handed each girl a slip of paper. "No wardrobe. We need only closeups. Charles of the Ritz will shampoo and set at the studio, and we may use some John Frederick hats. That's all. Thank you."

As they started to leave, the woman called Leya aside. "Miss Marks, I suggest that you get your photo book in order. Mr. Revelsky likes to have color shots of new girls."

"I'm getting it fixed today," Leya replied. "I can drop off some pictures later if you'd like."

"That won't be necessary." The woman smiled at Leya's reference to "pictures." It was the certain mark of a beginner. "Shots" and "photos" were the proper professional lingo.

Down on Thirty-fourth Street again, Leya left Dulcy and went to find a pay phone. There was no message from Arthur at the store. Leya wandered north on Fifth Avenue. At Fiftieth Street she turned into Rockefeller Plaza. Gusting wind, funneling through the complex of skyscrapers, tore veils of mist from the Prometheus fountain. The sky, darkening ominously to the west, set waiters to stripping the outside tables at the French Pavilion and the English Grill. Hurrying now, Leya crossed the Plaza and sought the shelter of the RCA Building's shopping arcade. As she passed the banks of elevators leading to the National Broadcasting Company's studios, she ran into Celine Cervier.

"Leya! It's spooky! I was just thinking about you!" She hugged her former classmate. "I've been wanting you to come to the theater."

"I'd like to very much," Leya replied. "When it's convenient."

"Come now! Please! I have a half hour before I dress for the next show."

In the cast lounge, Celine introduced her to half a dozen dancers, then led her to a sofa. They talked for ten minutes. Much of the conversation concerned Leya's new career as a model.

"It sounds wonderful!" Celine enthused. "But you miss all this, don't you?" Her arm swept across the groups of relaxing dancers with unconscious grace.

"Yes," Leya confessed. "I just hope to God I can do it again. What about you? Are you going to join Kent's dance group?" Leya hoped she was concealing her uneasiness.

Celine frowned. "I don't know. He wants eight ballet kids who know modern and jazz. I'm not really interested in that. But I enjoy watching it—and primitive, too. Katherine Dunham is still teaching primitive down at the Labor Theater. I watched her class last week. It's very exciting Afro-Haitian dance. But I don't think I could ever do it. All those sexy bumps and grinds. I'd be embarrassed. Anyway, I don't think my parents would be too happy about my dancing with Negroes. I wouldn't mind personally." She rolled her eyes in mock horror. "But I can see my father if he ever caught me dancing with a big Negro, performing together in one of those fertility rites!" She clasped her hands. "*Mon Dieu!* And my mother would get the vapors and swoon!"

Leya was amused by her friend's dramatic pantomime.

"Would you dance professionally with Negroes?" Celine asked.

"Yes, I would," Leya said. "I like ethnic dancing, but I don't suppose there'll be much chance of that now. I've got to make this modeling thing work until papa finds a steady job, and until I find out what this knee is going to do."

The girls talked until it was time for Celine to dress. "Come back during rehearsal," she said, "I still want you to meet Mr. Leonidoff. I've talked to him about you. He'll audition you anytime."

"Thank you, Celine. Maybe I will—later."

* * *

On the train home, Leya thought about the encounter with Arthur Lieberman at the Stork Club. She considered and rejected a call to him. By the time the subway emerged from the tube to run on elevated tracks, the full force of a summer thunderstorm had struck the five boroughs. Leya sat with her eyes squinted against the startling flashes until she reached her station. There, standing in shelter with others who were waiting for a lull in the storm, she patted the perspiration from her temples and the base of her neck and wondered whether or not her father had been caught, too.

Reluctantly, he had been borrowing money from her to follow still more leads. None of them had materialized. He had found two days' work helping the people in the store downstairs rebuild some shelving. It was the only money he had brought in since the job at the fairgrounds.

When the squall showed signs of lessening, Leya dodged from awning to awning and doorway to doorway, then lowered her head and ran the last half block to the flat. At the top of the stairs, she found some mail. One envelope was addressed to her father. It bore a U.S. government postage-free frank and a return to the Department of the Navy. Puzzled, Leya set it by her father's place at the table and went to the bedroom to remove her sodden clothing. She wanted to soak in a tub and work her knee but settled for a cold sponging, then went to the living room to pull the curtains aside and open the windows to the clean, cool air that always followed a summer storm.

Harry Marks found Leya asleep with a sheet pulled over her when he arrived at the flat shortly before seven o'clock. He had climbed the stairs more heavily freighted than ever with disappointment. There were jobs to be had, but there were no steady ones for men his age.

He tiptoed closer to look down at her and shuddered as he remembered, still again, that night—twenty years it would be in October—when his beautiful young wife had lain covered with a sheet and he had kneeled, streaming tears, to kiss the lips, bruised by her own teeth, before the ambulance doctor had arrived—too late—and pulled the cloth up to turn the sheet into a shroud.

Grief, self-pity, and anger welled up in Harry Marks. Opening his collar as he went, he made his way to the kitchen.

Several minutes later, joyous whoops echoed through the little flat. Alarmed, Leya called out, "What is it, papa?"

"So look!" he said, returning to the room to thrust the letter into her hand.

"Dear Sir," Leya read, "Records at the Navy Yard, Brooklyn, New York, indicate that you were employed there from five March, nineteen seventeen, to fifteen August, nineteen nineteen, as a master mechanic and steam fitter.

"Because of an unexpected increase in repair work, we are in need of skilled labor. If you are available for civilian service, will you please contact the Manpower Procurement Officer, Brooklyn Navy Yard, at your earliest convenience? Sincerely, Admiral W. O. Kellerman, Commandant."

Leya was as excited as her father. " 'Skilled labor' it says, papa! That's wonderful! You will go?"

"Of course I will go!" he chanted as he grabbed Leya to swing her in an exuberant dance.

"Papa, please!" Leya pleaded, pulling away from him. "You'll wind up with a bad knee, too!"

"I'll be a foreman! That's what I'll be!" he replied.

Leya wanted to caution him not to get his hopes too high, but she could not bring herself to spoil his moment of triumph. She watched, smiling, as he poured a large dram of slivovitz. "To celebrate," he said, holding it up. "*L'Chaim*, darling!"

"Leya!" Harry Marks burst through the door, spotted his daughter at the sink preparing supper, and rushed to her. Seizing her by the shoulders, he held her at arm's length. "You'll please look at your father the shipbuilder!"

Leya caught him in a hug. "Oh, papa, nothing could make me happier!"

Harry held her away. "I'm not too old. The lieutenant who went over my work records says for me fifty-two is perfect! I'll be foreman of an assembly section!"

"How much will they pay, papa?"

"Two-fifty an hour. Plus overtime. Also insurance and pension!"

Leya watched her father and marveled at the change. The good news had erased ten years.

After a hot-weather supper they lingered over tea, speculating about the future.

"At the yard, something big is happening," Harry said. "There's a Dutch cruiser in. Her port bow is smashed. Torpedoes, maybe. And our cruiser *Tuscaloosa* is in. She's getting fitted with new antiaircraft batteries. Also two mine layers and two sweepers are in for refitting."

"I know the *Tuscaloosa* is in, papa. Willie's friend, Lieutenant Sutton, is on her."

Harry Marks frowned. "Willie? So who's Willie?"

"William Vandercort. The Fourth."

"Oy!" Harry Marks clapped his palm to his forehead. "You'll excuse your father. Lately, I'm not on such friendly terms with millionaires."

"Oh, stop it, papa! You'd like Willie. He's a very simple person."

Harry shrugged. "I had a simple friend once. But he didn't have money, so they locked him up."

Leya appealed to high heaven. "Oh my God, papa, you must be feeling better! We should call Minnie. She'll be very happy for you."

When they entered the store on the ground floor, Mrs. Nathanson, wife of the proprietor, looked relieved.

"I have a message for you, Leya. It's a 'please call' from a Mister Lieberman."

"When did he phone?" Leya asked, close to shrieking. "Did he leave a number?"

"An hour ago, maybe," the woman replied. She pointed to a scratch pad by the telephone. "The number's there."

Leya opened her purse and took out a five-cent piece. "I'll leave the money, Mrs. Nathanson. Can I call from here?"

"So call," the woman replied.

Leya held her breath until she heard the ring. A confusion of thoughts raced through her mind. The phone rang four times, then she heard his voice.

"Arthur. It's Leya. I just got your message."

"Oh, hi! I'm glad you called back. I wanted to talk to you after the other night at the club. Then over the weekend I couldn't because my father's been ill."

"I'm sorry," Leya said. "I hope it isn't serious."

"The doctor says he'll be okay now if he takes his medicine and stays on his diet."

In the background, she heard a deep male chuckle.

"Leya—I wondered if you're busy this Sunday? The family would like you to come out to Long Beach for the day."

Leya's impulse was to accept, but two thoughts stayed her. She would need new weekend things, which would deplete her marginal cash reserve; and despite the unarguable truth of an ailing father, she wanted Arthur to experience a little of the anxiety that she had suffered while waiting for him to call.

"I would love to, Arthur, but I think I'd better talk with my family first. I heard papa say something about the weekend."

"Oh?" His disappointment was obvious. "When do you think you'll know?"

"I'll talk with papa as soon as I can. Could I call you when I know?"

"Of course. I'll be at the office all day tomorrow except for a business lunch between twelve and two-thirty. Call anytime before or after."

"Thank you for asking me, Arthur. I'll call just as soon as I can."

Wednesday, just before noon, Leya called Arthur Lieberman to accept. His delight bordered on the sophomoric. "Wonderful! We'll swim, go on the boat, make a barbecue on our dock. We'll have a fine day. I'll pick you up at ten Sunday morning. Wear something light. Very informal. You don't even need a bathing suit. My sister Shelly's got dozens of them, most of which she hasn't worn. Just bring yourself, that's all!"

Leya called Dulcy to tell her the good news. "Don't worry about clothes," her friend said. "Until you get set up, anything I've got in the closet is yours."

When Leya demurred, she insisted. "If Arthur wants to

show you off to the family, you've got to put on the window dressing."

"I'll feel like a dummy," Leya joked.

"You'll be one if you don't use every advantage!" Dulcy said. "Call me Monday and let me know how things went. I know you're going to knock them dead!"

Dulcy slipped out of her silk wrapper and returned to the bed. William Vandercort, IV, rolled his head toward her, content to just lie there and admire her smooth, unblemished skin. Then he reached out and traced a forefinger beneath her breasts. "Who was that?"

"Leya Marks."

"Oh? She's very nice. I'm glad I had a chance to meet her."

"She is also one hell of a straight young lady," Dulcy replied, "and I mean to do what I can to see that she stays that way."

Willie grinned and reached out to bring her down to him.

"You want to spare her all of the worldly woes you've known?"

She allowed herself to be brought down close. "With you I have no woes, Willie, worldly or otherwise. I just don't want a nineteen-year-old kid to have to learn the hard way."

"Is there any other way, really?" he asked.

She pulled away to give him an incredulous look. "Good God! Don't tell me that William Vandercort, the Fourth, knows anything about the hard life! Maybe old Willie Number One did, sugarplum, but not you!"

"It may amaze you to know that my life has not always been a bed of roses."

"Orchids?" Dulcy asked.

"No!" Willie replied. "I suppose you'll misunderstand, but sometimes it's just as hard for a Vandercort to get outside those big iron gates as it is for an outsider to get in. It's a small world I live in. A lot of things are proscribed."

"You mean like sleeping with scullery maids, underwear models, and other poor but honest working girls?"

"Cut it out!" he cautioned. "You know I love you. You also know that when the time is right, I'm going to marry you."

"I know, darling," Dulcy replied with mock seriousness. "We'll get married 'come the revolution.' "

"I mean, come the time when I'm in a position to make my decisions stick. I want to make sure I've met all my family obligations so nobody can accuse me of being irresponsible. Certain things are expected of me."

She pressed a finger over his lips. "I know, sweetikins. Just like certain things are expected of me." She kissed him for deliberate effect. When she felt him respond, she reached down and brought him to her. Efficiently and effectively—for him—she made love to him for the third time that afternoon. A half hour later, in the bathroom, she took the douche bag from the basin cabinet.

One of the things that had surprised her about Willie was his lack of pretension. As unlikely as it seemed, she hoped that it might be a trait common to the entire family. If so, it could make the going smoother, and Dulcy harbored little doubt about where she wanted to go.

She let Willie snooze until she was in her dress. Then she awakened him and led him to the shower. When he came out, he found fresh things laid out on the coffee table and the bed remade into a sofa.

He leaned close to kiss her. "If this is domestic bliss, then I'm all for it. You're spoiling me rotten."

"You'll get your chance to reciprocate later. Now get dressed and let's take care of your other male appetites. Females have some of the same, too, you know."

CHAPTER 17

At ten-forty-five Sunday morning, Arthur Lieberman made a right turn into a short street that dead-ended at Rockaway Channel in Atlantic Beach and pulled up beside a large two-story Colonial house.

"This is it," he said.

Before he could help Leya out, the front door opened, and a slender, smartly dressed, dark-haired woman in her middle years appeared. She came to Leya with her hand extended.

"Welcome! I'm Myra Lieberman," she said as she caught Leya's hand in both of hers. For a moment she studied her son's guest; then her smile turned to warm approval. The vibrant, elegant woman who, as Myra Mannix, had been one of New York's leading fashion illustrators, released Leya's hand. "You two made very good time," she observed as Arthur urged them toward the door.

"How's dad behaving?" he asked.

"Much friskier than Dr. Hoffenberg says he should. In fact, he's been pacing the floor, watching the road for the last half hour. But in all truth, his impatience has to do with brunch." She smiled. "So you won't misunderstand, Miss Marks, the doctor has been starving Martin for a week now."

The entrance—actually a side access—led into the end of a

long living room with two deep bay windows. Between them was a formal entrance that led down a brick path to the private dock on the channel.

Leya had never been in such a house. It resembled the Early American interiors she had seen pictured in magazines. The atmosphere bespoke solidity, comfort, and quiet affluence.

As they entered, Martin Lieberman came downstairs. "Welcome to our house, dear!" He gave his son a reproachful look. "But what took you so long? The Nova Scotia's getting warm, and the eggs are getting cold."

"Martin!" Myra Lieberman's dark eyes grew pained. "You're dreadful! Really!"

All innocence, Martin winked at Leya and turned to his wife. "What's so terrible? The girl is here. I'm in love already. So let's eat."

"Where are Shelly and Bert?" Arthur asked.

"Bert's down at the club," his father replied. "Shelly's with him. One of his clients has tax trouble. They'll come around one o'clock."

Brunch was a new experience for Leya. Two silver chafing dishes on the sideboard contained eggs scrambled with bits of matzoh and a fonduelike cheese concoction into which were dipped fingers of thin-sliced toasted rye bread. On the table were platters of pink Nova Scotia salmon, which Leya quickly discovered was more delicate than the darker, oilier "lox" her father enjoyed, and platters of smoked Great Lakes whitefish and sturgeon. She was awestruck not only by the quality of the food but also by the quantity.

"Take more, Leya," Martin urged. "You eat like a bird."

"So do you," Myra chided. "A vulture!"

Leya found herself enjoying the exchange. These were people who liked one another. The good-natured banter continued until they heard a car pull into the driveway.

Myra got up. "That will be Shelly and Bert."

"You'll like Shelly—and Bert, too," Martin said, turning to Leya. "They've only been married a little over a year. Shelly's first marriage didn't take, and I can tell you, Leya, I didn't weep. When everybody else was cutting velvet, her ex-husband, Lennie, was still cutting taffeta! Thank God things are better now."

From the length of the long room, Leya was struck by Shelly's resemblance to her father. The likeness of father and son made for a handsome offspring, but the similarity of father and daughter was less satisfying. Naturally a brunette, Shelly affected straw-blonde hair, which she wore in a Ginger Rogers ratted pompadour in front. The back fell into an uncurled page boy. It was a coiffure that made her perfectly groomed mother groan inwardly.

Bert Farber acknowledged the introduction with a pleased smile. "Believe me, it's a pleasure to know you, Leya."

Shelly, clearly taken aback by her brother's date, managed a perfunctory "Hi, Leya," then turned to give her father a quick kiss on the temple.

For the rest of the brunch the burden of conversation fell on Myra. She managed a few skillful probes into the Marks family background. Leya's direct answer about her mother's death and her own years in the Brooklyn home brought a telltale glistening to the older woman's expressive eyes.

After cheesecake and coffee, Martin Lieberman pushed away from the table with a satisfied sigh. "One thing the doctor told me, after a nice light lunch—"

Myra's eyes rolled. "God forgive the man!" she whispered.

"I should relax by the radio with the baseball game," Martin continued. "So if you'll forgive me, I'll go upstairs and listen to the Cincinnati game because McKechnie's come over from St. Louis to manage. I've got a small bet he'll win a pennant for the new owners."

Arthur grinned at his father. "Want to make another small wager that McCarthy does it again for New York?"

"Six fifty-one last year? And he's going to do better?"

Martin pushed his chair in and walked to the opposite end of the table to kiss the top of Myra's head. "You go have a nice time. Take the boat. Take a swim."

Myra gave her husband an affectionate pat on the behind. "You've been very good, darling—for you! The game's been on fifteen minutes already, and you've only looked at your watch five times. Run along."

Turning to the four young people, she said, "You all go do what you want to do. I'm going to stay here this afternoon and catch up on some reading. I've finally got around to Anne Morrow Lindbergh's book, *Listen, The Wind.* I want to see if she was taken in by that overstuffed Nazi sausage, Herman Goering, like her husband was!"

Arthur got up and slipped an arm around his mother. "The world is a worrisome place for you! Maybe Lindbergh wasn't really taken in. He's a colonel. It's possible he's trying to find out something. I read in the paper that he's making a report to the War Department now."

"I hope you're right, darling," Myra said. "Now go along. Enjoy yourselves." She moved between the girls as they were leaving the dining room and linked arms with them. "I don't know what Arthur plans this afternoon," she said to Leya, "but between Shelly and me we can fix you up with everything from beat-up old clamming dungarees to a floppy garden hat." She turned to her daughter. "Isn't that right, Shelly?"

"Sure. We've got a whole hand-me-down wardrobe for Arthur's weekend dates. You name it, we got it—in any size, too."

Myra's fingers tightened around her daughter's forearm. "We do fun things impulsively, Leya. We never expect our guests to be prepared." She called to Arthur. "Are you planning to go out on the boat, dear?"

"Whatever you all want."

"I vote for the boat," Bert said, "and plenty of cold beer."

"How about you, Leya?" Myra asked.

"Anything is fine. I've never been on a small boat."

"Well, ours is not exactly a *small* boat," Shelly said. "It's a forty-two-foot Chris Craft. It sleeps eight people."

Myra did her best to conceal her annoyance. Ever since Arthur had started bringing girl friends to the house, his sister had resented them. As a young girl, Shelly had not been attractive to boys. The result was a proprietary attitude toward her considerate big brother. If Shelly had not been able to monopolize him, at least she had always managed to be included. The jealousy had carried over into her teens.

Myra thought Shelly would outgrow it with marriage. Indeed, for a time it seemed that she had. Then, after the divorce, the trait had reasserted itself. The marriage to Bert Farber appeared to have diminished the jealousy only slightly. She thanked God that Shelly was no longer living at home.

"Come change upstairs, Leya. I've put your things in the guest room. Do you really have everything you need?"

"I do, thank you," Leya replied.

On the second floor, Leya could look down on the channel and the private dock where the *Myra III* was moored. After changing into her bathing suit, she gathered up the orchid terry-cloth robe that Dulcy had insisted she take and returned to the window.

Bert Farber, dressed in blazing orange bathing shorts, was lugging a case of beer aboard. Arthur appeared from inside the cabin. He was wearing dark-blue shorts and a shapeless white and blue FDR sailing hat that was both comical and stylish. His body was as she had imagined it—strong, well-muscled, but spare—and he was deeply tanned.

As she was about to turn away, Leya saw Shelly walk toward the dock. She was wearing a vividly colored tropical print Lastex suit that compressed her flesh. Instead of controlling her ample curves, the elasticized material forced her soft flesh into converging ridges along the deep V of the back, and the snug leg opening puffed out the flesh of her upper thighs. Leya knew that at twenty-five, Shelly Lieberman was well on the way to becoming what her father would define as a *zoftigeh.*

Aboard the *Myra III,* Leya was amazed at the luxury in the living quarters below. Arthur's quiet competence as he made the craft ready for sea gave her a sense of security. He was confident and dependable, and she found her attraction to him deepening as she watched from the observer's seat where he had perched her to keep her from getting "fouled up in the gear," as he had put it.

Arthur, for all of his apparent absorption in the familiar tasks of ventilating the bilges, checking the fuel tanks, and starting up the twin engines, was acutely aware of Leya's presence. It seemed altogether right and natural for her to be there. He meant to see that she was—often—and a part of him prayed that she would be a good sailor.

After they had cleared the private berth behind the house, Arthur headed the *Myra III* almost due east along the Rockaway Channel. Making way slowly, he maneuvered the craft between the markers until they came to Jones Inlet and the open Atlantic.

Relieved that no seaway was running, he followed the markers into open water and ran along the coast well outside the breaker line until they picked up the buoys marking Fire Island Inlet and the entrance to Great South Bay.

In less than a half hour they were opposite Point of Woods, the exclusive summer colony inhabited by a dozen or so well-to-do families. The weathered Victorian houses loomed like great stark hulks stranded atop the low dunes. Few of them boasted any planting.

Pointing to the fence surrounding the compound, Arthur said, "I don't know that it's true, but I've heard that you have to have blue blood to live there."

Bert Farber overheard and called from the after cockpit. "To get in there you've got to have two things, forefathers and foreskins. In Cherry Grove, you've got a better chance."

"Is that near here?" Leya asked.

Arthur indicated a dense stand of flat-topped native pines to the east.

"That's it, about four miles up the bay. How do you know about Cherry Grove?"

"I have a friend who has a place there. He was in my dance class at the Met."

Arthur smiled. "That figures."

"What figures, Arthur?"

"That a boy dancer would have a place at Cherry Grove. Don't you know anything about the place, Leya?"

"No."

"It's probably the safest place in the world for a female to be—with a male. Cherry Grove is getting to be the homosexual summer capital of the Atlantic Coast. What's your friend's name?"

"Kent Kendall."

"Is his mother a trustee of the Metropolitan Museum?"

"She has something to do with art," Leya replied.

"If it's the same family, his father is chairman of the board of Kendall Engineering. He's one of the giants in the construction business. He's also on the board of a half-dozen companies."

Both Bert and Shelly had been listening. Bert's generous mouth twisted into a leering grin. "He's worth fifty million, and he's got a *fageleh* for a son? What kind of luck is this?"

Arthur shot back, "Maybe he's just artistic."

"He's a very nice person," Leya said, unable to conceal her annoyance. "And one of the best dancers Madame Baronova has ever trained. She'll tell you that herself."

Arthur turned away from the helm. "If he's a friend of yours," he said, "he's a friend of mine, too. Would you like to run out there for a few minutes?"

Leya glanced aft at Bert and Shelly. "If nobody else minds, I think it might be fun."

Twenty minutes later, the *Myra III* fell in behind Captain Fred Stein's Fire Island ferry and followed it south across the Blue Point Oyster beds to Cherry Grove.

By the time they had tied up on the inside of the T-headed pier, the long, sleek converted rum runner, redesigned to carry passengers, was taking aboard a noisy crowd of weekenders heading back to the city. The majority of the passengers were young, male, with good, deeply tanned physiques that they displayed to maximum advantage in an extraordinary variety of skimpy summer costumes. One young man, attended by two adoring male companions dressed in nothing more than ornamented jock straps, affected oversize dark glasses, a straw coolie hat, and a long black caftan. As he boarded the boat, each of his friends kissed him and made over the miniature poodle he cradled in his arms.

By the time Arthur had assisted Leya and Shelly to the dock, the ferry was easing away. Those who remained on the island shouted comically "heart-rending" farewells. One tall, willowy boy moved to the edge of the dock clasping a large bunch of gladiolus to his heart.

"If you don't come back," he called to his departing companion, "I shall simply destroy myself!" Whereupon he closed his eyes and threw himself, flowers and all, off the pier. A scream of delight went up. The young man surfaced, acknowledged the applause, caught one of the floating stalks between his teeth, and struck out for the shore. By the time the ferry had turned and headed north across the channel to Sayville, the crowd was dispersing.

"Let's go up to the hotel for a beer," Arthur suggested. "It's something you ought to see once."

Leya and Shelly donned their beach coats, and the four of them walked up the weathered boardwalks that served in place of streets. Leya found Cherry Grove quaint and attractive. She hoped Arthur didn't mind the stopover. The outlandish exhibitionism on the docks had amused him. Shelly and Bert were plainly disgusted.

Soon after they entered the bar, a pair of hands closed gently around Leya's shoulders. Startled, she turned to find herself being embraced by Kent Kendall.

"What on earth are you doing here?" he demanded.

Arthur cut in with his hand extended. "I'm Arthur Lieberman, and this is my sister and brother-in-law, Shelly and Bert Farber. We're out on the boat for the day, exploring."

Ignoring Shelly's unsmiling gaze and Bert's perfunctory grunt, Kent acknowledged the introductions warmly. His arm around Leya, he turned back to Arthur. "Is it your first time here?"

"Yes, it is."

"Well," Kent said, smiling, "then, like Columbus, you've just discovered a new world. Welcome!"

"I told Arthur you had a place here," Leya explained, "but we didn't intend to—well—"

"—barge in unannounced," Arthur finished for her. "We just came up for a drink and a look around."

"But you are staying!" Kent replied. "And you're having a drink—at my place." Kent looked down the bar and motioned to a boy in his late teens. "I want you to meet my house guest."

Shepherding the dark-haired, well tanned lad with one

arm, Kent said, "This is Heather's brother, Matt O'Brien. He's one of the best young dancers in Boston, and he's coming down to make a career in the big city."

The introductions were acknowledged by all except Shelly, who continued to regard Kent and Matt with ill-concealed distaste. Kent covered the awkward moment by devoting himself to Leya and Arthur.

"I won't keep you long, I promise. But I've been dying to talk to this girl."

When Kent urged them toward the door, Shelly balked. Linking her arm through Bert's, she said, "I hope you're not too long. Bert and I will wait for you on the boat."

Kent's cottage faced on Great South Bay, not more than fifty yards from the old weather-beaten hotel and the little store. Unlike most of the others, it was freshly painted. Beneath the heavily mullioned windows were bright flower boxes filled with petunias.

Inside, the place was deceptively large. "I like it, Kent!" Leya exclaimed as she took in the unusual furnishings. Except for a driftwood bar and four matching stools and a colorful L-shaped sofa, the furniture consisted mainly of bright, odd-sized cushions and hassocks designed to be arranged as seats or to be pushed together as pallets on the grass-mat flooring.

Arthur smiled at the inventiveness and obvious utility of the furnishings.

While Kent fixed drinks, Leya chatted with Heather's young brother. Matt had his sister's classic "Black Irish" good looks—thick dark brown hair, vivid lapis-blue, heavily lashed eyes—and a superbly developed dancer's body. He was several inches shorter than Kent and more heavily muscled, but he moved with the same disciplined grace. Even so, he seemed ill at ease with the unexpected company.

When they were settled with their drinks, Kent turned to Leya. "How is your knee behaving? Have you tried dancing yet?'

"I've tried a little barre," she replied, "but mostly I've taken my exercise and therapy. Dr. Lewin thinks I'll be fine, but he wants me to take it easy."

"My interest in your knee is not entirely unselfish, Leya. I want to know if you'll be able to dance again. I mean, as you used to. Because if so, and if you want to, you're going to be a part of the Kendall group."

"Oh, Kent! Of course I want to dance again!" Leya replied.

Arthur found her enthusiasm unsettling.

"It's always been my life. You know that," she added.

"Thank God it still is, then, Leya, because I am determined to bring something new to the art form, and I need you to accomplish that. We will have eight dancers at the beginning. I plan that you and Matt are to be two of the principals. Peter Genova and his wife, Jean Baxter, will join us, and so will Marc Bright and Luanna Parker. I've given up on Celine, but I've asked Tanya Kuznetsov. Do you know her?"

"No," Leya replied. "But I've heard some of the kids talk about her."

"She's a pixie. You'll like her," Kent said. "But let me tell you what I want to accomplish."

For a full ten minutes, Kent Kendall expanded on his concept. He argued with conviction, and it was obvious to Arthur that Leya was caught up in his enthusiasm. He did his best to understand. It was becoming increasingly clear to him that these serious dancers were a breed apart.

Kent felt that George Balanchine had moved into new areas with his Broadway musical choreography even though Madame Baronova, secure in the purity of her old-school disciplines, deplored any departure from the classic forms. Matt O'Brien's knowledge of the dance surprised Arthur when, his reticence apparently gone, he suggested that Charles Weidman had broken through old barriers also, with such dancers as Bill Maton, José Limon, and Letitia Ide. Kent agreed, but he contended that there were still other concepts that could broaden the statements possible in dance. That, he explained, was why he had often urged Celine, among others, to study primitive and modern. Elements of both could be synthesized with the classic forms, and a new dance language would emerge—one better suited to contemporary stories. Katherine Dunham, Chicago's brilliant dancer-anthropologist, had been experimenting with such possibilities at the I.L.G.W.U.'s Labor Theatre. He had visited several of her classes and had come away more eager than ever to pursue his own inquiries.

Privately, Arthur would admit that he would rather be burned at the stake than sit through most grand opera, especially *The Ring*. But he had always enjoyed ballet, most especially the more modern works. Sono Osato and Tamara Toumanova had captivated him in *Union Pacific*. He had seen the premiere performance of Massine's ballet with his mother at the Forrest Theater in Philadelphia.

Kent apologized for monopolizing the conversation. "I'm full of it!" he laughed. "And now that the financing is arranged, I'm overflowing." He turned to Leya again with a speculative look. "When will you know about your knee?"

Arthur answered for her. "Max Lewin is a close friend and an honest surgeon. He thinks another week or two will tell."

"And if it takes more time, I suppose you'll continue to model?"

"I enjoy it," Leya admitted.

"Not too much, I hope!" Kent said, rising to replenish the drinks. Just then the *Myra III*'s horn began to blow insistently. Arthur checked his watch.

"I'm sorry, but I'm going to have to break this up," he said. "We've got a couple of hours of running yet, and I want to clear the channel before it gets dark."

Kent reached for Leya's hand and pulled her up into an affectionate embrace. "Get back on your toes, ballerina. I can't pay you as much as modeling, but I'll pay you more than you'd make dancing for Balanchine! That's a promise!"

The *Myra*'s horn was blowing in a persistent, nerve-jangling pattern. In the distance, several male voices shouted, "For God's sake, shut up!"

"Sorry about that," Arthur said as he moved to the door. "My sister is a captive crew today."

The return trip was made in an atmosphere of tension. Bert, after too many beers, flopped into deep sleep in the forward cabin. Shelly propped herself on the transom cushions, where she smoked incessantly and fired caustic comments about the afternoon in general and "*fageleh*" dancers in particular. Arthur endured it for a time. But when Shelly came up to the helm and persisted, he lost his temper. "Shut up, Shelly! You're being a complete little bitch!" He half whispered so Leya could not overhear. "You better know, I'm not going to stand for it!"

Pouting, Shelly retreated to the forward cabin to vent her unhappiness on her snoring husband. There was a brief explosion below and then silence. Grinning at Leya, Arthur said, "Good man, that brother-in-law of mine!"

It was past one o'clock in the morning when Arthur pulled the convertible to the curb in front of Leya's flat. It had turned chilly enough to put the top up. For most of the trip, Leya had curled her legs beneath her on the seat and snuggled into the cashmere sweater Myra had insisted she borrow.

Arthur turned off the ignition and angled on the seat to face Leya.

"Well," he said, "as far as I'm concerned it was a very short Sunday."

Leya resettled the skirt over her knees. "I guess I kept you too long at Kent's place."

Arthur reached out to take her hand. "I didn't mean it that way! I enjoyed meeting your friend. I just meant, with you, time always seems to run out too fast."

Leya smiled. "I know," she said softly.

Leya felt Arthur's hand tighten around hers, and a moment later, unresisting, she allowed herself to be eased into his arms. She expected to be kissed. She would have welcomed it. Instead, he cradled her face against his chest, with the crown of her head beneath his chin as it had been when he carried her from the photo studio. She heard the muted pounding of his pulse.

"May I ask you a question, Leya Marks?" He felt her head move in assent. "Is there anybody else you'd rather be saying good night to right now?"

"No," she whispered.

"Is there anybody else you'd rather have holding you?"

"No."

Suddenly, his restraint deserted him. His hand reached for her chin, cupped it, and brought her face up to his. Gently, at first, and then with mounting intensity, he kissed her.

For a moment, she resisted. Then, as his tongue brushed her lips, he heard a muted sound—almost a whisper—and he felt her mouth relax. An instant later, her tongue began to move timidly against his. Leya felt Arthur's left arm slip down against her hip and turn her body to his. Her breasts pressed against his light sport shirt. Leya knew that a part of her—a frightened part—wanted to hold him off, but curiosity and desire were moving her to respond. She could not separate the emotions—did not wish to try—as Arthur's left arm brought her still closer and his right hand sought her breast. Her nipple hardened and was pressing against his palm. His gentle circular motion started an electric something deep in her belly.

Since her teens, in her fantasies, Leya had allowed herself to be held by nameless, faceless, formless lovers. They were shadow entities, beings without substance. Now, in Arthur's arms, she knew she was close to abandoning herself to the restrained power of hard muscles, the eagerness of hungry lips, an exciting man scent, the sensuous abrasiveness of whiskers. When Arthur moved to bring her still closer, she responded willingly. Subtle movements in his lower body, gently persistent in the beginning, were now openly insistent, and her own responses, unconsciously sinuous, synchronized with his. When his lips left hers to trail across her cheek, then move to her ear and down the length of her throat, an involuntary shudder shook her, and she whispered his name half aloud.

An instant later, his fingers dug into her backside with gentle viciousness as he forced her lower stomach against him. Caught tightly in an embrace that charged her entire being, she was unaware for a moment of the pressure against her inner thigh.

Suddenly, Arthur felt her body go rigid. Her hands pushed against him as she struggled to move away.

"Please! Arthur! No!"

Arthur returned his lips to hers to silence her protest, but she twisted away.

"Leya!" His voice was strange. "Leya—I love you—I love you—"

"Arthur—please—I'm not ready. I love you, but I'm not ready—"

As she forced her body away from his, she felt his embrace relax. After a few seconds, she moved to the right-hand corner of the seat.

Arthur straightened slowly and sat up. When he lifted his head, the pain in his face punished her.

"Oh, God, Leya—I'm sorry," he whispered. "I didn't mean to let that happen." He started to reach out to her, then returned his hand to his lap. "I feel like a goddamned fool. I know there is nothing I can say—but please believe me—I love you."

Then, with a suddenness that startled her, he bolted from the driver's seat, came around to her side, and opened the door. At the bottom of the stairs, unable to find words, Leya flung herself into his arms for a moment, then ran to the top of the stairs. He was still standing, looking up, when she closed the door behind her.

CHAPTER 18

"Walter Winchell–Danton Walker–Hy Gardner–Ed Sullivan–Earl Wilson–" Kent Kendall tossed the clippings aside. "Every gossip column in New York but not one of the dance reviewers!" He gave Matt O'Brien an injured look. "They are not taking my Kendall Dance Group seriously!" He retrieved one of the columns. "Listen to this! 'Kent Kendall, handsome scion of the Kendall Industrial millions' "–he spat out the words–" 'whose father could buy the Ballet Russe and keep it on his estate to amuse his powerful international clients, has started his own dance group.

" 'Young Kendall has promised to "revolutionize" the dance with an entirely new approach to the classical and modern forms. We wonder if George Balanchine, Lester Horton, Martha Graham, Charles Weidman, Helen Tamiris, and Doris Humphrey are fingering their worry beads?' "

He poured himself a fresh cup of coffee and perched on the stool next to Matt at the driftwood bar.

"It's absolutely rotten that artists who dare to try something different have to be prejudged. But they did the same thing to Tamara Geva when they found out she was going to do a Broadway musical. And they were wrong!"

"They'll be wrong about you, too," Matt said.

Kent had let his guest sleep late while he planned his first tentative concert program. It was Matt's first overnight visit to Fire Island, and Kent did not intend that it would be the last. He had been delighted the afternoon before to expose Matt to Leya Marks and Arthur Lieberman, friends who were less flamboyant than those who usually dropped by.

Young Matt had not really come out, did not really know who he was yet. Kent knew that it was important to make him a part of his plans, to bring him closer through their mutual devotion to the dance, to bind him intellectually and emotionally to his own life-style. There had been other companions, but ever since the day he had run into Heather during one of Matt's visits from Boston, Kent had determined to know the boy better.

He was beautiful, and he was an extraordinarily versatile dancer for his age. Two more years of the sort of training he could get in New York and Matt O'Brien might well become star material. Except when he was talking about the dance, Matt contributed little to a conversation, sometimes embarrassingly little. But Kent knew that once exposed to the cultural advantages he could give him, the young dancer would grow. Time, and the boy could become the one companion who would completely fill his needs.

The day on the beach passed quickly. Because Kent discouraged the curious Cherry Grove regulars who dropped by to give the new boy a once-over, he and Matt were able to get much planning done.

For the premiere program they settled on a theme from the polygamous Oneida Colony. The piece would be tentatively titled "The Land of the Free" and would deal with the puritanical persecution of John Humphrey Noyes's "free-love" social experiment in New York state. Another would be called "Chautauqua." A third would be an intricate society satire—an entertainment romp set to original music—to be called "Big News at Newport." The fourth could be a challenge routine, a tour de force.

They quit the beach at four-thirty and returned to the cottage. Matt slipped into a faded cotton shirt and tied the tails in a knot above the belt line of his calf-length white duck beach pants. The outfit accentuated his deep tan and his dark good looks. Kent forced his thoughts back to Leya Marks, who could be the ideal choice to complete the group if she were still able to dance.

"As much as I hate to leave," Kent said, "I think I ought to go into the city tomorrow and see if I can get some answers. Not just from the kids but on a place to rehearse and, hopefully, on a theater, too. Would you like to come in with me?"

Matt understood that he was expected to. "Sure. Anyway, I'd like to see my sister."

"Marvelous! Why don't we do an after-the-show party for Heather at the apartment Wednesday? Heather and her current–" He broke off. "What shall I call him?"

"Why not call him by his right name–'gorilla.' "

"And her patent-leather gorilla," Kent corrected, "and Leya and Arthur, and certainly Celine. Who else should we ask?" The question was directed to himself. "Maybe I should ask some people who could help us with the business end of things." He made a distasteful face. "I might just as well begin my selling pitch."

Kent Kendall's penthouse was a revelation to Leya and about what Arthur had expected. Eight rooms with a broad-tiled terrace on three sides overlooking the river and Long Island to the east, lower Manhattan to the south, midtown and across the Hudson to New Jersey to the west.

It was just past eleven-thirty when Kent met them at the door. Leya was scarcely out of her host's embrace when Heather hurried to meet her. Carlo Romano, following her, smiled. "Look who's here! Miss Marks! It's good to see you!" He took her hand, and once again the man's thick, strong fingers closed around hers. Heather slipped her arm through his possessively and turned him to introduce Arthur. Romano released Leya and offered his hand. He noted that Arthur's was more finely made but as powerful as his own.

"Glad to see you, Lieberman," he said heartily. "We've got mutual friends. Johnny Damone organized the truckers in your local. Your shop's one of the best now. No strikes. We get along, huh?"

"That's the name of the game," Arthur replied.

"Too bad everybody in the industry doesn't understand that. Can I tell you?" Romano said earnestly, dropping a heavy arm across Arthur's shoulders, "If they did, it could be a beautiful world. Right?" He ignored Arthur's noncommittal response and turned back to Leya.

"Heather says you are a great ballerina. When are we going to see you?"

Leya glanced up at Arthur. "I've stopped dancing for a while."

Carlo Romano gave them a knowing look. "I understand. *Amore.* Makes the world go around."

Kent interrupted. "Come on, you two gypsies. You can catch up later. I have some people I want Leya to meet." He led them to a tall, assured-appearing man dressed in a conservative black mohair suit. Arthur recognized Howard Pryor immediately. The head of International Artists' Management was conceded on both coasts to be one of the most powerful and perceptive talent men in show business.

Pryor smiled and offered his hand to Leya. "I thought Kent had been exaggerating about you, Miss Marks. Now I must put him down as a master of understatement."

Still uneasy at small talk, Leya smiled self-consciously. Arthur relieved the awkward moment. "Coming from you, that's an extravagant compliment, but from my own prejudiced point of view, one that's not at all undeserved."

Pryor laughingly conceded the point. He admired a smooth performance, and young Lieberman was smooth, smoother even than his father, who, as an occasional show backer, had been a sometime business associate. More than that, young Arthur's girl was stunning. She was very young, he thought, and still a bit out of her element socially. The intuitive gift that had earned him his reputation as a discoverer of new talent prompted Howard Pryor to make a mental note to keep an eye on the Kendall Dance Group. Dance ensembles seldom made profitable clients. But the individual stars they often produced did.

As they were talking, a striking silver-blonde showgirl, fully six-three in her spiked heels, approached on the arm of a compact, prematurely graying man in his early middle years. Something about him reminded Leya of Martin Lieberman.

Howard Pryor introduced the girl simply as "Sheri." Her escort was Ed Matson. "Ed is an entrepreneur," he explained to Leya. "That's French for a man with no visible means of support. But that's unfair. A half-dozen stars plus as many Broadway shows would not have happened if Ed Matson hadn't recognized the right ingredients and mixed them together with backers' money."

Matson's smile was open and good. "I'm happy to know you two," he said. "What Howard is trying to say is that I'm a 'puter-er together-er.' If I'm involved with any preoccupation too long, I get bored." He glanced up at the showgirl. "Except, of course, with this beautiful lady—without whom, by the way, I appear much taller."

Sheri's green eyes glittered. "Dating me is good for Ed's ego," she said. "If people don't know him, they say, 'It must take a hell of a lot of man to handle that much woman.' "

Kent saw Leya laughing along with the others, but he read discomfort in her set smile. "Let me introduce Leya and Arthur to some other guests." He led them through the large modern living room to a long buffet and bar set up in the dining room. Pausing before a couple talking with dancer Marc Bright, he said, "Leya Marks and Arthur Lieberman, may I present three of the charter members of the Kendall Dance Group?"

He turned first to a tallish, sorrel-haired girl whose years of ballet training were evident in her poised, clean-lined body and to the slightly shorter, strongly built, and pleasantly pugnacious-appearing Italian-American beside her.

"Jean Baxter and her husband Peter Genova—and my good friend, Marc Bright, who on my own off days, may be the finest unmarried *premier danseur* in this country."

Bright, a spare, darkly handsome dancer with brooding eyes and evenly chiseled features, managed a laugh. "Kent's an accomplished liar, also."

Leya found herself liking the dancers Kent had chosen. With the exception of Matt, they were all several years older than she. All were professionals who had danced in concert and in shows. More than that, they were open and outgoing. She sensed that working with them would be fun.

In New York there were two pianists who were the undisputed darlings of café society. Dwight Fiske entertained with his cleverly risqué original songs at the Savoy-Plaza, and Cy Walter, a brilliant technician and innovator, commanded the customers' rapt attention at the Madison Hotel bar. Kent had persuaded Cy to compose an original score for two of the group's dance numbers. The score for the "Oneida" number had been blocked out, and the pianist had agreed to preview it.

Kent and the others kept Walter at the piano for over an hour. The composer's original themes and variations for the "Oneida" piece brought unanimous approval. Seated on the floor beside Arthur, Leya lost herself in the music's intricate rhythm. Involuntarily, her body moved, and Arther grew aware that, besides himself, three other men in the room seemed more preoccupied with watching her than with the music itself. Carlo Romano, seated slightly behind Heather, seldom took his eyes from Leya. Howard Pryor and Ed Matson studied her less obviously, but their attention returned to her more often than to the other members of the group, all of whom were finding it impossible not to react.

It was almost three in the morning when Arthur interrupted Leya's conversation with Kent and Peter Genova. "Come on," he urged, "before we get caught in the early-morning traffic."

Shortly after four Arthur pulled the Cadillac convertible to the curb on New Jersey Avenue in Brownsville and got out to open Leya's door. At the top of the stairs, he held her in a long, intense embrace. "There ought to be a law against what you've done to me, Leya Marks!" he whispered. "Will you phone me late this afternoon at the office? I have no idea what for, but I'll think of something."

For Leya, sleep did not come quickly. Cy Walter's music for the *pas de deux* in the "Oneida" number haunted her. She felt and, in her mind's eye, saw herself caught up in totally new rhythm patterns. She was weightless and free, liberated from the limitations of a body that required endless discipline to perform.

Her fantasy came to an end when she turned involuntarily and felt a stab of pain in her left knee.

Oh God, she thought, *what if I try to get back in shape again and find I can't?* Her body grew rigid as she stared up into the darkness, scarcely breathing, afraid to face the possibility and unable to deny it.

Finally, as the sounds of early-morning traffic reached her, she drifted into sleep.

On the Tuesday after Labor Day, Kent Kendall went to Ed Matson's office in the Scribner Building at 597 Madison Avenue. During the hour it took to persuade Matson to act as manager for the group, it seemed to him that the man was much more concerned with Leya Marks. In the end, Matson agreed to take on the management responsibility for fifteen percent of the net gross. He would try to interest I.A.M. in doing the bookings. Moreover, he had been adamant on one count. He insisted on personal contracts with each dancer.

"If they balk," Matson had said, "then you sign them to personal contracts, with the right to assign the agreements. I hope that won't be necessary, but it's the only way I'll go."

As soon as Kent had left the office, Matson placed a call to Howard Pryor at I.A.M. "Howard, the Kendall kid just left here. He's no dummy. He's skittish about the individual personal management deals."

"For you and me, Ed," Pryor reminded him needlessly, "those are the only papers that will be worth a damn. Incidentally, I talked with Romano at Kendall's party. Sight unseen, I've already got the group booked into the Golden Palm Club in Miami. Six or eight weeks at two thousand, but only if the Marks girl is a featured soloist in the group."

"She's the only one he can't count on."

"I'll handle it. I'll call Kendall and call you later, Ed."

Pryor's conversation with Kent was short and to the point. "The only reason we're interested in your group," he said, "is the possibility that you and perhaps one or two others may become 'saleable names.' That is not to say that your group can't become a well-paid attraction. But after all, we haven't seen your group, have we? We've only seen some of the dancers who have agreed to take a chance with you."

"They are all committed," Kent argued. "All but Leya Marks, and I'm sure she will be."

"Do everything you can to get her. Whether you like it or not, this is a business of personalities. Matson feels she has the appearance to come across on stage, and so do I. If she dances half as well as you say she does, then you can't afford not to have her." Pryor withheld any hint of the conditional Romano offer. He knew these "serious" art-for-art's-sake ballet dancers and their impractical aversion to anything less dignified than the concert hall. With anybody else he would have been blunt about the realities. But Kendall had the money to indulge his whims for a time.

"We want to see your people together as a group before we make any firm decisions. When can that be done?" Pryor asked.

"We can't really start until we have a full company and get the music finished, but we all take class three days a week at Carnegie Hall. You could see us there."

"When is your next one?"

"This afternoon at three. Room sixty-one."

"But the Marks girl won't be there—"

"I'll try to get her there, but she hasn't danced for a while."

Pryor leaned over to check his appointment calendar. "If you can get her there and persuade her to move a little, give me a call. Ed Matson and I may be able to drop by for a look."

Kent called the Powers Agency and found that Leya was doing some cosmetic shots for Revel. He left a message at the photographer's studio and went back to his program plans with Matt O'Brien.

The telephone rang just before noon. It was Leya.

"If you tell me you're busy this afternoon, I'll kill myself," Kent threatened. "I want you to come over to Carnegie this afternoon and watch the kids. We may try to block a few bars of Oneida after class. I want your opinion. Can you make it?"

"I think so."

"Leya?"

"Yes?"

"Do something for me? Come on over and take a class with us. No toe work. Just some barre so we can see how your knee works. Please?"

The request stirred up a small storm of confusion. More than anything else she wanted to begin dancing again, but Dr. Lewin had been firm in his warning about the consequences of impatience.

"Gee, Kent, I don't know if I should. And, besides, I don't have any dance things here."

"I've anticipated that! What size ballet slippers do you wear?"

"Four D."

"And a small leotard, right?"

"Yes—but, Kent—"

"They'll be waiting. I'll even have knee pads for you," he said. "Later you can come back here to shower and change."

"I'll come over," Leya said, "but I really don't think I should try to take a class."

"Then just do a little barre with us."

"I'll see. I've got to go now."

Kent hung up the phone and clasped his hands. "So far, so good!" he said as he dialed I.A.M.'s number.

Once in the studio, it took less than five minutes to persuade Leya to try on the new practice clothing. If she was surprised to find Howard Pryor and Ed Matson talking with Kent when she came out of the changing room, she gave no sign.

After twenty minutes of conventional barre with the others, testing her left knee, putting more and more weight on it, she was relieved to find that she could handle progressively more difficult exercises.

After barre, Virginia Lee called them to the center of the floor for a session in primitive basics. From the first moment, Leya had no difficulty imitating the stretches and contractions. When it was her turn to link several combinations together solo, she did so with ease and finesse.

At the break, Kent circled Leya with his arms.

"What I suspected about you is true, you know."

"You mean that I'm a natural born *klutz?*" Leya asked.

"Certainly!" Kent replied. "But I'm desperate, so I'll have to let you join the group, anyway—in the back row, of course."

Leya gave him a playful push and skittered across the spacious floor to the dressing room, doing little Russian *positions des bras* but with an amusing Oriental angle as she held her wrists and arms in the second and third positions.

Howard Pryor and Ed Matson motioned to Kent to join them at the door. "We've seen enough," the I.A.M. head said. "The girl is very interesting. Do you think she can handle it?"

"I know she can!" Kent replied. "You saw how her confidence returned after the first half hour or so. She'll be fine, and Virginia won't let her overdo."

"When you've got one or two finished numbers to show me, get in touch with Ed," Pryor said.

Kent went into the second hour filled with optimism. When the dancers returned to the floor, he beckoned Leya.

"Are you sure you're not overdoing?"

"I'm positive. None of this is as hard as our old classes with madame."

"It's easier because of the training she gave us," he observed. "We really should thank the old girl for the discipline."

"I do," Leya agreed.

Kent motioned to the teacher that the group was ready to resume.

"All right, kids, let's see how we do with contracted *pirouettes,*" said Virginia Lee.

Leya and Kent, partnering, linked together both left and right outside *pirouettes* in contraction.

"Make the turns with your middle caved in as though someone had kicked you in the stomach!" the teacher called. "Arch your shoulders forward still more!"

The position would have been unthinkable in classic ballet—regarded as ugly and off balance—and still, as the movement grew more natural, Leya sensed that a new dimension of freedom was to be found in disciplined intuitive movement.

By the end of the second week, she had been won over completely. As her confidence returned, her grace and quiet dedication seemed to energize the entire company. For Arthur, who dropped by several times late in the afternoon, there could be little question that Leya was in her natural element, that she belonged to the world of the dance. He determined to resign himself to the inevitable if possible.

Just before her twentieth birthday, Kent and Matt conspired with Arthur to give Leya a surprise party at the Beekman Place penthouse. The deception worked so perfectly that it sent Leya, between laughter and tears, flying into her father's arms. Harry and Minnie, their reluctance to appear in "society" overcome by Arthur's persuasion, had been the first to come out of hiding. After Harry's "Happy birthday, my darling daughter!" the others appeared—the dancers, Martin and Myra Lieberman, Shelly and Bert, Heather, Celine Cervier, and the new Russian dancer, Tanya Kuznetzov, who had joined the group several weeks earlier.

Leya laughingly obeyed as Kent and the others admonished her not to prolong the suspense of opening the packages. As she opened gifts—some had represented a sacrifice on the part of her dancer friends—Leya found herself close to tears. Finally, just two boxes remained.

"This is from Matt and me," Kent said, holding one out to her. Leya undid the bow, spread the tissue paper apart, and let out a delighted little screech as she held up a pair of lavender, hand-knitted leg warmers. On one knee was the initial "L" and on the other the initial "M."

"I'll never wear them!" she breathed. "I couldn't bear to get them dirty!"

"You'll wear them. They'll lend a note of elegance to those beat-up old practice clothes of yours!"

Leya gave both boys an impulsive hug.

"And now for the final one," Kent said, motioning to Harry.

Harry took the box from Kent and held it. "*Bubeleh,*" he said, "this wouldn't be a surprise, maybe, but except for our love, it is the only other thing we could give to you—to be yours from now on."

Leya accepted the foot-square box and hefted it curiously. Turning, she set it on the side table and removed the outer ornamental tissue. It covered a striped box that bore the imprint BERGDORF GOODMAN. Still more puzzled, Leya lifted the lid and set it aside. A hush fell over the room as the guests moved in closer. An instant later, Leya gasped and turned disbelieving eyes to her father.

"Your mother would want it like this, darling," Harry said quietly as Leya reached in to the tissue paper to remove the little music-box ballerina.

"Oh, papa!" Leya whispered. To conceal her tears, she involved herself in winding the key. When the ballerina began her pirouettes to the tinkling melody of The Sugar Plum Fairy theme from The Nutcracker Suite, Kent's feet moved to the third position. He placed his left hand on his hip and extended his right hand to Leya in an invitation to dance. To the delight of the others, the pair improvised a brief *pas de deux,* ending with Leya's finger spin on demi-point.

When the applause subsided, Kent summoned them all to the buffet for the unveiling of the cake.

There were more congratulations, and someone started the "Happy Birthday" song. Harry Marks stood off to the side, wishing such a party had been his to give. He took some small comfort from the knowledge that his present—his and Anya's—had been the only truly precious one his daughter had received.

Arthur managed to be near Leya throughout.

"My God!" Shelly whispered to Bert, "you'd think this was an engagement party!"

"If we're lucky that comes next," her husband replied.

"And if I were you, I'd thank God that Arthur's *meshuga* over this one. She's a nice kid. You want to prove you love your brother? Make Leya welcome. Be a sister."

Dulcy managed to get Leya aside to explain Willie's absence. "He sends his love, dear heart. He intended to come, but the family insisted he go down to Washington. Some sort of a White House dinner, something about that Hitler mess in Europe. Willie's father wants him to put money in an aviation thing that England and France need."

She dismissed the inconvenience with an impatient gesture. "I've missed seeing you," she said, hugging Leya again. "Being in love agrees with you, girl!" She glanced across the room at Arthur, who was talking with Celine and Kent and several of the dancers. "It agrees with him, too!"

After six weeks of rehearsal, the Kendall dancers presented their first concert at New York's Town Hall on West Forty-third Street. The date was November thirtieth, the day every newspaper in New York carried the screaming headline: RUSSIA INVADES FINLAND! The best seats were occupied by family and friends, whose appearance had less to do with love of the dance than loyalty to the dancers, and complimentary tickets. There was one notable absence: Alexandra Baronova, who had been among the first to be sent an invitation. Repeated telephone calls to her home had produced no answer.

At final curtain, everyone but the critics gave the Kendall Dance Group a standing ovation. They had risen on the final note and headed for the exits and their typewriters.

Kent Kendall was generous and charming with the curtain calls. "Now—if they'll just love us in Sheboygan," he whispered as they ran to the wings, "we've got it made!"

Before family and friends stormed the stage door, Kent gathered the company around him. "What can I tell you except that I love you? Thank you, kids!" As he looked at each one, his eyes filled. "How beautiful you all are!" He turned away and hurried to his dressing room.

Leya found that her own eyes had filled, too. Kent Kendall, the tall, handsome, amusing, and very talented young man whose faith in her had reinforced her own faith in herself and in a strange way had given her the courage to rebel against Madame Baronova's tartarous behavior, had opened a door for her that led to a strange and exciting new world of dance. During the rehearsals and the performance, the new-found freedom of movement, the controlled violence and earthiness of Kent's choreographic storytelling had elated her. She realized that she had not even given her knee a second thought on stage.

She dressed quickly. Arthur would be waiting to drive her to Kent's place.

Counting the dance company, family, and close friends, thirty-five guests attended the special night lunch.

For two hours, the dancers speculated on audience reactions, convinced themselves that the concert had gone extremely well, complimented each other generously, and listened eagerly to the reassurances of those who had been out front.

At two in the morning, Kent collapsed in a chair, happy to be alone with Matt. Twenty minutes passed before he stirred, got up, and peered into Matt's room. Through the closed door he heard the shower. Needing one badly himself, he stripped off his clothing and regarded his long, muscled, well-tanned body critically in the mirror. What he saw pleased him. He hoped, once freshened up, that it would please Matt, too.

Some minutes later, wrapped in a burnt-orange Belgian terrycloth robe with a monk's cowl pushed back, he knocked on Matt's door.

"My God!" he sighed as Matt cinched the robe belt around his middle and resumed toweling his hair, "I can't believe we actually did it!"

Matt lifted the towel from his face. "We did it—and I think they liked it."

"I know they liked it," Kent agreed, "but let's not be too impressed with ourselves yet. Let's see what the critics say." He settled on the edge of Matt's bed, leaned back, and propped himself on an elbow.

"I know I should try to sleep, but I'm so keyed up I'm sure I won't close my eyes. Do you mind if I stay and talk for a few minutes? You can get into bed if you wish."

"It's okay," Matt replied as he continued with his hair.

Kent straightened. "You were wonderful on stage tonight, Matt."

"I can do better. I thought Leya was great, though."

"She was dazzling. Now you know why I broke my balls getting her to join the group."

"The kids like her," Matt added. "They like the new girl, too."

"Tanya? I know," Kent agreed. "That's one of the things we have going for us. We all love each other, and it shows in the performances."

When Matt did not reply, Kent fell silent again and watched as the young dancer finished his hair by flailing it gently with the sides of his spread fingers. After a time, Kent loosened the belt of the robe, pretending to ease it.

"Matt, are you still sort of 'on'?"

"How do you mean?"

"I mean, are you really pleased about the way things went tonight, the way we were received?"

"Oh, sure. I feel real good."

Kent laughed quietly. "I feel keyed up—like I don't want to be alone."

Matt turned from the mirror and discovered that Kent was reclining on one elbow again. His robe had parted at the belt, exposing the lower half of his body. He turned back to the mirror.

"Look, Kent," he said, deliberately prolonging the uncertainty, "I'm not sleepy. We can talk if you want to."

Kent sighed. "Oh, God! I'm all talked out, Matthew dear. When I said I don't want to be alone, I meant I don't want to go back to my monk's cell of a room"— he paused —"and just say my prayers and shut myself away in the dark." He got up and crossed to the young dancer and took him by the shoulders. "Does that sound silly to you?"

From the beginning, Matt had no illusions about Kent Kendall and his predilection for boys. Kent had been very protective and discreet at Fire Island. Now the pretense of fraternal concern was about to drop, and the prospect excited Matt.

On more than one occasion during summer camp in the Green Mountains, he had engaged in sexual play with his tent mate. That had been exciting, and he had not suffered any particular guilt.

Neither had he felt any particular concern at fifteen, following several experiences with the seventeen-year-old neighbor girl who had initiated him into sex. What he had learned from her had been exciting, but the possibility that he might knock up the girl had introduced an element of anxiety. There had been no such worry with his former summer-camp tent mate.

The memory of those nights began to arouse Matt. When Kent's hands maneuvered inside his robe, caressing his bare flesh, he responded in kind. The older dancer embraced him and whispered, "Oh, my God, but I love you! I'll do anything for you, Matt! Anything!"

CHAPTER 19

The reviews were encouraging. There were no raves, but the principal papers gave credit to Kent Kendall and his group for attempting some innovative approaches.

Howard Pryor received another offer from Carlo Romano.

"Kendall won't accept a club booking right now," Ed Matson cautioned him. "He's hell bent to do concerts first. Later, when they're established as a legit group, we can demand top dollar as a class attraction in clubs."

Matson arranged bookings in Boston and Philadelphia. By April, Elizabeth Kendall could confront her husband with a satisfied smile and say, "I was right about Kent, dear. I hope you can accept the fact now that we have a very talented son."

"K. A." Kendall nodded absently and returned his attention to the deuterium oxide plants that Kendall Engineering was building for the Norwegian government. In the hands of Nazi scientists, the heavy water they produced might well result in weapons so terrible that the mere proof of their existence could cause the Allies to capitulate.

The Kendall Dance Group worked hard to improve its material. The "Brigham Young" dance was eliminated. The critics were right. It was too close in theme to the "Oneida" piece.

The George Sand number, "Mallorcan Idyll," danced to Chopin's "Preludes," was particularly well received. It was the most balletic of the pieces.

"Sinful Miss Sadie," danced by Kent, Leya, and Jean Baxter to an original Cy Walter score, added humor and eroticism to the Somerset Maugham short story, "whose plot," one reviewer wrote, "threatened, until tonight, to become one of the more mundane 'morality plays.' Since the ubiquitous Aimee Semple McPherson's capitulations to the 'Devil's Desire,' it is difficult to get excited about an all-too-mortal missionary who yields to temptation, then, in the ultimate act of repentance, does a swan dive off the Rock of Ages."

The reviewer continued. "Whether intentional or not, Kendall, as the tempted missionary, danced a fine line between satire and burlesque, and Leya Marks as the 'fallen woman' had this reviewer convinced that the reverend gentleman would have had to have been a stone Tiki not to succumb. Miss Marks was quite literally irresistible!"

Arthur attended the Philadelphia opening and used the occasion to call on several customers in the area. At the stage door, after the performance, he ran into Carlo Romano and Heather.

The club owner greeted him like an old friend. "Lieberman! How are you?"

Heather offered her cheek for a kiss. "We're very glad you're here, Arthur. Carlo has reserved a room at the Liberty Club. He wants to take the whole company there for a night lunch."

Arthur tried to conceal his annoyance. "Leya and I had planned to go somewhere and have a quiet bite."

Romano rested a hand on his arm. "In this town, no place is quieter than the Liberty Club, and the food is great." His fingers closed around Arthur's forearm. "I regard you as my friend. So you'll come."

There was a flat finality about the statement that angered Arthur. But it wasn't that simple. Romano's friendships reached all the way to the truckers who distributed Super Figure products. Frustrated, Arthur pushed on in. "Let's see what the others want to do," he said.

Ed Matson, pleased with the group's progress and thinking ahead to the money that would be available in the Romano club the following season, had counseled Kent earlier to accept Carlo's offer and urged Leya to go along. Outside the girls' dressing room, she appealed to Arthur. "Let's just stay for a little while, darling. Ed thinks the man has connections that can help us."

"I know all about those connections, Leya," he replied, "and they only help one person, Romano."

A half hour later, at the Liberty Club, Carlo commandeered Leya for a dance. Heather smiled and drained her scotch. "Okay, so you dance with me, Art. I want to talk to you, anyway," she said.

On the floor, Arthur tried not to glance too often at Leya, who, in his opinion, was being held too close. Heather looked up at him with an understanding smile. "Don't worry about Carlo being on the make. He's not like that, Art. Can I tell you what's really on his mind?"

"Please do!"

"He's hell bent to reopen the Miami club with an attraction that will get the money crowd because of the upstairs action, gambling. He's sure the Kendall Dance Group is right. 'Classy sex' is how he puts it. He'll pay anything I.A.M. asks."

Arthur, watching Carlo obviously trying to charm Leya, nodded. "I believe that!"

"Carlo would really appreciate it if you could put in a good word. He's very good about helping his friends."

"Heather, I have nothing to do with the bookings. That's entirely up to Kendall and Matson."

"Carlo knows that, Art! But Leya listens to you. She adores you, Art. And she's the only one Kent really listens to."

Anxious to end the conversation, Arthur appeared to capitulate. "All right. I'll sound her out. But no promises!"

Later, on the dance floor, Arthur couldn't resist questioning Leya. "What did Romano talk about?"

"He talked about Carlo Romano mostly. He did say some nice things about my dancing, and I thanked him."

"I'm surprised you could speak, he was holding you so tight."

Leya removed her head from beneath his chin and looked up. "You're holding me much tighter, and I can still talk. Anyway, I can talk enough to say that the only thing I don't like about the road is being away from you."

Arthur's hand moved up to the back of her neck, and he squeezed it affectionately. "Me, too, and want to know something? So help me God, I get jealous."

"Why?" Leya asked, a bit too innocently.

"I'm jealous of anybody who can spend time with you when you're not dancing. There's just got to be a bunch of 'stage-door Johnnies' hanging around."

"Of course there are, darling! But believe it or not, between performances and rehearsals, and at least eight hours for sleep, we don't have time for 'socializing.' Anyway"—her eyes were accusing him—"I have a lot more reason to be worried about you."

Arthur's lips brushed her forehead. "You have absolutely no reason to be worried! They've even accused me of converting and becoming a monk." He eased her away to look at her. "And as you know, darling, monks do very little monkeying around."

Leya groaned, then moved closer, smiling to herself. She was learning!

The new girl in the troupe, blonde, twenty-three-year-old Tanya Kuznetsov, a technically accomplished, Paris-trained ballerina, danced by with Matt.

"When does this command performance end?" she asked in a softly accented voice.

"Any time you say," Arthur replied.

Matt glanced over at Romano and Matson, who were talking earnestly. "Let's go!"

At the table, Arthur refused a fresh drink. "We've got some tired ladies here, Carlo. And I have to be back in New York for an eight o'clock thing."

"We really are beat!" Jean Baxter added.

Heather pouted. "It's early, kids. Don't go. Let's have another."

Carlo took the drink from her. "Sure, sure. For me dancing is fun. For them it's work." He pushed the chair back. "I thank you for coming," he said, looking at each in turn. "You have got the best act I've ever seen. You're artistic—but everybody understands. You will be a smash in my club this winter."

Kent managed a smile. "You're my witnesses, kids. We've just signed a verbal contract." He turned to Ed Matson, who appeared mildly amused. "I enjoy the luxury of having a manager," he continued, turning back to Carlo. "The artist is never the villain. When he wants more money, or when he wants to refuse an offer, he just says, 'Talk to my manager.' "

Romano leveled a dark glance at Kent. "No real artist ever has to ask me for more money. I give it to them first if they're worth it."

Heather added a bit thickly, "If you only knew what he paid for Joe E. Lewis and Jimmy Durante and—"

Carlo laid a heavy hand on her shoulder. "We don't talk business here. This is strictly social."

When Heather seemed about to persist, Carlo's pressure made her wince.

During the taxi ride back to the Bellevue-Stratford Hotel, where the company was staying, and where Arthur had taken a room for the night, Leya snuggled wearily against him. She could have gone to sleep in his arms, but he seemed troubled.

"Darling, let me ask you something."

"Yes?"

"Has Kent ever told you how he feels about playing Romano's clubs?"

"Not right out, no. But I've told him how I feel! I don't want to work clubs!"

"I know, darling, and you're right. But what about Kent—if Romano comes up with more money?"

"I don't know. Why?"

Arthur reflected a moment. "If the concert business is good, he won't be tempted. What did Matson talk about when you were dancing?"

"About the show—and about Matt and me."

"Would I be prying if I asked what he said? I'm not jealous of *him*, you know."

"Ed said we surprised everybody, that we are a very exciting 'attraction.' He said that Matt and I were—well—we're the ones who stand out, or something to that effect."

Arthur nodded. "He's dead right about that, sweetheart."

At the door of the small suite that Leya shared with Luanna Parker and Tanya Kuznetsov—"Kuzzy," they called her for short—they spoke softly for a moment. Then, after a precautionary glance around, they kissed.

In the room, Leya sank down on the bed. Each time she and Arthur kissed, it became more difficult to leave him. She knew that Arthur was longing to take her to his bed, and part of her longed to be taken. The conflict produced such an acute physical reaction that she undressed, bathed quickly, and hurried to bed to lose herself in fantasy.

At eight o'clock the following morning, Carlo Romano pulled on a dressing robe and glanced at Heather. As usual, lately, she was sleeping off too much Scotch.

Minutes later, Tony Spacco picked up the private line at the Romano waterfront estate in Miami.

"Tony, I want two things, quick!"

"Sure, Carlo."

"Heather says the Marks girl, the dancer, went to school in Brooklyn. Also, her old man works in the Navy Yard. His name is Harry. I want you to use connections. Find out everything about both, and get back to me. *Subito! Capeesh?*"

"Sure, Carlo."

"Call me here."

Romano was dressed and breakfasting by himself in the sitting room when Spacco returned his call.

"The girl went to the Hebrew Orphan Asylum in Brooklyn until she was fifteen or sixteen. They paid for her dance lessons when her old man couldn't. She's been doing some modeling—underwear and stuff."

"What about her old man?"

"He used to work for your father when the girl was still a baby."

"How do you know?" Romano demanded with sudden interest.

"From a guy named Hymie Solomon. He was our Brownsville outlet in the old days."

"I know him. What's Solomon do now?"

"Delicatessen—beer, wine, all Jewish stuff. Flatbush. You want his number?"

"Maybe."

Several minutes later, Carlo Romano reached his family home near Passaic, New Jersey. His wife, Angelina, answered.

"Carlo! It's good to talk to you, darling! Where are you? How are you?"

"I'm okay. How's the boy?"

The note of hope left her voice. "Sal? He's fine. He wants to see you."

"I want to see him. Where's papa?"

"In his room."

"Tell him I want to talk."

"Sure, Carlo. Wait a minute."

When Angelina heard the father and son greet each other on the extension, she returned the instrument to the cradle with a deliberate click.

"I'm in Philly, papa. I'm looking at a dance act for the club."

"So? You want me to come look at dancers?"

Carlo laughed. "Not unless it'll make you feel young, papa."

"Who's old?" Salvatore di Romano challenged.

"Not you, papa! *Non mai!*" Carlo's tone became serious. "I want to know about a guy named Harry Marks. A Jew from Brownsville. Did he ever work for you?"

"Sure!" the father replied. "I remember him. A good little guy, smart, kept his mouth shut. Why?"

"His daughter is the star of the act." Sensing his father's concern, Carlo chuckled. "Look, papa, before you get ideas, relax. Without this kid the act is okay. With her it's sensational. But she doesn't want to work clubs. She's legit—like ballet."

Salvatore di Romano was relieved. He was tolerant of his son's preoccupation with that other little "*meretrice,*" but screwing two of them was stupid.

"You need a little help to change her mind, right?"

"What work did he do for you?"

"On the docks he was a cargo checker. Later, a maintenance man at the Greenpoint place. His kid was sick. I gave him a job."

A smile warmed Carlo's face. "So Marks owes you one?"

Salvatore di Romano hesitated. "It's a long time back, but if you need it, he owes me one."

"I need it."

"Okay, *figlio*, you got it. I'll talk with Marks."

In the delicatessen on Flatbush Avenue, a worried Hymie Solomon peeled back the casing on a kosher salami. The place was empty now. He had been talking to himself ever since Tony Spacco's call.

"So why? All these years—nothing. Now a call from Sal's boys—for Harry. What did Harry do?" He froze in midslice. "What do they *want* him to do?"

The Di Romano family was mixed up in a thousand things. Loan sharking, the numbers, prostitution, casinos—dope, God forbid! And the unions. He closed his eyes. There was no end! "But why Harry?" he asked aloud.

Harry Marks found two telephone messages waiting for him in the grocery store when he arrived home after work. One was from his old friend Hymie Solomon. He didn't see Hymie so much anymore. There had been more time to visit when things were bad. He went to the wall phone and called the first number. Hymie recognized his voice.

"Hang on a minute, Harry. I want to talk from the back."

A moment later, the extension in Hymie's cubbyhole picked up, and he heard his friend holler to somebody out front to hang up.

"So how are you, Harry?"

"I'm fine. Fine. So how are you?"

"I'm fine, Harry. Believe me, I'm glad to hear!"

Puzzled by the man's tone, Harry frowned at the mouthpiece. "You heard different, maybe?"

"I didn't hear, Harry, only a call from a guy we used to know, asking about you. Tony Spacco. Remember him?"

"I remember! One of di Romano's musclemen." He felt the edge of anxiety press his middle. "What's he asking?"

"Nothing personal, Harry—where you live and where you work."

"Nothing personal!" Harry said. "Maybe also he wants to know about my bowels? Where I live is personal! Where I work is personal! What else?"

"Only if you have a telephone. I told him the grocery store."

"That's all?"

"Believe me, he was friendly, Harry."

"Friendly," Harry moaned. "How many friends these days call to ask only from health?"

"For health they don't call," Hymie Solomon admitted.

Minutes later, Harry swallowed to ease the dryness in his mouth and placed the call to the Cliffside number.

The phone was answered by a heavy male voice.

"Hello," Harry repeated. "Who is talking please?"

"Who wants to know?"

"My name is Marks. I received a message to call this number."

"Harry Marks! My old friend! How are you?" The voice boomed with hearty friendship. "This is Sal Di Romano. You worked for me. I gave you jobs when you needed them. Remember?"

Harry nodded at the mouthpiece. "I remember, Mr. Di Romano. How could I forget?"

"You remember? That's good! Now tell me, my friend, how are you?"

"I'm good, thank you very much. Lately I've got a steady job."

"I know, Marks—in the shipyard. You'll work as long as you want! And how's your kid? The one that was sick, remember?"

The reference to Leya knotted Harry's guts. "She's better. Very healthy," Harry replied. "She's a toe dancer in the ballet. Very high class."

"I know," Di Romano agreed. "I hear also she's a *bellissima ragazza*—very pretty now, eh? So—I'll tell you why I called. My son Carlo owns some clubs. Very high class. He wants to book your kid in Miami."

"She doesn't dance alone," Harry replied, his voice suddenly high-pitched. "She's only a part. She dances with others."

"I know, Harry," Di Romano said. "My son knows her. Your daughter's best friend is his friend. He's going to book the whole company, he tells me, at very big money and give them a big buildup. Let me tell you, Harry, my good friend, I called to congratulate you. I wish your daughter good luck. Also, I want to thank you for telling your daughter how much Carlo appreciates her talent. I'll regard it as a favor."

"I'll tell her," Harry managed. "She's out of town for a while."

"In Philly. I know," Di Romano replied. "When she comes home, you'll give her my regards. Right?"

"I'll give regards," Harry said.

"Good, Harry. It's nice to hear from you. We'll keep in touch."

CHAPTER 20

The Philadelphia concert engagement ended with a modest profit. On closing night, Carlo Romano appeared backstage with extravagant bouquets for each of the four ballerinas.

"Beautiful flowers for beautiful ladies!" he said. "My own 'beautiful lady's' in Boston." His eyes gleamed as they rested on Leya for a disconcerting moment. "I can't stay. I'm going on to Baltimore tonight, but I wanted to stop off and see what's happened with the act in a week. *Bravissimo!* There's nothing around like what you people are doing." His manner was so smooth that it made Leya's skin crawl.

"When you play for me, I'll make you the biggest class act in show business!" He started to turn away, then stopped.

"I nearly forgot!" he said, addressing Leya. "I just found out your father and my father are old friends. Did you know that?"

"No, I didn't." But suddenly she understood why the name "Romano" had sounded familiar.

Carlo's eyes became warm pools of Italian sentiment.

"When you were a *bambina,* Leya, you got very sick. Your father was out of a job. My father heard about it, and he gave him a job—a couple of times." As he reached for her hand, she forced herself to keep from pulling away.

"They talked on the telephone this week. Two old friends—so happy to find each other again. Do you want to know something, Leya? Your father is still thanking my father for a favor he did so many years ago." His heavy black eyebrows arched. "How often do people remember to be grateful? It's a miracle! My father would say, '*La forza del destino.*' " He turned to the others who were watching, transfixed. "You had better believe me, for such a special friendship, I will do everything I can!"

When he had gone, Kuzzy expelled a sigh. "Him and Rasputin! What do you make of that whole sentimental bit, Leya?"

"I don't know. That man makes me very nervous." She turned to Kent. "My father hasn't seen or heard of Salvatore di Romano since I was a baby. And they never were 'dear friends.' If the man helped papa, it was for some other reason."

Kent had booked parlour-car seats for the cast on the early-morning train. They arrived at Pennsylvania Station in Manhattan before noon. Leya went directly to the pay telephones to call Arthur. She was disappointed when she found him out of the office until after lunch.

She dialed the agency and found three calls. One was from Dorothy Simpson from some days back. The other two were from Gordon Revelsky's office. The second one asked that she drop by as soon as possible.

In the lobby of the Empire State Building, Leya checked the directory and took the elevator to the seventieth floor. After a brief wait, she was shown into Revelsky's enormous office.

"Sit down," he ordered, scarcely looking up from the rough billboard layouts being submitted for his approval by two art directors. One layout featured a photo of Dulcy's head to the left of the slogan HE'LL REVEL IN YOUR NEW GLAMOUR!

A similar one featured a brunette model whose face seemed familiar to Leya.

"That brunette won't do. She's been all over the media.

What's the blonde done?" Revelsky asked. "Has her face been spread around, too?"

"No, sir," replied the elder of the two art directors. "She's done mostly catalogue work, and she's been a chorus girl." *The son of a bitch,* he thought. *He knows all this as well as we do.*

Revelsky shuffled through some color photos on his desk and grunted. "The eyes and the coloring are okay. But find a face with more class."

"These were the ones you narrowed it down to, Mr. Revelsky."

The cosmetic manufacturer looked up. "You think I don't know this?"

"We're getting close to production deadline, sir. I just wanted to remind you—"

"So you reminded me! Now I'm reminding you. I want a new blonde. I want a face with more class. Find me one!"

Revelsky's summary dismissal of Dulcy shocked Leya. She felt her face flush with anger. When the embarrassed art directors removed their display material, she rose to leave with them. Revelsky looked up.

"Sit down," he ordered. "What's your name again?"

Stunned by his bluntness, she dropped back onto the chair. "Leya Marks," she replied in a tight voice.

He riffled through some color proofs and set several prints aside.

"We used you on a test ad, right?"

"I guess so," Leya replied. "I didn't ever see it."

Revelsky reached for two magazines, crossed to the dark-green Florentine leather divan, and sat. "You didn't see it because it didn't run here. We tested it in California."

He opened one of the rotogravure sections and spread it on Leya's lap. The ad featured an astoundingly glamorous full head shot of her. "This one pulled good."

He opened the second magazine, which featured a shot of Dulcy that made the most of her heart-shaped face and her huge, merry blue eyes. "This one didn't," he said.

"I don't see anything wrong," Leya murmured.

"I didn't expect you to." Gordon Revelsky tapped Dulcy's

likeness. "This kid's a beautiful blonde. But look at her eyes. She looks like she wants to laugh at something. You don't laugh when you're about to get laid!"

He ignored Leya's wince. "Now, look at this." He pointed to the first sheet. "A woman looks at this and sees the kind of eyes she wants to have when she's on the make."

He closed both magazines. "That little difference in expression makes a difference in sales of a thousand gross in just one test area." He returned the magazines to the desk. "What did we pay you to use that photo? Twenty dollars?"

"Yes."

"Okay. I'll make it twenty-five an hour for this job. Tell Conover. That's a special favor to him."

"When are you going to shoot, Mr. Revelsky?"

"What difference does that make?"

The man's manner continued to unsettle Leya. "Did the agency tell you that I'm with the Kendall Dance Group now?"

"You don't dance all day and all night, do you?"

Leya struggled to control her annoyance. "I guess I could work between rehearsals. How many days will it take?"

"What do you mean, days? Hours!" Revelsky glowered at her. "Look, Marks, I don't arrange my plans to suit models. We shoot Monday and Tuesday of next week. If you can work on one of those days, okay. If not, forget it."

Leya knew that rehearsals could be arranged with Kent to clear the time. She also knew that it would not be a matter of hours. It would take a day, more than likely two days. If so, she could make four hundred dollars. The prospect did little to relieve her unhappiness about Dulcy. She knew she should not interfere, but she could not resist.

"Is Dulcy Devine going to do any of the ads?"

The executive made no effort to conceal his annoyance. "I thought I told you. She's not sexy enough."

Leya felt an urge to laugh in the man's face. Dulcy, who by now must have done it all, not sexy enough? And little Leya Marks, who was still only daring in her dreams, sexy? The idiot must be blind!

Revelsky was studying her. "This Dulcy is a friend of yours?"

"She's my best friend."

"Look," Revelsky snapped, "she's not right for this particular line! She'll do other things for me." He dismissed the problem as inconsequential. "So call me tomorrow afternoon."

Leya went to the public phone and called Dulcy.

"I thought you had dropped off the face of the earth!" her friend exclaimed. "Get your little behind up here!"

Twenty minutes later, the two friends were caught in a happy embrace. Dulcy slammed the door and turned to inspect Leya. "I've never seen such a change in a person! Did you check the agency? They've got a bunch of calls for you." She shepherded Leya to the sofa and flopped into the chair opposite.

"I got the calls," Leya said, unable to conceal her unhappiness.

Dulcy regarded her closely. "There's nothing wrong with you and Arthur, is there?"

"No. I'll see him later, I'm sure."

"Then what are you down about, dear heart?"

"One of the calls was from Revelsky. I saw him a little while ago."

"And?"

"I can have the billboard job if I want it."

"What do you mean if you want it? Of course, you want it—just like I do—so bad you can taste it. Our faces on a couple of thousand billboards around the country—and in the magazine tie-in ads—can make us famous overnight. Not to mention the beautiful moolah we'll earn from now on." Dulcy felt Leya's anxiousness increase. "What happened? Did he try to get into your pants?"

Leya shook her head. "I don't know how to say it, Dulcy, but if you don't do the job, then I don't want to do it, either."

After a long silence, Dulcy closed her eyes and nodded. "Okay, dear heart, I get it. The bastard's found another blonde, right?"

"No," Leya replied in a small voice, "but he told his men to look for one."

"Did he say that in front of you?"

"Yes. He made me come into his office while he was still looking at the artwork."

Dulcy's eyes betrayed nothing. "Okay, bounce it on me," she said. "Just why does he want another blonde?"

Leya could not bring herself to repeat Gordon Revelsky's comment. "He did a test with both of us in California. The same ad, but one had a Wales test shot of me in it, and the other had yours."

Dulcy spared Leya the necessity of spelling it out. "Your ad pulled better than mine, and so now the guy wants a new blonde."

"I'm so sorry, Dulcy. I meant it when I said I won't do the job unless you do it."

"The hell you won't, Marks! You and I are friends. That comes before all the rest of this crapola!"

I know that," Leya replied. "But it's the way I feel."

"Bless you for that! But I'm not going to let you be a *shmuckess,* or whatever you call a female *shmuck.* I know what the problem is. Baby-faced blondes with big blue eyes are a dime a dozen. Copper-heads with slanty bedroom eyes are not. So forget it. Revelsky will try to make it with you. But if you sit on your goodies real hard, he'll give up, and you still get the job. One thing about the guy, he never gets his cock caught in the cash register!"

When Leya did not respond immediately, Dulcy shook her.

"Are you listening?"

"Yes."

"Okay, then, do what I said, girl. I adore you for leveling with me and for wanting to tell the miserable prick to shove it. But I can't let you make a Noble Nellie out of yourself. You do that job! Do you hear?"

"Yes," Leya said unhappily. "Incidentally, he told me to tell you that he wants to use you in some other ads."

"Really?" Dulcy let the question soar and settle. "What on? A new mud-pack facial?"

"He didn't say. But he wanted me to be sure to pass it along."

"Thanks loads. Now I've got something for you to pass back to him. Tell him I've just signed a ten-year contract with Max Factor!"

CHAPTER 21

It was nearly five o'clock when Leya carried her two bags up the stairs and let herself into the Brownsville flat. After she opened the bedroom window to get some through draft, she stood looking at the kitchen with a bemused smile. Her father had used every dish in the cupboard. A loaf of bread had been left out, partially unwrapped, and the drip pan under the refrigerator was only a few drops from spilling onto the linoleum.

Poor papa! she thought. Long work days and overtime had taken their toll on the little place.

She was luxuriating in a cool bath when she heard her father come in. They exchanged greetings through the door, and she hurried into a robe. Seconds later, unmindful of his soiled work clothes, she was in his arms.

"*Bubeleh,*" he said, glancing apologetically toward the kitchen, "I didn't get time to clean up."

"Go change, papa, I'll do it. We have lots to talk about."

While her father was bathing, Leya went downstairs to the store. A few minutes later, she had made order out of the kitchen and set the table with cold borscht and sour cream, gefilte fish, fresh onion rolls, cream cheese, and tea.

As they ate, she told her father of the Kendall dancers' reception in Philadelphia and Kent's plans for strengthening the show.

Harry sensed the undercurrent of concern in his daughter. "It sounds like you're enjoying, only—I'm hearing something I'm not hearing. What is it?"

"You're right, papa," Leya confessed. "Something did happen."

"So?"

"It involves you, papa."

Harry pressed his palms against his fresh undershirt. "How can something happen to me in Philadelphia?"

"Heather O'Brien's boyfriend, Carlo Romano, wants us to play in his club in Miami."

"I know. His father and I talked by the telephone."

"About what?"

Harry took a sip of tea and avoided her eyes.

"Did you talk about the weather, papa," she chided, "or did you talk about us and the Miami thing?"

"We talked about my health," Harry said unhappily.

Leya looked at him skeptically. "That's all?"

"Daughter," he replied, "when a man like Sal Di Romano reminds you of favors he did for you, he's talking about your health."

"But that was nineteen years ago, papa!" Leya said. "And you did him a favor, too, by working for him."

"Let me tell you, at the time it was a favor, all right! With these *momsers,* favors are like loans. They've got to be repaid." He shrugged. "So my loan is being called, and they are asking you to do the paying."

"But papa, you don't owe the Romanos a thing!"

"So let me explain. He helped me once. If there hadn't been trouble with Volpe, when things got bad again, I would have been very happy to work for him again. I can only tell you, *bubeleh,* in uncertain times—like now, with Hitler and the mish-mosh in Europe—maybe a good offer is not the worst thing that could happen."

"I don't like Carlo, papa. I don't want favors from him. I don't want to do him any."

"Maybe you think I liked Di Romano?" Harry got up heavily. "So you'll make up your own mind. You'll do what you have to do, and you won't worry about me." He fished a paper from his pocket. "You have some calls."

* * *

There were two numbers. Leya recognized Arthur's office phone. The other was the backstage phone at Music Hall.

She dialed Arthur from the store, and he came on immediately. "It's so good to hear your voice, darling."

"And yours, Arthur. I was afraid I'd miss you."

"I know. Me, too. Look, Leya, a day like this shouldn't happen to anyone. Dad and I have to take the early-morning plane to Chicago. We won't be back until day after tomorrow. I hope you're not going out again?"

"No, Arthur. I'll be here."

Several minutes later, she reached Celine. Her friend had just finished rehearsal. "I'm so glad you called, Leya. I can't talk long now, but Mikail Khazar is back in town. He's interviewing dancers for a new company he wants to form. He wants to see you as soon as possible. He's in Room 303 at Carnegie Hall. Will you see him?"

"After what happened with Madame Baronova?"

"He told me the old girl said you and Kent and I were the best dancers in her class."

"Somehow I don't believe that—about me," Leya said.

"Believe it, *chérie*. Baronova really liked you."

Leya dismissed any further discussion of what she considered a questionable point. "Are you going to join his company?"

"I'm thinking seriously. I'm getting bored with the same old variations here. It's a good living, Leya—but oh God, we are nothing but wind-up dolls in toe shoes and tutus!"

The analogy made Leya smile. She thought of her own precious little wind-up ballerina.

"Why don't you go see him, Leya? It can't hurt."

"Maybe I will," Leya replied, aware that she would be just one floor below during her own rehearsals. The girls promised to get together soon.

At one o'clock the following afternoon, she climbed the stairs to Room 303. A scattering of hopefuls carrying bags of practice clothes lounged around the spartan anteroom. When Leya gave her name, she was shown in immediately.

"Thank you for coming by, ma'moiselle!" Khazar said,

bowing over her hand. "I thought perhaps our enterprise did not interest you until I remembered that you were appearing in Philadelphia. You did well there, no?"

"We did very well, thank you."

"I saw you in Boston," Khazar said. "Very unusual concept your M'sieur Kendall has. May I tell you, with one, possibly two exceptions, I would be very happy to consider you dancers as prospects for my new company. Would such an opportunity be tempting?"

"I don't know about the others, sir," Leya replied.

"But you are here because it interests you?"

"I would like to hear about it."

"I shall tell you what I can." He raised a long finger in a dramatic gesture. "You will be excited!" For twenty minutes, the impresario talked with infectious enthusiasm about his plans to establish a major international ballet company with New York as its headquarters. He alluded to unlimited Italian financing, spoke of the great names who had expressed interest. Igor Yousekevitch, Tatiana Riabouchinska, Rosella Hightower, Lila Zali, and Michael Panaieff were among them.

"So," he said, rising to take Leya's hand, "I am trying to tempt a few exceptional young artists. You will call me soon and tell me that I have succeeded. Yes?"

"I'll call," Leya replied. "Thank you for thinking of me."

"The thanks are mine, ma'moiselle!" he said, bowing over her hand again.

Downstairs Leya changed and entered the rehearsal hall to work with Matt on some new variations in the challenge number. Kent gave her a knowing smile.

"I saw you go upstairs. If it weren't for the foreign financing, it might be tempting."

"Not really—as long as things go well for us."

Kent's eyebrows lifted. "I thought they were."

"I guess they are, Kent, but I'm worried about all this talk about playing Carlo Romano's club." She decided against telling him of the call from Salvatore Di Romano. "I don't like the man, Kent, and I don't think we should play supper clubs."

"Don't worry about that, Leya." Kent smiled. "It will never happen! Anything else on that busy little mind of yours?"

"Arthur wants me to do another catalogue job for him in a week or so."

Kent pretended to be aghast. "But no flying through the air this time. Promise?"

"No flying," Leya laughed. "Also, Gordon Revelsky wants me to do his new national cosmetic campaign."

"Great! Do it! It can only help to have your beautiful face staring at millions of people from coast to coast." Suddenly, he grew troubled. "I regret to say that so far we have two weeks free. The I.A.M. people say we've hit a bit of slack time."

The meeting in Revelsky's office was brief. Two art directors, who were asked for token reconfirmations of Leya's suitability, were dismissed after they had reported no success in finding an acceptable substitute for Dulcy.

Leya asked if she might suggest another dancer? She spoke of Celine Cervier's classic blonde beauty. When Revelsky indicated some interest, she agreed to reach Celine and have her call.

Between shows on Wednesday afternoon, Celine hurried to the rehearsal hall with the news that she had seen Gordon Revelsky and was offered the job. She had arranged to take her week's vacation beginning on Monday, when Jon Wales would be taking test shots. Celine waltzed Leya around in an ebullient embrace, then ran upstairs to keep a promised appointment with Mikail Khazar.

Kent kept the company working for two hours. Late in the afternoon, he called them together. "I had a meeting with Pryor and Matson this morning, kids. I wish I could tell you we're booked solid for six months. The plain truth is, everybody's doing the wait-and-see bit. They want to see if Roosevelt gets in for a third term. They want to see if we are going to get involved in the war because of the convoy thing. Pryor says producers won't sign anything but known attractions. So—here's where we stand. We're rebooked in Philadelphia for a week. We've got a week in Cincinnati and maybe one in St. Louis. If we draw as well as we did last spring, we can stay alive. That's about all. I'm truly sorry."

Peter Genova broke the uncomfortable silence.

"We've talked it over, Kent. Most of us can get other jobs. Khazar is interested in us. Jean and I have offers to work in *Panama Hattie* with Merman. Marc and Luanna can work in *Pal Joey* or *Panama Hattie.* So can Kuzzy. And Leya—" he grinned at her affectionately "—I haven't yakked with her, but any show we can work, she'd probably get picked first! Same for Matt. So don't worry about us. Let's play the dates and see what happens."

On September sixteenth, President Roosevelt signed the Selective Service Act. On October sixteenth, the first draft cards would be sent out to males between the ages of sixteen and thirty-five.

On September twenty-seventh, when Germany, Italy, and Japan signed the Tripartite Treaty, news commentator Raymond Gram-Swing oozed the news out on the airways without alarming his listeners. Lowell Thomas, in his clear, bold-type voice, made a solid statement of fact. Fulton Lewis, Jr., lent the news a note of earnest anxiousness. Gabriel Heatter and Walter Winchell gave the story apocalyptic overtones.

Since the previous June, when the Nazi Panzer divisions had turned the Maginot Line and overrun the Lowlands, and the French had signed the articles of surrender in the little railroad car at Compiègne, the fiction of the German army's invincibility had come to seem more and more like solid fact. The national unease manifested itself less among the patrons of popular escape entertainment than among the patrons of serious art.

Ed Matson dropped by the rehearsal hall after the Ohio date and took Kent aside.

"I've just been with Howard. There's nothing doing in concert for any group now. The only thing we can count on is the Miami date. If you won't take that, we're in trouble."

Kent pulled the towel from his neck and blotted the perspiration on his face and lower arms. The others were warming up at the barre. He could see their anxious expressions in the mirror as they bobbed up and down executing their *pliés*.

He dropped heavily into a chair. "I thought you agreed with me that unless we built a reputation as a concert attraction first, we'd wind up as just a high-class club act if we took Romano's offer."

"I did say that," Ed Matson conceded, "last spring. That's not true today, especially after the good concert reviews. Howard thinks a strong publicity buildup by Romano could turn the club date into an asset. I'm inclined to agree. I.A.M.'s sales people say they can make capital of it next season, when this war thing's been settled, and there's a concert market again."

"What makes you think the war will be settled? My father's not so certain."

"A lot of senators think Hitler will back off and settle for what he's got if he thinks we will come in. *Der Führer* has already squared up with France for 1918. He's given back Germany its self-respect. He's in a good bargaining position. Think about it. The timing was bad, even for a group as exciting as yours. Your only chance to keep together is to work quality clubs."

Kent braced his chin on his fists. After a time, he got up. "I understand, Ed. Let me sleep on it."

When Arthur had ordered for them at the Divan Parisien, he turned to Leya. "All right, darling, what is this earth-shaking matter that needs my advice?"

"I had a talk with Ed this afternoon. He and Mr. Pryor came over to the rehearsal hall to see me."

"I don't blame them. I wish I could!"

"Don't joke. Please?"

"What happened, darling? Bookings falling out again?"

"The ones we want are—the concert dates."

Arthur nodded. "With things the way they are in the world, I'm not surprised."

"Mikail Khazar is starting a company. He wants us," Leya said, clinging to a last tenuous thread of hope.

"I read the story," Arthur replied. "He's dreaming."

"I hope not, because that leaves only one possibility: eight weeks at two thousand a week for the group in Florida."

Arthur drew in a deep breath.

"Carlo Romano won't take no for an answer, Arthur," Leya went on. "Except that he won't book our group unless I stay with it. He says Matt and I are the real excitement."

"I hate to admit it, Leya, but he's right. Only I'd include Kent, too. His concepts are brilliant." He regarded her closely. "Have you made a decision?"

The question produced a pained expression. "If it were up to me, I'd turn it down—cold. I don't like Romano or the way he and his kind do things."

"That's not exactly news to my father and me." He leaned forward. "Look, Leya, Romano's not twisting your arm, is he?"

Leya was reluctant to tell Arthur about Harry's phone call from Sal Di Romano. That would mean revealing her father's bootlegging past, and would he understand? How could she expect the Liebermans, from their elegant Long Beach home, to understand what the Marks family went through in their Brooklyn cold-water flat?

"Not mine," she answered with deliberate evasiveness. "That is, not directly, but Ed and Howard made it real plain that if I won't go along with the booking, the group is finished. Kent's father won't lend him any more money." She shot him an appealing look. "Somehow, everything gets to be my fault, doesn't it?"

Arthur was certain the question was not asked out of self-pity. More likely, it was an attempt to win approval for a decision she was being forced to make out of concern for others more directly involved than he. Seeing plans fail, being out of work, were experiences this girl had learned much about.

"Look, darling, I've never been a good liar. The thought of you being away all winter, much less working for Romano, knocks me out. I also know that the Revelsky job could make you one of the top models in the business. You'd be earning ten times more than Kendall can ever pay you." He continued in a quieter voice. "But I also know where your heart is and that dancing isn't something you can do part time." He looked up. "Leya, let me ask you one question. Do you love me?"

Her answer came without hesitation. "You know I do, Arthur."

"Do you love me enough to marry me?"

"I've never loved anybody else. I never will."

"But you don't love me enough to marry me. Is that it?"

"I love you enough to marry you, Arthur darling. I've known that for a long time now, but please, I need time. First I want to find out who I am—and what I am. If we were married, you'd have every right to expect me to start making a home. I do want that, Arthur, but not for a while yet. Please understand. Please?" She broke off, but her eyes continued to appeal.

Arthur wanted to shake her, to shout at her, to tell her she was a damned little fool, that she could only go so far, that he would let her continue with her dancing for a year or so if it was really all that important. But he knew that none of these things were true. Leya Marks was an artist. It would be stupid—worse yet, cruel—to pretend otherwise, and it might cost him her love. That was a risk he was not prepared to take.

"All right, darling. I understand."

He linked her arm through his. Leya knew that he was holding her as he would hold something precious in danger of slipping away. Tears threatened. The words that Arthur wanted to hear were down there, stuck in the base of her throat. "Oh, yes, Arthur, I love you, and I want to marry you right now. I want to be held by you, I want you to take me in your arms as I dream you do, I want you to love me and make love to me, and I never want you to stop. God, yes! I want all that!" But those words were not to be said yet. The ones that were meant to be said—and they were no less honest—had been said. For now there was nothing more to say.

CHAPTER 22

Carlo Romano's Golden Palm Club occupied a one-and-one-quarter-acre coral fill on the shore of North Bay at Seventy-ninth Street. It was well north of, and across the bay from, the built-up section of Miami Beach. Romano and his associates augmented their legitimate liquor-importing revenues by operating Golden Palm Clubs in New Orleans, Phoenix, Las Vegas, Palm Springs, and a number of lesser gambling clubs in Midwestern cities in which "green grease" could be liberally applied.

The Miami location was the blue-chip club, with a two-level stage and dance floor large enough to accommodate elaborate production numbers, featuring twelve chorus girls and boys, eight six-foot, seminude showgirls, and almost any attraction short of a high-wire act. When Kent looked over the facilities with Carlo and Ed Matson, he knew the layout was made to order for the group.

On opening night, the club was packed with celebrities. Walter Winchell and his party were at ringside. Winchell's close friend, band leader Ben Bernie, and his guests were seated at the opposite corner of the low main stage. The word was passed by publicist Johnny Coyle that both Winchell and Bernie had threatened not to show if the other appeared, that management had finally persuaded them to come by promising that they would be kept as far apart as possible. Only the insiders knew that the famous feud was contrived by the old friends as a publicity gimmick and that it was being applauded privately as a classic of its kind.

The opening show, booked by I.A.M., was an unqualified extravaganza. Jack Carlson, an engaging young comedian, was the show's master of ceremonies. The featured "single" was Larry Alden, a harmonica virtuoso who had attracted Romano's attention at the Palm Springs club the season before. His version of the Gershwin melody, *Rhapsody in Blue*, was becoming a classic.

For the group's number in the opening show, Kent had made some dramatic changes in the challenge number. Ed Matson approved the choice for two reasons: It had been proved on the road, and it demonstrated the group's remarkably varied talents. During the tour, one reviewer had written, "At the risk of mixing a metaphor, the challenge is a sort of terpsichorean debating team in which each dancer, to display individual versatility, 'argues' both sides of the classic, modern, and jazz questions with such extraordinary skill that the only possible conclusion is to say quite simply that the audience is the winner."

The show's three production numbers, staged by Lillian Morrison, were the most elaborate Carlo Romano had ever presented. Heather danced in the chorus, and so did Ed Matson's friend, the spectacular six-foot showgirl, Sheri, who described her role to Leya by saying, "We girls prance while you kids dance."

Everything that happened on the stage, from the showgirls down front, whose minimally covered bosoms thrust out over the ringside tables, to the precise hoofing of the chorus line, drew prolonged applause. The master of ceremonies "gassed" them with ethnic jokes and "one-liners" that zeroed in on everything from Hollywood and Beverly Hills to the Catskills and "the Beach." The affluent Miami crowd laughed at themselves and loved it.

When the time arrived to introduce the Kendall Dance Group, Carlson turned serious and followed the script prepared by Ed Matson. "Ladies and gentlemen—tonight, we are privileged to witness a first! Those of you who are devotees of the dance have heard of the sensational Kendall Dance Group that has won raves from the toughest critics and audiences in the great cultural centers of our land.

"Tonight, Carlo Romano presents for their very first appearance in a supper club anywhere"—he paused and smiled toward Carlo's booth—"the Kendall Dance Group in their great challenge number, 'Show Up, Show Down'!"

The swift transitions that Kent had devised to the Cy Walter score made extraordinary demands on the dancers. Led by the spontaneous applause of those who recognized their virtuosity, the audience acknowledged each variation. The excitement out front transmitted itself to the dancers on the stage.

"The kids are working over their heads!" Pryor whispered to Matson. "They're great!"

The personal manager nodded.

In the challenge number, Leya portrayed three distinctly different personalities, the elegant, aloof prima ballerina; the amusing, hyperenergetic jitterbug; and the hoyden, whose seductiveness bordered on harlotry.

"Beautiful!" Romano muttered each time she finished one of her solos.

The ovation surprised no one as the dancers took their bows. Romano, pounding out his applause, turned to Ed Matson. "The best dancer I've ever seen. The kid's a star!"

"So is Heather's brother," Matson said diplomatically. "It's a great act, and this is a great showcase for it. We appreciate what you've done, Carlo. It is first-class."

"With me there is no second-class," Romano replied. "The kids can play the season here. Just change the number every four weeks. I'll up the ante, too."

When the closing patriotic routine ended, Carlo turned to his guests. "We got a couple of hours before the late show. We're going to eat now. Heather wants Leya to eat with us." He turned to Matson. "When you go backstage to get Sheri, bring Miss Marks along, too."

"*Heather* wants Leya to eat with us?" Ed smiled to himself as he made his way through the kitchen doors to the backstage entrance. "The hell she does!" he said half aloud.

The dressing room was bedlam. Half the kids in the chorus line were crowded into the Kendall group's quarters to congratulate them.

Ed found Leya standing a bit apart and wondered why she seemed so subdued. When he repeated Carlo's "invitation" to dinner, she gave no visible reaction.

"What's troubling you, little friend?"

"I was expecting some phone calls before the show."

"It wouldn't take a genius to guess who from, would it?" he asked.

"Arthur said he was going to call, and I sort of expected a call from my father."

Ed slipped an arm around her shoulders. "The long-distance lines between New York and Miami are crowded this time of year." He offered his arm. "I'll leave word to have somebody call you at the table if Arthur gets through."

Leya followed him to the main room. As they approached the table, Carlo rose and seated her on his right with elaborate attention.

"What can I tell you? You heard them." He indicated the customers at the tables and those on the dance floor, who were in the throes of a rumba being played with as much skill as enthusiasm by the Cuban relief band. "You kids were great." He signaled to the captain, hovering close by. "What are you going to drink?"

"A glass of iced tea, thank you."

"Sure," Carlo said, turning to Heather. "And one Scotch," he ordered. "That's all right?"

"One Scotch—on the rocks—that's all—*right!*" she mimicked him. Leaning across, she said to Leya, "After the second show, I do better!"

Distracted by the phone call that had not come through and by the need to lean across Carlo to converse with Heather, Leya found it impossible to enjoy herself.

Ed Matson, aware of her discomfort, invited her to dance. On the floor, she eased into his arms and was pleasantly surprised to find that he was an accomplished dancer.

"I thought I'd better let you rest your ear," he said.

"I like Heather very much," Leya said, "but she seems sort of—I don't know—on edge or something." Leya glanced at the table. Her friend sat toying with the ice in her drink and watching them.

"He treats her terribly. I wonder if he really does love her?" Leya asked. "I don't understand why, but I know she loves him."

Matson's eyes grew troubled. "Maybe I should tell you something, Leya. But if I do, I want you to promise to forget where you heard it." He looked down at her. "All right?"

"Of course. If you're afraid I'll break my word, don't tell me."

"I want to tell you because it may explain a lot about their behavior. Carlo is married and has a son. His family lives in New Jersey."

The revelation upset Leya. "But maybe Heather didn't know . . . ?"

"If she didn't know, little friend, she must be the only kid around the business who didn't."

"But maybe he really does love her, and he's planning on getting a divorce so he can marry her." She remembered then that Heather was a Catholic, and she presumed that Carlo must be, also. Most Italians were.

"Carlo's father is of the old school," Ed said. "He wouldn't stand for it. But he closes his eyes to his son's peccadillos, just like his peers did for him. These men like it this way."

"Do you think Heather knows now?"

"I think it's obvious that she's known for some time."

Leya only picked at the huge steak Carlo had ordered for her.

"What's the matter? If it's no good, we'll get another one." He was summoning the captain when Leya stopped him.

"Please, Mr. Romano! It's delicious, but it's too big. I can't dance if I eat too much."

"Okay, if you're sure." He turned back to Pryor, to whom he had been revealing plans for a still-larger casino with two showrooms in Las Vegas.

Heather had turned glum. While Carlo talked, and Leya and Ed pretended to be interested, she continued to twirl the half-melted ice in her glass. Carlo seemed not to notice that her meal was hardly touched. Covertly, Leya watched her former ballet classmate, and what she saw filled her with sadness.

Heather O'Brien was still beautiful. On stage, in her scanty dancer's costume, she was conspicuously attractive, even among the girls of the line who had been chosen as much for their beauty as for their ability to dance. Her legs still had the well-fleshed line that could only be described as "sexy," but there was a suggestion of puffiness around her middle now. Beneath the heavy show makeup, her face still had the old appealing freshness, but the energy and good humor that had attracted so many of her classmates was gone. Heather was no longer happy. It was obvious, too, that Romano was no longer happy with her.

Without seeming to, Leya studied Romano, Pryor, and Matson as they talked. In the light of the confidence Ed had shared with her, she could feel Romano's cold indomitability as a palpable force. Pryor was a hard man, too, malleable on the outside but every bit as inflexible at the core. Arthur had said Pryor and Romano were the opposite sides of the same coin. Romano controlled the market, and Pryor controlled the product. Ed had put it another way when he had explained to Kent and the others why he had changed his mind about club dates for the group.

"Romano and his friends are realists. They are primitive psychologists. They know what diversions people want and when they need them most. When times are bad, they help people forget. When times are good, they help them remember—and either way, they make them pay! That's why their enterprises are always in the black."

If she had not known Ed, as she watched him now, listening, nodding, occasionally taking part in the conversation, Leya would have taken him for a gentler, less threatening partner in the same enterprises. Arthur had explained him, too. "Don't be deceived, darling. Matson works both sides of the street. Good managers more than earn their keep, and Matson's a good one." As she sat with him now, Leya realized that even with Romano and Pryor, she felt safe when Ed Matson was present.

In the midst of her reflections, Heather pushed her chair back. "Hey, Leya, we've got to go change."

Romano glanced at his watch. "You got a half hour yet."

"I know," Heather replied. "But I want the wardrobe woman to fix one of the straps on that damned Eskimo costume. It's cutting my shoulder off."

Carlo looked at her suspiciously, then shrugged. "So—go."

Heather got up and gave Leya a questioning look. "You coming, too?"

Before Leya could respond, Romano glowered at her.

"She's next to closing. She doesn't have to change for an hour yet."

Ed rose and rested a hand on the back of Leya's chair. "Why don't we excuse the ladies?" he said amiably. "They haven't had time for much girl talk, and I know Leya wants to make a call to her father before it's too late."

"Sure, sure," Carlo said, hiding his annoyance. "Go talk."

In the dressing room, Heather turned to Leya. "Honey, I didn't have any problem with my strap. My problem is with that son of a bitch out there!" She jabbed a thumb in the direction of the main room. "I hate having dinner with him. It's always business. If it isn't one of the agents about the shows, it's Mike Parroco or Tony Spacco or one of his other torpedoes, talking about the clubs and the gambling and the payoffs and things. It bores the shit out of me!"

She opened her locker and reached into the back. After some rummaging, she removed a pint of Scotch and took a swig. "Another thing that fries my ass is being watched over like a campfire girl! 'One drink! That's all. Un'nerstan!?' " She mimicked Carlo's rough, authoritative tone.

Leya, noticing the wardrobe woman and several of the girls watching, grew uneasy. "Maybe he's got a lot on his mind right now," she said. "Opening the club here—and all the other things he was talking about at dinner."

"He's got a lot on his mind, all right," Heather said. She

took another drink, shuddered, and returned the pint to its hiding place. After she had closed the locker door, she caught Leya's hand and led her into the hall.

"One of the things he hasn't got on his mind these days is little old me," she said. "I was supposed to have a featured hoofing spot in the Eskimo number. Lil' Morrison set it, and Carlo made her cut it. When I asked him why, he told me to shut up and go buy some clothes." She released Leya's hand and lowered her head. "I do everything he wants me to—and God knows I don't like some of it." She looked up. "But lately it doesn't seem to make any difference. He's changed."

The sound of coins dropping in the pay phone distracted Leya. The anxiety returned. It was not true that she was expecting a call from her father. She would call him at Minnie's in a day or two. But Arthur had promised to call. She was only half listening to Heather's chatter "—he's dumb to treat me like this. I know an awful lot about him and his friends, and some of the things they do!—" when another thought, a sickening one, intruded. What if Arthur had decided that he didn't want to bother with a girl who wanted a career? What if he had decided to break it off—fast and clean—by not getting in touch again? She could feel the blood draining from her face, and then she felt Heather touch her and saw the concern in her friend's face and heard her voice.

"I'm sorry, Leya! Hearing me say those things must have scared you. I didn't mean to. Anyway, what Carlo does is no worse than the things any big businessmen do. Forget I ever said it. Please?"

It took Leya a moment to reorient herself. "I didn't hear anything," she said. "I was thinking about something else. I'm sorry."

The chorus boy hung up, and the coins from his incompleted call rattled into the return chamber. He fished them out and was about to leave when the instrument rang. "Dressing room. Yes . . . Who? Leya Marks—with the Kendall Dance Group . . . ?" He turned to her, questioning. "Yes, she's here. Just a minute."

"Hello, this is Leya—" She knew her voice was pinched and strange.

"Darling, it's Arthur. I've been trying ever since seven-thirty to get through to you. The damned circuits were busy! I wanted to wish you and the kids good luck before you went on."

Leya ignored his remarks. Caved in with relief, all she could do was repeat his name.

CHAPTER 23

The morning after the opening, those who had seen the second show were still talking about the performance given by the entire Kendall Dance Group. At brunch at the Roney-Plaza coffee shop, Kent gazed across the table at Leya.

"I don't know what Arthur said on the phone," he said, "but I want a recording made of it, and I insist that you play it before every performance!"

He laughed and turned to the others. "I swear, when I went to lift the girl in the challenge, she went up like a bird before I could get my hand under her bottom. By the way," he added, "is Arthur coming down?"

"This weekend," Leya replied, unable to conceal her delight. "Arthur and his mother and father are bringing down some relatives from Germany. They've taken a house on the beach."

Kent's eyebrows lifted. "Sounds like they're here for the winter, then." The possibility produced some troublesome thoughts that he kept to himself. Happy as she presently was, Leya was a radiant, exciting performer on stage. But the demands that Arthur, at leisure in Miami Beach, might make on her free time could prove to be a problem.

It dawned on Kent that through his persistent effort to bring Leya into the dance group, he had acquired an artist who was rapidly becoming indispensable.

Now that a continuing run in Miami seemed inevitable, Leya, in love with Arthur and uneasy with Carlo, could become a double liability. Neither was she the only one in the group who could become a mixed blessing. Kuzzy was getting to be particularly annoying because of her affection for Matt. And Matt? Kent promised himself that problem could be and would be handled. He felt some relief when Leya said, "I don't think Arthur can stay for very long. He's just coming down to open the house. The others are coming on the train. He said he'd have to go back to tend to business while his father has a rest."

Romano was delighted. Another gamble paid off. He let it be known that he wanted the chorus kids and the showgirls to dine with "special guests" between shows and that it would please him to see the Kendall dancers out front, too. Leya pleaded an indisposition to avoid dining at the private table. When Heather told him, he had insisted on calling a doctor. "For Chris' sake, Carlo," she had said. "At least once a month can't you just let a girl be a girl?"

Kent arranged rehearsals so Leya could meet Arthur at the Miami Airport on Friday afternoon. Oblivious of the amused onlookers, he picked up Leya and swung her around like a rag doll, then lowered her.

"How did you get out here?" he demanded.

"Heather wanted to drive me, but I took a cab. I didn't want to share you with anybody."

"Thank you, darling! I don't want to be shared." He took her arm and walked toward the terminal without taking his eyes from her.

"You look fantastic, Leya. But why no tan?"

"Have you forgotten that I'm on display every night? Sunburn lines don't look very glamorous in the costumes we wear."

Arthur laughed as he visualized the lubricious, overroasted females he had seen for years in the Florida hotels and clubs, women whose bathing-suit lines were more circumspect than the plunging necks and backs of their evening gowns.

They retrieved Arthur's single bag, hailed a taxi, and headed for the beach.

The ocean-front house was a rambling one-story Spanish stucco. A Cuban couple, engaged by the owner as maid and houseman, led them into a well-kept living room whose French doors opened onto a tile patio. A wooden walk meandered across the white sand to the high-tide mark. It was a bright, happy house.

"What a perfect place!" Leya exclaimed. "It seems like heaven!"

Maria and Amador Gutierrez disappeared, smiling discreetly, as Arthur enveloped her in his arms and kissed her. When their lips parted, she clung to him, her cheek pressed against his chest.

"It's so good to have you here, Arthur. How long can you stay?"

"Until Monday. But I'll be back before Lincoln's birthday for ten days or so if Dad feels up to holding the fort that long."

Leya reached up to smooth the hair above his ear. "That means three more weeks without you, then maybe two weeks with you, and then—"

"No time-keeping!" Arthur ordered. "I'm here now. Don't start missing me until I leave." He released her and looked around. "Let me check through the house so I can phone the family and reassure them. Then you tell me what you have planned."

Nothing needed to be done except to stock the refrigerator with cold drinks and some snacks. Arthur gave Amador money and sent him to the delicatessen, then excused himself and changed. It was four-thirty when he came out to the patio in swim trunks.

"How about a splash?"

"But Arthur, my bathing suits are at the hotel. Besides, I had my swim earlier. It's good for my knee. Why don't you go in? I'll wade and watch you."

Arthur was reluctant to swim without Leya, but once beyond the gentle surf line, he found it pleasant to be alone with his thoughts. After a few strokes, he rolled over to float on his back with his feet toward shore and watch Leya as she occupied herself with bits of flotsam along the scalloped tidal line. He had known many girls who were desirable as decorative dates—some as willing bedmates—and a few, very few, with whom he could share an occasional confidence. But this girl—this quiet, lovely Leya Marks—had, from the outset, moved him in other ways. He did not deny her physical desirability, for the prospect of holding Leya and making love to her could be unbearably exciting if he allowed his imagination to run. But Leya made a prior claim on his emotions. For want of a better word, he thought of it as a need to protect her, to cherish her.

He smiled. "Cherish" seemed such an old-fashioned word. "To love and cherish . . ." he said to himself as he rolled over and swam with strong, leisurely strokes along the shore. When Leya saw him swimming again, she waved and smiled.

What a wonderful moment, this one, Arthur thought, a moment to be cherished among countless others that they would share in the future.

In the future! Arthur rolled over to float again, and his thoughts turned to the conversation after dinner the night before with two relatives recently arrived from Germany.

"The future seemed so perfect for Ruth and me," Dr. Abraham Lowenstein had said. His eyes had reflected the pain of once-happy memories turned to nightmares.

"Who could have foreseen the irrationality of the German people?" the former associate professor of geo-politics at the University of Munich had asked. "The Allies had just begun to understand the value of Germany, a nation that has contributed so much to science—and to social stability, with the first practical application of social security for workers. With so many good things!" In the man's eyes Arthur had seen mirrored shock and mystification. "Who could have foreseen this monstrous Hitler? Who could have foreseen such a tragedy for our people? Who could have believed that such insanity could have infected one of the most civilized societies on earth?"

Dr. Lowenstein and his wife, whom Lieberman dollars had seen safely out of Munich to Budapest and finally to England and the *Queen Mary* to New York, unfolded the chronicle of barbarism masquerading as political, economic, and ethnic necessity.

Arthur had felt rage rising in him when Dr. Lowenstein had said, "If this can happen in Germany, then no civilized country—no democracy—is safe! Who is to say that some demagogue here could not exploit the ancient lie of the Jewish conspiracy to poison America, to misdirect the fear and frustration of an organized working mass caught in some future economic depression?"

Not until tears traced rivulets down Ruth Lowenstein's face had the professor ended his warning. "Every Jew in America should give his last dollar, if necessary, to get our people out of Europe and to stop the Nazi plague. If we are to have a future, we must never cease being vigilant!"

As the old man's warning echoed in his memory, Arthur looked at Leya on the shore. She was on her toes, waving to him to come ashore. The thought that there could exist even the remotest possibility that some unthinkable political holocaust might become a personal threat, might rob him of his future with this precious girl, sent a wave of alarm coursing through him. He rolled over and began a powerful crawl stroke. Swimming parallel to the shore, he was aware that Leya was laughing and, with her skirt tucked into her waistband, scampering to stay opposite him. He could see her run, stop, watch, laugh, and applaud. Finally, using the swells as an aid, he surfed toward her until his feet touched bottom. Bushed from the exertion, he struggled ashore and flopped face down on the hard tidal pack.

Leya knelt beside him. "Poor baby," she pouted as she picked apart his matted curls. "What were you trying to do? I thought a monster was after you!"

Breathing heavily, Arthur braced his upper body on his elbows. "One was! But I think I got away." On his feet again, he looked back at the water. "It's beautiful out there. Warm as chicken soup—and just as good for you. Tomorrow you go in with me, okay?"

"Of course," Leya replied, taking his hand. As they approached the covered patio, she detained him to look at the house. "It's such a nice place, Arthur."

"Dad and I may buy it," he said. "The people who own it live in Illinois, but they're getting older now. They want ninety thousand for it."

The sum had no reality for Leya. "I don't know if that's too much or not," she said.

"It is, but it won't be in a few years—that is, if the world doesn't fall apart. I may go half with dad, and you're welcome to my half." He took her face between his hands. "With the understanding that I go with it, of course."

"But of course, Mister Lieberman!" Leya replied.

While Arthur showered and dressed, Leya waited on the patio. Off to the southeast, a line of cumulus clouds seemed to rest on the horizon like great blobs of whipped cream spooned by some celestial hand. Closer, she could make out two vessels, both deep-loaded tankers, heading north. During their weekends on the *Myra III*, Arthur and his father had taught her to recognize the silhouettes of most of the ships that plied the coastal lanes. The ones that especially excited her were the great transatlantic liners. In her private fantasies, she cast herself as a famous ballerina returning on the *Queen Mary* and being photographed in elegant furs, her shapely legs demurely crossed as she perched on the cap rail with a life preserver in the background. Anna Pavlova had posed that way. So had most of the movie stars. Now she, Leya Marks, was an internationally famous ballerina home from a triumphant European tour. She had performed only in the great capitals and had been celebrated in all.

She did not hear Arthur when he stepped into the doorway looking trim and handsome in a new double-breasted Palm Beach suit. For a time, he stood watching her. Sitting cross-legged on a big blue-and-white patio hassock, her chin propped on her fists, she reminded him of Shelly when she had been lost in her preteen daydreams. A child. A girl. A woman. Leya was all three. The memory of their parting in New York still lingered for both of them. He knew that. It had taken all of his control then to keep from taking her to his place, dominating her emotionally and physically, and by the sheer force of his passionate need, making her capitulate and accept his decision for their future. He hadn't. An hour after he had left her, he stood naked, still half tumescent, in front of the bedroom mirror. Lifting the double-Scotch nightcap that he did not deny he needed, he had saluted his image.

"*L'chaim*, noble white knight with the bent lance!" he had said. "You know what you're in, don't you? You're in love, Artyla!"

He moved quietly across the patio. Leya, sensing his presence, turned and was startled to find him so near. He laughed and leaned over to kiss the top of her head. "Where were you? You looked like you needed a passport!"

"I was just sitting here, enjoying, thinking." She took his hand and pulled him down beside her. "I like Florida, Arthur. I didn't think I would, having to work here and all." Then, as though seeing him for the first time, she got to her feet. "Please stand up, Mr. Lieberman," she ordered.

He obeyed and found himself being subjected to a minute scrutiny. "Well?" he said. "Do I pass?"

Ignoring the question, Leya braced her fists atop her hips. "That's who you look like, all right!"

"Who?" he demanded.

"Robert Young."

"Who said that?"

"Heather. I never even thought about it until now. But you do, you know."

"No! No! No!" Arthur disagreed. "She's wrong. Robert Young looks like me!"

Leya angled her head critically, then came close. "On second thought, you're right, darling," she agreed, "but you're much better looking." When she felt his arms tighten around her again, she eased away. "We've got to go now. It's going to take me an hour just to get ready for the first show. I don't feel confident on stage unless I do my knee exercises first."

She led him into the house.

CHAPTER 24

If the news of Arthur's impending arrival in Miami had been sufficient to inspire Leya to an extraordinary performance, his presence at Carlo Romano's table enabled her to reach a peak of technical skill that brought whispered "I don't believe yous!" from Kent several times during their adagio.

When the company took their bows after each show, Romano himself led the standing ovation. Kent forced Leya to step out for the solo curtain calls generally accorded the *danseuse ètoile* in a traditional company.

While they were waiting for Leya and Heather and Sheri to join them at the table, Ed Matson wondered how much ot a factor Arthur Lieberman might be in his personal future plans for Leya Marks. Arthur could no more conceal his love for Leya than Carlo Romano could conceal his elemental delight in the girl's beauty—or than he himself could deny his envy of young Lieberman.

Matson, a forty-year-old widower, did not delude himself. His interest in Leya Marks had become more than professional. The night before, when Sheri had stirred beside him, he had found himself wondering what it would be like to hold a smaller and far more agile female. The prospect tantalized him.

Romano brought him back to reality by rising when he saw

the three girls appear in the service door and make their way to the table.

Arthur wanted to kiss Leya but decided against such a proprietary gesture in the presence of several hundred curious customers, some of whom had started applauding again when they recognized Leya in her ballet-length summer evening dress.

Carlo put his arm around her as Arthur held the chair. "You know what I have on my hands, don't you?" he asked, addressing the others. "I have a star!"

The girls had hardly settled at the table when Carlo turned to Heather. "So, *cara mia,* tell them what we're going to do tonight," he ordered.

Heather summoned more enthusiasm than she felt. "Usually, we have a party at the house on opening night. But we waited this time until Carlo's father could get here. It's wonderful Arthur can be here, too. So tonight's the night, kids! We're moving the whole celebration over to our—over to Carlo's place on the key."

Ed caught the disappointed glances that Leya and Arthur exchanged. He leaned across Sheri and tapped Arthur's sleeve. "We can cut after an hour or so," he whispered. Arthur shot him a grateful look.

Carlo rose and led them through the service entrance to his private parking area. A burgundy Cadillac convertible was waiting with a driver behind the wheel.

Ten minutes later, they crossed a private bridge and stopped in front of wrought-iron gates opening into an estate surrounded by a high coral block wall.

The driver, an expressionless man whom Carlo Romano had introduced collectively by saying simply, "Meet Tony Spacco," touched the horn, and the gates opened. Once inside, Leya was amazed at the size of the place. On both sides of the driveway were broad expanses of close-cropped Bermuda grass studded with palms, hibiscus, and trumpet vine trained on free-standing trellises. The entire area was illuminated softly by concealed floodlights. The driveway curved left around a mosaic swimming pool that glowed like a giant oval aquamarine. They stopped at the foot of a flight of broad marble stairs leading to a balustraded verandah that extended along the entire front of the two-story mansion. At one end, a bar had been set up. At the opposite end, a rumba band was playing.

"It's a modest little place, but we call it home," Heather quipped. Carlo pushed the front seat forward and assisted Leya from Arthur's lap. "Eat, drink, dance, swim." He waved an encompassing arm. "Anything you want, we have. You are welcome to my house."

By the time Carlo had shown them up the steps to the verandah, the Cadillac had disappeared along a spur of driveway that circled behind the house, and the headlights of several other cars were visible near the gate.

"You know whose place this was?" Carlo asked as he led them toward the entrance. "It belonged to Senator Philbin. He's the friend that got things done for the oil companies." He indicated the neoclassic marble statues on pilasters at the end of the balustrade. "They got things done for him, too," he laughed. "Wait till you see the inside!"

The floor of the foyer was inlaid with alternate squares of pink-and-black marble. The walls were white plaster, and the ceiling was elaborately bordered with hand-tinted Italian staff work. Directly in front of them, a curving marble staircase led to the second floor. Bronze Dianas flanked it. On either side were hallways leading to other ground-floor rooms and through the lower floor to a back garden that reached down to Biscayne Bay and a private boat landing.

On the left, through twelve-foot hand-carved doors, Leya could see a huge formal room cluttered with heavy Italian furniture. To her right was a room of equal size in which an enormous buffet had been set up.

"Ten bedrooms in this place," Carlo explained. "And each one's got its own bathroom and toilet. That's one thing I want—plenty of bathrooms." He aimed a thumb in the general direction of the ceiling. "You know something? My bedroom's bigger than my father's house used to be when I was born."

More cars were arriving, and Leya could hear women laughing.

Carlo smiled. "That's good! People come. Heather, you take the ladies upstairs." Turning to Arthur and Ed, he indicated a doorway near the main entrance. "You use this toilet down here. Anything you want—ask. Okay?"

When Leya and Heather rejoined the others, the verandah was half filled with guests and more were arriving. Carlo saw them and steered a solidly built older man through the crowd.

"I want you to meet my father, Salvatore Di Romano," he said, making no attempt to present them individually. After an awkward moment, Heather undertook the task.

Arthur was fascinated by the elder Romano's seamed face and intense dark eyes. It was a strong, confident face and somehow familiar. Beneath the carefully barbered iron-gray hair, it seemed almost benevolent.

Suddenly, Arthur remembered. In the past year, Di Romano's likeness had filled several editions of the New York papers when he had survived an attempted assassination in a New Jersey café. Several weeks later, the garroted bodies of two men had been found near the Erie Railroad right-of-way, not far from the Hackensack River flats. The papers related the two incidents and attributed them to a move by an upstate mob to muscle into the Di Romano family's union and loan-shark rackets.

"So Miss Marks," the older man said, "my friend Harry's sick little girl got well and grew up to be a beautiful lady!" He took her hand and patted it. "I'm so happy to see you. I want you to give regards to your father. Tell him I appreciate his friendship. Also, I want you to know, Carlo and I appreciate having you at the club." He gave her hand a final pat and released it. "Don't forget, *bella ragazza!*"

Heather watched Carlo and his father move easily through the crowd. The respect accorded Salvatore Di Romano was clearly founded in fear.

"Hey—" Heather breathed, "you really rate with the old man!"

Leya was aware that both Arthur and Ed were studying her curiously.

"You'd be surprised if you knew who was here tonight,"

Heather went on. "See the man in the light-blue linen suit? He's the–"

"Heather," Ed cut her off with a friendly smile. "I don't think we're really curious about Carlo's guests. It's recommendation enough if they're friends of his."

A slender, sharp-featured man materialized next to her. "Come on, Heather. Dance with me while Carlo's introducing his father. Okay?"

Leya saw Heather flinch as the man took her by the arm. "Sure. Okay, Mike."

Sheri's eyes followed them. "That's Mike Parroco. When he was a kid he worked for Carlo's old man. He's Carlo's right bower now–smooth and easy, like a good razor!"

Leya slipped her arm beneath Arthur's and welcomed being drawn close. "I thought this was going to be a party for the kids in the show," she said.

"Let's call it a party for Romano's friends," Matson said.

Leya glanced around. Except for their own group and some of the chorus dancers and showgirls who seemed to be paired with older men, she recognized no one.

Several times, Heather and Mike Parroco danced in their direction. It was obvious from her dead-faced expression that she was an unwilling partner. Parroco danced well, but he seemed preoccupied. His eyes moved over the crowd. Arthur noted that the man seldom turned his attention away from Carlo and his father, who were moving from one group to another.

As Arthur and Leya walked around the end of the dance area toward the buffet, Kent Kendall, dancing with Luanna Parker, brushed close and whispered, "Hail, hail, the gang's all here!"

Leya glanced around apprehensively as Arthur laughed and turned her away. A moment later, they passed Peter and Jean dancing next to Matt and Kuzzy. Peter grinned at them. "Hey," he said, rotating his open hand at the wrist, "*Fantastico! Questo mi piace molto!*" Jean reproached him with a little jab in the ribs. "Don't make fun!" she warned.

"Who's making fun?" he replied. "The *gumbas* know how to throw a party. No?"

"No!" Jean hissed, and steered him away.

The food, presided over by a Jamaican chef and four immaculately dressed helpers, ran almost the entire length of the dining room. Flanking an elaborate ice sculpture of the Golden Palm Club's symbol, whose crystal fronds were beginning to drip into a large flower-bordered basin, were glazed hams, roast turkeys, whole cold salmon in gelatin, large slices of red Cuban papaya, imported prosciutto, surrounded by green-rind melon, a dozen kinds of cheese, four huge salads, trays of giant Gulf shrimp, and chafing dishes filled with chicken tetrazzini, scampi, spaghetti with chicken livers, and a squid concoction. On a side table stood a five-gallon cut-glass bowl filled with Asti Spumante punch.

Arthur surveyed the ostentatious display in amazement. "My God! And they accuse us of committing suicide with a knife and fork!"

Balancing filled plates, Ed and Sheri led them through the hall to the terrace garden at the rear of the house. There, at wrought-iron lawn tables overlooking Biscayne Bay, they were joined by the rest of the Kendall dancers.

By the time they had finished, the party was getting noisier. Shrieks of laughter reached them from beyond the house.

"Sounds like the real action's down around the pool. That's where the drinkers are!" Peter Genova observed.

Ed Matson turned a concerned look toward Leya and Arthur. He would try to find a graceful way to leave before things got rough.

Carlo came by, followed somewhat unsteadily by Heather. When he saw their empty glasses, he turned to her. "Go tell them to bring Spumante. A couple of bottles." When Heather did not respond immediately, he took her by the arm and turned her toward the house.

Embarrassed, Arthur got up. "I'll get it. Let Heather visit with Leya."

Romano stayed him. "She needs the exercise."

Leya watched Heather start toward the house. On an impulse, she got up and followed. Romano called after her. "She doesn't need any help. Come back and enjoy yourself."

Leya gave him a level look. "I'll enjoy myself more after I've been in there."

Carlo grinned. "Sure, sure, I understand. Go."

"The son of a bitch!" Heather hissed when Leya overtook her. "He's treating me like shit!" On the verge of tears, she parroted his orders. "*Chiusa la bocca!* That's all he says anymore. Shut the mouth! Open the legs!"

Holding her friend close, Leya walked Heather to the house. At the buffet, she told a serving boy to take the Spumante to the garden table. On the way out, as they passed the staircase, Heather paused.

"Leya, wait here for me for just a minute, will you?"

"Do you want me to come with you?"

"No, honey. I've got to get something. I'll be right down."

As unsteady as she seemed, Heather negotiated the winding flight quickly. Leya remembered the bottle in the locker at the club and found herself wondering if Heather had stashed bottles at home also to escape the constant surveillance. Certainly, in the last few days and evenings, she must have been consuming more liquor than she had drunk openly. Her friend's obvious need to escape saddened Leya.

Carlo entered the hall. "What are you doing here? Where's the kid?"

"She went upstairs for a minute. I'm waiting for her."

Carlo hesitated briefly, then loped up the flight. Leya heard a door open. Seconds later, she heard his angry voice, but the words were unintelligible until Heather appeared suddenly as though she had been shoved. "I told you, honey, I just ran up to get something. That's all."

The door closed again, and Carlo reappeared, took her arm, and escorted her down. His grip made her wince. He motioned to Mike Parroco. "Take her back to the table. I Want to talk to Miss Marks for a minute."

Heather shot Carlo an appealing look. "Please, honey—"

He watched impassively until they were outside. "I'm sorry about her," he said. "She shouldn't leave you waiting."

"It was perfectly all right, Mr. Romano."

Carlo's eyebrows arched. "Old friends should not be formal. My father calls your father Harry. You call me

Carlo." He took Leya's hand. "I will call you Miss Marks because ever since the opening, you are a star, and you will be treated like one."

When Leya attempted to free her hand, he caught it in both of his. The feeling of possessiveness was frightening.

"I am going to give Kendall's group a buildup in every city where we operate supper clubs. By the time you come back here next winter, you will be the star of the highest-paid class act in the business. That's how I'm going to show my appreciation for you. I never forget my friends."

Leya did not see Arthur approaching until Carlo looked up and released her hand.

"I was just telling Miss Marks how much I appreciate her talent," he said, smiling easily. "Wait until you see the buildup Kendall's going to get."

Leya reached for Arthur's arm. It felt strangely unyielding, and his voice sounded strained.

"I'm sure Kent and the others are equally grateful to you, Romano," Arthur said. "You've given them a fine presentation."

Carlo's smile broadened. "It's only the beginning." He squeezed Leya's shoulder affectionately. "I'll see you outside in a few minutes. Have more to eat and drink."

When he was out of earshot, Arthur pulled her toward him. "Come on, Leya. Let's say our good nights and get the hell out of here!"

When they returned to the table, Heather was seated dejectedly.

"We're going now," Arthur said. "Leya's had a tough day."

"But it's only a little after two," Heather protested. "Please stay a little longer."

"She can't," Arthur said flatly. "Where's Carlo? We'd better say good night to him."

"He went down to the pool with his father. He'll be back in a minute."

"We'll find him," Arthur replied, steering Leya back toward the house.

"If you have to go," Heather called, "Tony will drive you back to the hotel."

"We can take a taxi, thank you, Heather."

Mike Parroco came over. "Taxis don't come in here, Mr. Lieberman. Tony will take you. The car will be around at the side."

"Okay, thanks," Arthur said curtly.

They went through the house, and Arthur led Leya to the opening in the boxwood hedge that marked the entrance to the pool area. While they were still some yards away, a figure came running toward them. It was one of the showgirls, fully dressed and soaked to the skin. "God, it's wild!" she called. "Go on in, honey, the water's fine!"

A moment later, a man clad in wet boxer shorts passed them in pursuit. From the pool, hidden by the trimmed hedges, came several splashes and a chorus of female shrieks followed by raucous male laughter.

"Why don't you wait here while I go find him?" Arthur suggested.

"I want to stay with you," Leya replied.

On the broad mosaic apron surrounding the pool, they saw twenty or more guests standing around, watching several naked couples disporting themselves. The elder Di Romano stood on the far side, smiling as a balding, barrel-bellied man clung to the splash trough with one hand while he cradled with the other the behind of a naked girl whose legs were locked around him. When the supporting hand would move under the girl, she would squeal and lift herself up wildly, so that her full breasts smothered the man's face. Each time the spectators would hoist their glasses and shout encouragement.

"Oh, for God's sake!" Arthur muttered. "Look at those idiots! Let's go." As he was about to turn Leya back to the path, a shout caused them to look back in time to see a heavily built younger man strip naked.

"For Chris' sake, old man," he shouted, "if you can't find it, I'll show you where it is!" A delighted cry went up as he plunged in and came up beside the couple. An instant later, all three were submerged. The underwater lighting distorted their figures, but it was clear that the older man had been deposed, and the girl was now locked tightly to the newcomer. In a few seconds, they surfaced, blowing out their breaths explosively. The girl's head was thrown back, laughing and choking.

"*Fare! Fare!*" a male voice was shouting. "Show her what it's for, Angelo, baby!" another kept repeating.

Disgusted, Arthur all but dragged Leya from the scene.

Carlo returned to the table and looked around. "Where's Miss Marks and Lieberman?"

Mike Parroco supplied the answer. "They went looking for you to say good night, Carlo. Tony's taking them back to the hotel." As his man spoke, Carlo saw the burgundy convertible pull away from the parking area on the right side of the house. He glowered at the car until it disappeared around the side drive; then he turned to Heather.

"Go upstairs!"

"What for, Carlo?"

"Go—up—stairs!"

Terrified, Heather hesitated for an instant, then whirled and ran toward the entrance.

"Where's Matson and his girl—and the others?" Carlo demanded.

Peter Genova pointed toward the house. "I think they're dancing, Mr. Romano."

"Good. Eat. Drink. Have a good time. I'm very happy," he said, and turned to follow Heather.

"Compared to him, Count Dracula is laughing boy!" Jean Baxter muttered. "Poor Heather! I wonder what she did?"

"Don't wonder, baby. Eat! Drink! Be merry! And be goddamned glad you're married to my kind of a 'ginzo'!"

Heather was standing by the desk in their bedroom when Carlo entered. He stood in the threshold for a moment, then closed the door hard behind him.

"Where did you get the liquor?" he demanded.

"I only had what you said I could, Carlo. Honest!"

"You're a liar. You got a bottle up here somewhere. Get it or I'll beat your brains out!"

Heather seemed about to protest. Then, shaking visibly, she went to her wardrobe and took a half-empty bottle of Scotch from behind her rows of shoes. Carlo snatched it from her, examined it, then tossed it onto the bed. An instant later, she was staggered by a sharp slap across the cheek. As she fell back, he grabbed her arm so brutally that she cried out.

"How many times do I have to tell you," he demanded, shaking her like a rag doll, "not to shoot off your mouth?" He slapped her again, and she slumped to the floor whimpering.

"Tony heard you! Mike heard you! You said things to the girl!"

"I was mad at you, Carlo. You hurt my feelings," Heather sobbed. "I didn't mean anything, honest!"

"When you tell the Marks kid that I treat you like shit, you don't mean anything?"

"You treat me like a child, Carlo," she sobbed. "You don't treat me like you used to." When she tried to get to her feet, he pushed her against the side of the bed.

"You know why?" he demanded. "Because you don't act like a lady now!" He stood for a moment, appraising her critically. "Why don't you act like your friend? You don't hear rough talk out of her mouth. You don't see her trying to sneak drinks. Don't tell me that's because she's a dancer. You were a dancer, too. before you got like a—" He broke off with an exclamation of disgust. Suddenly righteous, he jabbed his chest. "You don't give me respect! No respect!" His hand swept the luxurious surroundings. "I give you everything—like a princess. And you shoot your mouth off so my friends can hear. You want to go? You don't like it here anymore?"

Heather could barely control her voice. "I don't want to go, Carlo. You know I love you. You know that from what I do . . ."

"Sure! Sure! What I want is a lady! A lady who keeps her eyes open—" He moved a step toward her and raised his arm as though to hit her across the mouth with the backs of his fingers. "And the mouth shut!"

Leaving Heather crumpled and wracked with sobs, he backed toward the door. "Now stay here. You're a mess! You got a headache, understand?"

Tony Spacco dropped Leya and Arthur off at the Roney Plaza after a brief ride made in brittle silence. It was twenty minutes to four. Arthur stopped in front of the waiting elevator.

"Leya, I'd like to talk to you. Let's go to Wolfie's. I can say what I want to say over coffee."

Something in his manner troubled Leya. "All right, Arthur, if you'd like."

They took a taxi up Collins Avenue to the famous all-night delicatessen. At four in the morning, the place was as busy as it was at four in the afternoon. Leya ordered hot tea and a wedge of cherry cheesecake. Arthur wanted only coffee.

Leya gazed across the booth at his troubled face. "What do you want to talk about, Arthur?"

"Us," he replied, "and that creep who was holding your hand—and his lousy club business you're in—and what I think you ought to do about it." He leaned forward. "Look, Leya, I want you to quit the show right now and come back to New York with me. I'm not asking you to give up dancing. I never would. I want you to get away from these animals. They corrupt everything they touch! If you don't want to model, I'll find you a Broadway show. I'll make you a dancing star if I have to back the whole show myself!"

"But Arthur, I have a contract with Kent. And one with Ed Matson. You know that. I couldn't do that to them."

"There are ways to get out of a contract!" Arthur snapped. "They can be bought up. Or, God forbid, you could get ill. Doctors can be persuaded to attest to it. Max will re-examine your knee. You're doing too much. You must rest it."

"But you're asking me to lie and hurt the kids and start all over again—give up roles that were especially choreographed for me—" She shook her head. "Please, Arthur, it's not fair!" She reached out to him. "You know how much I love you, darling. There couldn't be anybody else. And you know how much I love dancing, and you say you want me to dance. But I can't start all over now, after everything that's happened—"

"You wouldn't have to, darling. I want you to dance for as long as you want to—until you get it out of your system. But you belong in a different setting, one with class. We'll find a show that's worthy of your talent. When Kent is free, we'll make him a part of it, too—and the others. In the meantime, you can be presented in concert at Carnegie Hall."

"As a soloist? Without a company?" Leya laughed in spite of herself. "Darling Arthur, I'm sure we could rent the hall and an orchestra and all. But nobody's going to come to see Leya Marks all by her little self on a stage for an hour and a half! Even Pavlova couldn't get away with that! And besides, how could we explain my sudden recovery? We'd **be** sued!" Leya covered his hand with hers. Her eyes were pleading for understanding.

"Darling, until we went to Carlo's place tonight, you thought I was doing the right thing, didn't you?"

"Yes," he agreed reluctantly. "It's more honest to say that I thought it was the best thing for Kent to do—under the circumstances. But for you there are alternatives."

"I don't have to associate with them, darling—I mean, after tonight. I don't have to eat with them, do anything with them."

Arthur gazed at her in amused wonder. "You really are Little Red Riding Hood, aren't you?"

"What do you mean by that?"

"I mean you believe that, don't you?"

"Of course I do."

Arthur nodded. "And that's what scares the hell out of me! You don't see, not even after that bacchanal tonight. You girls are part of the offstage entertainment, too!"

Leya's eyes widened, and she drew her hand away. "Arthur, are you suggesting that any of us kids in the ensemble would do things like that?"

"Of course not! But I know human nature, and I know men like Romano. They take what they want!" He banged his fist on the table. "Argue if you want to, Leya, but every one of those men tonight undressed you. Every single one of them saw you dancing those erotic roles, and they're the kind of pigs who figure if you do that on stage, you could probably be persuaded to do it privately." He thumped the table again. "Goddamnit, Leya! I want you out of that! And *you* should want out of it, too!"

Leya felt her middle begin to cave in. It was more than the fatigue of two demanding shows and the tension of a party she detested. Arthur's words struck like blows. Earlier, in

New York, when he had reassured her that there would be no more glamorous dates for him to be noted in gossip columns, she had believed him. Leya wanted to remind Arthur of that now, to demand the same trust from him, but she found herself unable to speak.

A tense silence had fallen between them. He reached for the hand she had withdrawn. "You understand what I'm saying, don't you, and why I'm saying it? I love you, Leya. I don't want you exposed to any of this."

Suddenly, a great weariness settled on Leya. She closed her eyes and lowered her head. "Arthur."

"Yes, darling?"

"Can we go now, please?"

"But we haven't decided anything."

"I can't decide anything right now." She looked up, appealing.

"What do you mean, right now?"

"I want time to think it over. I can't just say, 'Yes, Arthur, I'll go back on my word, I'll leave Kent and the kids, contract or no contract.' I can't do that, Arthur."

"Are you sure it's just Kent and the others that you don't want to disappoint?" The undertone in the question caused Leya to look at him closely.

"What does that mean, Arthur?"

"It means," he said, hedging now, "that—" He threw up his hands. "I don't know. It's just that I feel you're not telling me everything!"

Leya straightened, and her eyes blazed with hurt and anger. "You're calling me a liar! That's rotten, Arthur. You know me better than that! The only obligation I have is in my contract. I need time to think. If you really love me, you won't force me to make a decision at five o'clock in the morning after two shows and a horrid party. I want to go to the hotel now, Arthur, if you please?"

The sky was beginning to lighten when they got out of the cab. At the door to the suite she shared with Luanna and Tanya, she turned to face him.

"I'm sorry I can't say what you want to hear right now,

Arthur. I'll get up at ten and meet you for breakfast if you'd like. We can talk more then."

She stretched up to be taken in his arms. Instead, he held her by the shoulders, gave her a searching look, then kissed her lightly on the forehead.

"I think you ought to get your rest, darling. Good night."

He turned quickly and disappeared around the corner leading to the elevators.

In the room, Leya was relieved to find the other girls were still out. Numb with fatigue, she did minimal things about removing makeup and fell into bed. For several minutes she lay rigidly, fighting the tears that had been threatening since Arthur's abrupt leave-taking. Suddenly, with a choked cry, she buried her face in the pillow and gave in to them.

Leya awoke with a start at ten past ten. Luanna and Kuzzy were face down, dead to the world, in the darkened room. Moving quickly, she took her things to the dressing room, pulled the phone after her, and called Arthur's room. There was no answer. She called the restaurant and had him paged. Again—no answer. Without knowing why, she called the front desk and asked if he was waiting in the lobby. After she had been asked to hold for several minutes, the desk clerk came back on the line.

"I'm sorry, Mr. Lieberman's checked out."

Leya gasped "thank you" and hung up. From the lobby, minutes later, she called the Miami airport.

"Yes. A Mr. Arthur Lieberman changed his reservation. We found him a seat on our eight o'clock flight to New York. The flight is due in LaGuardia at three."

Dazed, Leya moved from the desk and stood for a time, unmindful of the curious stares. Then, mechanically, she turned and walked through the corridor of lobby shops to the door leading to the pool and the beach. Scarcely noticing the brilliant beauty of the new day and the cool, unusually dry breeze, she wandered onto the sand. After a time, she slipped out of her sandals, reached down for them, and linked a finger through the ankle straps. Unaware of the surf that eddied around her bare legs and splashed on her skirt, she wandered aimlessly along the shore.

CHAPTER 25

"The whole matter is academic, Kent! You heard Leya. She refuses to honor the option to dance in clubs again—*any* club—but most particularly in clubs controlled by Romano. She played out her contract to protect you and the kids. So far as she's concerned, doing that has cost her a lot more than anyone should be asked to pay."

Ed Matson left his desk in the suite at the Roney Plaza and walked to the window overlooking the Atlantic.

"There's no way that Romano's going to rebook the group without Marks," he continued, "and there's no way I can persuade him to. More than that, Kent, you know damned well what the odds are against keeping Matt O'Brien out of the service. He's a solid One-A with a low-order number. With all due respect to you and the others, Leya and Matt are the two outstanding dancers in your group, and that's because you yourself recognized their special qualities and choreographed to make the most of them. You realize that, don't you?"

Kent Kendall sagged under a burden of obvious truth. He brushed away an errant shock of sun-streaked blond hair. "I know." The muscles in his jaw tensed with anger. "Arthur's a stubborn jackass not to trust that girl. If he had, everything would have been all right."

"Most men in love with beautiful women are stubborn

fools—or jealous fools—or both. But don't forget that little Miss Marks is stubborn, too."

Kent looked up. "You called Arthur, didn't you?"

"Yes," Matson admitted, "I was dumb enough to try to patch things up. He was convinced that her career is the most important thing in her life, so there wasn't much I could do."

Carlo Romano had found out within hours that Arthur had left Miami unexpectedly. Because he was worried about what Leya might do, he had asked Matson to call and reassure Lieberman that she would not be required to socialize. "I want her to see only her friends, including Heather and me. But nobody else. Tell him!"

Matson had been much less specific. It was, in fact, a translation, carefully rephrased to be self-serving. He had said, simply, "I'm telling you, Arthur, you hurt the kid badly. You're wrong not to trust her. I know the girl. She's a true artist. Instead of crying her heart out, she'll dance her heart out. And that's all she'll do."

"Obviously, she's doing what means most to her," he had replied. "So what can I say except good luck to her?"

Now Kent rose and walked toward the door. "So—there's nothing else to do."

"Not at the moment. I told you Howard and I would try very hard to find a replacement for Leya—and one for Matt, if necessary—and do everything we can to find the group some bookings."

"If those bookings are up north, do you think Leya will stay with the group?" Kent asked.

"I'd urge her to—for a while. But I want to say again, Kent, if we get mixed up in a shooting war, you can kiss our kind of concert attraction goodby, and the classical ballet, too."

When Kent left, Ed picked up the phone and called Howard Pryor in New York. "What did you find out on the coast?"

"What I expected. A lot of Hollywood's male stars are draftable."

"I'm not sure that's going to make the customers weep, Howard, the way the box office has been lately. The only money the exhibitors are making is their cut of Screeno and

Bingo. You saw the Gallup Poll. The box office take for the industry is down to fifty-five million paid admissions a week from eighty-five million."

"I saw it," Pryor replied. "And I also know why that's happening. The profile of the typical head-of-family moviegoer today is very simple. He is twenty-seven years old, makes twenty-eight dollars a week, and wants escape. He and his family don't want to hear about the horrors of war. I maintain that if we get involved, it will be the singers and dancers who make it. Does that make sense to you, Ed?"

Matson laughed. "Am I going to disagree with a man who's just leased two more floors in Radio City? We're coming up on the Seaboard tomorrow. I'll call you when we get in."

On the eighteen-hour train ride to New York, the atmosphere was strained. The dancers, with no certain immediate prospects now that Romano's offer was out of the question, bore some predictable resentment toward Leya. Without being obvious, Ed Matson shielded her from it by spending time with Kent and the group making plans, most of which he knew had little chance to be realized. They talked about the possibility of Broadway musicals and revues—and of a new form of dance concert in which an entire story would be done in dance pantomime and poetry, aided by an orchestra and a chorus.

Matson's strategy was essentially humane. Kendall was an exceptional talent, a fine dancer, but more than that, a really imaginative choreographer. Marks would be a star, was well on her way as a result of Kendall's talent and perceptiveness. At some point, in some way, they could be mutually useful again.

Several days later, Pryor's concert department found two spring dates at minimum fees strictly for dance aficionados: one at Jacob's Pillow in Massachusetts and another at Provincetown. Leya agreed to dance both dates.

At home in Brownsville, Leya did her best to conceal her depression. After dinner at Minnie's place, Harry Marks poured three small drafts of slivovitz. "Now," he said, "we are going to drink to a great surprise." He glanced at Minnie. "Maybe even a miracle!" He seemed merrier than Leya had ever seen him. "So—I'm taking a wife!"

Minnie, whose eyes had been averted, looked shyly across the table at Leya and rested a chubby hand on her ample bosom. "So—I'm being taken!"

The wedding was arranged for the Saturday night before Leya left for Jacob's Pillow. It was held in Minnie's flat, where the newlyweds would live. Only a dozen people witnessed the ceremony. Leya was the maid of honor. Minnie's boss, Arnold Zimbalist, was best man. Shirley Zimbalist helped Minnie prepare the wedding feast, insisting that a bride should not have to work in her own kitchen on her wedding day. Minnie was philosophical.

"At my age, Shirley, please tell me in which room I'll do better?"

Early Sunday morning the couple left for Grossinger's Catskill resort in the secondhand knee-action Buick sedan that Harry had bought for four hundred dollars and reconditioned in his spare time. One of his neighbors had offered him seven hundred dollars for it—"And I'm *meshuga,* Marks, to offer hard cash for an old car with forty thousand miles on it!"

Harry had smiled. "I'll tell you, Mandell, I'll do you a favor. I wouldn't sell it to you. I don't want you to have it on your conscience that you stole from a crazy man!"

The concerts at Jacob's Pillow and Provincetown were well attended despite the air of pessimism that was beginning to pervade the country with the news of recent Nazi successes in Europe. Early evidence of persecutions, brought out of Germany by those few who, like the Lowensteins, were fortunate enough to escape, was proving to be a gross understatement. Waves of anger and revulsion swept over the country. In the American Jewish communities, there was another, equally profound emotion. Fear. Isolationists such as Father Charles Coughlin and Gerald Smith used national radio to arouse large audiences of sympathizers. Realistic Jews in the United States found much to fear from the popular rantings of German American Bund Führer Fritz Kuhn, William Dudley Pelley's "Silver Shirts of America," the Christian Fronters, and Christian Mobilizers, who were abusing Jews. In mid-May, with the Nazi invasion of Crete, it seemed that the end of a free Europe must come in a matter of weeks.

Ed Matson journeyed to Provincetown to find some merciful way to tell the Kendall Dance Group that its days as a concert attraction were over. On the return trip to New York, he spoke with Kent.

"If you want, Kent, I'll tear up our management agreement. Howard will, too. But I hope you don't, at least not until we've had a chance to assess another opportunity that may be in the offing." As he had expected, Kent decided to let their relationship stand.

When they detrained at Grand Central Station, Matson carried Leya's bag. "Call me tomorrow morning. I've had a very interesting phone conversation with Howard Pryor about you. Refusing to dance in any more clubs may just have been the wisest thing you could have done—under any circumstances."

Weary but hopeful again, Leya walked to the public phones to call her father. A sense of loneliness settled over her as she dialed. Always before, there had been no need to call. Her father's flat in Brownsville had been her home, too. For a moment, she felt again the dull ache in her throat that she used to feel as a child when her father returned her to the Brooklyn Hebrew Orphans Asylum after their weekends together.

Minnie's home was no less her home; that had been made clear. A cot had been put in the little sewing room, and her father had added extra shelving in the closet. But somehow it was not the same. She did not feel free to come and go at will. Her father's plans no longer revolved around her. Minnie was the principal female in his life now. And that was as it should be.

The phone rang three times without an answer. She let it ring several times more. Then she hung up and called Dulcy.

"Hey, Pavlova! Where are you?"

"In Grand Central. I'm killing some time until I can reach my father."

"Well, jump in a cab and come on up."

At the door, Dulcy greeted her with a wheezy squeal. "Just shake hands—in case, honey. I'm just getting over a cold."

She gave Leya a thorough looking over. "I've never seen such a change in one girl in all of my life. You're grown up!" She linked her arm through Leya's and led her to the divan.

"Dear heart, I know what a smash you guys were in Florida. I followed the reviews. But what happened with you and Arthur? He was back in town for a while this winter, making like the footloose bachelor again."

She paused and gave Leya an anxious look. "Am I out of line?"

"No," Leya replied. "He came down to Miami to see me. Some things happened and he got all upset and told me I'd have to leave the club or else."

"In the middle of a run?" Dulcy's blue kitten eyes mirrored indignation. "He knows better than that! What really happened?"

"Arthur didn't like me working in clubs. And he didn't like some of Carlo's associates."

"Tell him to get in line," Dulcy replied. "Neither does the FBI and the IRS and the attorney general. Are you sure he wasn't using that as an excuse to get you back up here to marry him?"

"That was part of it. He said if I insisted on dancing, he'd find a show for me up here."

"Bullshit! I think he saw what a sensation you were making, and he got nervous and jealous. If I were a Jewish mother"—she held up a finger—"which, of course, is unlikely, I'd be in there hocking my precious *boychick* to hang a ring on you with all possible haste! Arthur was—*is*—nuts about you. That I know!"

"Maybe so," Leya agreed unhappily. "But that doesn't give him the right to ask me to give up everything just like that!"

"But you did, honey! The *Variety* story said you guys were going to work the Golden Palm Clubs all this year. So why are you here?"

"We worked out our contract in Miami. Carlo wouldn't sign the group for the other dates unless I stayed with it."

"I don't blame him, dear heart! But for God's sake, didn't you guys try to talk to each other after he left?"

"His mother and father came to the club three or four times."

"Were they trying to patch things up for Arthur?"

"They tried to explain how he felt, and they tried to get me to come back. Mr. Lieberman told Ed Matson that he'd put some backers together and finance a show for us."

"Great, sweetie. I hope you didn't spit in his eye."

"Of course not. But Ed said it would have to be a revue with a lot of other entertainment in it, and he didn't think it was as good for me as some other things he and Howard Pryor have in mind."

Dulcy's eyes narrowed. "Really, now! And just what does the king of the flesh peddlers have in mind?"

"I won't know until tomorrow."

"So—" Dulcy gave her a resigned smile. "Are you going to try to see Arthur?"

Leya shrugged. "I suppose I should."

"Jon said he's gone up to Montreal," Dulcy offered. "He's been working with some organization that's getting Jews out of Europe. Jon contributed a grabber of a photo for the posters. They're up all over town. I got Willie to send a check, too. I told him if he didn't, I'd hock my jewelry and make the contribution in his name."

Glad for a chance to change the subject, Leya asked about Willie.

Dulcy brightened. "Are you sure you want to hear about my secret love life?"

"You heard about mine. I hope yours is happier."

"Mine is exactly where we were when you left in January. Only—" She clasped her hands to her breast dramatically. "At long last, I'm going to get to meet mother and father Vandercort—in the Persian Room of the Plaza Hotel—next weekend. It seems 'mothah deah' is sponsoring a Bundles for Britain ball, and Willie's finally got up enough courage to bring me out of the closet." She jumped up so suddenly she startled Leya. "Hey! Want to see what I'm going to wear?"

Without waiting for an answer, she went to the closet and brought out a pink evening gown with an enormous gossamer skirt. Holding it up to herself, she spread the material.

"Twenty yards of French *tulle* in the skirt alone. It moves like a dream!" She did a graceful pirouette and extended her arm in an elegant handshake. "I shall drop my eyelashes and be dreamy and demure so 'mothah' won't suspect what a scheming, uncouth, little—" She broke off in midsentence. "Hey! Why didn't I think of it before? You remember Gardner Sutton, don't you?"

Leya remembered the attractive navy lieutenant very well. "Of course. Why?"

"He's on leave. He always asks about you. If I can fix it up, would you date him and go with us?"

Without really intending to, Leya heard herself saying, "Sure, why not?"

CHAPTER 26

When Willie Four and Gardner Sutton arrived at Dulcy's a few nights later, it was hard to tell who was the more amazed—Lieutenant Sutton, when he saw Leya Marks in the amethyst Charles James evening gown, or Leya, who was all but gawking at the tall, tanned, blond naval officer, resplendent in formal dress uniform.

Gardner let his gaze wander from one girl to the other.

"You know something?" he said. "It's worth every bone-freezing hour on those tin cans off Iceland just to come back to a pair of lovelies like you two!"

Dulcy rolled her eyes with comic wistfulness.

"Oh, tell us more, kind sir!"

"Come on. You'll spoil them rotten," Willie grumbled. "I've got Oscar waiting downstairs."

Dancing with Gardner Sutton to the music of Eddy Duchin and his orchestra, Leya found that Miami, the Golden Palm Club, Carlo Romano, Heather, and the others seemed part of another world. And so, strangely enough, did Arthur. Earlier that evening, she had thought of him several times. Each time, there had been a stab of loneliness. But as the evening progressed, the stabs became less frequent and less troublesome.

By midnight, Leya was certain that she had never enjoyed a date more. When Duchin played, "What Is This Thing

Called Love?" and "You Do Something to Me," she and Gardner moved in perfect unison. His right arm embraced her, and his jaw caressed the left side of her head. She closed her eyes and abandoned herself to the music and the movement.

At the table, just before they prepared to leave, Gardner turned to Leya. "As an officer and a gentleman, I should tell you in advance that I have no intention of letting you get away. That is why, with diabolical cleverness, I have persuaded Willie and his lady to join us for a day at my family's place at Stony Brook tomorrow." He gave her a stern look. "Which they say they will do if you'll agree to come along—which you will, of course, Miss Marks, because I'm used to giving orders, and that is a command."

Leya made a gesture of submission. "Ballet dancers are used to taking orders, so I guess I have no alternative but to say yes, sir!"

"Perfect!" Gardner exclaimed, beaming. "Willie and I will pick you and Dulcy up at ten."

For Leya, the word "estate" had always conjured up a picture of forbidding crenelated walls, enormous iron gates, and a mansard-roofed manor house surrounded by acres of rolling lawn. A few minutes after eleven, when Gardner drove his roadster through the low, white, freshly painted post and rail fence and along the lazy-S drive, bordered by lush green maple, elm, and chestnut trees, and parked beside the rambling home that had evolved from the original saltbox structure, Leya smiled to herself. Dulcy had referred to the "Sutton estate," but "country place" seemed a more apt description. Gardner led them around to a broad expanse of lawn that fell away gently to West Meadow Beach.

Pointing off left, he said, "That's Stony Brook Harbor. I keep my sailboat there." To his right, beyond the wooded hills, he indicated Port Jefferson and the summer ferry that crossed the Sound to Bridgeport on the Connecticut side.

"Let's barge in and surprise the family." He took Leya by the hand and led her toward the entrance overlooking the water. "I called before we left and didn't get an answer, which means that they could be having brunch at the club.

It's sort of ritualistic—melon, in season, and eggs Benedict. I once did a calculation. In the years since I was born, mother and father have eaten five thousand six hundred and sixteen poached eggs Benedict for breakfast. And roughly half that many melon or grapefruit halves."

He tried the door and found it locked. Puzzled, he said, "Mrs. Murphy should be here. Excuse me."

He disappeared around the house. Several minutes later, they saw him making his way through the living room to the front door.

"Welcome to East Euphoria!" he said.

The house was larger, but Leya found the interior reminiscent of the Lieberman home. Except for the personal items—the paintings and family portraits and pieces of cut glass and Spode china—everything was genuine and old.

"I forgot," Gardner said apologetically, "Mrs. Murphy, bless her soul, is probably attending mass unless mother and dad gave her the day off. But we can shift for ourselves. It looks good for sailing out there today. Does that ring any bells?"

Dulcy turned anxious eyes toward the waters of the sound. They were ruffled with small whitecaps. "It looks a bit windy."

"It's perfect for sailing. Clear and brisk."

"Would you be offended, Gardner dear, if I asked how large your boat is?"

"I'd be offended if you didn't. The *Jezebel* is a thirty-foot sloop, planked with Port Orford cedar. It has teak decks and a clear pine stick. It has a forty-five-hundred-pound lead keel, a head—which means a 'rest room' for you landlubbers—a galley, a dining area that converts into a double bunk, and two bunks forward. It is an able, fast, and safe boat that can be sailed single-handed."

"That's the best part!" Dulcy murmured. "Single-handed—because so far as I'm concerned, I want you to sail it alone. On boats I tend to throw up a lot."

Gardner looked to the others. "Well, we'll think of something else."

"I have been ever since you mentioned sailing," Dulcy said. "But what about 'tennis, anyone'?"

"Or bridge?" Gardner asked.

"I don't play," Dulcy said. "Do you, Leya?"

"I've never played cards."

Willie moved up beside Dulcy. "I'll tell you what—" He turned to Leya. "Have you ever been sailing?"

"If you mean on a boat with sails, no."

"But you have been on the water?" Gardner asked eagerly, "and you don't—uh—throw up?"

Leya laughed. "No. I love it!"

"Well," Gardner said, "it follows that if we don't sail, Leya will be disappointed, and if we do, Dulcy will. So, the only fair solution is to do two things. You and I can sail for a while, Leya, and Willie and Dulcy can play tennis or honeymoon bridge or whatever."

"Don't worry about us," Dulcy said, welcoming the chance to be alone with Willie in something approximating his natural environment. "Go sail for a couple of hours. When you get back, Leya and I can do the domestic bit—if Mrs. Moiphy will allow us in her kitchen."

It was over a mile to the private moorings in Stony Brook Harbor. When Gardner handed Leya aboard the *Jezebel*, she was filled with misgivings. The sloop looked like a hopeless tangle of rigging and wrapped canvas. Sitting out of the way in the cockpit, she watched as Gardner, with the sure hand of a skilled sailor, got the boat ready for sea and started the auxiliary outboard.

Clear of the harbor, Gardner killed the engine and let it drag while he set the jib and the mainsail. As the sails caught the wind, the popping and thundering of canvas alarmed Leya. Once, when the *Jezebel* heeled sharply, she braced herself with an involuntary cry.

Gardner, holding the tiller hard over and pulling on the main sheet at the same time, gave her a reassuring smile. "Everything's okay, miss. Lieutenant Horatio Windblower's on the quarter deck. Sit here beside me and I'll teach you to sail."

Leya found the lesson thoroughly enjoyable. She grew accustomed to the perpetual list as Gardner let her take the tiller and helped her steer to take full advantage of the wind.

Boiling along briskly, they ran north and east toward Bridgeport. On the north shore of Long Island Sound, they came about and beat down the Connecticut shore to Port Chester. When they headed east again to run before the wind on a course to Port Jefferson, Gardner looked over at Leya and grinned.

"You make a perfect first mate!"

"I love it," Leya replied. "I think it's the most peaceful thing I've ever done."

He squinted up at the sail and trimmed in a bit on the mainsheet. Leya watched him, absorbed in his task—in his element, a tall, strong, bronzed Viking whose eyes seemed to mirror the blue of the sea and sky. Intent as he was on his task, Leya understood that Gardner Sutton was seeing and feeling in dimensions that must be denied to all who do not love the sea and who are not consumed by a passion to master it.

She felt a pang as she remembered Arthur had loved the water, too. But the *Myra III* was an implement of recreation, an extension of the Lieberman summer home. The *Jezebel* was an extension of Gardner Sutton. The dancer in her understood the relationship between the physical and intellectual challenge and the spiritual satisfaction in meeting them. She could read in the little squint lines at the corners of Gardner's eyes the satisfaction beyond pleasure that came from knowing that he was equal to the challenge.

Gardner Sutton was a new experience, a man her father might characterize as a *shaygets* or, in Gardner's case, a *shayna goy*. Yet there was no sense of strangeness about him.

She saw Gardner glance at his watch. "Haven't we been gone a long time?"

"Does it seem like a long time?"

"Oh, no!" Leya replied. "I lost track of time. Only I wonder about Dulcy and Willie."

"Don't worry about old Willie. When Dulcy's with him, the rest of us cease to exist. Besides, I imagine my mother and father are home by now. In that case, my inquisitive mother will be trying to shinny up Dulcy's family tree, and my broker-father will be asking discreet questions about the

Vandercort empire, the answers to which poor Willie is not yet privy to!" He looked at her closely. "Let's just worry about you. You haven't said ten words in the last half hour. Still enjoying?"

Leya nodded. "Very much, Gardner."

"Are you warm enough? Do you want to go below and get a windbreaker?"

"I'm perfect, thank you."

"Yes," he said grinning. "That's the word for you, all right—perfect!"

They sailed for ten minutes more, then altered course a few degrees to the starboard. Off to the northeast, Gardner pointed to several large shapes on the horizon.

"Those are British ammo ships coming down the Sound to the New Rochelle anchorage. They'll drop their hooks there until they're cleared for Liberty Anchorage in lower New York Harbor. We'll load them with high explosives, and they'll head for Halifax to join a convoy."

He paused. "Sitting here like this, it's hard to believe that in ten days I'll be back out there, quite probably helping to get those same vessels safely over as far as Iceland, where the Royal Navy takes over."

He fell silent again. "And, very likely, one of those three will take a Nazi torpedo or a bomb from the new Luftwaffe bases in Norway." He squinted again at the vessels riding high in ballast. "Very few sights are more horrible than seeing one of those ammunition ships go up."

"Have you seen that?" Leya asked in a small voice.

"Yes. Several times since I've been on the *Kearney.*"

Leya shuddered. "Does anybody ever get off? Alive, I mean?"

"In the North Atlantic, Leya, you pray for two things: that you'll make it, or that if you don't, the end will come instantly. The only options are to freeze to death or be eaten alive."

Leya closed her eyes and shuddered. A moment later, she welcomed the comfort of Gardner's arm. Leaning close to him with her head against his shoulder, she thought of the Lowensteins and what Arthur had told her they and others had endured, were enduring, and how the people of Britain were suffering under the *blitzkrieg*. She shuddered again.

"Sure you're not cold, Leya?"

"No," she answered without looking up. "I was just thinking."

He removed his arm to retrim the main.

"I'm sorry," he said when he had resecured the sheet. "It was thoughtless of me."

Brightening, he directed her attention to a point of land. "That's Eaton Neck. Let's run along the north shore and I'll show you my secret pirate's cove. It's a sand and gravel pit that's been abandoned for years. It's tricky to get in and out of, but it's very quiet and peaceful. Like to see it?"

"If we have time," Leya answered.

"Leya," he said, "I have so little time to enjoy myself that I'm going to be completely selfish and stretch every possible minute with you." He grinned down at her. "So—let's go exploring!"

In twenty minutes of sailing, the *Jezebel* was standing off the unmarked entrance. The tide was about an hour from low. Gardner could see from the shore that it would be a five- or six-footer. The *Jezebel* drew a shade under six feet, which meant they had just enough clearance if the unmarked channel had not shifted.

"I'm going to douse the main and power in," he said. "It's been a couple of years. I want to be sure."

Minutes later, the *Jezebel* picked her way along a canal-like channel made some years earlier by a clam dredge that had eaten its way into the shore and dug an artificial harbor an acre or so in area. The place was secluded, closed in on all sides by high, symmetrical mounds of gray gravel. The water was millpond smooth. Once inside, Gardner killed the engine and let the *Jezebel* drift.

"Only three or four of us used to know this place. We used to skinny dip here in the summer."

Leya stood up and stretched. "I like it here," she said. "It's kind of spooky, though—like we're in another world."

Gardner got up and pushed the boom aside to clear the cockpit. "I have been—all afternoon."

Leya smiled. "I know. I've been watching you. When you're sailing, you're really absorbed, aren't you?"

"Yes, but that's not what I meant." Leya's ingenuous expression amused Gardner. "I meant that today, with you, was very special."

The change in Leya's eyes prompted caution. He laughed. "I'm terrible with speeches, Leya! I'm really more at ease if I stand ramrod straight, like this, and bow slightly and say, 'Miss Marks, I cannot find words suitable to the occasion, but in my poor halting way I would like to advise you that your presence aboard the *Jezebel* has transformed her into a veritable dream ship.' " He saluted, then relaxed and grinned. "How's that?"

Leya laughed. "Very good, sir!" she said, returning the salute. An instant later, she was being held close as they laughed together. Gardner let her go and turned serious.

"Ever since I met you that lucky night in the Stork, I've not been able to get you out of my mind. I even bribed Willie to get a photo of you to keep aboard ship."

He paused to study her reaction. Her wariness seemed to have disappeared.

"So—there you have my inept confession. If you hadn't come with me today, I'd have sailed off into the sunrise. Years later, they would have found me, a tattered, scraggly-bearded ancient mariner, lashed to the mast, sail in shreds, bony hands clutching a salt-stained photo—and through the ages, forever more, lonely sailors would hear my voice in the night wind crying, 'Leya—Leya . . .' "

She broke into peals of laughter at Gardner's melodramatic performance. Gardner pretended indignation, then reached out and drew her to him. When he felt her respond to his kisses, he brought her closer and moved his lips to her ear and to her neck, then back to her lips. Leya's hands found his face, smoothed his cheeks, moved around to embrace his neck. Gently, he eased her down to the cushioned cockpit seat and turned her body so she could lie across his lap.

Diverting her with kisses, he slid his left hand from her back to her ribs, beneath her arm until it cushioned her breast. When she did not protest, he eased his right hand down to the curve of her hip and gathered her still closer.

"Oh, Leya—Leya—" he whispered. "You'll never know how many times I've dreamed of holding you like this. Have you any idea how much I love you? Have you?"

"I think so," she whispered. Instantly, his lips were on hers again, and she felt his tongue probe her mouth. There was a tiny shock of awareness; then her own tongue responded. She felt his body stiffen as he shifted her, rolling her hips closer. Soon there was nothing but feeling, and she abandoned herself to it.

The fury of his passion brought a cry of protest. He was gentler then, but as persistent. He gasped and whispered her name hoarsely. Then, gathering her like a child, he carried her below into the cabin and laid her gently on the upholstered settee that ran along the port side.

Her right arm was still around his neck when she felt him drop to his knees. His hands left her and fumbled with his white sailing shorts. A moment later he reached for her free hand and brought it down to him. For an instant, Leya did not react. Suddenly, she cried out and thrashed frantically. "No! No, Gardner— No!"

"Leya! For God's sake, darling—" He grabbed her hand and tried to force it back.

"No, Gardner! No! I don't want to!"

Pinning her down roughly, he tried to kiss her into submission. She avoided his mouth.

"Leya! You said you understood! I thought you felt that way, too! What's the matter, darling? Let me love you! Oh, God—please . . ." His voice trailed off in an agonized whisper.

Leya pushed him away. Hobbled and off balance, Gardner fell back. As she struggled upright, Leya saw that his loosened shorts had dropped down around his knees. The sight of him, exposed and erect, made her cry out again as she swung both legs off the bunk and drove her feet into his chest. The force of the blow slammed his head against the edge of the cabin table.

Stunned, he slumped to his side and watched dumbly as she stumbled up the cabin ladder and disappeared into the cockpit. Several minutes later, he found Leya huddled against the bulkhead on the far side of the cockpit, her body wracked with dry sobs. Moving closer, he knelt down.

"My God, Leya, I'm sorry. I thought . . ." He groaned and rose. "I don't know what I thought!"

Seated with her back to Gardner, Leya could feel his pain. She wanted to turn and say something, to try to tell him—what? That it was as much her fault as his? That toward the end she and Arthur had kissed with as much passion, but it had been different then?

In the midst of her self-recrimination, the *Jezebel* lurched and abruptly lost headway. Leya heard Gardner curse as he loosened the outboard's tiller handle, shoved it hard over, and twisted the throttle full open. For an instant, the sloop seemed to respond. Gardner sculled the vessel's rudder in an effort to dislodge the keel, but it had knifed deep into a sand shoal. After several more seconds, he twisted the outboard throttle to idle and walked forward with a boat hook to probe the water under the bowsprit. The hope that he might be able to go over the side and heave the sloop free faded when the probe showed the depth to be nearly over his head.

He glanced at the sky and at his watch. It was six-thirty, and the long twilight still lingered.

Leya stood up and gathered her sweater around her. "Are we stuck?"

"In the same boat!" Gardner replied with an ironic smile. He went below and returned with a sheepskin-lined jacket.

"Put this on," he ordered.

Grateful for the warmth of the jacket, Leya settled down on the cockpit seat again.

"Look," he said, sitting beside her. "I made a complete horse's ass out of myself. I have no excuses to make. But I am sorry."

For a time, he stared toward the dark open water of the Sound. Then he brought one leg up on the cushion to face her.

"Whatever else I am, Leya, I'm no liar, and that's all I'm going to say in my defense. I did not engineer this trip so I could get you out here to seduce you. That much I would ask you to believe."

"I believe it," Leya said in a small voice. "It was my fault, too."

"For what?"

"For—" the words were coming hard. "For letting you think—"

"That you might feel about me the way I feel about you?"

"Yes."

Gardner Sutton's brow wrinkled. "Well," he said, "let's just say that if I had used my head, I would have figured out some things—like I have a vivid imagination, and that it's dangerous when you've been at sea a long time to let it run rampant." He got up suddenly. "What the hell! I've loused myself up with a beautiful girl whose photo looks at me with loving eyes every night at sea, and for that I am very damned sorry."

For another half hour they sat, talking to no point, both being careful not to let the subject get too personal. In the middle of one of Leya's replies, Gardner checked the aft anchor line. It was slack.

"Excuse me," he said, jumping up. "I think we've got water under us again."

A few vigorous turns on the windlass handle confirmed it. The *Jezebel* grated gently and moved astern.

"We're saved!" he called. "Let's rejoin the human race!"

CHAPTER 27

Conversation all but stopped in the Waldorf Astoria's Peacock Alley when Leya entered to meet Ed Matson for cocktails.

Dressed in a simple Claire McCardell spring wool crepe, her copper hair pinned in a braided ballerina bun, a bit of liner accentuating the subtle uptilt of her eyes, the dancer commanded attention. Several of the patrons whispered among themselves, certain that they recognized her. Quite apart from her talent, it was Leya's unconscious ability to turn heads that Matson had been counting on as a prime factor in furthering her career.

"You've just made me the envy of every man in the place," he said as he held the chair.

"And you've made me the most curious woman in town with your call. Why couldn't you tell me on the phone?"

"Because I have something special to tell you, and I regard this as a proper setting. What will you drink?"

"Just a ginger ale, thank you."

The manager ordered a Scotch on the rocks for himself. "Now, then, so we won't prolong the suspense, it's my very pleasant duty, Leya, to tell you that you and Kent and Matt and I are flying out to Hollywood—to Paramount Studios, to be precise—to do a screen test."

Leya seemed not to comprehend.

"You did hear what I said, didn't you, little friend?"

"Of course," Leya answered.

"Well, aren't you excited?"

"My gosh, Ed, I guess so."

"You guess so? Good God, girl, fifty million pretty chicks in the country would be squealing with ecstasy by now, and you just guess so?"

"Of course I'm excited, Ed! You just took me by surprise. I really don't know what to say."

"Why don't you say, 'Great, Mr. Matson! You are a superhuman manager. You work miracles! I'm very glad I signed with you!' For starters, I'd settle for that."

"All that is true, Ed. I think it's wonderful. Really. When do we go?"

"This coming Friday. The test is really yours, Leya. But I want them to see you in excerpts from the challenge number. That is why I.A.M. and I are paying to take Kent and Matt along, too."

Leya frowned and traced a fingernail through the frost on the side of her drink. "Do they know that it's really my test? Won't they have a chance, too?"

"Certainly! Strategy-wise, it is much better for me to try to sell you alone and sort of let them ride in on the tail of the kite. You will all get equal exposure, and if there is interest in Kent and Matt, it will come to the surface automatically. In fact, I'm counting on that, and so is Howard Pryor." He regarded her with a smile. "Are you really excited?"

Leya moistened her lips. "My insides are going like mad, and I'm a little scared, too. Is there any chance that it won't happen, Ed?"

"No. We have a firm commitment. Why?"

"Because I'd like to know how things really are. A lot of times in my life when I wanted something very badly, something else came up, and it didn't happen." She smiled apologetically. "I'm very excited. Honest. But, like papa says, 'I don't want to mess up my *mazel.*' "

"Take my word for it, your *mazel* has just started, Leya!"

For the next half hour, Ed assessed her prospects. "Your

only chance for a dancing career now is in pictures. Or possibly Broadway. But that's a long, hard road unless you have a name. Hollywood can build that name for you in a matter of months—if you have it. Obviously we think you have, or we would not be making this investment in you. Forget serious ballet companies for a while. Mikail Khazar's dream just blew up. His so-called Italian financing is *finito!* He's finished, at least until after the mess in Europe is over." He nodded. "This is not only the right way, it's the only realistic way to see that your talent gets a full chance. I hope you agree?"

"Of course I do, Ed. I'm very grateful that you and Mr. Pryor are interested enough to do all of this for us."

"For you!" He drained the last of his Scotch and sat back. "I don't have a crystal ball, and neither does Howard. But we do have a lot of experience, and the fact that the studio is interested at all tells us that we are sizing up the future box office realistically. There will never be a better time for a dancer with your looks and ability to make it."

"I guess not," Leya said, still half afraid to believe what she had been hearing.

"I *know* not, little friend, and let me tell you something. We can thank Revelsky and that billboard campaign for a lot of the interest. It was a lucky break."

A half hour later, in Dulcy's apartment, where she was staying with increasing frequency since her father's marriage, Leya found a note propped against the dressing-table mirror. "Gone to interview. Back at five-thirty. Wait for me if you can. D."

Leya slipped out of her pumps and called Jon Wales's studio. Dorothy Simpson answered.

"Leya! My God, how are you? We haven't heard from you for months." The stylist's voice was tense with suppressed excitement. "Are you coming back to work again?"

"Not for a while," Leya replied. "I'm going out to Hollywood the end of the week. I promised Jon I'd call and let him know my plans."

"How casual you sound! May I ask why you're going?"

"Ed Matson has set up a screen test at Paramount."

"I knew it would happen!" Dorothy cried. "So did Jon. The Revel ads did it. Right?"

"They helped," Leya admitted.

"Since you went to Florida, Jon's looked at the Revel billboards a thousand times and called you every kind of an idiot in the book for giving it up. Have you any idea how much money you could be making? Thousands! And I don't mean posing for underwear." She paused. "By the way—you know about Arthur, don't you?"

The question sent an apprehensive shock through Leya. "We haven't been in touch, but Dulcy told me that he was in Montreal."

"He's joined the Royal Canadian Air Force, dear." When she heard no reaction, Dorothy continued. "He didn't want to wait until we got in. On the last photo date, he seemed very upset. He looked like the devil, not himself at all. I heard him telling Jon that his father was bringing in a new man to handle his work. The old man's a wreck!"

Seized by guilt, Leya felt certain that her refusal to leave the show in Florida had been as much a part of Arthur's decision as his hatred of Hitler. She was hardly conscious of acknowledging Dorothy Simpson's good wishes and saying her good-bys. For a time, she stood by the phone, trying to decide whether or not to call the Liebermans.

What would she say to Martin or to Myra? *Tell Arthur to change his mind? Tell him to come back, please, and I'll do what he wants? Tell him again that I love him?* The shock and remorse were too much to contain. She dropped heavily onto the hide-a-bed sofa, let her head sink into the crook of her arm, and sobbed.

After a time, she sat up. Slumped in the corner, she thought of Arthur, of Heather and Carlo, and of Kent and Matt—and Kuzzy, too, and the hurt look in her eyes when Matt allowed himself to be monopolized by Kent.

People in love! People in love with the wrong people! People who had lost their way or had deliberately turned their backs on love, as she had!

As she thought of Gardner Sutton, her throat tightened.

Tears threatened again when she remembered the excitement she had felt in his arms hours earlier—and the hurt and consternation in his face when she had gone wild with fright.

The lobby buzzer startled her. It was the doorman. "There's a delivery boy down here, Miss Marks. Shall I send him up?"

"Please," Leya replied. By the time she had taken a quarter from her purse, the door bell sounded. The messenger handed her a box. A letter-sized envelope secured beneath the ribbon bore the address:

Gardner L. Sutton, Lt., U.S.N.
U.S.S. Kearney
Fleet Post Office
Third Naval District
New York, N.Y.

Leya had trouble coordinating her hands as she slipped the ribbon from the long box. Laid in green tissue were two dozen American Beauty rosebuds. Inside an envelope was a single sheet of note paper. She unfolded it and read:

My dear Leya,

Ever since we met, really by accident, two summers ago, you have been a part of everything that has happened to me. You transferred with me from the *Tuscaloosa* to the *Kearney*. You've been on convoy to Iceland. You've listened to my confessions of fear. And when I finally got your photograph (by some not entirely honorable means!) you shared and endured it all.

Poor girl! How could you know that I survived simply to see you again. And when I did see you again Saturday, the dream and the reality merged in a confusion of feeling that you could not possibly suspect, much less understand.

I've never known a girl such as you, Leya. And—tragic loss—I never shall again! The memory of you in my arms I'll cherish forever. And I shall pray that merciful time will erase the memory of my stupidity.

If I dare not ask for forgiveness, dare I ask for understanding? The truth is simple. I fell in love with you that night in the Stork. I've loved you deeply ever since. I always shall. Not much in this crazy world is forever. But, so help me God, that truth is!

Always,
Gardner

The roses had not been removed from the box, and Leya was still holding the note when Dulcy let herself in.

"My, my, my!" she purred as she lifted several of the buds. "Who sent them?"

"Gardner," Leya replied, trying to conceal her emotion.

Dulcy's eyes widened. "Oh ho!" Then she saw the note, and her smiled broadened. "Roses and a 'forgive me for being a jerk' note, huh?"

"Yes. He feels very badly."

"I'll bet he does!"

"I do, too," Leya confessed in a tight voice.

Dulcy settled on the edge of the sofa. "I thought you two had made it up by the time we drove home."

"Mostly, we had," Leya agreed. "But it wasn't the same as before."

"No matter what happened on that boat, it couldn't be, honey." She indicated the note. "Did he apologize nicely?"

Leya handed it to her. After reading it, Dulcy handed it back. "I think it's a hell of a note from a hell of a gentleman. What about you?"

"I think it's—well—probably he's very sincere."

"Bet on it, sweetie!" Dulcy got up and crossed to the dressing room. Looking at Leya's reflection, she began to undress. "You're going to stay with me tonight, I hope?"

Leya considered briefly. At home she would ask Minnie about Arthur. Minnie would say that she would have told her sooner if she had just come home. Then they would sit around the samovar and talk about the shop and the I.L.G.W.U. and the shipyard and a lot of other things that somehow had lost their interest. Later, she would go to her cot in the converted sewing room and lie awake most of the night wondering about Arthur, reliving the times with him and the weekend just passed—Gardner and the *Jezebel*—and these, too, she thought as she reached for the flowers.

"If you have nothing planned, I can stay."

"I have nothing planned, doll," Dulcy said, "beyond deciding when and how I should tell William Vandercort, the Fourth, that his fertile darling is just about two months overdue—tomorrow."

CHAPTER 28

Minnie stood in the doorway watching Leya pack.

"So why can't you ride the train? Your father's very nervous, you know."

Leya smiled to herself. Before he left for the Navy Yard, he had knocked on her door and come in to say, "To tell you the truth, *bubeleh,* I'd like to try a ride in an airplane, but your cousin, my wife—" He had rolled his eyes heavenward. "Can I tell you—a strong man couldn't take such *tsouris!* So I won't fly, and you'll tell me what it's like when you get back."

"We have to be at the studio on Monday." Leya put her arms around Minnie. "Mr. Matson says we're going to fly in a new airplane, the biggest one in the air."

Minnie was dubious. "Big is heavy. In the air, heavy is bad. What if the motor stops? You'll tell me, please, where are you going to pull over?"

"There are four engines. Twice as many as they have on the other planes." Leya hugged her again. "Don't worry. Please! I'll be safe."

"Sure, sure," Minnie said. "So I'll pray. Also, I'll have Mrs. Harrigan next door make with her beads."

She followed Leya downstairs to the taxi. When it pulled away, Leya looked back to wave and saw her stepmother dabbing at her eyes with a handkerchief. *The truth is,* Leya thought, *I'd just as soon be taking the train.*

At the airline counter, she found Kent and Matt checking in. Kent pointed to a magazine stand some yards away. "Ed's over there buying the place out. Are you excited about flying?"

"No. Just nervous," Leya answered. "But if it gets us there quickly, that's all I care about."

Ed Matson approached, carrying an armload of reading matter, including several Hollywood fan magazines. When he saw Leya, his eyes took in the John Frederick hat and the smart tailored traveling suit Dulcy had helped her pick out; then he turned to Kent and Matt.

"Think she'll do?" he asked.

Matt grinned. "I'm not taking any chances. I'm getting her autograph now."

Suddenly, they saw a figure running toward them, waving. It was Tanya Kuznetsov. "I'm so glad I got here in time," she panted. "I have something for you kids." She reached into her handbag and removed three packets wrapped in tissue paper.

"They're Saint Christopher medals—for travelers. They've been blessed by the Bishop at Saint Seraphins. It's Russian Orthodox, but we have a Saint Christopher, too."

She made the explanation without taking her eyes from Matt. "Here!" She handed him the first one and gave the other two to Kent and Leya. Looking at Ed apologetically, Kuzzy said, "I didn't bring you one, Mr. Matson, because I didn't know if you'd appreciate it."

Ed laughed. "Don't worry about it, my dear. We Presbyterians leave saints to others who need them more than we do! Anyway, if it makes you feel better, I'll canonize myself on the spot. I am now Saint Edward of Manhattan," he said in a sepulchral voice, "patron saint of ballet dancers who fly through the air."

Kuzzy's china-blue eyes rebuked him. "I'm very serious about blessing my friends," she said.

"Don't worry, Tanya. We'll all be safe. And if everything works out, we'll all be together again soon."

Leya and Kent hugged her. Then Kuzzy turned to Matt. "Good-by, Matt," she said softly. Before he realized her intent, Kuzzy went up on her toes and planted a kiss on his lips. "God keep you," she murmured. Then, after an embarrassed smile at the others, she turned and hurried through the crowd.

Kent stood looking after her. "Well," he said, his tone betraying both amusement and indignation, "I guess Rome and Constantinople aren't so far apart after all!"

A driver from the Beverly Hills office of I.A.M. was waiting for them in front of the terminal. Within the hour, grateful to be free of the enervating drone of the engines, they were installed in comfortable rooms in the Hollywood Knickerbocker Hotel.

Leya was still not settled when the phone rang. It was Kent. "I haven't seen Hollywood's answer to the Great White Way since I was a kid. Want to take a stroll with Matt and me? We've gained three hours, you know."

Leya begged off. "I'm still groggy from the airplane, and really, the only thing that appeals to me now is a hot bath and bed. Tomorrow?"

"Of course, only I don't know that the boulevard will stand the light of day. It's a bit like a seedy overage actor!"

On Saturday, Ed Matson took them to brunch at the Vine Street Brown Derby. When owner Bob Cobb singled them out for special attention, necks craned in the nearby booths.

"On Saturday, you're not apt to see too many celebrities here," Ed explained. "But during the week the place is a *Who's Who* in pictures and radio." He consulted a small notebook.

"We have tomorrow off, except that at some point we should talk over the things we want to do in the tests. We're due in makeup at Paramount at seven Monday morning."

"How long do you think the tests will take?" Leya asked.

"All morning. Perhaps all day. We'll have to keep ourselves available in case the brass wants to talk specifics. I think we can fly back toward the end of the week."

After lunch, they walked up Hollywood Boulevard as far as La Brea Avenue and returned on the opposite side. Leya was disappointed. "I think it looks like a little country town trying to be someplace," she said.

Ed laughed. "You'll change your mind when you get inside

the studios. That's where the real Hollywood is, even if most of the studios are no longer actually in the place. Hollywood's a state of mind—much like heaven and hell—and too often, more like the latter for those who don't make it!"

On Sunday, Kent and Matt accepted an invitation to visit Kendall's family friends in Bel-Aire. Ed took the agency car placed at his disposal and drove Leya out Sunset Boulevard to the beach. The day was brilliant. They drove north to Malibu, lunched at a passable cliffside restaurant near the film colony, then turned inland on a canyon road leading through the barren Santa Monica Mountains to the San Fernando Valley. It was after dark when they returned. Rather than change, they dined at the hotel.

At nine o'clock, Ed saw Leya to her door and took her hand. "Like the place a little better now?"

"The ride was beautiful, Ed. I enjoyed every minute of it. Thank you. I really feel ready to do the test in the morning."

"Great! I'm betting that you kids'll make them sit up in that projection room and take notice." He kissed her lightly on the forehead. "Good night, Leya, and thanks for making my day, too."

In her room, using the dresser as a barre, Leya reviewed the day with Ed Matson. He was easy to be with. She realized that until now she hadn't given much thought to Ed Matson, the man. As a manager, she felt secure with him. Now, she admitted, she found herself at ease with him as a man, also.

Ed, Leya, Kent, and Matt arrived at the Paramount main gate at seven. The guard checked the names on his clearance sheet and directed them to a parking area in back of the writers' building.

A conservatively dressed young man waited for them. "I'm Marty Maizlish from the Beverly Hills office of I.A.M.," he said, offering his hand to Matson. "Mr. Pryor wants me to stay with you and help in any way I can."

After the introductions, the young agent excused himself. When he returned, he was smiling broadly. "We've arranged for Mr. Westmore to make up Miss Marks."

Ed turned to Leya. "That's a break, little friend! Usually, the Westmores only work on stars. Somebody up there likes us!" He pointed to the second floor of the main office building.

"I have better news than that," Maizlish said. "The test is going to be directed by Mitchell Leisen. He wants to look at you all for a musical he's planning. We're due at nine-thirty on the assembly stage."

Leya began to understand what Ed Matson had meant when he said the real Hollywood existed in the barricaded private world of its movie lots.

On beyond the writers' building, which Ed told them had housed, among others, Marc Connelly, Maxwell Anderson, Gladys Leyman, Carey Wilson, Sam Hellman, Grover Jones, Norman Krasna, Herbert Fields, Virginia Van Upp, Oscar Hammerstein, II, and Preston Sturges, Leya saw the huge boxlike sound stages. Ahead of them, a hand dolly containing four ornate merry-go-round horses was being rolled from the property department. On the far side of a high fence that separated the studios, she could see the RKO lot with its landmark water tower.

In the makeup department, an assistant stopped by Leya's cubicle. "Mr. Westmore will be with you in a few minutes, Miss Marks. He's touching up some makeup for Miss de Havilland and Miss Goddard. They're doing some retakes for *Hold Back the Dawn.*"

Several minutes later, a man stopped outside to chat with two women. Leya recognized Olivia de Havilland and Paulette Goddard. After several good-natured exchanges, the man entered and offered his hand to Leya.

"Hello, Miss Marks. I'm Wally Westmore." As he spoke, Leya was aware that he was studying her face.

"I'm very happy to know you," Leya managed.

"Likewise," the makeup artist responded absently as he moved around to examine her profile. He handed her a smock. "Slip this on and we'll tuck a towel under your chin and try not to improve on nature."

An hour later, made up and coiffed, Leya looked at herself, amazed at the transformation. Instead of the exaggerated makeup required for the stage, Westmore had done little beyond giving her a deeply tanned look.

"I've lightened the area under your cheekbones to de-emphasize them a little," he explained. "When I do Carole Lombard, I have to do the same thing to her jawline—and her cheekbones. And I've opened up your eyes just a wee bit," he said. Pointing with the tip of a fine camel's hair brush, he indicated the two fine white lines along the inside of her lower eyelids. "By the way, our artificial lashes look a lot better on camera than stage beading. More comfortable, too. Most women will use them before long. So," he smiled "I've taken care of my department. Now Judy will take care of hers, body makeup." He pointed to the waiting assistant. "Thanks for coming in, Leya, and good luck."

Leya found the body makeup messy and uncomfortable. Instead of the light dusting of powder she had used on stage, the makeup woman, working with a large sponge, painted her neck, shoulders and upper breasts, arms, midsection, and her legs to the edges of her pubic hair. The Max Factor pancake makeup, sponged on cold and wet, raised goosebumps.

As she smoothed out the last splotch, Judy backed off for a final inspection.

"You're going to feel like a whitewashed outhouse when it dries, honey. After you've put your costume on, I'll touch you up again on the set."

Outside, Leya found Kent and Matt waiting for her. Both were made up and in costume. Ed Matson and Marty Maizlish arrived a few minutes later and led them to the assembly stage behind the writers' building.

"There's a big dance set still standing. It was used in the *Road to Zanzibar*," the agent explained. "They're going to light part of it for your test." He opened the sound lock doors and moved through the inner vestibule to the huge stage itself. Leya stopped stock still.

The cinematographer, Leo Tover, was standing with his head gaffer discussing the light plan in the midst of a jungle clearing surrounded by exotic trees and plants. The realism astounded Leya.

Everywhere in the organized disorder of the stage, men

were going about their tasks. An attractive woman, dressed in a corduroy skirt and a matching pongee blouse, approached. "I'm Eleanor Broder—Mr. Leisen's assistant." Ed introduced himself and the dancers.

"Mr. Leisen will be here in a moment. We have the recordings Mr. Pryor sent, and we've dubbed the music onto track. Perhaps we should decide which number to do first and how much of the routine you think we'll need for a useful test."

Leo Tover came over and was introduced. Leya knew he was studying her face as he made pleasant small talk. After several minutes, he returned to speak to the head electrician, who relayed some orders to his men on the shadowy catwalks fifty feet or more above them.

They had hardly settled in the canvas chairs when a tall man with thinning gray curly hair, a precisely trimmed mustache, and the bearing of a grand duke approached. Ed rose to meet him.

"Hello, Mitch!" he called. "I'm more than happy to see you on a couple of counts! First, because you were good enough to do this test for us, and second, because I want to tell you what a hell of a job you did on *I Wanted Wings*. Milland and Holden are going to be heard from. Constance Moore was great, and so was the new kid, Veronica Lake. How in hell did you get that little blonde with the crazy hair to act like that in the final scene?"

Mitchell Leisen's blue-gray eyes twinkled with amusement, and his celebrated smile revealed perfect teeth. "It's good to see you again, Ed! Veronica's another story!" he said, laughing as he remembered the trouble. "I'll tell it to you some time—over a martini!" He turned toward the three young dancers, who had risen. Eleanor Broder undertook the introductions.

Tall and slender, a picture of casual eloquence, Leisen epitomized the Hollywood superdirector. Marlene Dietrich, Carole Lombard, Jean Arthur, Claudette Colbert, and a dozen other top female stars demanded him and changed their plans so he could direct them. No other director in Hollywood had the Leisen magic with women. He knew as much about scenery and gowns as the best of the designers. He knew as much about composition and lighting as the best of the cinematographers. Many of them admitted having learned composition from him.

He made a major contribution, usually without taking credit, to the stories that he and producer Arthur Hornblow, Jr., brought to the screen. A living legend, Leisen was known above all for the way he instilled confidence in his casts, from the brightest star down to the merest trembling hopeful.

As the director held her hand, Leya silently thanked Ed Matson for telling her about his long-time friend during their ride. In his presence now, she felt less awe than confidence and security.

Leisen took his time over the introductions to Kent and Matt. It was odd, she thought, that Kent and the director, who were similar physical types, seemed to have struck some instantaneous bond between them. In future years, she could see Kent, in his forties then, as assured, charming, and knowledgeable as the director.

Leisen also seemed to take a special interest in Matt O'Brien, whose dark good looks promised exceptional screen possibilities.

Resting a hand on Matt's shoulder, he directed the sound technician to start the musical track.

They heard the preliminary popping and frying sound in the speakers as the film leader ran through the pickup heads. An instant later, a timpany roll thundered through the cavernous sound stage, and the full orchestra blared the opening bars of the challenge music.

Leisen turned to Leya. "The part we want is the jazz and classical adagio, right?"

Leya turned questioning eyes to Kent. "That's right, Mr. Leisen. I'll dance the classical portions with Leya, and Matt will do the jazz sequences."

Leisen nodded and took Leya by the hand. "A tour de force for the prima ballerina. Good! Let me see your costume, dear."

Leya stood up, removed the makeup smock, and moved into the clear, where she did several contained turns. Fifty feet above them, from the lighting catwalks, came low whistles of appreciation. Embarrassed but pleased, Leya acknowledged their appreciation with a curtsy.

The track was rewound and run down to the adagio.

"All right," Leisen called, "take a few minutes to warm up. Then you kids walk through the adagio bit so Leo and I can see what we have to work with."

In an area several times larger than the stages they were accustomed to, Leya and the boys did some improvised barre for fifteen minutes; then Kent asked for the playback.

At the end of the adagio, the crew and spectators broke into spontaneous applause. Leisen was unquestionably delighted.

"Ed told me you were good! Now I want you to run through the complete routine for me so we can block the shots. Then we'll go for a take. All right? Take a few minutes more to limber up if you think you need it."

Although the adagio took less than five minutes on stage, it took an hour to block the shots. Leya found the monotonous start-stop-start-stop fatiguing and, after a time, somewhat frustrating. It was difficult to sustain rhythm and tension. By noon they had managed two takes.

"Before we go to the commissary, let me see the costumes for the other number," Leisen said.

Eleanor Broder removed them from the large cardboard box and held them up. The director nodded. "They'll do. I wish we'd had more time. I'm sure we could have run up something that would have photographed better." He swept them with his infectious smile. "Let's break for some food."

Four pictures were shooting, but two of them were on location. Leya recognized Beulah Bondi, dressed as a frontier woman, lunching with several others in costume, and just before they finished their meal, Bing Crosby and Bob Hope came in with several people she did not recognize. Leisen sensed her disappointment.

"I'm sorry we couldn't manage a better show for you in here today. I suspect about now some of our biggest names—including Gary Cooper—are eating box lunches up in Inyo County or over in Arizona."

On the assembly stage again shortly after one o'clock, the tedious process was repeated, this time using several excerpts from the Oneida number. It was almost four o'clock when Mitchell Leisen and Leo Tover were satisfied.

"Okay, kids. You boys can break and get dressed. I have one more thing I want to do." He turned to Leya. "Miss Marks, I want to get some close-up footage of you." He took the cinematographer aside and spoke with him quietly for several minutes. Then he motioned to Leya.

"I want you to sit here while we light you," he said, indicating his director's chair. "Then I'm going to sit just out of camera range, and we'll talk informally for a few minutes. That's better than giving you some dialogue to read. All right?"

"I'll try," Leya said, unaccountably nervous.

During the ten minutes it required to reset the lights, Leya's makeup was repaired. A hanging back light snapped on, and Leya's distorted shadow appeared out front. A moment later, a key light struck the right side of her face, blinded her momentarily, then dimmed down. A fill light came in on the opposite side and was softened with silks until Leisen, sharing the ninety-millimeter viewer with the cameraman, murmured, "Good!"

He pulled his chair close under the camera facing Leya, nodded, and said, "Roll it." In the darkness behind the camera, a voice said, "Speed." An assistant held up a slate and slapped the clack boards to synchronize the sound track with the picture. Leisen smiled reassuringly at Leya and said, quietly, "Ready? Right? Action."

Speaking with his left cheek close to the camera's sound blimp and looking directly at Leya, the director said, "Miss Marks, do you mind if I ask you some personal questions?"

Leya glanced around, looking for Ed. When she did not see him in the darkness behind the camera, she shrugged. "I guess not."

"Good!" the director said. "I know very little of your background, Leya—may I call you Leya?"

"Please do."

"I must say one thing. You are not only very attractive, but you are a very accomplished dancer. That must have taken many hundreds of hours of hard work."

"It did," Leya admitted, remembering those early years of lessons and later, Madame Baronova and her demanding discipline—and her long malacca staff!

"I always wanted to be a dancer," Leisen said, "but I broke my ankle, and the surgeons were never able to repair it properly. So I became a balletomane instead." He paused. "Do you have a family in New York, Leya?"

"Just my father."

"May I ask about your mother?"

"She died when I was born."

"So your father had to be both mother and father—is that right?"

Leya, remembering her father's efforts to manage job hunting and housekeeping and cooking, smiled. "He was wonderful—papa. *Is* wonderful!"

Unseen by her, Leisen turned to Tover and nodded. "You love him, all right!" the director said. "It's written all over that lovely face of yours."

He paused again to allow the camera to record a few more feet of reaction. Then, without warning, Leisen fired a blunt question. "Are you in love?"

Leya's eyes widened, and she caught her breath. "N—no—" she stammered.

"Have you ever been?"

Leya shot an anxious look into the darkness where she had last seen Ed Matson. Against the lights, she could not make him out, kneeling in the shadows, smiling in anticipation.

"Pay attention to me, Miss Marks!" Leisen commanded icily. "I asked you—have you ever been in love?"

Leya's throat constricted, and her eyes began to fill.

"Yes—"

"But you're not now?"

Leya's face mirrored the sudden emotional confusion.

"I—uh—no!" she blurted.

"Why not?" Leisen snapped.

The camera, forgotten by Leya now, continued to roll.

"Answer me, damnit!" Leisen ordered. "I want to know

why you're not in love anymore, and don't tell me it's none of my damned business because it is!"

The camera panned up slightly as Leya grew rigid and straightened in the canvas chair. In the finder, Leo Tover could see the telltale glistening in her eyes. Leisen pursued the questioning relentlessly.

"Can't you talk, girl? Silent pictures went out ten years ago! Now tell me why you're not in love anymore. You like men, don't you?"

Once again Leya looked desperately off camera. Ed Matson moved closer and made a fist, signaling to her to fight back.

"You *don't* like men. Is that it?" Leisen purred sarcastically.

Leya gasped. "My love life is none of your damned business!" she cried. "I came here to dance, not to be psychoanalyzed!" She glared at the director. "What kind of a screen test is this, anyway?" she demanded, rising so abruptly the camera had trouble following her.

"Cut!" Leisen called. Catching Leya in his arms, he held her against his gray cashmere sport jacket. "I'll tell you what kind of a screen test this is—it's a great one!"

Leya, trembling with anger, struggled to free herself as he pushed her away to look at her. Crooking his index finger beneath her chin, he said gently, "When your knees hurt, darling, and you get bunions, quit dancing, and I'll make one hell of an actress out of you!" He slipped an arm around her waist and led her off-camera. Several male voices up in the grid called, "Bravo, kid! Bravo!"

It took Leya a full minute to come out of it. She knew she had been tricked. She realized that if she hadn't been, she would have been frightened, self-conscious, and stiff as a broom handle. Even so, she couldn't rid herself of the resentment.

Mitchell Leisen understood. Holding her affectionately, he said, "If you haven't seen *I Wanted Wings,* Leya, get Ed to take you. I want you to watch Veronica Lake in the final scene where she finds that she's trapped in the plane." He laughed. "Compared to what I put Veronica through to get her to cry, you and I have just played patty cake!"

CHAPTER 29

At the Hollywood Brown Derby, where they dined after the test, Kent voiced few misgivings. "I know we danced well," he said. "But the important thing is, Mr. Leisen took time to do that sneaky bit at the end." He laughed as Leya closed her eyes and clasped her head in embarrassment.

"You were beautiful, dear!" Kent continued. "The fire in your eyes nearly scorched his jacket. Ed said you were sensational. He's never used that word before, have you, Ed?"

The personal manager smiled. "Not in precisely that context—lately. Anyway, conjecture is useless. We'll know in a day or two. The film goes into the lab tonight. They should have an answer print in the morning."

At the hotel, they found a message asking them to meet Eleanor Broder at the reception office at 8:30 A.M. for the screening.

Leya excused herself and went to her room. Matt and Kent, keyed up, went to the bar. Ed Matson made a call to an erstwhile actress whose off-screen talent had been recommended by Howard Pryor.

The following morning, when Eleanor Broder took them to the screening room, Mitchell Leisen, Leo Tover, and several other men were already there.

The director greeted them warmly. "Sit here," he said,

indicating the vacant rows of upholstered seats reserved for stars and studio executives.

"My God, look at that!" Kent breathed, clutching Leya's arm as the wide shot of the *Zanzibar* set came on the screen. Then, as the camera dollied in to a medium shot, they saw themselves as they made their entrances. Behind them they were aware of voices making comments, but the sound level was running so high that they could not hear. Several times, in passages that were rough from lack of practice, each of them fidgeted and groaned. Once, when a lift had seemed a trifle labored, Kent audibly called himself a "*klutz!*" For the most part, however, they watched with a curious detachment. After the early minutes of novelty, three dancers were performing on the screen, and they were watching each variation with critical objectivity.

When the last variation ended, and the lights did not go up, Leya stiffened. The wax pencil marks squirmed for a third time, the slate appeared, the clacker snapped traplike, and suddenly, there was her face filling the screen.

"God, girl! Look!" Kent breathed, "You're dreamy!" He reached across Leya to jab Matt. O'Brien nodded without removing his eyes from the screen.

Then they heard Leisen's voice on the soundtrack, smooth and deceptively amiable, coming from off-camera.

Kent slipped his arm under Leya's to clasp her hand. "Look at your eyes!" he whispered. "Absolutely gorgeous!"

As she watched, Leisen's quizzing built ruthlessly. The face on the screen registered surprise, confusion, the edge of terror, and finally blazing anger. The lights went up, and there was dead silence in the screening room.

Leya sat frozen, afraid to move. Then she heard the director's voice close by. She turned to find him standing in the aisle, smiling down at her.

"Well, would you like to know what I think?"

Leya covered her face. "Oh, Lord, I don't know!"

The director laughed sympathetically. "It's not all that bad. You three dance superbly. I've told you that. And you all photograph very well, too. But this is addressed especially to you, Miss Marks." Leisen's eyes twinkled. "Of course you are beautiful. But when you are angry, you are positively ravishing!"

When Leya found herself unable to answer, he turned to the others. "Thank you for coming. The test came off very well, and I intend to say so in the right places."

He turned to Kent. "I want to compliment you on your choreography, Mr. Kendall. If you ever decide you'd like to create some routines for pictures, let me know. I'll be happy to open some doors."

Addressing Ed Matson, he said, "I'm going to talk to the front office about this over lunch. I'll try to call you this afternoon."

On the ride back to the hotel, Ed endured the dancers' overdramatized agony with patience and did his best to answer unanswerable questions. Conjecture, anxiety, and wishful thinking occupied them through an early lunch. As dancers, each of them had tried out for roles in the theater that could mark pivotal points in their careers. He knew that in each of those competitions there was an element of the "what if?" traumatism that afflicts all performers and none more so than the classically trained dancer who knows that in the popular theater perfection of style and technique may count for less than perfection of figure and features.

Matson knew that Leya Marks, angled beside him on the banquette with her favored left leg curled beneath her, had the rare gift of both requisites. If she were a lesser talent, her remarkable physical assets would not suffice in a major ballet company. But Hollywood was not so demanding. What he had just seen in the screening room reaffirmed his conviction that Leya Marks could occupy a conspicuous place in either world—if she wanted to.

Matt O'Brien would do very well, also, once he decided who and what he was. As for Kent Kendall, any disappointment in store for him as a screen performer could be more than offset by new opportunities as a choreographer. His concepts were unique. He demonstrated impeccable taste and imagination in choosing and developing themes. The end results, proved on tour and at the Golden Palm Club, were solidly commercial. With proper management, Kendall could take his place beside Busby Berkeley, Jack Cole, Hermes Pan, and the others.

So, Matson thought with more than a little satisfaction, three strong possibilities out of three is not a bad average—if . . . ! "The hardest work in the world is waiting," Matson said aloud. "Leisen said he would try—repeat, try—to call me this afternoon. But I know studios. We'll wait today, and if we don't hear by tomorrow, we'll take the early plane back Wednesday morning."

"You mean we'd go back without knowing?" Kent asked.

"Yes. It's costing over a hundred dollars a day for us to sit around. Whatever the studio's decision, it can be telephoned to I.A.M. in New York. It may be that Howard has already talked to Leisen. Maizlish was to phone New York right after the screening. Howard can pose questions that I can't very well ask at this point."

He paused to order three beers and an iced tea. "I'll call him at home around our dinner time here."

"Oh, God," Kent murmured. "I much prefer a show situation. At least you know if you're dead or alive in a couple of days."

"Me, too!" Matt seconded with deep conviction.

Leya seemed lost in thought. Ed could guess at her anxiety, but no hint of it was visible. Suddenly, he found himself comparing this girl with the compliant young starlet he had dated the evening before. In return for nebulous promises, she had been more than willing to accommodate an important personal manager and a friend of Mr. Pryor's, in that order.

Hang on, Matson, he said to himself. *There will be at least two times when this girl will need you badly: when you tell her the good news, and if you have to comfort her because the news is disappointing. Patience, man! The little black book—and Sheri, too—will help ease the pain of waiting!*

"In the meantime," Ed said with more enthusiasm than he felt, "Let's drive up to Mount Wilson. Go get some sweaters. It's almost six thousand feet up there. It can get chilly."

At the mountain overlook, the spectacular view of the Los Angeles basin, stretching off to the west to the sun-dappled waters of the Pacific, left them awe-struck. Through the coin telescope, Ed pointed out the Santa Monica Mountains, the beach cities, the Palos Verdes peninsula, the harbor area, the skyscraper apartments dominating the Long Beach skyline, the green checkerboard of orange groves along the San Gabriel Valley, and the clean little foothill towns.

"Very few views on earth can match this," he observed.

"Except the view of lower Manhattan from the top of the Empire State Building," Kent interjected, half in jest.

At nine-thirty, they were back at the hotel. Ed found a message from Mitchell Leisen and a private number where the director could be reached. Pretending that it was personal, he pocketed it without comment. He placed the call in his room. A moment later, the director was on the phone.

"Arthur Hornblow and Frank Freeman screened the test at five-thirty this evening, Ed. We are particularly interested in the Marks girl. They like Kendall and the O'Brien boy, too, but they want to know about draft status. Freeman wants New York to look at the test. You can take the reels back with you. I've left them in your name at the main gate."

Things were happening about as Matson had surmised they might. The news that New York wanted to see the test was encouraging. Final decisions to invest in a name buildup were made there.

"We're going on the early plane tomorrow, Mitch. I'll pick them up at six A.M. and take them personally to the Paramount Building Thursday morning."

"Good. You can drop them off at Paul Raibourn's office, if you will."

"Okay, Mitch, and thanks again for taking a personal interest in the kids."

"The thanks are to you, Ed. The Marks girl is very interesting. Think about finding a better last name for her, though."

Matson laughed. "I'm way ahead of you! I've got one—my own middle name. Leslie. Leya Leslie— How does it sound?"

"Sell it to her," Leisen answered without hesitation. "I'll noise it around here, too. And by the way," he added, "your last name would work very well, too!"

Smiling, Ed replaced the receiver and sat on the edge of the bed. Paramount's New York corporate executives relied less on intuition than on what they considered demonstrable values. Ideally, what Leya needed now was a Manhattan booking to which the Paramount brass could be invited—after I.A.M.'s press department had planted some solid stories in the trade press and in the daily columns. If New York did not entirely trust Hollywood's opinion or, for that matter, its own, he knew from long experience that the balance could be tipped in his favor by a few current hard-hitting press breaks.

He glanced at his watch. Too late to call Pryor in New York. Restless with anticipation, he was tempted to go down to the bar. Instead, he stripped off his clothes, showered, and settled into bed with a copy of Ernest Hemingway's new novel, *For Whom the Bell Tolls.* At the end of the first chapter, he put the novel aside and picked up the current issue of *Life.* A half hour later, he tossed the magazine aside and turned out the lights.

For a time, with the streetcar and automobile traffic on Hollywood Boulevard as underscoring, he thought about Leya Marks. Not Marks— Leslie! Leya Leslie. It was a good name. Easy and memorable. It had a star sound, the sound of a star he had every intention of hitching his wagon to—as her personal manager and as her man.

The return flight was a merciful hour shorter.

Minnie and Harry had been in bed for an hour when Leya called. "I'm here, papa! At LaGuardia Airport. Were you asleep?"

"Who's asleep? When are you coming?"

"Soon, papa. Please don't stay up for me. Get your rest. I'll tell you all about things tomorrow."

"We'll tell you about things, too. Oy! Have we got news for you!"

"What are you talking about, papa?"

"Come home and we'll tell you. What do you want to eat?"

"I've eaten, papa. They served dinner on the airplane."

"Up in the sky they cook?"

"Yes, papa. I'll be there in about forty-five minutes."

Kent and Matt said their good-bys to Leya while Ed Matson made a phone call. Some minutes later, as he carried her bag and his own, Ed was tempted to tell Leya the results of the call to Howard Pryor but decided against it until there was definite news. The head of I.A.M. had talked with both Leisen and Hornblow. They had been encouraging—if New York agreed.

On the plane, sitting beside Leya as she dozed with her pillow wedged between the seat back and the window, he had studied her face. The girl's exquisite beauty stirred emotions not much remembered since his first adolescent loves in high school in Kansas City. What this young dancer had started in him was disturbing and exciting. He wanted to do things for her—and with her—make himself indispensable personally and professionally in such a way that she would learn to depend on him. They would make a good team, Leya Marks and Ed Matson, and each would need the other equally.

"I'll phone you tomorrow," he called through the window as the driver closed the door.

"Let me call you, Ed. I'm beat. I think I'm going to sleep around the clock!"

"Okay, little friend," he agreed. "Call me in the late afternoon at the office."

At the Brownsville flat, Harry came running down, struggling to maneuver the remaining suspender strap over his shoulder. "*Bubeleh!*" he called as he clasped Leya, "we're so glad you're safe!"

Minnie, wrapped in a shapeless cotton robe, stood waiting at the top of the stairs. Her head was sprouting paper curlers. "So," she nodded, "You're famous all over billboards, and now you are having moving picture tests. What is next, please tell us?"

"What is next, darling," Leya said, hugging her, "is a glass of milk and some plain cake—and then about eighteen hours of sleep."

"We'll talk while we eat," Harry said, depositing her bags in the hall as Minnie urged her to a chair in the kitchen.

Leya smiled wearily and caressed them with her eyes. No longer did she feel like an intruder. It was good to be home. So good! An hour ago, she had been looking down on a panorama of jewel-like lights flung in random patterns across miles of a dark unseen surface below. Now, surrounded by all that was familiar, everything that had happened in California seemed unreal. She had dreamed it all!

"There isn't much to tell yet," she began. Then, between bites, she recounted the details of the test and the screening and cautioned them about the hopeful but still uncertain outcome.

"Tomorrow I may know more. Mr. Matson will have heard something by then," she concluded. "But what is this news you've got for me?"

Minnie gave Harry a cautioning look, a clear warning that this was her moment. "You know your friend—Dulcy?"

Minnie's tone sent a stab of anxiety through Leya. "What about her? What happened?"

Minnie folded her arms and smiled smugly. "What's happening hasn't happened yet. But it will. Your friend Dulcy is marrying maybe one hundred million dollars!"

"Dulcy? Marrying Willie Four?"

"William Vandercort, the Fourth," Minnie confirmed. "It was in the paper yesterday."

Leya closed her eyes and recalled what Dulcy had said the last time they were together about being two months overdue. Of course! She should have guessed.

"So?" Minnie said. "It's a surprise?"

"Not entirely," Leya admitted.

"He's going to be very important in Washington," Harry offered. "It also says this in the paper."

"And in another, also," Minnie interjected, "it says they will make their home in Washington."

Harry rubbed his finger along the side of his nose. "So—he's going to help President Roosevelt. It just goes to prove that money doesn't count if you have brains."

Leya slept ten hours and awoke with a start. For a moment she was disoriented. Then she smiled and stretched. Nothing to do! No anxiety about a performance! She thought about Mitchell Leisen and laughed at her embarrassment when she discovered that, like Veronica Lake, she had been tricked into giving an impromptu emotional display. She liked the director. Perhaps someday she would get to work in one of his pictures. If that happened, she would give him the best performance in her.

For a time, Leya allowed herself to daydream. In the midst of the leisurely flow of thoughts, she remembered Dulcy. Fastening her robe, she went to the telephone.

"Oh, dear heart!" Dulcy shrieked. "Am I glad to hear from you! Did you hear the news?"

"It was the first thing papa and Minnie told me last night when I got in. Tell me everything."

"Oh, not on the phone," Dulcy wailed. "Come on over. I'll tell you the whole crazy story. Then you can tell me what happened out in movieland, okay?"

At a quarter to twelve, Dulcy opened the door and caught Leya in an enormous waltzing hug.

"God, I'm glad to see you! When the whole thing happened, I was dying to call you on the coast, but those bastards at I.A.M. wouldn't tell me where you were staying. I called your father, too, and he wasn't even sure about the studio."

She pushed Leya away and gave her an eager inspection. "What do you want to eat?"

"Anything. I just had coffee. What about eggs and toast?"

"Coming right up! Come on over here so we can yak."

Dulcy paused long enough to put the things she needed on the sink top, then turned to Leya. "I told you I thought I was late, didn't I?"

"Yes."

"Well, sweetie, when I went to my GYN, it turned out that I was later than the Late George Apley. Apparently, I had started making little Vandercorts weeks earlier."

She broke four eggs in a mixing bowl and beat them with a fork. "So—it's nervous decision time. I know a fine, upstanding M.D. on Gun Hill Road in the Bronx who will reduce the population for two hundred bucks. But I also know that sulfa pills won't always stop septicemia." Dulcy paused. "More than that, and this may gas you, I really want Willie's baby."

She cocked her head quizzically. "So, suddenly the vision of me being noble and dying screaming in Bellevue to protect the good name of Vandercort seemed sort of idiotic."

Dulcy poured the batter into the pan.

"What about Willie?" Leya asked. "What did he do?"

Dulcy grinned. "I called him in Washington and asked him when he was due in again. He came up for the weekend—all ready Eddy. You see, in Willie's inventive mind, my call meant that I had an insatiable need for his beautiful body."

Leya closed her eyes and expelled a long "Oh, no."

"Oh, yes, dear heart," Dulcy said, tending the eggs with a spatula. "He came bounding in with that little trinket." She pointed to a large cloisonné box. "A mere four hundred years old! I'm afraid I wasn't very subtle. I said, 'Speaking of boxes, darling, it seems we're in one.' "

"Oh, my God," Leya moaned. "What did he say?"

"Well, sweetie, Willie's not very good at puzzles, so I had to spell it out for him. Then, for about twenty minutes, our Willie Four didn't say a damned thing. You see, he was busy growing up." Dulcy divided the scrambled eggs and reached for the plates.

"After a while, he quit staring out the window and came over to me. Then he sort of laughed and said, 'I thought we were taking care of things.' I said that I thought so, too, but that there are times when it's human to err. But do you know what my four-square little darling did? He put his arms around me and said, 'I guess there's no use putting things off, is there?' Then he held me as gently as a child. I was so shocked that I'm a son of a bitch if I didn't start to blubber!"

Seated at the table with Leya, Dulcy recounted the rest of the events. "We're going down to Elkton, Maryland, Sunday night. They don't make you wait there. Willie's got a line on a justice of the peace. And, by the way, have you ever been a maid of honor?"

"Only when Papa and Minnie got married. Why?"

"Well, you're going to be one again, dear heart—mine. And guess who's going to be Willie's best man?"

Willie's choice was obvious.

"But I thought Gardner was on his ship again," Leya said, experiencing a twinge of pleasant anticipation.

"Not yet. The *Kearney*'s been delayed in the Boston Navy Yard. So, Madame Butterfly and Lieutenant Pinkerton are going to attend us, and if you say no, I'll cut you off without a million!"

She reached over to take Leya's hand. "Seriously, sweetie, tell me you will. There's nobody else I want beside me."

For an instant, Leya hesitated. Sunday was only two days away. "Of course I'll be with you," she said. "I'd love to!"

"Willie would like that very much, too. And do I have to tell you that Gardner will be in seventh heaven just to see you again?" She squeezed Leya's hand. "Be nice to him, dear heart. My god, how he's suffered! He's done everything but put his epaulets on a hair shirt!"

Ed Matson hung up his office telephone and tipped back in the chair. For a time he sat with lips pursed, considering and discarding possibilities of finding Leya and the group a suitable local showcase to which the Paramount New York brass could be invited. Howard Pryor had seemed annoyed by his pressing. He agreed that a decision about Leya could probably be expedited if the Paramount men could meet her and see her work in person, but neither he nor any of the I.A.M. organization could turn up a practical New York City date.

As he was about to reach for the phone again to leave word for Leya to call, a name scribbled on a memo pad caught his eye. A young personal manager, Billy Brenner, had phoned earlier, ostensibly to find out how Leya's screen test had gone. Brenner was young, personable, and quietly aggressive. He had signed Celine Cervier and placed her in the new Jack Beckman revue, *Riddle Me This,* after the blond ballerina had attracted national attention with Leya as a Revel girl. Beckman had produced a ten-minute modern "pop" ballet routine around her, using two male dancers. The overall reviews of the show had been good. Of the individual acts singled out, Cervier's reviews were favorable but far from the "raves" Leya had received.

Suddenly, Matson sat bolt upright. "Son of a bitch!" he said half aloud, "I must be slipping to have missed *that* possibility!"

Minutes later, Howard Pryor was listening with a bemused smile as Matson outlined a plan to secure a screen test for Celine Cervier as soon as possible and to use her absence as an excuse to offer Beckman the Kendall Dance Group as a temporary substitute. It could be the perfect showcase, one that would also attract wide press attention.

"Tell me, Howard," Matson continued, "is there any reason why your Hollywood office couldn't arrange it?" He paused. "I mean a screen test, in quotes, if necessary—and soon?"

He heard Pryor laugh. "You know, don't you, Ed, that you're an evil genius? Why don't you come to work for I.A.M.?"

Matson pretended surprise. "I thought I was! Well, what do you say?"

"I'd say it probably can be arranged—while my conscience is out to lunch."

"What studio?"

"M-G-M. I'll call Eddie Mannix. He owes me, and they're always looking for new girls for L. B.'s stable. By the way, who handles Cervier?"

"Billy Brenner. She doesn't have an agent. She's been with Powers for a while."

"She should have an agency."

"Could I.A.M. fit her in?"

"If we can help her—yes."

"When will you get back to me?"

"It's four o'clock now, one o'clock on the coast. I'll try to get through at two their time. If I can't reach you, call me back later."

Matson held the cutoff down and buzzed his secretary. "See if you can get me Billy Brenner, please."

While he waited, Matson thought about time. It was pretty tight—if things were to be arranged ideally. Assuming that a test for Cervier could be set up and assuming that she was interested, Leya would have to be sold to Jack Beckman. The producer was new to Broadway, but he was smart. And he had a hit. Pressure could be applied through allusions to big I.A.M. names for his next show. No problem there. Allusions are not commitments. Then Beckman would have to be talked into substituting Kent's proven challenge routine until Celine returned. It all "logicked" very well, he thought as the buzzer sounded, except that "assume" was probably the most dangerous word in the English language.

"I have Mr. Brenner for you, Mr. Matson," the secretary said.

Ed pressed the line key. "Billy?" He hoped familiarity would flatter the young manager.

"Yes, Mr. Matson. Thank you for calling back. How are you?"

"Great. And you?"

"Fine. I'm not close to winning the personal manager of the year award yet, but I'm in there pitching."

"You sure are, Billy. I understand your Cervier girl is attracting a lot of attention."

Brenner managed a rueful laugh. "Some of it we could have done without like Richard Watts's review! But it's shaping up. Audiences like her. Especially women, because of the Revel campaign."

"I don't doubt that," Matson observed with conviction. "What can I do for you, Billy?"

"Well—" Brenner laughed nervously. "It's probably none of my damned business, but I've been wondering what happened to Leya Marks's tests?"

"Everything went fine for all three kids. We should hear any day now, Billy. Why? Is Celine interested in pictures, too?"

"Not as much as I am, probably. But I think she has possibilities not only as a dancer but as an actress."

"I don't doubt that," Matson agreed. "Do you have any contacts at studios?"

"No top-level ones."

"Could I make a suggestion?"

"You sure can, Mr. Matson. I'll be very grateful."

"I'm happy to do what I can, Billy. I hear that M-G-M is interested in new female faces. Why don't you call Howard Pryor and see if he can open some doors? I'll call him, too, to make sure you get through. And let me know if there's any other way that I can be useful. I know that Leya will be very excited about such a possibility for Celine."

"Thank you, Mr. Matson. We really appreciate your interest."

They talked briefly about the revue; then Ed hung up. He was pleased with himself. Now, in all honesty, he could tell Leya that definite moves were afoot to expedite a favorable reaction at the Paramount Building.

The wedding service, generally short-formed, often recited from a faulty memory, was painstakingly read while Dulcy beamed and William Vandercort, IV, feeling a strange tightness in the chest, tried not to fidget. A half step behind him, Gardner Sutton, still in winter uniform, stood like a pillar of dependability, stealing sidelong glances at Leya.

Her radiant beauty beneath the gossamer strawberry mousse of a hat that Dulcy insisted on buying to go with her pink spring suit unsettled his insides as much as the recollection of his libidinous blunder aboard the *Jezebel.* He had driven Willie down the day before to make arrangements for a wedding brunch at the hotel. The newlyweds would go on to Washington by train. He would drive Leya back to Manhattan, where she had agreed to stay in Dulcy's apartment until the Vandercorts' plans were sorted out.

Gardner and Leya saw Willie and Dulcy onto the three o'clock train to Washington and stood waving until the parlour car was out of view.

"Do you want a tea break now, Leya?" Gardner asked. "Or would you like to stop along the way?"

"Let's get back, Gardner. I still haven't recovered from the Hollywood trip."

Gardner regretted that time did not allow them to drive down to Anapolis, then across the eastern shore, to return by way of Chesapeake City and on up to Wilmington. On his next leave, he would propose that, with all of the reassurances and safeguards that he felt would be required.

When Leya asked about the war and the Nazi U-boats that were taking such a toll of supplies and life, he described duty on the Iceland runs. Though he made no attempt to dramatize the experience, he felt her shiver beside him when he told how the U-boat wolf packs stalked and killed. When his assessment of Britain's poor chances to hold out without direct armed intervention from the United States alarmed her, he deliberately tried to put an optimistic face on the long-term prospects. Leya, remembering the Lowensteins and the other victims of Nazi brutality, asked how much truth he felt there was in the stories of atrocities coming out of Europe. Gardner shrugged. "It's so hard to tell. Propaganda is a weapon, like ordnance, and sometimes it's more effective."

When they approached the Holland Tunnel, Gardner glanced at her. "Shall we find a restaurant now, or do you want to go to the apartment first?"

"What time is it?"

He glanced at his wristwatch. "Ten after eight."

"Why don't we eat first? I can put up my loose ends in the powder room while you're having your drink."

They dined on East Fifty-third Street at Louise Junior's restaurant. During dinner, Gardner questioned Leya about Hollywood. The good red Bolla relaxed her, and she recounted most of the experiences, but she refused to speculate on the outcome of the tests.

"I have no way of knowing, Gardner. I talked to Ed Matson Friday afternoon. He said some encouraging things—but then he's my manager, so I suspect him."

"How do you feel about giving up the ballet for a career in Hollywood?"

Leya toyed with the stem of the wine glass. "Well, for starters, I don't like the place. Under any other circumstances, I wouldn't even consider going out there, just to 'be in pictures.' On the other hand, with serious ballet having such a rough time right now, I would give it a try if I thought I had a chance to be a dancing star—without having to become a hoofer to make it. I agreed with Ed. It seems the sensible thing to do."

"What happens if the studio has second thoughts, and the decision is negative?"

Leya frowned. "Who knows? I'm a professional dancer. I suppose I would look for work in my profession—in musicals, perhaps in one of the Balanchine shows—if my knee can still take the amount of work necessary for classical ballet."

"What about modeling?"

"That is strictly a bread-and-butter job, Gardner."

"I suspected as much. But haven't those Revel billboards made you a star of sorts in that game?"

Leya made a deprecating gesture. "They helped get the Hollywood test. And they helped Celine get into *Riddle Me This*. By the way, have you seen it?"

"No. My family has. They say it's very funny. It has some marvelous pokes at Hitler and Mussolini."

"It's very smart," Leya agreed. "Celine's going to get a long run out of it."

Gardner gave her a pixie grin. "Is your friend as talented and as lovely as you are?"

"She's a very talented dancer," Leya hedged. "About the other, you've seen her billboards. What do you think?"

"I don't think any female in this world is as lovely as you are," he said.

The personal turn made Leya wary. Seeing Gardner again, being with him, produced a confusion of feeling. She did not deny that she had been attracted to him and still was, more than ever. That day aboard the *Jezebel* had come to seem unreal, something that had happened with an anguished boy, not with this handsome, self-assured officer beside her. Leya wondered what it would be like to be in Gardner's arms again. In the next instant, she drove the thought from her mind, troubled by the realization that quite probably she would not resist.

"When do you have to be back on your ship?" she asked.

"I'm due at the Boston Navy Yard at noon tomorrow."

"Then do you go out again?"

"Yes, if they've finished modifying her. All of us on old Four Thirty-two will feel a lot better with some new antiaircraft guns aboard, particularly if we start escorting merchantmen farther north and east. Those Nazi bombers are reaching way out now since they've got bases in Norway."

Leya looked at Gardner Sutton with wonderment. "Aren't you frightened out there?"

"I'll answer your question with another question," he said, turning toward her on the banquette. "Aren't you frightened just before you go out on stage?"

"I'm nervous—until I start dancing. Yes."

"Well, that's how I feel. I'm nervous until the action starts. Then there isn't time to be. Thank God!"

"Don't you ever worry about being hit?"

"Yes and no. Most of us feel it always happens to the other guy."

They lingered another half hour over dessert, and Leya admitted to herself that she was enjoying Gardner's company. Later, they found a parking place on East Forty-seventh Street close to Dulcy's apartment, and Gardner looked at her almost timidly.

"May I see you up to the door?"

Leya smiled at him. "Of course."

At the door, he took her key and let her in. She turned. "It's late and I'm tired, so I'm not going to ask you in for a drink. But I do want to thank you for driving me back this evening—and for dinner." She paused and looked down. "And I want to tell you that I'd like to be friends and that anything that happened—" She looked up, smiling. "—or didn't happen—is forgotten as far as I'm concerned." She held out a hand, and he caught it in both of his. "I want you to be safe, Gardner. And when you come back on leave, if I'm still in New York, please call me if you'd like to."

His hands tightened around hers. "If I'd like to?" He paused and looked into her eyes. "Miss Marks, darling, you'll never know how much I'd like to!"

Leya moved closer and raised her lips to be kissed.

"Good night, Gardner," she said in a half whisper, "and thank you for everything."

Gardner Sutton kissed her tenderly on the mouth, hesitated for an instant, then wheeled and closed the door behind him.

CHAPTER 30

Ed Matson stopped pacing and propped himself against the edge of his desk.

"It's the best possible showcase for you as far as Paramount's New York brass is concerned. The timing of Celine's screen test is perfect."

"I know all that," Leya replied. "I'm just thinking about her understudy. She's been praying for a chance to go on."

"Forget her!" He lifted a hand. "I don't mean that literally. One of the things I love about you is your unselfishness. But if Celine's test turns out, her understudy will get her chance sooner than she expects." He resumed pacing.

"Take it, little friend. When breaks like this come along, it's a crime not to make the most of them!" Ed stopped in front of her. "Bet I know what you're thinking."

Leya averted her eyes. "Ed, what happens to Celine if the test doesn't turn out, and Jack Beckman decides he wants a stronger spot in the show after seeing us?"

"If that happens, Celine will get up in your role, and we'll talk Beckman into putting Kent and Matt with her in the challenge. It's a simple solution. She doesn't have your fire or your talent for jazz, but she'll come off very well with a few changes in the routine."

When Leya did not respond, he added, "I'm being selfish, too. If that happens, it means I have a great Broadway showcase for Kent and Matt."

Leya sensed that there was more to this unexpected break than she was being told. "All right, Ed. If you can convince Mr. Beckman to make the substitution, go ahead. Have you talked with Kent and Matt?"

"Yes. They're out at Fire Island. They're very excited."

"What if Matt gets drafted?" Leya asked.

"Kent will have to find himself another—" He hesitated. "—another dancer with Matt's all-around qualifications."

"All right, Ed. Let me know so I can make plans. Jon Wales has some work for me if I can fit it in. So does Powers."

Matson frowned. "Do you need the money?"

"I can use some, but it's not urgent."

"Then hold off. I don't want it noised around that you're working again unless its another prestige job like Revel."

When Leya called the Powers Agency to say she would not be available for a while, she was given a message from Myra Lieberman. "She's very anxious to talk to you, Miss Marks," the appointments girl said.

Leya thanked the girl and dialed the Liebermans' Manhattan number. A maid answered, and in seconds Myra picked up an extension.

"Leya, darling! Martin and I just returned from Canada and found out that you're just back, too! We hear that interesting things are happening for you. How are you?"

"I'm fine, Myra, thank you. There's the promise of exciting things if everything works out."

"I want to hear all about it, and I hope you have some free time. I have some things to tell you, too." She paused, then continued in a less confident tone. "Martin says I'm being presumptuous, and perhaps I am. But I finally said, 'To hell with that!'—so I'm calling to ask you to lunch with me tomorrow. Please say you can!"

A nameless anxiety filled Leya. What "things" would Myra be so anxious to share? Of course, it would be something about Arthur. Bad news, perhaps? But if it were that, certainly she would have just called and been done with it.

Leya glanced at her appointment calendar. "I'm free, Myra."

"Oh, good! Let's make it one o'clock, then, at Le Pavillon—one eleven East Fifty-seventh."

For an hour after the call, Leya tried to fathom the purpose of the lunch. She ruled out the possibility that Arthur had asked his mother to become a peacemaker. That was a job he would insist on doing himself if he had finally decided to relent.

In the midst of her wondering, Gardner Sutton called from Boston. At the sound of his voice, Leya's insides knotted. Why did Myra have to call and stir up all of that old pain again?

"We'll be shoving off for Newfoundland soon," Gardner said. "I just wanted to tell you that nobody in the entire United States Navy is going to sea with better morale, thanks to the most beautiful and compassionate young lady in the world. I'll call you when I get back, and I promise on a stack of Blue Jacket's Manuals to conduct myself in an exemplary manner."

"When will you be back?" Leya asked.

"In about three months—some time in September. How will I know where to reach you?"

"Powers will know. Call them—or International Artists Management. And please, Gardner, be safe."

"Forgive me, Leya, but I promise no chilling news from Iceland. Good-by, darling."

For a time after Gardner's call, Leya wandered around the apartment feeling confused and alone. She would rather have been with her father and Minnie, but for the time being, it was more convenient to be in Manhattan. A quick inspection of the refrigerator showed little but eggs and bread and butter. Leya wrinkled her nose. "More damned eggs!" she said aloud. Suddenly, she laughed. It was the first time she had consciously used the word "damn." It amused her that in Dulcy's apartment she was beginning to sound like her friend.

* * *

Myra Lieberman, chic and trim, was waiting when Leya entered Le Pavillon. Her face lit up, and without a trace of self-consciousness she embraced Leya, then stepped back to admire her.

"What a marvelous change, Leya. I don't know how you could possibly grow more beautiful, but you have!" She nodded to the maître d'hôtel. "Come on, I've got a thousand things to tell you. First of all, Martin sends his love."

It was odd, Leya thought, as she followed Myra into the dining room, that somehow she resented being bound emotionally without ceremony. "Martin sends his love!" It was as though the sending of love placed her under subtle obligation.

At the table, Myra ordered an Amontillado sherry. Leya refused an aperitif.

"I'm so happy we could get together, dear," Myra said. "Do you realize that it's been six months since I have seen you?"

"Yes, I do," Leya replied, deliberately letting the older woman place on it any construction she wished.

"If that means you've missed us a bit, Leya, just let me tell you that we have missed you a great deal. Even Shelly has said a dozen times that she wished you could come see us."

No mention of Arthur! Leya tried to fathom Myra's motive.

After they ordered, Myra rested a hand on Leya's arm. "Jon Wales, that utterly dependable source of divine photographs and devilish gossip," she said, "told Martin that you had simply bowled them over at Paramount and that you were going to sign a long-term contract."

Leya was amused. "If that's true, Jon knows some things that my personal manager and my agent don't know, at least not as of this morning."

"Do you think you will go West, dear, assuming the studio plans important things for you?"

"I'll make that decision when I hear what my guiding lights have to say," Leya replied.

"If you've talked to Jon Wales, then I presume you know that Arthur threw himself into the task of getting our people out of Germany and finally, in frustration, ended up joining the Royal Canadian Air Force?"

Leya nodded. "I don't know the details, but I had heard."

Myra lowered her head. "We're proud of him, Leya, and frightened. We think he acted hastily."

Leya braced herself for an accusation, but it did not come.

"We knew that Arthur would get into some sort of direct action. Martin is certain that our company will be called a critical industry and that Arthur would not have to go into service. But Arthur rejected the notion—absolutely." She gestured helplessly. "What does a mother say? If it were only a stupid political war . . ." Myra knew that it was not necessary to recite the other considerations that would make an able-bodied young Jew want to strike back.

"We did everything we could to deter him, but he wouldn't listen. He's training in Ontario now to be a bomber pilot. I don't know precisely how to say this, darling—" She searched Leya's eyes. "Martin and I saw Arthur over the weekend in Toronto. He asked about you. We told him the little we knew—" The older woman broke off, obviously bolstering her courage. "Surely, Leya, it is no secret that Martin and I love you. So—however futile it may sound, let me illuminate the obvious and say that Arthur's feelings have not changed one iota, either. What has changed—had changed weeks ago—was Arthur's attitude toward your career. The last thing he said when we left him—really just hours ago—was, 'Please tell Leya that I'm trying very hard to get over being a bullheaded idealist.' " Myra smiled sadly. "There's a fine irony in that, darling! It is his idealism that is making him risk his life to fight Hitler."

When Leya betrayed no visible reaction, Myra took a sip of coffee to mask her uneasiness. She wanted to reach over and shake the girl and say, "Why don't you say something? Or don't you give a damn anymore?" Instead, she turned an inquiring gaze on Leya.

"I would understand completely, dear, if you are not

appreciating being burdened with this, but I wanted to tell you for Arthur's sake, in the hope that it would bring some understanding to my son's behavior."

Leya lowered her head. Her throat ached, and it took a moment before she dared to trust her voice.

"Will he come home before he has to go?"

"He will have a week after he graduates and gets his wings as a bomber pilot. I think that will be around the first of July." Myra's eyes were suddenly pain-filled. "Oh, Leya, I hope you will be here then. Arthur is so much in love with you, darling. Even if you two had not—" The words were difficult. "If you two had gone on as you were before, Arthur would have still insisted on going—perhaps a little later—but he would have gone. What he heard from the Lowensteins and the others affected him profoundly. 'We can't turn our backs just because we are a few, chosen by fate, to be safe. All the more reason,' he said, 'that we do all we can!' "

Abandoning any further attempt at restraint, Myra took both of Leya's hands. "Please try to understand my son! By the time he had got his thinking in order, you were gone, and he had to go to Montreal on that refugee business. You were still on the road when he got back, and he had to turn around and go back to Canada just before you returned and went to the coast. It was tragic timing all around! He wanted to tell you that nothing had really changed, that he was not shocked by that nonsense at the Romano party. They are just dirty little children at play! But we know those people, Leya—their other side. We are forced to deal with them in our business. If we don't, our trucks don't roll, or our merchandise is lost or damaged in warehouses—all sorts of dreadful things happen. Most people don't believe it, but once they have a hold on you, there is simply no getting away!"

She looked at Leya intently. "You know that I'm not exaggerating, don't you?"

"I know it's the truth," Leya said. "My father had dealings with them, too, when I was a baby."

Myra nodded. "We know that, Leya. It was one of the things that worried Arthur so dreadfully. He did not know the details, and you didn't want to tell him."

"But it was years ago," Leya protested.

Myra Lieberman's smile was knowing. "That makes little difference. They have memories like elephants and tentacles like giant octopi!" She leaned forward earnestly. "Leya, you must believe that Arthur was not jealous of a man like Carlo. Only afraid for you. He did not want you exposed to the pressure such a man can exert. Arthur knows now that he was wrong in asking you to break your contract, that you could not have done it without damaging many others. When Martin and I first heard, we were more than willing to do anything here to further your career. We would have backed the Jack Beckman revue, with the proviso that you and the others were starred. But Arthur told his father he didn't think you would want that. Was that true?"

"No," Leya said simply. "We would have loved that after we finished our obligation at the Golden Palm. None of us liked the clubs. But when Arthur demanded that I walk out—" She touched her left knee. "—on the pretext that my injury was troubling, I simply couldn't do that to Kent and the others."

Myra nodded. "I know. My God, how Arthur regretted that bit of stupidity! It was the first time since his coming of age that he did not think straight!"

Myra fell silent then, suffering again the pain of those earlier misgivings. After a moment, she looked up.

"You loved Arthur, didn't you, dear?"

"Yes," Leya replied. "Very much."

"And you still do—?"

"I loved him very much," she repeated in a low voice. "But so much has happened, Myra, so much. Suddenly, Arthur was a stranger—" She turned, appealing for understanding. "I honestly don't know how I feel anymore, Myra. Can you understand that?"

"I can. Yes," the older woman answered reluctantly.

"Please try, Myra. Nobody could ever take Arthur's place—but don't ask me to make a commitment. Not now, please."

"I understand," Myra said. There was another brief silence. "Tell me, Leya, if it were possible, would you see him again and let him speak for himself?"

"Of course I would!"

Vast relief settled over Myra Lieberman. She had been right about the lunch. Martin had insisted that beneath the gentle exterior the girl was an artist with a will as tough as steel. A will, yes. But her heart was made of more malleable stuff!

"I know Arthur will want to write to you, Leya. Where should he address a letter?"

"At my father's new place." She gave Myra Minnie's address and explained, "I'm sort of apartment sitting now—for a friend who got married."

Myra smiled knowingly. "I can guess! The papers were full of that wedding! It was quite a fashionable elopement. And you were the maid of honor." With studied innocence, she added, "Some people got the impression from Earl Wilson's column that there were two romances represented there! It must have been very exciting!"

Leya ignored Myra's oblique probe about Gardner. "I was pleased to be asked."

When they parted, Myra was forced to admit that she could not find much more to cling to than a tenuous thread of hope that time would heal the wounds her son and Leya had inflicted on each other through their righteous stubbornness. Later that night, as Martin held her, Myra could no longer resist crying over the "might-have-beens."

Shortly before noon the next day, Leya met Celine, who had proposed an impromptu luncheon at the Stage Delicatessen. Celine was apologetic. "I hope you don't mind such a chic joint! I have to go over to the rehearsal hall and work some bugs out of the routine with the kids, so I can't linger."

The girls settled at a minuscule table in the far corner.

"I'm so happy we could get together," Leya said after they had ordered. "I think it's very exciting that M-G-M is going to test you. Imagine! Tests for both of us! And just weeks apart." She shivered in anticipation. "I wonder what old Madame Baronova will say when she hears."

Celine glared down her nose. "What do you expect, child?" she demanded in a credible Russian accent. "Those young ladies are my *protégées, C'est vrai, elles sont mes enfants!* Everything they are, they owe to me—Madame Alexandra Sonovavitch Baronova!"

The two dancers giggled. "Poor old madame," Leya said. "She means well, and she's still the best in the profession."

"Mikail Khazar says so, too," Celine confirmed. "Isn't it lucky I didn't sign with him? I would have wasted all that time before we found out that his backers couldn't send money over here. I can thank Billy for warning me about that."

Leya looked wistful. "I still think it would be the most exciting thing in the world to be an honest-to-God prima ballerina in an international company, like a Danilova or a Markova."

Celine frowned. "Do you still feel that way after the screen test and all? You sound more like me than I do!"

Leya inclined her head. "I always see myself like that."

"I know," Celine said. "Me, too. But with the show and—well, some other things in the offing—I'm not so sure now." She leaned forward eagerly. "Anyway, please tell me what to expect. Already I'm scared pea green!"

After fifteen minutes of listening, Celine felt a bit reassured. "Do you think I should sign with I.A.M.?"

"What does Billy say?"

"He says if I sign now, I may get lost. If the test turns out well, then they'll be interested and push me, like they're doing for you."

"He's probably right," Leya agreed. She felt like a veteran now, filled again with the confidence she had enjoyed when the kids in the home crowded around after her first successful solo. "Just remember, if you do a good test, the whole thing is sort of automatic. After all, the studio people must have been watching if they asked you to come out. *Riddle Me This* has done for you what the Florida date did for us—plus our Revel ad, of course. It works that way. Ed says they never set up a test unless the artist has a real chance."

"Keep talking, chérie!" Celine rolled her eyes comically. "Ooo-la-la! I'm getting all the breaks! A screen test, my best friend's taking over for me in the show while I'm gone—" She gave Leya's hand an impulsive squeeze. "Who knows? Maybe one day we'll all be in the same picture!"

That night Leya watched the revue from house seats with Ed Matson, Kent Kendall, Matt O'Brien, and Jack Beckman. The following day they would rehearse with the company, and the following night they would appear in Celine's place.

Leya agreed that the show deserved its good reviews. The bright young players missed nothing newsworthy in their clever satirical sketches and songs. Because the material changed with the headlines, many in the audience were attending for the third and fourth time.

Celine's spot was a ballet fantasy. Beginning as a preteen student in pigtails, taking a few tentative steps on demi-point, she progressed through a series of underdressed quick changes made behind free-standing scenery, decorated with time-transition symbols. At the end of the routine, Celine had gone from awkward tyro to ballet star to demanding arthritic ballet mistress, all danced to the accompaniment of a medley that moved from "Glow Worm" through "Sugar Plum Fairy" to Debussy, Stravinsky, a contrapuntal Bartok fragment, choreographed spastically, then back to an amusing bop version of "Glow Worm" in counterpoint to a paraphrase of "The Volga Boatman" theme. Leya was amazed at Celine's subtle humor. She turned to Jack Beckman.

"I had no idea she was that good."

"She's great," the producer agreed. "Did you see the way she mugged? She may turn out to be as good an actress as dancer."

Ed Matson nodded. "Cervier's great, Jack. She may have a real chance in pictures. Do you have her for the run of the play?"

"Yes," the producer answered. "And now I wish I had her under personal contract, too!"

Ed gave the producer a conspiratorial smile. "Work out a partnership with Brenner."

Sitting between the men, listening to the exchange, Leya found herself growing uneasy. Ed's machinations with I.A.M. to secure the Florida dates and her own screen test were evidence enough that a young artist can be a pawn in a three-handed power game played by talent agents, personal managers, and producers.

When Ed dropped her off at the apartment well after midnight, a special-delivery letter from Dulcy was waiting. They had found a house in Silver Spring, Maryland. Willie had been in touch with his father several times, and it was clear that the family was not overjoyed at the new addition and probably did not yet know that the new additions would number two shortly after the first of the year. "I want to keep the apartment," Dulcy had written. "Both Willie and I feel we want a little retreat of our own—just in case the family burns the welcome mat. But it's yours, dear heart, for at least six months.

"What can I tell you about life with Willie? Almost every night we have cocktails or dinner with State Department characters. If you could see the government bigwigs leering into the decolleté gowns, it would make you wonder! So far, I'm very popular—with the men—the new girl in the house. But I must tell you that the Vandercort name is a great advantage. I am respected because I wear it, envied because I managed to get it, and safe because nobody screws around with the Vandercort women—unless, of course, the Vandercort women let it be known that they don't mind.

"If you go back to the coast—and I pray you do because that means the break you deserve—just lock up the apartment and let us know where you can be reached. I miss you, dear heart. Any word from either of your two devoted slaves? Don't hold out on me!"

Dulcy signed the note, "Mrs. William Granville Vandercort, IV," and added, "(I couldn't resist!)." At the bottom of the page was the Maryland address and the private telephone number, together with Willie's number at the State Department.

The rehearsal at the theater the next morning went very well. As the challenge routine reached its climax, the cast members, watching from out front, burst into applause.

Later, at the soda fountain, Ed said, "Those kids were not just being polite. Neither was Jack Beckman. I could see his brain working. He's trying to figure how to shorten the other material so he can keep both dance numbers in the show."

Kent frowned. "Is there a chance—if the Paramount thing doesn't happen?"

"Yes. Beckman could move Cervier's number up earlier and put you kids next to closing. Actually, it would help."

Neither Kent nor Matt was as certain. "With so much of the special-material songs being staged—maybe not really choreographed but staged—wouldn't that make the revue too heavy with dance?" Matt asked.

"A dancer asking if a show is too heavy with dance?" Matson laughed. "You just worry about your spot. The main thing now is for you to knock over the Paramount brass tonight. I'm taking them to dinner before the show, and I'll bring them backstage afterwards."

When he returned to his office to clean up the late calls, Ed found a message from Johnny Coyle. The publicist, who had worked in Miami during the winter season, had come north to work with Sokol, Pyne, and Dahl on summer-theater promotions and on several of the Broadway shows that braved the hot weather. Unable to afford the new air conditioning, the Alpin Theater, which housed *Riddle Me This,* had installed a primitive system utilizing ducted fans and five-hundred-pound cakes of ice housed in an insulated structure on the roof. It kept the audiences reasonably comfortable, but on hot nights the cast still sweltered backstage.

When the publicist came on the line, Ed pulled a note pad close. "Who's lined up for tonight, Johnny?"

"Everybody who's anybody in town. I've got all the papers and news magazines—and *Life,* too."

"Great. Can we count on any of them to be especially useful?"

"They'll use all of the acceptable adjectives," Coyle assured him. "Some of my promises to them will be deferred until next winter in Florida, Ed, but have faith. Under Romano's tutelage, I have refined the art of obligation to an exact science!"

* * *

In Leya's dressing room before the show, Kent looked at her closely. "Are you nervous? I am."

"A little," she admitted. "I shouldn't be, though."

"My trouble is the moguls out front. I really dislike this waiting for the gods to speak. Damn them all! I like our concerts better."

Leya smiled at him in the mirror and continued to bead her lashes. "Try not to care too much."

"You care, don't you?"

"Yes. I'd like to find out if I'd be any good in pictures."

Kent laughed. "You amaze me, Leya. In your quiet way, you have as much star drive as Ethel Merman!" Confidentially, he added, "And so does Matt. Does that surprise you?"

"No, not really."

"Well," Kent sighed, "I guess that spells me out in letters a foot high. I have absolutely no ambition to be a movie name at all." He paused, and Leya saw a pensive expression soften his face. He got up and paused with his hand on the doorknob. "I discovered the truth about me when we were on the Coast. I enjoy dancing, and I won't ever quit. But I get my greatest kick out of dreaming up the ideas, then choreographing them." He opened the door. "Be that as it may, dear, let's go out there and win one for the Ripper!"

True to its reputation, Jack Beckman's bright young revue offered continual surprises. The group of satirists who called themselves "The Jaundiced Eye" introduced special material that only one week later would prove to be devastatingly accurate. The sketch was called "Heil, Tovarich!" It depicted Hitler, Goering, and Goebbels sitting in the Kremlin explaining to Stalin that it had been necessary to take him into protective custody to keep the Reds from being infiltrated by the Dies Committee on Un-American Activity.

The sketch, which came a half hour after the intermission, was followed by the Kendall Trio. From the moment Leya and her two partners appeared on stage to begin the challenge number, the audience was theirs.

Ed Matson, sitting with Howard Pryor and their two guests from Paramount, wore a satisfied smile as Leya, dancing difficult, often stately, classical-ballet routines with Kent, changed, seemingly in midstep, to accept the challenge to dance both sensuous modern and hard-driving jazz with Matt. Their performances earned frequent outbursts from the audience. After four curtain calls, the three left the stage to sporadic, diehard applause.

In the wings, soaked and sucking in great breaths, the trio stood in the draft of the fan vent above the lighting board. Jack Beckman pushed through to them.

"Sensational!" he whispered. The electrician and the two stage hands, nearby at the fly rail, grinned and circled their thumbs and forefingers in signs of approval.

Kent expelled a long breath and let his arms dangle. "We did it! Maybe nobody liked us but the public, but we did it!" He breathed heavily for a time, then straightened. "Well, let's get rid of the eau de armpit and polish up our manners. Ed says we're to be displayed at Twenty-One."

CHAPTER 31

Ed Matson's call awakened Leya at nine.

"I'm sorry to get you up in the middle of the night, little friend, but you kids left the party before the morning papers were on the street. Are you curious to know what those dastardly reviewers said?"

Leya's voice was thick with sleep. "I don't know. Am I?"

"You should be! Want me to read them before Howard and I go over to Paramount? We've got a meeting at ten."

"Did anybody not like us?"

"You be the judge, little friend. I'll read you the worst one first."

Some minutes later, after her manager had read the reviews in the *Herald Tribune*, the *Times*, the *Daily Mirror*, the *Daily News*, and the *Brooklyn Eagle*, Leya allowed herself to believe that it had really happened. They had played Broadway, and the critics had echoed the audience's opinion.

"This is called a 'bouquet of raves,' " Ed Matson said when he had finished reading the last one, an extravagantly favorable review that singled out Leya and placed her in Broadway's most rarefied air—"despite the lovely dancer's youth."

Later, as Leya was making coffee and "eggs damnation," as she had come to call them, Kent phoned. Matt was on an extension.

"I was afraid Ed would beat me to it," he said. "I wanted to read them to you first. I would have—at eight o'clock—if I weren't so humane! Anyway, dear little Leya, we, and without one whit of jealousy, I say, 'mostly you,' were a smash! I had a call a few minutes ago from Billy Brenner at the Garden of Allah in Hollywood. Remember the place? The ghost of Valentino stalking around? Brenner wants to know if I'll choreograph a new act for Celine."

"It would be wonderful if you could, Kent," Leya said. "Will you?"

"Certainly—if I'm here to do it. Let's wait and see what happens with the test. Any hunches?"

"No. Ed and Mr. Pryor are over at Paramount now."

"Oh?" Kent paused. "Well, while we're sitting around waiting, the clicking noise you hear coming from Beekman Place will be Matt and me doing our beads!"

Leya had no sooner hung up than Dorothy Simpson called.

"I saw *Riddle Me This* last night, my dear. It was absolutely superb!" She laughed a bit too gaily. "When I think of you as you were when you first started to model for Super Figure, and I see you as you were last night, I simply cannot reconcile the two images! Incredible!"

Leya answered Dorothy's questions about the prospects for pictures objectively, without elaboration.

"Lord, but you are cool, girl!" Simpson exclaimed. "I'd be absolutely up in the clouds!"

"I am excited," Leya admitted, "but I'm trying to keep one foot on the ground."

"And your pretty little level head on your shoulders!" Dorothy added. "Anyway, my dear, you know that Jon and I wish you the very best of luck. We're sharing it all—vicariously!"

Suddenly, it was clear that everything Dorothy Simpson really wanted, she had been forced to experience vicariously. Again Leya found herself feeling sorry for the stylist, and she was stirred by an unexpected wellspring of compassion.

Leya was pouring a second cup of coffee when Ed Matson called back.

"You better have an unlisted phone put in if you want to

receive your good news on time. I hope you're decent because Howard and I are coming over to talk to you—now!"

Ed Matson and Howard Pryor spelled out in detail the understanding with Paramount in New York. In spite of their reassurances, Leya was disappointed. She had hoped for more than a one-picture deal.

It was not the first time these talent men had been forced to cope with the impatience of young ambition. It was aggravating, particularly when they knew that, ability aside, they had overcome tremendous odds to win a good contract for a relatively untried artist.

When Howard rose abruptly, Ed shot him a cautioning look. Turning to Leya, still in her robe and slippers, Pryor said in an even voice, "I want to tell you again that this is not, as you may suspect, 'just another screen test' simply because they are offering you only a one-picture contract. We don't want a standard seven-year contract. That's Wampus Starlet stuff. You'll get lost. We want you to start the way Dottie Lamour did—in a featured role that was such a good showcase she jumped to stardom. In her second picture, *Swing High, Swing Low,* she played second lead to Carole Lombard. The same thing can happen to you. But you've got to take one step at a time."

"What we're betting on, Leya," Ed Matson interjected, "is that you'll no longer be an unknown after your featured spot in *Hollywood Holiday of Nineteen Forty-Two.* You're slated for the two biggest dance numbers in the picture. You *are* the dancer—a principal."

"I'm very happy, really," Leya said, smiling at last. "I just thought we'd be going out for a longer period."

"You'll probably be going out for fifty-two weeks, Leya," Howard said. "If we had any doubt about your option being picked up, we would not have made the deal. By the way," he added, "who is 'we'? Do you mean Kendall and O'Brien?"

"Of course," Leya replied.

Ed sat down beside her. "They're both going out for the challenge spot, little friend," he said, "but they're not under contract for the full term. Just six weeks."

He read both disappointment and anxiety in Leya's eyes. "Now don't get worried. It's quite likely that Matt will stay on if the draft board doesn't get him. And we're working out an agreement for Kent to choreograph a second number for you. So you three will be doing the challenge and then a big number with thirty or forty kids, a sort of Busby Berkeley production thing."

Howard nodded. "It's a perfect showcase for you, Leya. Jay Sanford is producing and Lew Frederix is directing. Kent's going to work with them directly in creating the big finale. It's a great break for him, too."

Leya allowed herself a tingle of excitement. "Will I have to do any acting, too?"

"Yes, you will," Ed replied. "There's a story line running through the musical. It won't win the Pulitzer Prize, but it's commercial."

Leya turned to Ed. "Who are the stars?"

The personal manager laughed. "A couple of new kids. Patti Day and Frankie Naples."

"The band singers?"

"The same. They have a big following because of their records. They'll draw at the box office. They're being booked into the Paramount Theater for a week with the new Gary Cooper picture. Incidentally, little friend, you wouldn't remember this, but Gary Cooper got his break on the Paramount lot just ten years ago in a thing called *Paramount on Parade*. And I seem to remember that he was pretty worried about how long he was going to last, too!"

Howard looked at his watch. "There's just one more thing, then I have to run," he said, walking over to Leya and Ed. "I know Ed goes along with me, Leya, that it would be best if you did not discuss the terms of your agreement with Kent or Matt. If they ask you about it, find a way to avoid telling them without making it obvious."

Ed agreed. "It's important, Leya. Whether or not it makes you uncomfortable, the chief interest at Paramount is in you."

Leya studied each man in turn. "I understand," she replied, "but I think I ought to warn you—I'm a lousy liar."

"That, dear Miss Marks," said Howard Pryor, smiling now, "is why you have us!"

Just before the end of the Kendall Trio's first week of substituting for Celine in *Riddle Me This,* Howard Pryor received a call from Billy Brenner on the Coast. It was obvious that he was unhappy.

"Can I ask you something, Mr. Pryor? When Leya Marks and the boys did their test at Paramount, did they have to wait around for days?"

Pryor, well aware of what was happening, laughed sympathetically. "I'm afraid that's par for the course," he said. "What seems to be the holdup?"

"First it was no stage available. Then something about re-recording the track. Today it was no top cameramen, and the director they wanted was doing retakes. Celine's getting very upset. And I must say, this isn't helping my budget, either."

"I know how it goes, Billy. One of the biggest faults with the studios is the way they waste time. The test will be done, I promise you. In the meantime, the kids are holding the fort for Celine here."

"Yeah," Brenner replied. "That's another thing that's worrying Celine. She's seen the trade reviews."

"Good!" Pryor enthused. "They're great, aren't they? It wouldn't have helped any of us with Beckman if the reviews had been lukewarm. My neck was out a mile because I talked him into doing it. Don't worry, Billy, and tell Celine again that I.A.M. is very much interested in her career."

After more reassurances, Pryor hung up and placed a call to Marty Maizlish at the West Coast office. When the young agent came on the line, Pryor was blunt.

"What's the screw-up at Metro with the Cervier test, Marty?"

"Nothing, Mr. Pryor. It's in the mill."

"Well, get it out of the mill. I want Cervier back here so I can get Marks and the boys ready for the start of the Paramount picture."

"We'll shoot it tomorrow," Maizlish promised. "I'll have her back in New York by the weekend."

"Okay. Don't let anything hold it up."

CHAPTER 32

The message from Paramount to fly to the coast had come on such short notice that the New York office had been forced to use pressure to secure reservations. Leya was anxious to start working, but the realization that she would be gone when Arthur returned on his graduation leave depressed her. Ever since the luncheon with Myra, her free time had been given over to thoughts of Arthur—a meticulous reviewing of the events preceding and following the damned Romano party. A hundred times she had thought about a reconciliation, about the things she would say. Then Arthur would say the things Myra had tried to say for him. She would listen and understand, and when the words were finished, she would come to his arms again, willingly now.

At night, alone in Dulcy's apartment, Leya allowed herself to imagine their first real coming together as lovers. Later, she would dream, and the image of Arthur would get confused with Gardner. She would wake up, startled by her own cry of protest.

Leya called Myra minutes after she got a travel schedule from Ed. "I'm sick, Myra. We are going day after tomorrow. I have to be there for at least ten weeks and maybe longer, depending on the shooting."

"Dear, you are no sicker than I am!" Myra moaned. "Is

there no chance that you might get a day or two off, just time enough to fly in or maybe to fly as far as Chicago? We would gladly sacrifice that time with Arthur if we knew you two could be together."

"I don't think there's a chance," Leya said.

"Could he call you? Could you talk on the telephone, Leya? Do you think that would be—well, an acceptable substitute?"

"Of course we can talk, Myra. I'm dying to. I'll call you and let you know where I'm living as soon as it is arranged. And I'll get a studio number, too. Ed says that once in a while they'll let a personal call come through to the sound stage—if it is arranged in advance."

"All right, then, my dear," Myra replied. "I'll wait until I hear from you, and I'm not going to tell Arthur about this rotten timing now. I just can't!"

As they moved along the aisle to their seats on the transcontinental plane, Leya was embarrassed by the stares of the passengers who had already boarded. Most of them had spent the waiting time with their faces pressed to the round windows of the big Constellation as the publicity men from the studio finished posing the shots with her.

The curious whispers in their wake as they moved to their seats amused Ed Matson. When they were airborne, and the long silvery ribbon of the Hudson River had slipped behind them, he loosened his seat belt, tipped back in his aisle seat, and rolled his head toward Leya.

"About six months from now, little friend, very few people are going to have to whisper, 'She looks familiar. Who is she?' They'll know Leya Leslie."

Leya turned from the window. "What about all the people who know me as Leya Marks from the billboards and ads?"

Matson laughed. "What about the people who knew Carole Lombard as Carole Peters and the ones who knew Dorothy Lamour as Dorothy Kaumeyer? 'Leya Leslie' is euphonious and memorable. Associated with a girl like you, little friend, it could become immortal!"

"Is it settled? Am I to be Leya Leslie?"

"Unless you can come up with a name I like better."

She dismissed the matter with a frown and turned back to the window. Ed studied her surreptitiously. The girl was many things, but most of all she was an enigma—at the same time dependent and self-reliant, open and aloof, and a more desirable female than any he had ever known. Ed wondered, as he watched her now, just how much of her introspection concerned Arthur Lieberman. He wondered, too, whether or not the unhappy end of that romance had made her vulnerable. He intended to find out by exploiting her professional and, hopefully, her personal dependency on him. In this girl—talented and beautiful—seated tantalizingly close to him, he perceived an avenue to all that he himself wished to achieve personally and professionally. But her confidence in him would have to be built with meticulous care.

"Leya Leslie," he repeated to himself several times. He could visualize the name on the screen. It had a star sound and a star look. He hoped she would not resist the change.

The trip West was tedious for Leya. The novelty of flying was gone. She was relieved when the plane touched down at Burbank.

Marty Maizlish had found two furnished apartments in a new building on Burton Way, just below Sunset Boulevard's famous "Strip." It was out of Hollywood, as Leya had requested, but close enough to Melrose Avenue and the studio. She, Kent, and Matt would stay there. Ed would occupy a bachelor apartment, one of two in nearby Sunset Towers, kept by I.A.M. on an annual basis.

It was past nine P.M. by the time Marty had made them comfortable. I.A.M. had attended to everything, including phones. Standing on the second-floor balcony near the doors to the adjoining apartments, the young agent mentally ticked off the last of his responsibilities.

"We have a meeting at the studio with Jay Sanford and Lew Frederix at ten on Monday. That means you've got a long weekend to get settled." He held out a card for Leya. "If you need anything, here's a number where I can be reached on Sunday. Tomorrow you can get me at the office. I'll pick you up here at nine-thirty sharp on Monday. Have a good rest."

It was after eleven when Leya slipped into the double bed and turned off the lights. For a time, she abandoned herself to feeling. The mattress was firm. The sheets against her naked body were cool and smooth. The new blankets were warm and light, and there was twice the space she had made do with in Dulcy's apartment. She was content to let go, to unravel in the unfamiliar stillness. Two small wrinkles bracketed her brow. That was it, she thought—the quiet! And in that quiet, while sleep came quickly, it did not come untroubled.

The meeting with producer Jay Sanford and director Lew Frederix ran through lunch and into the afternoon, when the writers joined them. In the commissary Mitchell Leisen deliberately diverted some attention to them when he came over to congratulate Leya. Standing behind Kent and Matt with a hand resting on each, he said in a voice intended to be heard at nearby tables, "I wanted very much to do this musical picture with you all, but the front office has got my poor white body sold down another river. You'll be great. Lew's the only director on the lot I'm afraid of!"

"That was a charming crock," Frederix laughed when Leisen continued to his own table to join Jean Arthur, Edward Arnold, and Ray Milland. "He's a wonderful guy. I'll try to do as well by you."

A second meeting was set up the following morning with the two band singers who were about to play their first starring roles. Patti Day was a pretty girl with an incipient weight problem and a bracket of charming freckles that spread from the bridge of her nose down to either cheek. Her first million-seller record was a sentimental ballad with a country and western beat called, "Valentine Blues."

Frankie Naples was a thin, boyish lad in his early twenties. A shock of coarse, unruly black hair dominated his narrow face and made his head look a bit too large for his body. Leya found his bashful-boy manner appealing. His current million seller was a song he called "a saloon grabber" titled, "Love Is a Lonely Road." It had been number one on the *Cash Box* and *Billboard* charts for eleven weeks. Both singers would feature their hits in the picture.

Revised scripts were handed out with the admonition to the principals not to do more than familiarize themselves with the basic idea because more changes were in the works.

At the apartment with Ed and the boys later that evening, Leya had trouble taking the story seriously.

"My gosh, I'm a home wrecker!" she said, scanning a line from a scene with Patti and Frankie. "Listen to this. 'It's all your fault, Betsy Brown! If you hadn't been so you-know-what bent on a career, you would have seen that poor Eddie was in love with you. He didn't leave you for me. You drove him away with your selfish ambition! I didn't steal him! I didn't have to!' " Leya's eyes were incredulous as she turned to the others. "Do you believe that? And my name is 'Laura Lamarr!' "

"I think the scene is positively touching!" Kent grinned. "And if you want to know what it's touching, it's the bottom!" He turned to Matson. "You know what the big finale song and dance number is to be, don't you?"

"Yes, I do," Ed said, "and don't knock it!"

" 'The Haymakers' Hoedown!' " Kent said to the others. "We're up to our asses in corn!"

Ed stubbed out his cigarette and gave them all a level look. "I want to tell you kids something. No young talent has had such a good break in years. Don't underestimate Jay Sanford's judgment. He's done a half-dozen of these pictures. All of them have earned six to eight times negative cost. That, my children, is success."

His manner sobered them. "And I'll tell you something else," he continued, "when you talk about this script outside, it's the greatest musical production since Nero played a hot fiddle in Rome. When Lew Frederix gets this on its feet, I want to see all of you put everything you've got into it—country corn and all. 'The Haymakers' Hoedown' finale with Day and Naples is there for a very good reason. The girl goes back home to Texas as a big singing star. So does her milkman boyfriend, and so do the rest of you—all good friends now. That was put in to grab box-office receipts in the corn belt—the 'Lum and Abner' and the 'Grand Ole Opry' country. It's good thinking. You kids from New York tend to think Manhattan's all there is."

He turned to Kent and aimed a finger at him. "What you should be doing is dreaming up a hoedown routine that will be the classiest corn ever seen on the screen! Corn doesn't have to be cheap, Kent. You've got a chance to make another breakthrough, and you can have a ball doing it. All of you!"

Kent worked for a week with Stan Silbert and Morrie Diamond, two of the studio's most promising young songwriters. In the end, they came up with a two hundred and sixty-four bar arrangement, including the coda, that ran eight minutes and fifteen seconds. It included variations on, and paraphrases of, every melodic and rhythmic country and western cliché in the books. When it was finished, Kent was overcome with delight. The three dancers worked for hours with the rehearsal pianist blocking out routines that would feature Leya in a solo, Leya with Kent, Leya and Matt, and the three of them backed by the Covered Wagon Boys and thirty-two contract dancers.

"It will be an absolute gas!" Kent enthused. "Ballet—modern—traditional—a whole new concept! Ed was completely right. It is real 'uptown' classy corn. I love it!"

At the apartment, after the second week of rehearsal, Leya collapsed on the sofa, rotating her neck and massaging the muscles in her shoulders. She smiled when she realized that she was administering relief to those muscles and not to the ones in her left knee. She scarcely thought about it once she was involved in the routines. Silently, she blessed Dr. Max Lewin's genius and Arthur's thoughtfulness and concern that had put her into such skilled hands. It had been those same qualities of compassion and responsibility, misdirected, that had separated them and had moved him to go to Canada on the first refugee mission.

Suddenly, she sat bolt upright. Arthur might well be home now! The days had flown at the studio, and she had promised to call Myra. She glanced at the clock. It would still be only nine o'clock in New York.

Leya went to the phone in the bedroom and dialed the long-distance operator. After a series of frustrating delays, an unfamiliar voice answered.

"Is this the Lieberman residence?"

"Yes."

"This is Leya Marks calling from California. Is Mrs. Lieberman there?"

"No, ma'am. Neither one is at home. They left this afternoon for Canada. Just a minute, ma'am—"

A few seconds passed, and the maid's familiar voice came over the wire.

"Miss Marks, this is Bernice. Mrs. Lieberman left a note in case you called. She said for you to please leave me a number where you can be reached, and she will call you back to explain."

Leya gave the woman the home and studio numbers and instruction about the best time to call. Trying to keep the anxiety from her voice, she said, "Can you tell me, is everything all right? I thought Mr. Arthur was to come home—"

"I don't know what happened. A call came this morning, and Mr. and Mrs. Lieberman went rushing out of here. There was some kind of a change. That's all I know."

"Thank you. If they call you, tell them to call me anytime. Anytime at all."

Leya hung up and dropped to the edge of the bed.

"There was some kind of a change—" the maid said. If it had been anything really bad, wouldn't she have said so? The only thing she could do now was wait.

Leya had just pulled on her bathrobe and started for the tub when Ed Matson called.

"It went well today, little friend. Everybody's happy with our department. But there are some problems in the shop. Shooting's going to be delayed. That means you've got more time for rehearsals, and that also means that Kent and Matt are going to get an extension."

"Oh? For how long?"

"I talked to Howard this afternoon and told him Jay Sanford thought three weeks. I told him to settle for six, movies being what they are."

The news did not particularly please her. "Do you really think it will take that much longer?"

"I always try to bet the odds, Leya. I'd say it will. By the way, would you like to dine out tonight?"

Leya's shoulders slumped. "Oh, no, Ed! Thanks very much, but I'm beat. I'm going to make up a great big eggnog and collapse."

"See what happens when I don't bet the odds?" he laughed. "Have a good rest."

Leya had barely begun to stir when the phone on the bed table startled her. Blinking at the clock, which read ten after six, she groped for the instrument and fumbled it to her ear.

"Leya?" She recognized the voice immediately.

"Yes, Myra."

"I'm so glad we could reach you. Bernice told us you had called when I called home this morning. I hope it's not too early, but we've waited as long as possible."

"Oh, no," Leya assured her. "I was just getting up. What happened?"

"There has been a change in Arthur's orders, dear. Terrible things have been happening over France and England. Apparently the Nazis have something called an ME-109 that has decimated the RAF bomber squadrons. Arthur's unit is going straight from graduation to a base in England. All the leaves are cancelled. Martin and I are renting a car and driver and going a hundred miles to Arthur's base. We'll just have a few hours with him—if that."

Myra's words left Leya without a response.

"It's absolutely shattering," the older woman continued. "I can't even let myself face it yet. The only good thing seems to be that he will not go into combat immediately. He will be trained on different equipment first."

"Could he call me before he goes?" Leya managed.

"I'm sure he will! It will be the first thing we ask him to do when we see him at noon. I won't keep you now, dear.

Martin's waiting with the driver. Please keep in touch and remember that we love you, Leya, all of us!"

The hurried call left Leya numb. For ten minutes, she was, unable to force her thoughts from Arthur and the new turn of events. She would dress and be at the studio for another round of needless rehearsal, on which she would not concentrate as she should, knowing that any minute the phone might ring, and she would have to find the right things to say to Arthur.

When, by midafternoon, no call had been put through despite explicit instructions to the head operator, Leya quit in the middle of blocking a sequence.

"I've had it for today, Kent," she said. "Going over and over this is ruining it for me. I'm going stale! You're worse than Madame Baronova!"

Kent tried to handle her unexpected outburst with humor. "Of course, darling, I'm worse than Baronova, but you must admit I'm prettier!" Frowning, he came close and studied her.

"Cramps?"

"No dammit! Boredom. Sheer boredom!"

Kent flopped onto a canvas chair and mopped his face. "You know something?" he said to Matt, "she's right. Let's knock off."

Leya checked the operator twice more before she left the studio. At home, after a hasty shower, she wandered aimlessly in her robe, threw together an unpalatable cheese sandwich, poured a glass of milk, and turned on the radio. Some minutes later, she heard Kent and Matt come bounding up the outside stairs, laughing. The sound increased her sense of aloneness. She couldn't remember, but if Toronto was in the Eastern time zone it would be nearing eight-thirty there. "We'll just have a few hours with him—if that," Myra had said. Half sick with disappointment, Leya slipped deeper into despondency.

She was not sure how long she had been lost in introspection when she grew aware of the newscaster's staccato voice. Rousing herself at the mention of the RCAF initials, she listened intently to the remainder of the story:

—according to word from London tonight. One squadron of ten Blenheim bombers had all but two of its aircraft shot down in flames by the new German Messerschmitt fighters. That brings the toll of RAF bombers to thirty-seven in the past three days . . . eighty for the week. Winston Churchill, in an urgent message to President Roosevelt, has requested aid from the United States at the earliest possible moment. "Despite the fact that we are drawing to the utmost on reserves of men and equipment from Canada, Australia, and New Zealand," he said, "we are in desperate need of bombers to carry the war to the mainland and relieve the terrible devastation at home."

"Arthur's unit is going straight from graduation to a base in England," Myra had said. Leya wondered now if, in fact, Myra and Martin had been able to find any time at all with Arthur.

Moments later in the news broadcast, the announcer inserted a late flash. Seventy-one light bombers of the Advanced Air Striking Force had been hit over Sedan by a swarm of Messerschmitts. Only thirty-one managed to get back to their bases in England. Half the RAF striking force had been destroyed in a matter of days.

Sick at heart, as much for Myra and Martin as for herself, Leya gave in to tears of disappointment and loneliness.

Shooting finally began early in August. Ed Matson, concerned about Leya's apparent disinterest in the production and unable to worm any explanation from her, was relieved when he saw her begin to get into the spirit of the numbers.

The challenge routine, expanded and elaborated, was set in an upstairs hallway in Carnegie Hall. There were two doors, screen right and left. One was lettered THE ROMANOFF SCHOOL OF CLASSIC BALLET, the other, THE ACADEMY OF MODERN AND JAZZ DANCE.

The choreography was modified to carry the action

through one door and into the rehearsal room, then out again and into the other. It worked so well that Kent decided he would stage it similarly in concert.

The call to Leya from Myra Lieberman came shortly before eight o'clock on the evening the routine's protection shots were finished. There had been trouble getting clearance onto the base, more trouble locating Arthur, who was in a last-minute briefing, and time only to try to repeat the things each had finally been forced to say to the other through Myra.

Resigned now, Leya sought relief once again in her dancing. Her total concentration in the sequences told both Kent and Ed that what they had suspected was true. And once again the manager found himself secretly relieved that fate was moving to his advantage.

"The Haymakers' Hoedown" was shot on the assembly stage. One entire side had been converted into a Thomas Hart Benton rural scene featuring an elaborate red barn, an American Gothic farmhouse, and a grove of stylized elm trees. The painted background cyclorama was a series of symmetrical rolling fields sprouting bright-green corn stalks from rich brown earth. On beyond was a cerulean spring sky. The foreground had been covered with a turflike substance to simulate a country yard. Saw horses, a grindstone, a chopping block, a wheelbarrow, a clothesline, a fence, and a barnyard gate were all used as props in the dance.

Counting setups, the challenge had been shot in five hours. "The Haymakers' Hoedown" took two full days. After that, the shooting progressed on schedule, and the picture was completed on time.

A sneak preview was scheduled in a neighborhood house in Long Beach. Jay Sanford's strategy in choosing the location had been expressed simply: "There are more celluloid collars and corset bones in Bixby Park than there are in all of Iowa now. If we get a good reaction in Long Beach, it will tell us a lot."

On the night of the preview, Leya had a bad case of the butterflies. Bill Pine and Bill Thomas, Paramount's publicity heads, had reserved two rows of seats for the studio people in the back of the house. There was a flurry when the principals made their entrance. Some of the girls recognized Frankie Naples and set up a commotion. Both Patti and Frankie signed autographs, and several fans shoved their books at Leya on the assumption that she must be somebody. She found it embarrassing.

The front marquee advertised *Hold Back the Dawn*, with Charles Boyer, Olivia de Havilland, and Paulette Goddard. The two end panels read: "Sneak Preview tonight. 9:00 P.M."

"The regular feature's a Leisen picture," Ed pointed out. "That's a good break for us."

Leya, sitting between Kent and Ed, struggled to suppress her anxiety. When the Paramount symbol came up on the screen, and the first strains of the hoedown overture blared, Kent took her hand. "God," he breathed, "am I ever nervous!"

Suddenly, the first scene was on the screen, a medium closeup of Frankie in his white uniform and cap at the wheel of his milk delivery truck rolling along a small-town street, singing the picture's bouncy opening song "Gotta Pretty Little Girl Waitin' For Me—A pretty little someone I'm longin' to see—She's as pretty as a 'pitcher'—she's as pretty as can be!"

From the moment Frankie arrived at Patti's house and jumped out with his wire bottle basket and swung in rhythm through the gate, most of the feet in the theater were tapping.

The running time for the picture was ninety-three minutes. Halfway through, Jay Sanford and Lew Frederix were certain they had a picture. The producer, sitting next to Ed Matson, leaned close at the end of the challenge number, a show within a show scene in which Frankie, following the split with Patti over her career, comes to New York to see the show, hoping for a reconciliation, and meets Leya backstage.

"It's working," Sanford whispered. "Your kids are great."

It took almost an hour after the show for the cast members to sign their autographs. Leya and Matt signed as many as Patti and Frankie.

On the drive back to Hollywood, Kent summed up their

feelings. "I'm a human yoyo! I was at the bottom of the string driving down there tonight. Now I'm all wound up tight! I don't know what you people are going to do, but Matt and I are going out to celebrate!"

Ed Matson smiled. "That's easier to do in New York. We'll go back to my place and see if the champagne is cold yet." He turned to Leya. "How does that strike you, 'Laura Lamarr' ?"

Leya laughed with the others. "Fine, Ed. I'm like Kent and Matt. Suffering through that preview was just as hard as doing the routines. I'm drained!"

"In a way it was worse," Matt said. "Sitting right in the middle of the audience could be dangerous. At least on the stage they can't get at you!"

"It's obvious none of you kids have ever been to an English music hall!" Ed gave each of them an affectionate look. "Well, we're over the first hurdle now, so we deserve to give ourselves a party."

They had been at Ed's apartment in Sunset Towers for only a few minutes when the rest of the crew principals from the picture began arriving.

Leya confronted Ed in the kitchen. "How did you know we wouldn't be sitting *shiva?*" she demanded.

Ed kissed her on the forehead. "Little friend, one of the things I'm paid for is to guess right—at least fifty-one percent of the time." He glanced around to make certain he was not being overheard. "I'm going to make another guess. Your option is going to be picked up—we'll get a contract for Matt if he doesn't sign one with the army first, and we'll get Kent a deal as a choreographer if he wants it."

Leya gave him a hug. "Thank you, Ed! You're super wonderful," she whispered.

Ed laughed. "It would be a lot easier to live up to if you'd make it just plain wonderful." He nodded toward the others. "Go out there and tell Jay and Lew they're wonderful, too. You've no idea what it can do for their egos and your career!"

It was two in the morning by the time the last of the crew members, euphoric with champagne, steered their uncertain courses to the elevator.

Ed came up behind Leya, who was standing at the big picture window overlooking a spectacular panorama of Los Angeles and the beach cities.

"It's not yours yet, little friend," he said quietly, "but it will be."

CHAPTER 33

Shortly before noon on the following day, Leya received a call from Howard Pryor in New York.

"Please don't tell Kendall and O'Brien that I called. Ed will tell you everything we know at the moment. I've just talked to him. And congratulations, Miss Leslie." He emphasized the name. "You're about to start on an interesting journey. I'll tell you more soon."

The call from Ed Matson came within minutes. "I'm going to pick you up at one o'clock, Leya. We're lunching at Lucy's with Sanford and Maizlish. Can you be ready?"

"I think so. Do you want me to tell Kent and Matt?" she asked.

"No. I'll talk to them later. Meet me downstairs. We'll be running kind of close."

Lucy's was an elaborately decorated Italian restaurant opposite the Paramount main gate. It was the "in" lunching place for the top-echelon executives and stars from the Paramount and RKO lots and for the hangers-on and the curious who could afford the tariff.

Jay Sanford and Marty Maizlish were waiting at the bar when they came in. As they walked to a table in a corner alcove, a number of people smiled at Leya and murmured their congratulations to the producer.

Ed, walking beside Leya with his arm linked through hers, smiled and whispered, "The word along the grapevine is good, honey. God help you if you make this walk and nobody looks up!"

At the table, Leya accepted a Dubonnet on the rocks "to celebrate." When the captain handed her the menu, the first thing that caught her eye was the luncheon special. Eggs Benedict! Smiling to herself, she mentally saluted Gardner Sutton and ordered it.

The producer had a breakdown of the preview cards from Long Beach. "They're very interesting," he said. "The only negative responses were those saying we didn't give you enough to do, Leya. Those came mainly from the above twenty-one group." He turned a knowing smile to the others. "So, we're going to remedy that in the next picture."

Ed rested his hand on Leya's shoulder.

"We don't know what the picture's going to be at the moment, honey. But the writers are working on a story that will feature you."

The producer nodded. "We'll have something on paper in about two weeks. The way we're thinking now—and this must remain strictly between us—is that we'll put you opposite one of our new leading men. What I'm thinking about is a ballet story—something very close to real life, perhaps—with the conflict between your love for a man who's not connected with show business and your love of dancing. Tough decisions to make, very dramatic. Do you get the picture?"

Leya smiled cryptically and tried not to look at Ed, who was studying her with an amused twinkle in his eyes.

"I think I get the picture," she replied.

"In the meantime, the front office has decided to pick up your option for a year." He beamed at her. "So—that's really what this celebration is all about. Congratulations, Leya!"

The balance of the luncheon was devoted to speculation about the picture industry and the possible effect a war would have on it if the United States became actively involved.

"I'd say we're pretty damned actively involved right now," Jay Sanford observed, "what with convoying British ships as far as Iceland. You know, don't you, that a Nazi U-boat let a couple of torpedoes go at the *Greer* last week? They only missed by inches! If they'd hit the old destroyer, that would have given FDR the excuse he's been looking for to get us in all the way!"

Marty Maizlish laughed. "I feel in all the way already. I'm One-A! But I'm counting on a warped mind and a bad back to keep me here offending the home front!"

"By the way, that reminds me," the producer said, "where does O'Brien stand with the draft board?"

"Right smack in the front row," Matson said unhappily. "He's One-A, and as healthy as Bernarr MacFadden. As much as I hate to say it, I think we'll have to write him off for the time being."

"What about Kendall?" the producer asked.

Ed Matson frowned. "I suspect that problem will solve itself at the draft board."

Sanford smiled. "If he doesn't have to go, he's very well liked in the front office." Matson, remembering his lecture to Kendall, was quietly amused.

Later, Ed took coffee with the three dancers at Leya's apartment and hoped that she would respect her promise not to tell Kent and Matt about her option until he had figured out the best way to break the news. The damned trouble was obvious. The trade papers would pick it out of the air in a matter of hours.

"What happens next?" Kent wanted to know.

"Nothing, for the moment," Ed answered. "As a matter of fact, I think we should go back to New York until the studio decides what it's going to do. I don't know about you kids, but I've got things to do. Also," he added, "any long-term decisions will have to be made there. I'd like to be close to the corner office, from which all blessings flow."

Leya could sense the tension of unasked questions in Kent. The need for silence made her feel guilty. All that had happened to her had happened through Kent.

She wanted to phone home and cry, "Papa, we're rich!" but to do that would be to tempt fate. What was it papa always said? "Good luck, *bubeleh,* you keep to yourself.

Nobody will believe. From bad luck you *shrei.* Everybody will enjoy!" Soon, now, she could do for her father and Minnie. She promised herself things would be done.

The night before her departure, Leya called her father in Brownsville. As always, when speaking long distance, Harry shouted. She laughed and held the earpiece away. He had a new sedan. Another Buick. He got nine hundred dollars for the old car. The old one was better. They didn't build the new ones "so good" now. He and Minnie had a bigger flat in the same building. More room now. Only the mailbox was different.

At the airport, Leya heard her father before she could locate him. After a tumultuous reunion, Ed Matson slipped away. Leya insisted on having a porter carry the five bags. When she tipped him a dollar and a quarter, Harry closed his eyes. "I couldn't look!" he moaned.

It was past midnight when they were finally talked out. On the chest of drawers in her new bedroom, Leya found an album. Every clipping had been pasted in, and space had been reserved for the reviews of the new movie.

As she was about to turn out the light, Minnie knocked and opened the door a crack.

"Your father's asleep already. Could we talk a minute?"

"Of course, Minnie." She patted the bed. "Sit here."

Minnie settled her bulk. "So you go back to California?"

"Yes. I'm going to do another picture soon. I'll have a leading part this time. It's a story about a dancer."

Minnie nodded. "So you won't come home for a year?"

"Of course I'll come home!" Leya laughed. "First of all, I don't have to go back to Hollywood for two or three weeks, and it only takes a couple of months to shoot a picture. Then I'll come home again for another visit." Leya propped herself up and regarded her cousin curiously. "What's the matter, Minnie? I thought you two would be happy about things, especially about the seven hundred and fifty dollars a week they will be paying me. Remember?"

"Could I forget seven hundred and fifty?" Minnie challenged. "The money I remember, darling. But also I remember something else." Her foreboding expression made Leya smile.

"For goodness' sakes, Minnie. What is this dreadful thing you remember?"

"I mean, with money comes temptation!"

A frown furrowed Leya's brow. "Temptation to do what?"

Minnie shrugged and averted her eyes. "When money comes easy, you have temptation—and from temptation you can succumb."

"Succumb to what, for heaven's sake? And who has more temptation than somebody who is broke?"

"I'm talking about men. You should have a man, Leya. You should have an Arthur."

Minnie's presumptuousness made Leya gasp.

"Minnie—" she said slowly, "if you hadn't gotten me the job where I met Arthur, I think I could almost hate you for opening that up again—just when I'm happier than I've ever been. Don't you trust me? Do you think I need a keeper?"

"Temptation is temptation—ever since Adam and Eve!" Minnie said defensively. "Every woman needs a man. Ask me. I know!" She aimed a pudgy finger at Leya. "And especially a woman like you—beautiful—and rich now! Every smart alec—every *gonif*—will be figuring. You'll need a smart honest man to protect you. Somebody you can trust!"

Controlling her voice, Leya reached out and patted Minnie's knee. "I have a man I trust," she said gently. "Ed Matson. My manager. He's the one who made all this happen for us, Minnie. He's with me all the time. And I have Howard Pryor, too. He's the most important talent agent in the country. He and Ed advise me. I don't want—or need—a husband right now, Minnie. I don't want to be in love, and I don't want anybody in love with me. Something very exciting is happening to me now," she continued quietly, "and I don't want anything to distract me. I don't know what's going to happen in Hollywood. I don't even know if I'll like it if things do work out. My heart has always been set on being a ballerina—here in New York."

Minnie gave her an incredulous look. "Do you mean seven hundred and fifty isn't satisfying you?"

Leya shook her head. "Of course the money satisfies me! It takes care of the outside things. But I'm talking about here—" She rested her hands on her middle. "I just don't know yet."

Leya let her body slip down onto the pillows. "Please don't you and papa worry about me, Minnie. I really love you for caring, but you have nothing to worry about." She smiled. "I'm a big girl now!"

For fourteen weeks now she had been sending two hundred dollars to the Marine Midland Trust Company to add to that little savings account that was started with the catalogue job for Super Figure.

Super Figure—and Arthur! She would call Myra soon, return the luncheon, and get caught up. Meanwhile, two calls needed to be made first—to Dulcy and Celine.

She reached Dulcy at the private number in Silver Spring, Maryland.

"Leya! Where are you?"

"I'm at papa's. I just got in from the West Coast last night. I want to know how you are."

"I'm out to here with a little Vandercort. How are you? What's happening with the picture? When will it be released? I'm dying to know!"

Leya caught her up without embellishment, reported the results of the sneak preview, and confided that her option had been picked up for a year. Dulcy yelped with delight.

"But please, Dulcy, keep it to yourself. Kent and Matt don't know yet. Ed's working out a deal for Kent as choreographer, and they love Matt, but they won't sign him until they find out about the draft."

"My lips are sealed!" Dulcy said. "Look, sweetie, when am I going to see you? Can you come down for a few days? We've got bedrooms to burn in this old place. I still think Bela Lugosi roams around here in the middle of the night!"

"I can't—now. How about you coming up here?" Leya asked.

"I'm in my second trimester, honey. Already I look like I'm smuggling a watermelon. But if you can't come down, I'll bring all one and two-thirds of me up there—somehow."

"Have you kept the apartment?" Leya asked.

"Of course! It's there for you. We use it once in a great while if Willie has to come up overnight. I'm still not exactly being welcomed with open arms. I don't even want to think about the pressure they must be putting on poor Willie. I can always tell when he's been through the family wringer. When he comes home, I have two babies."

"Have you been to the family at all—with him?"

"No, dear heart. The mountain came to Mohammed. Mothah and fathah visited us here in August, and I damned near froze to death! Truth is, Leya, I'm bucking heavy odds. But Willie is being a real thoroughbred. He says when the baby comes they'll melt all over the place. Little Whoozit'll be the first born in this generation. Willie says if we are making a boy everything will be copacetic. He'll be Willie Five, and I'll be a heroine."

The time for a visit was left open. "I must tell you, sweetie," Dulcy confessed, "a lot of sociopolitical bitches futz around here because I'm Mrs. Willie You-Know-Who, the Fourth. And what they lay on me over tea with their pinkies stuck out would fertilize the whole state of Maryland. You don't know how good it is just to hear your voice! Please call again—soon!"

Some minutes later, Celine's greeting was as cold as Dulcy's had been warm and open.

"Have I called at a bad time, Celine?" Leya asked.

"No. Of course not. When did you get back?"

"Last night. Late. I'm dying to know how everything's going in the show. And what about the test?"

"The show goes all right. Jack Beckman wants to put a couple of other kids with me." Celine laughed humorlessly. "The Kendall Trio proved to be a tough act to follow!"

"But that's not fair of him to compare your routine with the one we did."

"You may be right, *chérie.* Nevertheless, that's what happened."

Leya was puzzled by her friend's coolness and the fact that she had ignored the question about the test. "Let's have lunch tomorrow and get caught up."

"I can't. I've got a meeting with Billy. Then I'll be taking class at three."

"With whom?"

"Jimmy Starbuck."

Leya thought for a moment. "You know something? I'm going to bring my things in and take a class with you. Then we can visit after. Okay?"

"Sure," Celine replied without enthusiasm.

Leya placed a call to Ed Matson.

"Are you caught up with your sleep, little friend?"

"I'm fine, Ed. Listen, I just talked to Celine, and she sounded very strange, not friendly at all. It's something to do with our taking over for her."

"Well?"

"Well, if we made trouble for her, I'd like to know about it," Leya said sharply.

"Now don't get yourself upset," Ed soothed. "I'm sure it's nothing serious, and I think you know what it is—if you're honest with yourself."

The words stung. He was right. There was no need to guess. Celine had as good as spelled it out when she had said the trio was "a tough act to follow."

"I am being honest!" she protested, more annoyed with herself than with him now.

"That's a very good idea!" Ed replied with exasperating calm. "As a matter of fact, I've been thinking of talking with Jack about having Kent pick a couple of kids and do a variation of the trio around her."

Leya considered for a moment.

"What about Peter and Marc?"

"Peter won't work without Jean. Besides, I think the kids are all going to want to come to the Coast."

Leya had wondered about the possibility.

"Could they?"

"Probably—if we put on enough pressure."

"Are you going to talk to Jack Beckman about Kent?"

Ed Matson laughed. "You make it sound like I should do it right this minute!"

"I think you should. I'm going to take a class with Celine

at Carnegie tomorrow at three. Maybe I can find out more then."

"I'm glad you tipped me off. I'll hold off calling and just happen to drop by tomorrow, looking for you. I may be able to make things fit together then."

"Please try, Ed. I'm very unhappy."

"How about dinner tonight—to cheer you up?"

"I can't. I'm eating with my family. Thanks, anyway. So, I'll see you tomorrow—at three."

CHAPTER 34

When Leya walked into Number 61, Carnegie Hall, Celine gave her a perfunctory kiss, then left for the dressing room. A moment later, Billy Brenner came over.

"Hi!" he said with a tight smile. "I heard a rumor this morning that you've got a hit on your hands and a long-term contract. Congratulations."

Leya was taken by surprise. "They say the picture turned out well, but I don't know anything about a long-term contract." She placed deliberate emphasis on "long-term."

Billy shrugged. "You know the grapevine."

"If I did," Leya replied, "I'd know how Celine's test came out, too, wouldn't I?"

"It came out predictably—considering."

"You're talking over my head, Billy. Considering what?"

"Considering that the studio was never really serious about the test."

Leya met his gaze. "I don't believe that. Studios don't make tests they're not serious about!"

"Well, let's just say that some tests are more serious than others. We haven't heard anything yet."

"Have you called Mr. Pryor to see what he can find out?"

"That's how we got the test, honey—calling Mr. Pryor."

Billy glanced toward the door as Matson entered the studio.

"Anyway, let's just say we're still waiting to hear."

As he crossed the room, Ed Matson could sense the tension. His greeting was warm but not overly cordial. "I heard some interesting things about your Coast trip this morning over at I.A.M., Billy. Congratulations."

"For what?" Brenner's glance moved from Matson to Leya and back. "Being alive?"

Ed Matson pretended to be puzzled. "Am I talking out of turn?"

Brenner shook his head. "No, you're talking in riddles."

"Well, perhaps I'm assuming more than I should," Matson agreed, "but I was told that Metro is very interested in Celine as a featured dancer in a new musical they're planning with Nelson Eddy and Jeanette MacDonald—" He cocked a skeptical eyebrow. "You're putting me on, aren't you?"

Brenner laughed. "Now you're reading my lines, Mr. Matson!"

Leya grew impatient. "If Ed says it, you can bet on it," she said. "Celine got the same buildup on the Revel billboards that I got. And she's a wonderful dancer. What's so strange about the studio wanting her?"

"There's nothing strange about it," Brenner agreed. "Just miraculous, especially in view of the fact that the studio was never really looking for a dancer. We never quite got over the feeling that somebody was doing somebody a favor." He looked directly at Matson. "I really thought I.A.M. was doing us the favor, but the way it's turned out, it seems that we were doing I.A.M. the favor."

Ed controlled his anger. "Billy, it's obvious that you've got a burr up your tail. I'd like to help you get it out." He turned to Leya. "If you're going to take class, why don't you go change?"

Relieved to be excluded from what promised to be a disturbing encounter, Leya left them.

"Come on, Billy," Ed said amiably. "Scotch? Coffee? Celery phosphate? Let's hack this out."

It was nearing five o'clock when the two men returned. Leya and Celine had not exchanged a word since they had come out in practice clothes to start barre. In the moment before James Starbuck led them around the hall in a tour of *grands jetés,* both girls sensed that the atmosphere between the two men had cleared a bit.

In the dressing room, after their showers, Leya found herself still troubled. Turning to Celine, she said, "How about a cup of tea or something? We've really had no time at all to visit."

"I can't, Leya," Celine replied. "I will barely have time to get home and change and get back to the theater. Let's make it some other time."

"Of course," Leya replied, concealing her hurt. "I'll be in town for a while."

Later, when they parted on the sidewalk, Leya confronted Ed. "What was going on between you two? You look like the cat who swallowed the canary."

"He did the swallowing!"

Leya regarded him with suspicion. "And you did the conning?"

"Not entirely. You see, somehow Mr. Brenner got the idea that we arranged the test for his girl so you three could go into the show here to be seen by Paramount brass."

"Where on earth did he get that idea?"

Matson grinned. "Mr. Brenner is a very smart young manager. What he lacks is experience, which he's getting now, like crazy."

The suspicion in Leya's eyes deepened as she studied Matson's impassive face.

"Ed?"

"Yes?"

"Did you and Howard arrange for Celine's test?"

"Let's say that Howard arranged it at my suggestion."

"And she never really had a chance out there?"

"Not true! They do want her after the first of the year. Howard confirmed that to me a little while ago."

"After he arranged that, too, at your suggestion?"

Matson's smile vanished. "Now look, little friend," he said in a level voice, "taking into consideration everything that's happened, who would you rather have managing you, old Ed Matson or young Billy Brenner?"

When he saw the anger in Leya's narrowed eyes, his tone turned milder.

"The chances that Cervier would get a screen test—anywhere—were about ten thousand to one. Brenner can't even get through the front gates yet. We have the connections. It was more than a fair exchange. Your friend Celine got exposure where it counts. So did you and Kent and Matt. You got a contract. Celine will get six or eight weeks on the MacDonald-Eddy film, and her career will get a big boost. I suggest you think that over before your dudgeon gets any higher."

"No wonder she's giving me the cold shoulder! Never mind Hollywood. Her career in *Riddle Me This* didn't exactly get a boost, did it?" Leya snapped. "Mr. Beckman's not happy at all."

"Not true, damn it! Mr. Beckman's very happy—as of noon today. He's signing Kent to do a version of the challenge especially for Cervier. She doesn't know that yet, but she will tonight. So how about it? Am I still a villain, or am I really your best friend?"

Leya regarded him with what he characterized as her "silent slant-eyed third degree." "What you are, Ed Matson," she said, "is something my father says in Yiddish, which, unfortunately, I'm not fluent in!"

"What I am, dear little about-to-be movie star," he said, taking her hands, "is a movie *mavin* with *chutzpah*." She let him link her arm through his. "Come on. I'm going to put you in a cab."

On the ride to Brownsville, Leya could not rid herself of the sense of uneasiness. There had been no mistaking Celine's coolness, but despite Ed's plausible explanation for everything that had happened, Leya recognized the probability for a hurtful misunderstanding.

For some reason, she remembered Arthur's counsel about not accepting favors from men like Carlo Romano—that favors imply obligations. If that were true, Leya thought, then actually Celine and Billy had little cause to be unhappy. It had been her recommendation to Revelsky that had got Celine the billboard and ad campaign. The campaign had given Celine the recognition necessary for Billy, as her manager, to get her the featured role in *Riddle Me This.* And the interest she herself had engendered in Ed and Howard had resulted in Celine's screen test, and soon a featured role in a major musical picture. If anything, Leya thought, the favors were owed to her—and to her manager and agent.

By the time the taxi pulled up in front of the house, Leya found herself feeling a little disappointed in Billy—and in Celine.

The New York play date was set in the Paramount Theater for the first Wednesday in October. Seats were reserved in the first balcony for the Paramount officials, the players, and their friends. In addition to her family, Leya invited Dulcy and Willie Four and all of the gypsies from the original Kendall Dance Group. A special invitation was telephoned to Madame Baronova.

When Leya explained the purpose of the call, the old ballet mistress was deeply moved. Finally, in her heavily accented voice, she said, "I don't go out much at night anymore. But I thank you for your thoughtfulness, and I hope for your success if this is what you truly want."

Leya called Kent to tell him of Madame Baronova's refusal and ask him to help persuade her. Kent grew indignant.

"She's got to be there! My father's in Japan. His driver's just sitting around. I'll see that she's driven to the theater and to the party."

After its premiere, there was little question that *Hollywood Holiday* would be well received. The theater was packed with Pattie Day and Frankie Naples fans, who bedlamized the huge movie house.

The numbers featuring the two singers and the two major dance numbers brought wild applause. During the challenge, Leya watched Alexandra Baronova out of the corner of her eye and smiled as the ballet mistress, elegant in old-fashioned black, accented by her exquisite Russian cameo jewelry, nodded in time. During the "Hoedown" finale, she stared at the screen through a lorgnette balanced close to the tip of her nose. Later, at the Paramount reception in a banquet room at the Astor Hotel, she stood leaning on Kent's arm.

"I must tell you, dear children, it is difficult for me to reconcile myself to the hybridization of ballet. All of this—flip-flopping, jumping out of windows, dancing on fences—it is very amusing and very disciplined. But can we really call it ballet? For that matter, is Eugene Loring's *Billy the Kid* ballet? Or is it ethnic, like Cossack dancing?"

"It's ethnic," Kent rebutted, "like cowboy dancing in America—but more like Michael Kidd's concept."

The ballet mistress raised questioning eyebrows. "What-ever!" She looked off wistfully. "Change is inevitable, I suppose. Perhaps it is as unrealistic of me, as it was of Fokine some years ago, not to expect ballet to undergo change. Perhaps there should be more to the ballet than mannered posture, an erect spine, and a perfect turnout. But if there is to be, I would hope the new direction is founded on the same rigid classical discipline."

After a moment, she drew Leya close with her free arm and studied her. "So many gifts! I wonder where they will take you?"

Ed Matson's concern about the boys' reaction to Leya's year-long contract proved to be groundless. Kent would get a contract. Matt O'Brien's draft number was pulled within a week of the preview. After suffering the indignation of a naked, mass "short arm" inspection at the hall in the Grand Central building, the young dancer was accepted and ordered to Fort Dix, New Jersey.

Kent's going-away party for Matt at the Beekman Place penthouse was a seriocomic affair. In addition to the Kendall Dance Group, there were a number of other gypsies, friends who had been in other shows, summer friends from Fire Island, and more than a few show-business and dance sycophants who had wangled invitations or simply crashed. After a few drinks, Kent's forced gaiety verged on the hysterical. He sulked when Matt allowed himself to be monopolized by Tanya Kuznetsov.

Heather O'Brien arrived late. Leya was shocked at her appearance. Not only had the former dancer put on weight, but her face was puffy, and her eyes betrayed the glaze of one who is seldom completely sober.

She greeted everyone effusively—friends and strangers alike—and embarrassed her brother with her oversolicitous attention. Leya found it difficult to be with Heather now. It was even more difficult to accept those who smothered her with false affection and good wishes and, in doing so, could not conceal their envy. When she was certain she would not be missed, Leya asked Ed to take her back to Dulcy's apartment.

They released the taxi at the all-night newsstand on Lexington Avenue and Fiftieth Street just as the vendor slashed the bindings around the top bundle of the morning edition. A seventy-two-point banner headline leaped off the front page:

U.S.S. KEARNY TORPEDOED!
Heavy Loss of Life

For a moment, Leya stared at it. Then she uttered a wordless cry. Ed turned to find her on her knees by the stack moaning, "Oh, God—oh, God—no! Please!"

"Leya! What's the matter?" He dropped beside her and took her by the shoulders. He felt her body shudder with dry sobs. "Do you have somebody on that ship? Tell me," he urged as he raised her gently.

Leya stared down at the headline, her fingers pressed against her lips. She seemed not to hear.

Ed shook her more insistently. "Tell me!" he repeated.

Trembling, Leya wrenched free and looked up at him wildly. "Take me home, Ed. Please! Take me home!"

Dulcy slipped off the champagne-dyed sheared beaver coat and took Leya in her arms.

"I can't get as close to you these days," she said, indicating her pregnancy, "but I had to come up when I heard about Gardner. Poor Willie is absolutely desolate. I've never seen him cry, but he did when he talked with Gardy's family. So did I!" She held Leya closer. "He was really a wonderful guy, and you know, Willie believes he was truly in love with you. You liked him, too, didn't you?"

"Very much," Leya whispered.

"There's a memorial service for him on Sunday at the family church out on the island. Will you go with Willie and me?"

"I'd like to," Leya said, trying to control the threatening tears. "Thank you for asking."

Willie and Dulcy picked up Leya at nine o'clock Sunday morning. "I hope you had coffee," Dulcy said. "The service is at eleven, and we thought we could have a late brunch somewhere on the island after—if that's agreeable?"

"I'm fine," Leya replied. "I managed some toast and jam."

The bright crisp autumn day made the drive out to Stony Brook almost pleasant. Because it seemed to ease Willie's grief, the girls listened as he remembered the adventures he and Gardner had shared in their youth. After they had driven in silence for a time, Leya asked Willie what he thought the consequences of the sinking would be.

"Will be!" he corrected. "The president issued an order to the navy to fight back as of last Monday. We've had a marine garrison in Iceland since July when we took over from the British. They've got their shooting orders, too. A bunch of new antiaircraft batteries are being set up. In short, what the United States is doing is backing into the European war. There'll be a lot more *Kearny*'s this winter—God help us!"

In Stony Brook, the church parking area was nearly filled. Off to the right were several official U.S. Navy automobiles. An honor guard was assembling.

At the door, Willie pointed toward the back. "Save me a seat. I want to talk to the family for a moment."

Leya and Dulcy watched him make his way to the front row. When he leaned down to whisper to a woman whom they could not see, a tall, slender man with graying hair rose. His appearance startled Leya. As he stood with an arm around Willie's shoulder, his face mirroring deep sorrow, time seemed to warp. She was seeing Gardner as he would have been at his father's age. An odd perversity of conscience made her feel guilty about that Sunday—such a short time ago it was, really—that deprived the Suttons of their son's company because of his preoccupation with her. She wished she could give them back those hours—and the time-worn jokes about eggs Benedict and cantaloupe halves. But what if she could? Then Gardner would have been the deprived one. Until those last hours on his boat, he had been happy in the way people in love are happy. If he had been her first, if she had taken him into her, as she had wanted to until the very last tormented moments, would he have left happier? Would she be feeling any less remorse?

Willie returned and settled between them. "Because they'll never find Gardy, it doesn't seem real to them. They are holding in—dreadfully."

Leya had never attended a memorial service. From time to time when she was in the orphans' home, she remembered that her father and Minnie had gone to services for the dead. As she listened to the minister intoning scriptural words of promise, somewhere, from the deep recesses of memory, came the echo of an ancient incantation: *"yis-ga-dal v'yis-ka-dash sh'may ra bo."* She remembered the sounds, not the meaning, but the meaning was always the same.

At the close of the services, Willie escorted his wife and Leya to Gardner's parents, who were greeting friends on the steps of the church.

When she was introduced to the slender, gray-haired woman with the youthful face, Leya saw the quickening of interest and the searching look.

"It was so good of you to come, Miss Marks," she said. She turned to William Vandercort. "And thank you, Willie. It was very thoughtful. Good-by."

Leya glanced at her watch. "Before we find a place for brunch, Willie, could we do something?"

"Of course."

"Could we drive over by the harbor?"

Several minutes later, Willie pulled the car into an area above the landing, and Leya got out.

For a time, she stood, trying to orient herself. The sloop had been secured to a mooring in the harbor. They had rowed back and forth in a dinghy. A number of the buoys were empty now, and the dinghy—she thought it was the same one—was turned bottom up on the landing.

She saw two men working on some cables that stretched into the water. She called, and one of them came over.

"I was looking for—for Gardner Sutton's boat—the *Jezebel.* I thought it was tied up out there."

"It was, ma'am. Before he went off, Lieutenant Sutton asked us to haul her." He turned and pointed to a covered, demasted hull resting in a storage cradle. "There she be, ma'am."

Leya murmured her thanks and walked toward the sloop. Nothing was visible except the keel, encrusted here and there with clusters of mollusks. Somehow, angled up on the shore, stranded in its weathered cradle, the *Jezebel* seemed misshapen, ugly, an empty, lifeless hulk covered with a soiled shroud. For a moment, Leya stood looking up at the craft, remembering the feel of life in her as she heeled to the spring breeze gusting up the Sound, hearing again Gardner Sutton's sympathetic laughter as he tested her knowledge of nautical terminology, found it wanting, and chided her by saying, "A sheet, dear little girl, is not something you put on a bed. It's the line—the rope—that controls the angle of the sail in relation to the wind." Then he had pointed to the cable bracing the mast. "And a shroud is not something they cover a corpse with!"

CHAPTER 35

On the first of December, after what seemed to Leya an interminable wait, preproduction work began on *Miss Twinkle Toes.* She was to be costarred with Bert Bennett, who, as a bankable star, would get top billing.

Ed Matson leased a three-bedroom house with a pool for her in Laurel Canyon.

During the weeks in New York, at the studio's suggestion, she had begun voice lessons with Lydia Sturtevant.

"The girl has an interesting speaking voice," the coach had said to Matson after the audition. "Also she has a natural sense of rhythm. I can't make a Jeanette MacDonald or a Grace Moore out of her. But in three months she will make an acceptable sound—a true, supported tone—certainly sufficient for musical comedy."

When Jay Sanford listened, he made a decision. "The coaching has done everything it needed to do for the time being, Leya. We'll hire a voice to record the singing. The training in New York will make a lip-sync track easy for you." His eyes twinkled. "Just promise me one thing. When you hear the finished track, don't ask Matson to renegotiate your contract because you have such a sensational voice!"

While the sets were being readied, Leya and Kent spent long hours in ballet class. At the studio, Kent worked with her on modern and jazz. Together they conceived and blocked out the dances that would be featured in the film. At the end of the week, when Ed told them that the studio had agreed to engage Peter and his wife Jean as well as Kuzzy and Marc and Luanna, Leya insisted that Tanya Kuznetsov share the house with her.

Matt would not be with them, but Howard Pryor had been able to boost Kent's spirits by telling him that there was a good chance Matt could be assigned to a Special Services section, probably in Hollywood. By Saturday, December sixth, the future had never looked brighter for Leya.

Twenty-four hours later, the entire world came tumbling down around them as they listened to Webly Edwards' eyewitness account from Pearl Harbor and, later, to President Franklin Roosevelt describing Sunday, December 7, 1941, as "a day of infamy." Leya and the others sat stunned as the president declared that a state of war now existed between the United States and Japan.

Three days later, the Japanese captured Guam, and Hitler and Mussolini declared war on the United States. Blackouts were ordered for the entire Pacific Coast as Leya and the others waited for word from the studio. Their contracts contained clauses that enabled the studio to cancel its obligations in the event of war or other "acts of God." The dancers spent hours at Leya's house in Laurel Canyon waiting, conjecturing, for the most part afraid to indulge in the luxury of hoping.

For a week, the entire film industry placed itself in a state of suspended animation. Production was shut down in midscene. Actors and crews were ordered to stand by. Those who held reserve military commissions were called to active duty. Those who held order numbers not yet pulled held their breaths.

On the fifteenth day of December, Kent received his "greetings." To Leya, it seemed to be the final blow. Ed Matson's apparent unconcern angered her.

"He's as strong as an ox!" she argued. "I can't imagine them not taking him—just like they took Matt."

"Little friend," Ed said soothingly, "there are a lot of

things in this world you still can't imagine. One of them is our paradoxical Judeo-Christian Victorian morality. I've had a talk with Kent about the efficacy of candor when he is interviewed by the army psychologists. I can't tell you what's going to happen to the motion-picture industry, but I can predict with absolute certainty what's going to happen to Kent Kendall."

Two days later, at eight A.M., Kent Kendall reported for his physical. By noon he had been returned to a civilian status carrying a card marked 4-F. Within a week Peter Genova and Marc Bright were also exempted from service. Peter's married status and the fact that his elderly parents were valid dependents proved sufficient to pass him over, with the proviso that he might be reclassified in the future. Marc was given a 4-F when the physicians discovered what they thought was an anomaly in his heartbeat.

"When they examined me," he said at the spontaneous celebration at Leya's house, "all I did was imagine how I'd feel if I was stuck up to my knees in jungle mud and a Jap was coming at me with a bayonet. I nearly gave myself a heart attack, but I got away!"

"You guys escaped service," Ed agreed, "but if things get back on the track here, we'll do our part by entertaining the troops. Howard Pryor told me that a number of service organizations have gotten together with something called the USO. They're planning over a thousand canteens. One is being set up here." He smiled. "If I may paraphrase Milton, 'They also serve who only sing and dance.' So I'm going to make damn sure that's what you kids do in your spare time. And," he added, "there's a subsidiary benefit. Your devotion to patriotic duty will be duly reported by the nation's press."

Leya studied Ed Matson and wondered if he ever planned a move that did not contemplate a "subsidiary benefit."

For several days, tensions seemed to ease. Then, early on the morning of December twenty-third, the news came that the Japanese had captured Wake Island and were now within air striking distance of the United States mainland. Within hours, the Los Angeles area was riddled with rumors that Japanese reconnaissance planes had flown along the coast and submarines had surfaced and shelled city hall. Blackout violators were arrested. When shell holes failed to appear, when refineries and harbor installations remained intact, and the only evidence of shellfire proved to be shrapnel from our own antiaircraft batteries that had fired spectacular salvos at apparitions, Southern California settled down and with it the film industry.

Production resumed on *Miss Twinkle Toes* in mid-January. Ed Matson's optimism, guarded during the weeks after Pearl Harbor, revived with the evidence that an America at war still needed entertainment.

The press carried front-page stories of Hollywood's great going off to war. Frank Capra, James Stewart, Clark Gable, Ronald Reagan, Alan Ladd—the roster grew daily, and as it did, so did the opportunity for new faces, both in front of and behind the cameras.

One of those new faces was Celine Cervier, who was cast in a featured dance role in the new Nelson Eddy-Jeanette MacDonald musical.

Leya offered to put her up during her stay, but transportation proved to be a problem. Because she did not drive, Celine took an apartment in Culver City, close to the Metro-Goldwyn-Mayer studios.

The two girls saw each other only twice. Ed Matson and Leya had a special dinner for her and Billy Brenner at Romanoff's in Beverly Hills. The next evening they drove them to Union Station to catch the *Chief* to Chicago.

On the drive back, Leya could not rid herself of a lingering guilt. "Somehow," she said to Ed, "I can't get over the feeling that Celine's really getting the short end."

"Will you stop worrying about her?" Matson replied. "She's going back to a hit Broadway show. There's no way your precious Celine will ever be a star in pictures, little friend. She has absolutely everything she needs but the one indispensable quality, that indefinable X ingredient that comes from the inside. You have it. She doesn't. It's as simple as that. Leave it lay where Jesus 'flang' it, as my grandmother used to say when the wind blew the washing off the line."

Rushed through final production, *Miss Twinkle Toes*,

Leya's first starring feature, was to be ready for preview in New York early in March. Several days before she and Ed and Kent were to go East, a special-delivery letter arrived from Dulcy. The envelope contained an announcement of the birth of Gwendolyn Evelyn Vandercort, weight seven pounds three ounces, on January fourteenth, nineteen hundred and forty-two.

The hand penned note read:

> Look who's a Madonna! Don't tell me there's no such thing as an Immaculate Deception! I didn't make a son and heir, and I'll probably never be forgiven for it! But I did make the most adorable little golden-haired cutie imaginable. Willie absolutely worships her. I'm not too keen about the "Evelyn" moniker, but it was a political move to please Mother V.
>
> I know you'll want to send a silver spoon or something. Please don't. Just autograph a glamorous picture of yourself and sign it, "with love, from Aunt Leya."

The note went on to say that Willie was deeply involved in procurement for the War Department, that his father had bought an interest in several companies with defense contracts "to make certain they were properly financed and managed," and that the apartment was still available for Leya on a moment's notice.

Leya welcomed the news of the baby. Less welcome was the allusion to continuing family disfavor. During their last visit, Dulcy had intimated that a young William Vandercort, the Fifth, might go a long way toward easing familial friction. But she had borne a girl child. So far, Willie seemed to be behaving like a responsible husband and father. That was all to the good!

Transportation to New York proved to be extremely difficult because of a new system of priorities. Somehow, the studio managed space on an overnight flight.

In New York, the war seemed more remote than in California, where the whole coastline was on the alert day and night and bewildered Japanese-Americans were being sent inland to detention camps. Hitler was occupied in Russia and North Africa and, if one could believe the dispatches, wishing he were not. The Japanese had steamed into the Java Sea. They seemed unstoppable now that they had a major base in Singapore.

Miss Twinkle Toes, starring Bert Bennett *with* Leya Leslie, opened with modest fanfare at the Brooklyn Paramount and played to capacity business. There was no studio party, but Ed Matson hosted a supper in honor of the principals at the St. George Hotel in Brooklyn Heights.

In spite of the enthusiastic reaction from the Paramount people in New York and from the I.A.M. staff, Leya felt depressed. The next morning, she called Myra Lieberman.

"Leya dear! I read that you were in, but I didn't want to call until after the preview," the older woman said. "We haven't heard a word from Arthur since a censored letter saying that he's been assigned to an R.A.F. bomber group 'in the vicinity of London' and that he's promised a transfer to the United States Army Air Force in the event that becomes 'feasible'—whatever that means."

"Would he come home first?"

"I think not, Leya. By the way, I do have a picture of him in his flight officer's uniform. He wanted you to have it, and I'm sure you'll agree that he's the handsomest looking thing in it!"

"Of course I will," Leya responded.

"I know how busy you are, dear, but could we have you for dinner before you go back? Could you join Martin and me tomorrow—just the three of us—at six?"

"I have a sort of standing date with Ed Matson, Myra, but I'm going to break it. It will be such a relief not to spend the evening trying to outfigure my manager—and Paramount."

On the return flight to Los Angeles at the end of the second week, Leya stared down vacantly at the snow-blanketed Midwestern panorama slipping by twelve thousand feet below. From time to time, the quadrated fields and wood lots were obscured by tatters of wet, gray clouds scudding beneath the wings. Half hypnotized by the drone of the engines, she allowed her mind to drift back over the past fortnight. In her purse, protected between two pieces of cardboard, was the color print of Arthur in uniform.

The dinner with the Liebermans had been a refreshing change. The spacious top-floor apartment overlooking Central Park was furnished with comfortable, homey things.

Martin had told her that Arthur was to be copilot on the Stirling bombers that were designed to carry the air war into the heart of Germany.

"He asked to be assigned to the biggest planes that could carry the biggest bomb loads," he said. "Can I tell you, Leya dear, our Arthur is an angry man. If it were up to him, even God couldn't save Hitler!"

God hadn't helped poor Gardner, Leya thought bitterly. And now there were so many to pray for. She found herself picturing Arthur at the controls of the bomber, holding resolutely on course through black bursts of flack while the Nazi fighters, their guns spitting tracers, dove in for the kill. "God help him!" she whispered. "And God help me, I love him."

She rolled her face toward the window to conceal her tears. In her mind, she visualized the snapshot. It had been taken outside the officers' club at the base in Ontario. Arthur, leaner than she had ever seen him, was smiling broadly. His cap was set at a jaunty angle, and his chest was thrust out to make certain the family would see the embroidered RCAF wings above the left pocket of his tunic. "Oh, yes, yes, Arthur," she whispered again, "I do love you—God help us all!"

CHAPTER 36

The studio limousine Ed had arranged for met Leya at the airport and drove her to her Laurel Canyon house. Kuzzy, dressed in worn black wool practice leotards and a disreputable old hand-knit sweater, greeted her at the door. Her blonde hair was pulled straight up and caught in a "silly knot" atop her head. Her sparkling eyes round with wonder, she caught Leya in a huge embrace.

"*Padrooga,* he's here! He's here! Kent's having a party for him tomorrow!"

Leya turned Kuzzy so the driver could put the suitcases inside, "Who's here?"

"Matt! They got him transferred. He's been at some place up north. Fort Ord. Now he's with a special air corps unit. Do you know who his commanding officer is? Ronald Reagan!" Kuzzy ran to the telephone. "I'll call Kent. He wants to know if he can have the party here?"

"Oh, no!" Leya moaned. In spite of the bone weariness that always afflicted her after the twelve-hour flight, Kuzzy's eagerness amused her. Holding her friend's arm, she led her to a large L-shaped sofa that faced the two arched windows overlooking the canyon.

"Now rewind the track, Tanya, and play it back again. Matt's going to be stationed here—?"

"Making training films," Kuzzy cut in.

"And Kent wants to give a party, naturally—"

"Here," Kuzzy agreed, "because his place is so small, and he wants to ask some of the kids who worked on *Holiday* and some from *Miss Twinkle Toes*, too!"

Leya closed her eyes. "Oh, my God! How many?"

"Maybe only twenty—tomorrow night?"

Leya rose wearily. "All right. Anything for the war effort." She leveled a warning look at Kuzzy. "Just make sure you don't get wounded in the battle!"

Tanya Kuznetsov's expressive eyes saddened, and she clasped her hands below the sagging sweater front. "I know, *padrooga.* You think I'm crazy, just like Jean and Luanna do."

"Not crazy," Leya said. "Just unrealistic—and a little reckless, too, unless you don't mind risking Kent's friendship among other things."

Kuzzy nodded. "I know. But I'm sure about Matt—when he's with me."

It was after eleven when Leya stepped out of the sunken Spanish tile tub that, Ed had observed, "must have been left over from an old DeMille picture."

During the bath, Kuzzy had seated herself cross-legged on the yellow angora mat, talking and handing Leya the soap, back brush, and wash cloth. It was a funny thing about Kuzzy, Leya thought as she allowed herself to be tucked in. You had to love the little Russian with the perpetually surprised expression and the hard, round dancer's body, if not for her good sense, then certainly for her good humor. Instead of "The Mad Russian" or "The Sad Russian," the other dancers called her, not without affection, "the Cuckoo Cossack."

Perched on the side of the bed, Kuzzy kept up a barrage of questions until Leya reached up and pressed a hand lightly over her lips. "One of the smartest things I've ever done was to ask you to share this house with me, Kuzzy. But you've got to get the hell out of here now and let me get some sleep. My head's still on New York time." She loosened the covers.

"Twenty people? With Kent that means thirty!" She pulled the blankets up over her head. "Good night."

The party was fun. Bruce Cydney, Kent's film-wise assistant choreographer at the studio, and several of the lead contract dancers and their companions were present in addition to the original Kendall Dance Group. As Kent had promised, there were twenty in all. With the exception of Marty Maizlish and his aspiring actress date, the guests were gypsies. A few of them looked longingly at the unheated pool and decided that the end of February was still too early to swim even though the days had been up in the high sixties.

Kent and Matt brought over an elaborate buffet, which Leya and Kuzzy set up on the extended dining table.

After the guests had served themselves, most of them settled on the floor. Kuzzy took a seat a discreet distance from Matt, who was ensconced at the end of the sofa next to Kent.

Matt O'Brien seemed to have come out of his shell. Under Kent's questioning, he amused them with his account of the events at Fort Dix in New Jersey and his subsequent assignment to Fort Ord near Monterey, California, for basic training.

Kent, elated at having Matt with him again, and slightly campy from the brandy-spiked champagne punch, pointed to the medal and ribbon on the uniform jacket.

"I really believe our boy earned the marksman's medal," he said, rolling his eyes and gesturing extravagantly, "but a good conduct medal? My God! How careless of the army!"

Everyone but Kuzzy laughed. When Leya saw her companion's indignation, she called Kuzzy to the kitchen to help replenish a couple of platters. The little Russian's eyes were gleaming like clean blue porcelain.

"What's the matter with Kent?" she asked. "He's swishing all over the place tonight—and drinking too much."

Leya put an arm around her. "Kuzzy, darling, what are we going to do about you? Matt's living the life he wants to live. You shouldn't try to defend him from what he wants."

"He doesn't know what he wants!" Kuzzy retorted. "We've had a lot of close personal talks ever since Florida.

You won't believe me, Leya, but I know a lot more about him than he does!"

"That may be, little friend—" *Little friend?* Startled, Leya wondered why those particular words had come out. "But it might be a lot smarter to let him find out about himself in his own time. Don't get in the middle, Kuzzy."

"I'm not going to, Leya. But I think more of him than any guy I've ever known, and I know I can help him."

Leya fixed Tanya with a disbelieving look. "Come on, Kuznetsov! Don't be a hopeless wishful thinker!"

The little dancer set her jaw. "You'll see!"

The party broke up at half-past one with an overearnest promise by Kent that he and Matt would come by in midmorning to help clean up.

Shortly before noon, Matt appeared in Kent's station wagon. He was rested and in good spirits. "Kent got his nose too wet last night," he explained. "He's wiped out."

Kuzzy was unable to conceal her delight. She commandeered Leya's apron and shooed her out of the kitchen. "Get into your suit and go doze by the pool. We'll clean up here."

After a token protest, cut short by Kuzzy's pleading look, Leya went to her bedroom. In the midst of changing, a long-distance call came from Ed Matson. He would be out in midweek to set up an office in Hollywood. Paramount was pleased with the business *Miss Twinkle Toes* was doing, and a second picture was in the planning.

Ed had seen Heather and Carlo at Toots Shor's. Heather looked like "hell warmed over." Carlo was taking credit as "Leya Leslie's discoverer" and had hinted that he would regard it as "a great favor" if Leya would dance in his Las Vegas club between pictures. "And Sheri sends her love."

When Leya hung up, her insides were churning. "A great favor," Carlo had said. There isn't enough money in the world!

Carrying a large beach towel, Leya poked her head into the kitchen. Kuzzy, dressed in brief shorts and a skimpy halter, had done up her hair in a ponytail that seemed to squirt from the back of her head. She was standing in bare feet at the sink, in third position, up to her elbows in suds. Matt's GI sun tans were protected by a frilly flowered kitchen apron.

"He's learning," Kuzzy said as she rinsed a platter. Grinning self-consciously, Matt took it from her and swaddled it in a damp dish towel.

"If you've got to draw KP on leave," he laughed, "this isn't such rough duty!"

Leya moved between them and embraced them. "I feel guilty, but I'll try to live with it. Come join me at the pool when you're through."

Late in the afternoon, Matt ran up the stairs to the house to answer the phone. It was Kent, sounding poutish.

"I feel absolutely abandoned," he said. "Why don't you come home? There weren't *that* many dishes, for God's sake!"

"They want you to come over here and help us finish the food. There's enough left to feed an army," Matt replied.

"I can feed the army here, too, you know," Kent said. "But if they insist, I suppose you can come and get me. I'm still half a basket case!"

When Matt returned with Kent an hour later, both girls made little sympathy sounds.

"I know," Kent said defensively, "you don't have to tell me. I look like a fugitive from the morgue. I can't drink anymore!"

"If you mean, any more than you did, nobody can!" Matt said. "You really fell into the punch bowl last night."

Kent gave him a dismal look. "Well, I have reason to, don't I?"

Leya diverted the conversation to safer ground.

By nine o'clock, Kent, who had insisted a "hair of the dog" would make him feel better, was having trouble keeping his eyes open. Leya, ignoring Kuzzy's appealing look, sent them home.

Kuzzy padded into the big bedroom cinching a wrapper around herself. "Do you know, Leya," she said, "I think today was one of the best days of my life."

Leya was brushing her hair. "Doing dishes for two hours? Do you feel all right, Kuzzy?"

"I feel wonderful, *padrooga!*" She perched on the edge of

the bed. "Do you know something else? I had the best talk with Matt, too. I know you don't think so, but I'm positive that I'm right about him."

"You are the world's most determined optimist," Leya replied.

"If you are a White Russian, you have to be optimistic," Kuzzy said.

Leya slanted a glance at her through the canopy of gleaming copper hair. "If you really want to know about optimism, you should try being a Polish Jew."

"The hardest part of this job," Leya wrote to her father and Minnie, "is sitting around waiting. Matt O'Brien, who is in Special Services here, says the army calls it 'Hurry up and wait!'

"The new picture is called *The Girl with the Golden Shoes,* or at least that is the working title. I'll be with Bert Bennett again. He still gets top billing, but this time it's '*and* Leya Leslie,' and they promise me top billing on the one after that. They may try for another leading man. I hope so. Bennett is married and has three kids, but he always wants to play house with me. It got so bad that Ed told Jay Sanford, the producer, I was his girl and he wanted Bennett to lay off. I'm not happy about that, but Ed says it is better for the complaint not to have come from me.

"Anyway, here it is almost May, and they are still revising the shooting script. The kids will work with me again. Kent is doing some fantastic dance routines. There is more classical ballet in this picture because I'm a ballerina. (That will please madame!) I still take class with Carmelita Maracci, and I really look forward to rehearsals. This sitting around drives me crazy, even with Tanya living with me. I think Jay is going to give her a comedy role. She doesn't have to act. All she has to do is be herself!

"I'm glad you liked the snapshots of the house. It's very private being up the little dead-end road in Laurel Canyon. I would give anything if you two would come out for a visit this summer. You could watch the shooting on the set, and on weekends we could go exploring. Please think about it!

"A couple of weeks ago, I watched them shoot the final scene of *Take a Letter Darling* with Rosalind Russell, Fred MacMurray, MacDonald Carey, and Constance Moore. When Mitchell Leisen introduced me, they were so nice. They all said I didn't need an introduction. They had seen *Miss Twinkle Toes!* Charles Arnt, who is an extremely nice person and a very clever actor, even asked for my autograph!"

Harry Marks, squinting through the reading glasses that Minnie had finally persuaded him to buy, lowered the letter.

"What can I tell you? My little Leya socializing with movie stars! Who would believe?"

CHAPTER 37

The first of the three major dance numbers in *Golden Shoes* was a dream sequence in which Leya, as an aspiring teen-age ballerina, stops on her way to class in Carnegie Hall and sneaks into the auditorium to watch the dress rehearsal of a great Russian ballerina's debut in America. Concealed in the balcony, she sees herself in the role. At the end of the elaborate production, when she is receiving a great imaginary ovation, she is returned to reality by an amused custodian who escorts her to the lobby. There, dressed in her bobby-sox outfit and soiled saddle shoes, the teen-ager assumes the prima ballerina's glamorous pose depicted in the lobby poster.

Director Lew Frederix, delighted with the pathos Leya managed to impart to the fantasy, shot the sequence in two days. On the second day's lunch break, Frederix stopped by Mitchell Leisen's table and spoke with some wonder about Leya's surprising dramatic talent. Leisen smiled a bit smugly.

"I suspected a volcano behind that cool façade."

Toward the end of the eight-week shooting schedule, Ed Matson received a call from Howard Pryor in New York.

"I hear your girl is doing fine," he said. "The talk around the Paramount Building is good."

"Out here, too," Matson replied. "Will Johnny Coyle manage a *Life* cover?"

"He'll try. We'll get it if the kid comes through in this picture. He's pitching the 'underwear model to movie star' angle. Cinderella with a switch."

"How's *Riddle Me This* doing?"

"Holding up. The Cervier girl is doing very well in Kendall's new act. And that reminds me—Irving Berlin's doing an all GI musical for Special Services. O'Brien is being tagged for it. Is that going to create problems with Kendall?"

Matson mused. "That's hard to say. Somehow, I get the feeling that those two are not as cozy as they used to be." He paused. "We'll just have to handle the ruction, if it comes."

"Has Kendall finished his work on *Golden Shoes?*"

"Almost. He's got a very good assistant—a kid named Bruce Cydney—and by the way, I'm keeping an eye on Peter Genova, too. The lad has aspirations. He's also got a happy marriage to a dancer. If it turns out that he can choreograph, that could save me a lot of gray hairs!"

"I know him," Pryor said. "We'll give him a chance if we can." There was a pause. "Speaking of gray hairs, Ed, I've just got some news. It's not good. If you haven't already heard, you'd better know that Arthur Lieberman has been shot down on his first mission over Germany."

"Oh, Jesus Christ!" Matson murmured. "How did you find out?"

"Through Bert Farber, his brother-in-law. He's got his own C.P.A. firm. Bill Lazarus, one of our accountants, socializes with him. I got it third hand, but I believe it's solid news."

As he listened to Pryor, Ed Matson found his guts churning. If the news was confirmed, he was in for a bad time with Leya in the middle of her most important picture.

"When she finds out, Howard, I'll be asked a million questions. Do you have any more details?"

"Only that his wing was flying with the RAF on the first Thousand Bomber raid over Cologne on the thirtieth of May. Apparently, they flew out of a Lincolnshire base. From what Farber told Lazarus, the losses were awful."

The next morning on the set, Ed was alert for some sign that Leya might have heard. A carefully steered conversation about the war produced no hint that Leya was even reading much about events overseas. A few days earlier, the Germans had surrounded Marshall Timoshenko's forces while the Russian was trying to retake Kharkov. They had captured a quarter of a million Red soldiers and all of their equipment. Doomsday predictions had dominated the press and the airwaves. Even so, it was obvious that Leya was concentrating on her work.

Ed waited until the next scene was under way before he went to Lew Frederix's office to phone New York.

"Mrs. Lieberman, this is Ed Matson, Leya Leslie's manager."

"Oh, Mr. Matson," Myra said, "I'm so glad you called."

"I've called because I heard some distressing news that might have affected your family."

"Oh, my God, has it!" Myra said. "We're worried sick."

"I have no doubt that you are," Ed replied, wishing that he had found a more appropriate response. "I called to see if you had told Leya about Arthur as yet?"

"No, we haven't," she replied. "Martin and I weren't certain it was the right thing to do."

"I wonder if you would mind if I were the one to break it to her—at the right moment?" Ed said.

"So it won't disrupt her work," Myra finished for him. "Of course not! When you tell her, call me again if you don't mind. I'd like to talk to her also."

Matson was relieved. Just how he would break the news still had to be thought out. And so did his response in the event she got wind of it earlier.

Kent, immersed in rehearsals for the finale of *Golden Shoes,* accepted the news of Matt's transfer to New York philosophically. "I know! Just call me a gold-star mother." He turned back to blocking a sequence with Bruce Cydney.

Kuzzy's reaction was not so casual. "But Matt's going into the show, Leya! If Berlin's doing it, it will play forever!"

"Suppose it does?" Leya asked. "In that case, Kent will probably go home, too."

"I don't think so," Kuzzy said. "Things aren't the same with him and Matt now."

"That's wishful thinking!" Leya chided.

Kuzzy looked exasperated. "All right! I'm dreaming! But I love that boy even though I know he's a little mixed up—"

"He's mixed up deliberately," Leya pointed out. "Matt's AC-DC, Kuzzy. He goes either way. Where's that going to leave you?"

Kuzzy's eyes met Leya's without blinking.

"*Padrooga,* when I get through with him, he'll only be DC—direct current—between him and me! When I snuggle my little round butter cakes up against those beautiful pectorals of his and run my fingers into those sexy dark curls, I promise you I'll make him forget all about Kent's tricks. I'll eat the little bugger alive!"

Leya's expression made Kuzzy pause.

"I'm shocking you, huh?"

"No," Leya laughed, "but you're an earthy little Rusky, aren't you?"

"Dollink," Kuzzy clowned, planting her feet wide apart and cupping her hands beneath her bosom, "*I* am Mother Russia!"

Shortly before *Golden Shoes* completed shooting, Jean Baxter came over to Leya on the set.

"Is it true that Kuzzy's going East when we finish?"

Leya tried to conceal her surprise. "I suppose most of us will—for a visit at least."

"No," Jean explained, "I mean to stay?"

The possibility had occurred to Leya, but she felt some annoyance that Kuzzy would have told others first. "I don't know, Jean. Who told you?"

"Nobody, really. Peter deduced it from a crack Kent made." The dancer looked around to make certain she was not being overheard. "Also, we heard that Kent has asked Bruce to move in with him."

"I wouldn't know about that, either, Jean. Anyway, that's his business."

Looking a trifle hurt, Jean excused herself. A few minutes later, sitting beside her husband, she said, "Our Miss Leslie is beginning to act like a movie star."

Peter patted her leg. "You know Leya, honey. She's a very private person. You shouldn't have asked her."

"You know why I did, don't you? Because I want you to get your chance to choreograph. You're every bit as good as Kent."

"Thank you, sweetheart. When I get the job, I'll make you a star."

"Never mind that crap," Jean replied. "Just make me a living. Your lovin' wife's getting too creaky for this work!"

Ed Matson paced the large corner office in the suite he had leased at Sunset Boulevard and Doheny, a few blocks west of his Sunset Tower apartment. Leya, ignoring him, sat leafing through the motion-picture reviews in weekly *Variety*. The shooting had been completed, and the dubbing was underway. Pending confirmation from preview cards, Paramount was planning a major promotional campaign. That was all to the good. What was not to the good was Leya's mood. Since the previous day, she had shown signs of being unusually upset.

He stood facing her. "Generally, little friend, I do not inquire into your moods, but it's clear to me that something is bugging you. Is it anything I can help with?"

"Yes. Two things are 'bugging' me as you put it. Those damned driving lessons, which scare me pea green, and Kuzzy leaving me alone in the house."

"I suggested Luanna Parker. Remember?"

"It wouldn't work out," she replied. "That girl's a weirdo—with her yoga and her health food. And she has no sense of humor."

Ed smiled. "I can't refute that. But both of those problems are easily solved. Finish the three lessons you've got left and forget the idea of Luanna." He moved back a step and leaned against the edge of his desk. "Knowing what makes an artist happy or sad is part of a good manager's job. And I can't believe that this down mood you're in is really caused by driving lessons and roommates. Is it something between us? Something I have done—inadvertently?"

Leya closed her eyes. "No, Ed. You've been wonderful—and very patient."

"You know, don't you," he encouraged her, "that you can

tell me anything you feel like spilling without ever fearing that I'll break a confidence or secretly laugh at you or judge you?"

"I know, Ed." She paused, then gave her head an annoyed shake. "Look, damnit! I'm worried about Arthur."

The admission caught him off guard. He was on the verge of saying, "Then you've heard—?" when Leya continued. "I wrote Arthur a long letter when we came back here—after I had lunch with his mother. It was the sort of letter I know he would answer because it was about some personal things between us." She gave him a direct look. "I'm sure you could have guessed that."

"I can understand your concern," Ed agreed. For an instant, he thought of reassuring her that in time of war mail deliveries were uncertain at best, but he realized that such an excuse would be foolish. Later in the evening, after the three important press interviews the studio had set up at Ciro's, he would tell her.

"Leya," he said gently, "there's an explanation for everything. I'm sure the reason for it will be clear soon. What I think you ought to do now is let me drive you home so you can rest and take your time about getting dressed. One of these days, you can return the favor and drive me."

Leya's skeptical glance made him laugh. "Don't hold your breath, Mr. Matson!"

An hour later, in his apartment, Ed Matson poured himself a Scotch. As Leya's manager, he wanted to spare her any anguish that might affect her career. As a man who at last had found the combination of talent and beauty that he could cherish personally and use professionally to move him into pictures as a producer, he knew that Arthur's death might well have removed a major obstacle.

Once again he felt an old sense of guilt. Years before, when the going had been rough, his wife, an ambitious girl whose personal income had helped establish him, had found her patience wearing thin. They had argued a lot, and he had often wished her out of his life. And then, one day she was dead, killed in a head-on crash on the Boston Post Road near

Bridgeport. When her will had revealed the measure of her devotion, his conscience had nearly been his undoing.

Ed Matson glanced at his watch. Four-thirty. Five or six hours before he would have to tell Leya about Arthur. He dreaded the repercussions.

During dinner at Ciro's, legmen for Louella Parsons, Hedda Hopper, and Jimmy Fidler dropped by the table. Leya listened with admiration as Ed gave each of them an "exclusive" that would gladden the hearts of the studio's publicity staff. As she watched him, genial, easy, and deceptively sharp, Leya felt a twinge of remorse that she was—perhaps only sometimes—a bit hard on him. She could not imagine having no Ed Matson around to make things easier. He still had several other artist clients to be concerned about, but it reassured her to know that he felt her potential warranted at least eighty percent of his time.

After the interviews, when the attendant brought the car to the front, Ed tipped generously. The sharp boy had taken great pains to say, loud enough for the knot of bystanders to hear, "Good night, Miss Leslie. Your picture is a smash! Our whole family loved *Twinkle Toes*." That was part of the game.

Ed turned the car up the private drive that led to Leya's home, parked, and went around to open the door for her.

"Leya," he said, "I've got some unhappy news for you." He watched her curiosity turn to anxiety. "It's not about your work or your family. Everything's fine with them."

Leya sensed that he was having a difficult time. Her mind raced. Not the family. Dulcy, then. Or Celine—or Arthur's father. He hadn't been well. Or—she could not bring herself to think that it might be Arthur—

"There was a big RAF raid over Cologne, Leya," Matson was saying. "A lot of planes were shot down. Arthur's was one of those reported missing."

He broke off when he saw the color drain from her face. In an instant, it had become a flawless, inscrutable mask.

"I could say things that might make you feel better," he went on. "A lot of crews managed to parachute from their planes. If they landed safely at night, they had a good chance to get away. They are taught how to survive behind enemy lines. They are even given the names of sympathetic Germans around the target areas." He took her hand. It felt cold and dead. "There's no way of knowing right now."

Leya withdrew her hand and stood immobile, staring past him down the canyon to the wedge of distant city lights.

"Who told you?" she asked in a tight voice.

"Howard."

"How long have you known?"

"Several days. I didn't want to tell you, Leya, until you had finished shooting."

She nodded. "Because you thought I wouldn't be able to work?"

"No—not exactly. I just didn't want you to work under any unnecessary pressure, particularly in the final scenes."

Her steady gaze unsettled him. She was not reacting at all the way she had to the news of Gardner Sutton's death. If she loved Arthur Lieberman, how could she suddenly become a stoic?

"Ed—"

"Yes?"

Suddenly, her eyes blazed. "Why in hell didn't you tell me? Why did you keep play acting this afternoon and tonight? Is it because you think I'm a defenseless child? Is that what you really think of me? Goddammit, tell me the truth! No! Don't tell me! I know!"

An instant later, the door slammed behind her, and the dead bolt clicked.

Kuzzy glanced at the kitchen clock. It was almost two-thirty in the afternoon. Peter and Jean would be by any minute to help with her bags and drive her downtown to Union Station, where she would catch the *City of Los Angeles* to Chicago. There had been no way to get a priority, so she would sit up in the parlour car and take her chances in Chicago.

She went to Leya's bedroom door and pressed her ear against it, then knocked lightly. When a second knock brought no response, she eased the knob, opened the door a crack, and peered in. Leya, fully dressed in her evening gown, was sleeping face down on the spread. Kuzzy tiptoed closer. Lying at the edge of the bed was a color enlargement. Curious, she picked it up, recognized it instantly, then returned it to its place.

Hastily, she looked around for a letter or a card, any clue to a possible explanation. There was nothing. Frightened now, she returned to the bed, dropped to her knees. Mascara at the corners of Leya's eyes betrayed earlier tears. Kuzzy lingered, trying desperately to understand what could have sent Leya to bed so late—hours after she herself had retired—in such a state that she had collapsed in tears without undressing. Leya did not drink. Neither did she ever use any medication to make her sleep. Obviously, there had been some deep personal problem. She wondered about Matson.

When she heard Peter's car grinding up the steep driveway, she rose and went out on the front porch. Pointing to the packed bags she had hauled there, she called down to the couple.

"Give me a couple of minutes, you guys! I'll meet you in the patio."

In the living room again, Tanya stood for a moment staring toward Leya's bedroom. Finally, she went to the writing table. On a sheet of note paper, she scribbled,

"Dearest Padrooga—I came in to say good-by, and you were dead to the world. I could see that you must have had a very difficult night. I wanted to put my arms around you and thank you for all you have done and tell you how much I love you, but it didn't seem like the right time to awaken you.

"Peter and Jean are waiting for me, so I must go now. I feel a great Russian love for you and a great Russian sadness, too! I will write as soon as I'm settled in New York, and I'll telephone you as soon as I can afford it!

"God keep you, Leya darling! Kuzzy."

Car doors slamming beneath her open window awakened Leya. She returned to consciousness slowly, like one coming out of a drugged slumber. The sound of a motor sputtering to life brought her upright. For an instant, she was confused to find herself atop the bed, still dressed. Then, brushing aside a tangle of hair, she struggled to her feet and groaned at the image of herself in the mirror. From outside came the familiar labored grinding of worn gears. A moment later, she heard the squeal of brakes on the steep drive.

"Kuzzy?" she called, hurrying to the door. "Where are you?"

She glanced at the clock as the brakes protested again, and a warning horn sounded down at the intersection. Leya ran to the window in time to see Peter's old green sedan disappear around the steep turn that led to Laurel Canyon Boulevard.

"Oh, no, Kuzzy!" Leya cried. "You should have gotten me up!"

As she ran to the big arched picture window in the hope of catching a glimpse of the car as it reached Hollywood Boulevard at the mouth of the canyon, she saw the note impaled on the handle of the desk-set pen. She read it, uttered a cry, and snatched the drapes aside. For a time, she stood trying to make out the car in the stream of traffic. When she saw that it was useless, she turned away.

"Why did you leave so soon, Kuzzy?" she moaned. Then she remembered that her friend had been advised to be at the station an hour and a half before train time to make certain of her space. She had not left early, really.

Suddenly more alone than she had ever been in her life, more alone even than she had felt when she used to wave good-by to her father from the dormitory window at the home, Leya stared out over the city.

After several minutes, she returned to the bedroom. From the doorway, she saw Arthur's photo on the floor. She dropped beside it and stared at it numbly. Then, with the full realization of what had happened, she slumped against the edge of the mattress. Abandoning her silent struggle, she gave in once more to the shattering grief.

CHAPTER 38

Golden Shoes was released in the fall and soon was playing to capacity business everywhere.

Life magazine did not do a Leya Leslie cover. That prime exposure was reserved now for the great men and the events of the war. The magazine did run a two-page photo story of "Leya Leslie, Hollywood's most promising new dance star." The studio was far from disappointed. "It's a hell of a lot better for the long haul than a boxed blurb on the inside page," Jay Sanford opined.

Leya went home for the Christmas hiatus. After the first painful call to the Liebermans from California, follow-up calls were less difficult. Myra and Martin appeared to have achieved a philosophical acceptance of their son's fate. On the third call, Leya was relieved when Martin, speaking from his Florida place, said, "Darling, you have so much on your mind. If there's any word, I promise that you'll hear as soon as we do, whatever it is," he added, almost as an after thought. "We love to hear from you, darling, but please don't worry about us."

Leya decided to stay on until mid-January to attend Gwendolyn Vandercort's first birthday celebration at the Lexington Avenue apartment.

"When one thinks of a Vandercort party," Dulcy said,

"one thinks of striped garden tents on vast lawns, string quartets, an army of butlers and maids carrying silver trays"—she pantomimed elegant ladies looking down their noses through lorgnettes— "and mobs of the wrong people to make a fun party. So," she said with a smile, "we're having a small, very exclusive potty, and only the right people have been invited. Namely, you, Miss Leslie!"

Frowning, she repeated the name. "Leslie? Well, why not? It's a little hokey, but it slips off the tongue and sticks in the mind."

Shortly before Christmas, Leya had gone to visit Jon Wales, who had insisted on shooting some portraits. Leya autographed one, "To Gwendolyn on her first birthday, with love from her Aunt Leya," and had it framed in silver and gift wrapped.

"My God, you remembered!" Dulcy said, hugging Leya. "I think my mascara's going to run." She pulled away and dabbed at the corners of her eyes. "Grandfather and Grandmother Vandercort have only seen photos of their granddaughter. Their birthday remembrances were particularly appropriate—two one-hundred-dollar war bonds." Dulcy pointed to an open Bonwit Teller gift box sprouting squared petals of tissue.

"Busy daddy gave doting mommy a blank check and told me to go buy the things little Gwendolyn needs. I went to Bonwit's and asked if they had any fatherly love. The lady stared and told me to try Helena Rubenstein."

Dulcy smiled contritely. "That's not fair, really. I'm very proud of my Willie. He's working his balls off at the WPB, goosing this factory and that to get out more guns and shells and airplane parts and uniforms and God knows what. Truth is, dear heart, in many ways my timing stunk. But who in hell could guess that idiot screaming prick, Hitler, was going to stab Chamberlain in the *tukus* with his own bumbershoot?" She shook her head. "I put a split of Cordon Rouge thirty-six on ice. You and I are going to drink a toast. And from her little George Jensen silver spooney, Gwendolyn doll's going to have a sip, too. I don't know how her life will end up, but I want to make sure she starts it with champagne."

Leya touched the infant's silk-fine blonde hair as Dulcy put a drop of champagne to her lips. The effervescent fluid made the baby wrinkle her button nose. "Bubbly does the same thing to mommy, darling!" Dulcy cooed.

On the way to Brownsville to have dinner with her father and Minnie and to face again the curious neighbors whose pretexts for dropping in seemed endless, Leya wondered at the change in Dulcy. Superficially, she was the same beautiful, kitten-eyed blonde, slicker now, better groomed, Town and Country chic. But the humor was more brittle. There had even been a hint of self-pity when she had said, "God knows I try to be what he wants me to be. The point is, when you wear the Vandercort moniker but don't have the proper variety of ivy crawling up your family tree, you get caught between Plymouth Rock and a hard place."

It was the first time, Leya realized, that she had not completely enjoyed being with Dulcy.

On her return to Los Angeles, the studio photographer and the airline PR man shot Leya posing with the stewardesses and with the captain and copilot. When she finished the monotonous chore and came down the steps with the brown Karakul coat slung over her arm, Ed Matson hurried toward her. Taken by surprise, Leya allowed herself to be held in a tight embrace.

"Have I ever got good news for you, little friend!" he said, releasing her. "I know you're beat, honey, but you've got to ask me up."

"You're asked," she replied, truly glad to see him. "What kind of news?"

"Not the kind I'm going to fluff off on the run. You're going to get this sitting down—with a glass of Asti Spumante."

When the last of Leya's bags had been lugged upstairs, and she reappeared in slacks and an old sweater, he handed her a glass of the sparkling Italian wine.

"Here's to the brightest new star that dances in the night, Leya Leslie. Salary, two thousand dollars a week, new leading man, that baritone heart throb of *tutti degli Italiani,* Ricardo

Ricordi, and a two-million-dollar budget for her next picture, *The Sweetheart of Company B.*"

Leya's uptilted eyes ovaled in disbelief. "Two thousand dollars a week?" she whispered.

"That's right—gross. And I should say that while I.A.M. is content to accept its customary ten percent, I would be happy to renegotiate my contract with you so you will never again worry whether or not my commission covers my cigarettes and booze."

"Oh my Lord!" Leya laughed. "Draw up the paper, Ed, then blindfold me and I'll sign it." She looked through the big Spanish window to the dark trough of Laurel Canyon and the familiar fragment of city glittering below.

"Two thousand dollars a week!" she repeated. "Leya Marks, daughter of Harry Marks, master mechanic, Brooklyn Navy Yard—cousin and stepdaughter of Minnie Tabotchnik Marks, head seamstress of Super Figure Under Garments—Incorporated? I don't believe it!"

"Believe it, sweetheart! And drink to it!" Ed touched his glass to the edge of hers.

"And I want to congratulate you," he said, "on having had the wisdom to choose the smartest, most charming personal manager in show business."

Leya scrutinized him. "All right, I'll drink to that, Mr. Matson," she said, elevating her glass.

Ed laughed. "Now, then, Miss Leslie, we're not through with the good news. As of the first of the month, you don't have to drive this canyon anymore. In fact, you don't even have to drive yourself, anywhere" —he leaned closer—"because you're moving down to Malibu. Mitch Leisen insists on decorating your new place. Also, you will find a shiny new convertible—a gift from the grateful men at Paramount—and a dependable combination chauffeur and butler whose wife just happens to be your new cook and housekeeper."

Leya closed her eyes and sank into the corner of the sofa. "Ed, what are you trying to do to me? I'm very tired."

"It's no joke, Leya. We'll get into details tomorrow. But I want to tell you that Kent Kendall has bought a house on the beach just a few yards north of yours. And he also has a new seven-fifty a week contract as a choreographer with the understanding that he'll not be given an assignment that conflicts with our production. Also, if he dances in the picture, he gets an extra two-fifty." He paused. "How does that strike you?"

"I still think I'm going to wake up some morning in the Brooklyn Hebrew Orphan's Asylum on Ralph Avenue and find that I've been in a coma all this time, just dreaming."

Leya's misgivings dissolved during her first inspection of the rambling tile-roofed, one-story, white clapboard house on the beach in the Malibu colony. She had assumed that the house would be leased. When Ed told her that she was buying it for a mere eighty thousand dollars, she cried out in alarm.

"Eighty thousand dollars for a house is insane, Ed!"

"Poor baby," he soothed. "Getting used to being rich is not half as difficult as getting used to being poor. Please have faith, darling. I've checked this out with the best heads in the real-estate business. After the war, the price of this place could go up two to three hundred percent. And by the way," he added, "Kent paid ninety thousand for his, or rather his family did."

In her new house, Leya could not dispel the recurring sense of unreality. "It can't be happening," she whispered to herself as she watched Mitchell Leisen, whose consuming hobby was interior decoration, fussing with a swag of pearl-gray silk over the massive front window facing the beach.

When the antique white Empire furniture he wanted was not available in the market, Mitch ordered it built to his design in the Paramount carpenter shop. In three days short of a month, he worked a miracle. "Leya's Layout," as he called the Malibu house, had an enormous white-carpeted combination living room, dining room, and bar that gave onto a twenty-by-forty-foot glazed tile patio shaded by a permanent metal ramada. Its perimeter was fenced by rows of large classic urns in which dwarf cypress had been planted.

The house contained four bedrooms and three baths and a special Scotch shower room fitted with overhead sun lamps and a massage table.

When the last of her things had been moved in, Leya stood alone in the luxurious setting and could not rid herself of the feeling of resentment that had grown with the realization that in her own home—her very first—she had not been permitted to make a single basic decision.

Photographers from the newspaper "home sections" and from *Sunset Magazine* spent hours shooting "Leya Leslie at home." Paramount's photo crew followed with shots showing Leya playing with a dog on the sand or ready to plunge into the surf. Also, there were layouts purporting to show her practicing on the sand with Kent Kendall and his assistant. At the end of the week, Leya was out of patience.

"For God's sake, Ed," she flared, "I have more privacy on the set. I need some time alone! Tell them, *please,* to get the hell out of here, at least until I've seen all the rooms!"

The outburst surprised Matson. Leya had been edgy at times, but this was her first temperamental outburst. He thought that she might be suppressing more emotion than she suspected over Arthur's fate. There had been no new word. He knew that her reserve was a protective tactic. He mollified her by promising a week entirely free of business.

Leya could not remember a more relaxed time. Jack Squires—he insisted it sounded "more dignified" if he were simply called "Squires"—and Ellen took almost no getting used to. They were simple, comfortable folks from Oklahoma who, as a young couple, had been forced to give up their dry land ranch and come to Southern California with the other Okies.

The free days passed too quickly as Leya accustomed herself to her new home, inventoried her clothes, and tried to accept the idea that she no longer had to skimp, that now she could buy what she wanted without undue consideration for her actual needs.

Leya went to Kent's place almost daily. Usually, as she explored the beach, bundled against the moist bluster, Kent would appear with Bruce Cydney and insist she come in for a "glass of tea," his harmless little chauvinistic joke. He and Bruce were living together now, more out of convenience than conviction, Leya suspected.

Kent's house was not as large as hers. Neither was it as lavishly furnished. But it did have a large playroom with a parquet floor. Kent had installed mirrors and a barre along one wall and insisted that she practice there.

On the Sunday morning before her free days were up, Ed Matson called. "I hope you notice that I've kept my promise. I haven't even called."

"I appreciate it, Ed," Leya replied, "but you didn't have to carry it that far!"

"You should have told me. I've been dying to come down and take you to dinner—or better still, be invited to one!"

"You are—tonight—if you can make it. I'm having Kent and Bruce over. Ellen insists that I've got to stop dining in the kitchen and behave like a movie queen."

Shortly after noon, Kent came down the beach carrying a large paper sack. "Have you ever seen these?" he asked, opening the top to reveal a half-dozen green globes.

"What are they?" Leya asked.

"Papayas. Tell Ellen to wrap each one in brown paper and leave them out on the kitchen counter. They'll be ripe in a couple of days."

Leya thanked him, assuming that he had walked down simply to bring the fruit. It became apparent that he had something else on his mind.

"Bruce is sleeping on the sofa. He's like an old cat!" he said in a scornful voice. "I got tired of tippy-toeing around my own house. I know you're getting ready for tonight, but—"

Leya laughed and interrupted him. "I'm not doing a thing, Kent. Ellen would fire me if I tried. How about a 'glass of tea' for you?"

"Or Scotch?" he asked.

Seated out of the breeze in a sheltered corner of the ramada, Kent's mood changed.

"You heard about Matt, didn't you?"

"No," Leya replied, suddenly uneasy.

"Are you sure? Maybe you just want to spare me," Kent charged.

"Of course not!" Leya replied. "If I had heard anything about Matt, I certainly would have said something. What's happened?"

"Did you know he's engaged to be married?"

"My God, no! How did you find out?"

"In Hy Gardner's column. I still have the New York papers sent. Otherwise, I'd feel like I'm living in the land of Oz!"

"It's Kuzzy, of course."

"Well, God knows it isn't me!" Kent snapped. Suddenly, his face contorted. "That sneaky little Siberian slut! Ever since I signed her, I've regretted it." He sprang up from the wicker hassock and paced. "She decided from the very first that she was going to get him." He stopped to glare at Leya. "She knew goddamned good and well that he was with me—that he was gay and liked the life with me, didn't she?"

"I really couldn't say, Kent," Leya replied. "I try not to get involved in my friends' personal affairs."

"Of course you don't! That's why I'm spilling to you, Leya dear. I trust you!" He knelt down in front of her chair. His indignation turned to anguish as he reached for her hand. "My God, Leya, I do love Matt! It may shock you, but I would do anything for him. Anything!"

Leya wished she could say something comforting. She had watched Kuzzy with Matt at the Laurel Canyon place. "I'll eat the little bugger alive!" the Russian dancer had promised. Leya also remembered an observation Peter Genova had made. "She'll pretend to help him, then trip him and beat him to the floor," he had said, half in jest. Now it looked as though he had been right.

Controlling himself, Kent looked up at Leya. "I'm sorry," he said, searching her face. "You loved Arthur, didn't you?"

Leya masked her surprise. "Yes."

"Then you can understand, can't you?"

"I think so."

"Love doesn't hurt any the less because it's happened

between two men. Ever since school, I've fooled around with a lot of guys. It's the way I went, for whatever reason. I have no guilt about it. That kind of relationship gives me friendship, companionship, sex, everything but the responsibility of raising a lot of squalling kids. My babies are ideas. Perhaps someday I'll die a lonely old man wishing I had children. If that happens, Leya, I promise I won't pluck at the covers with bony fingers and whine at God for making me gay. I'll try to remember to thank Him for the good creative things I've done, for the happiness I've given people, for the loving friends I've known—" He broke off and lowered his head onto her lap.

Leya smoothed his shoulders and felt them heave with a huge sigh. "And," he continued in a muffled voice, "I'll try very hard to forgive."

Ed Matson arrived at four bearing a five-pound box of Mrs. See's mixed candy, an enormous bouquet of white chrysanthemums, and two bottles of Moet champagne. The four of them sat on the patio until darkness fell, then moved inside to the long semicircular white sofa until dinner was announced.

The talk drifted from pictures to Broadway and the phenomenal success of the new musical, *Oklahoma!*, that had opened the previous week. Some critics had buried it in Boston; but a change of title, an exceptional book and score, and Agnes DeMille's innovative choreography moved the New York critics to unqualified raves.

Several times during dinner, Leya caught Ed watching Kent. After a fourth glass of champagne, the dancer's gaiety threatened to get out of control. He laughed with little provocation and gestured with flamboyant grandeur. Bruce Cydney, barely managing to conceal his disapproval, made the first move to take Kent home shortly before ten o'clock.

"We're going to start early, planning the training-camp obstacle-course number. Mr. Sanford has to know what props we'll need so the designers can get them in the works," he explained.

"Wait till you see what I'm going to do with that number, Leya! God's socks," Kent giggled, "the sixteen boys we pick will have to be acrobats!"

"What will the sixteen girls be doing all this time?" Ed asked.

"The girls?" Kent repeated, frowning. He braced his right elbow in the cup of his left hand and toyed with his chin. Suddenly, he brightened. "I've got it! I'll make them army nurses. They stand around and pick up the boys when they fall on their asses!"

Exasperated, Bruce took him by the arm and led him to the door.

Ed watched until the two had disappeared into the darkness. "Can we talk for a few minutes now?" he asked.

"Certainly," Leya replied. "Would you like a nightcap?"

"No, thanks," he frowned. "What I'd really like is a run-down on Kent. How long has he been like this?"

"You mean, sort of overplaying all the time?"

"I mean sort of drunk," Ed said bluntly. "Do you think it has anything to do with Matt O'Brien leaving him?"

"Look, Ed," Leya said, annoyed. "I don't get involved in Kent's personal affairs. I know he misses Matt. He's said as much. But if you're asking if he's trying to drown his sorrows—" She shrugged. "I simply wouldn't know. Nor do I want to know."

Ed Matson gave her a level look. "Little friend, you'll want to know pretty good if Kent's personal problems start affecting you. He's your choreographer, primarily because I insisted that you would do your best work with him." He laughed humorlessly. "I don't give a damn what he does in bed—or with whom or with how many—just so long as his troubles don't show on the set. If they do, I promise you, Leya, I'll have him kicked off the picture." He lit a cigarette and flipped the match onto the embers in the fireplace. "One of the many things I love about you, Leya, is your loyalty. Just don't let it get in your way."

His mood mellowed abruptly. "Know something I've not done for years? Walked on the beach at night." He glanced at his watch. "How about a barefoot half hour to walk off the three helpings of stuffed veal and two helpings of Devil's Food cake"—he raised his right hand in a pledge—"if I swear not to talk about business?"

Leya brightened. "Good idea. Give me a minute to get a heavier sweater."

On the hard, wet tidal margin, Ed started to turn north.

"Let's go the other way, Ed," Leya suggested, reaching for his arm. "I always walk up toward Kent's."

Several hundred yards along, the only illumination an occasional patio light, Ed caught her hand as they parted to avoid a dark mass of stranded kelp. When he continued to hold her hand as they came together again, Leya made no move to pull away.

They walked a half mile around the gentle crescent of the Malibu colony, then turned and retraced their steps. It was a quiet walk, punctuated by the muffled tumbling of the surf and the occasional cry of an unseen shore bird.

They brushed their feet clean on the patio, and Ed pulled on his socks and shoes. In the parking area, he opened the car door and stood with his hand on it.

"I've had a wonderful time, little friend. I realize now how much I've missed you. It's been a long week."

"It's been a short one for me," Leya mused. "I was thinking of asking you to arrange another."

"That just might be done if you could take a few hours off to read the first draft of *Company B.*"

"I'm anxious to, Ed."

"Good. I'll have it sent down tomorrow."

"How does it look?"

"With a war on, it looks like a million—or two—or three."

"What about Ricordi? What's he like?"

"He's a horny Italian who thinks he's God's gift to women, and when he sings, most women agree. But remember, little friend, I'll always be there to protect you."

"If he gets out of line," Leya replied, "somebody'd better tell him that Leya Leslie is noted for her precision kicks."

Ed laughed. "I'm sorry you said that!"

Leya looked up at him innocently. "Why?"

"Because I was trying to get up enough courage to point

out that in the nearly four years we have worked together, I have never kissed you good night."

Leya pretended to think back. After a moment, she nodded. "I do believe that's correct, Mr. Matson." She moved close and slipped her arms around his neck. "You may take care of that now."

CHAPTER 39

Early in April, Leya received a note from Tanya Kuznetsov. "Darling," it read, "Matt and I finally managed to get away long enough to get married. He's marvelous, an absolute dear, affectionate (How I love that!), and doing very well in the show. He's even singing now. Leave it to the Irish to have a good tenor voice!

"I've been working as a swing girl in *Something for the Boys* just to stay in town with him. We are living at the Royalton Hotel at 44 West 44th. Our room doesn't exactly have a view, but it's okay for the time being."

The letter went on to say how proud all the "gypsies" were "who knew you and worked with you." It ended with a phrase written in the Cyrillic alphabet. Kuzzy translated it in brackets. ("You begin your voyage. May it be a happy one!")

The Sweetheart of Company B started shooting in mid-April. At Leya's first rehearsal, Ricardo Ricordi came over, kissed her hand, and said, "*Tutti nostri auguri!* You are Maria Taglioni incarnate, *signorina!* I shall call you my 'Angelina di Tentazione'! You have the face and body of a temptress, but you dance like an angel. I am your devoted fan!"

Kent came over after Ricordi had gone. "If you slip in that spaghetti sauce, dear, don't land on your back!"

Leya gasped as Tom Grayson, from the studio's publicity department, approached.

"Miss Leslie, Bill Pine wants me to set up a couple of dinner dates with you and Ricardo. He wants shots for a 'seen together' fan-mag layout."

"Please tell Mr. Matson about it," she replied. "He wants to approve anything like that."

When she and Kent finished working on some rough transitions in a difficult adagio, Matson came up to discuss Grayson's request.

"Do I have to do it?" Leya asked.

"Let's put it this way, little friend, it's a wise thing to do."

Leya looked across the stage at Ricordi, who had stopped to sign autographs for a group of fawning female visitors.

"Oh, God," she groaned, "this is the part I hate!"

Ed Matson laughed. "Ricordi's okay, Leya, but if it will make you feel easier, I'll find a date and just happen to be along, too."

"Oh, fine!" Leya said, giving him a baleful look. "Then who keeps an eye on you?"

A pleased smile lit Ed Matson's face. "The girl I bring will when she sees how lovely you are!"

At eight o'clock, Leya met Ricordi in the lobby of the Towers. She was dressed in a strapless black lace over white taffeta evening gown that Edith Head had designed for the picture and a white ermine jacket borrowed from the costume department. A series of so-called candid shots were taken as the handsome Italian singing star helped her into the rented Rolls Royce cabriolet. Two blocks down the Strip at Billy Wilkerson's Trocadero, they were photographed toasting each other and dancing. As much as she detested the phoniness of the set up, Leya found herself at ease with Ricordi. He was a superb dancer, and he possessed an unexpected sense of humor.

The next morning at rehearsal, Ed Matson chided her. "If you weren't enjoying yourself, little friend, you managed a very credible act. I might as well have been out in the parking lot."

His injured expression caused Leya to burst into laughter. In a reversal of roles, she took his hand and pretended to comfort him.

"Ed, darling, if I hadn't known that you were lurking there in the shadows, ready to desert your adoring date on a moment's notice, I'd have been petrified. Honestly."

"Don't swear to that or you may get hit by lightning!" he grumbled. "Anyway, don't be upset when you start reading in Louella Parsons's and Hedda Hopper's columns that you and Ricordi are 'an item.' That's what this is all about, you know."

Leya looked up at him innocently. "Will I also read about what you and your date did after you left?"

The Sweetheart of Company B was previewed at Camp Pendleton, the huge marine corps base midway between Los Angeles and San Diego. Allowing for the exuberance of the "grunts" and "ground pounders" who had just survived eight weeks of bone-grinding training and were waiting to be shipped to Pacific combat zones, the picture, which used stock footage of the base, was another box-office "money grabber."

To Leya, it seemed that the writers' building at the studio had been put on twenty-four-hour shifts turning out musical stories for her. Ed had said two more were in the works. When she asked him if the writers were using rubber stamps on the plots, he was plainly annoyed.

Almost nobody in Hollywood was out of work. Box-office receipts stayed at ninety million paid admissions each week. Producers and productions proliferated.

The Palm Springs winter vacation that Ed promised Leya was not possible. In July, with three weeks free before she would begin rehearsals on her next musical, Ed suggested they go to San Francisco and on to Lake Tahoe. "I have friends who own a big house on the north shore. George Roderick is a Ford dealer in Sacramento. His wife, Ellie, is an artist. They've given me an open invitation to bring you for a visit, and this would be a good time for you to get away."

"Oh, Lord," Leya groaned, "I'm afraid it will be just like

my visits to papa and Minnie. Everybody in the neighborhood wants to come over for a look at the 'big movie star'!"

Ed smiled. "You don't give me enough credit, little friend. I'll make them swear there'll be no mention—and for sure no parties."

San Francisco was a revelation. They rode the cable cars, strolled through Chinatown, feasted at Fisherman's Wharf on freshly cooked crab, and walked it off along the byways of North Beach. Ed kept surprising Leya with vignettes of the city's history. She especially liked the story of Lotta's Fountain, a gift from the grateful New York-born actress, Lotta Crabtree, who as a child in the Gold Rush days had been a *protégé* of the controversial dancer, Lola Montez.

The bay fascinated Leya. The forbidding island prison, Alcatraz, shrouded in gray early-morning fog, made her shiver. She spent hours watching the harbor, busy now with ghostly gray-painted military vessels transporting troops and materiel to the Western Pacific, where the tide of battle was slowly turning in favor of the Allies.

"I love San Francisco!" Leya said. "It feels so much like New York!"

"The two places have a lot in common," Ed replied. "They're both world ports, both cultural melting pots."

"Whatever the reason," Leya said, "I love it. It's alive!" She drew in a deep breath of moist sea air. "When I do that, I feel refreshed!"

Ed borrowed a car and some gas-ration coupons from the Paramount distributor in the Bay area and crossed the Golden Gate Bridge to the Marin County side to show Leya the famous Muir Grove of redwoods. The gigantic trees, rising like columns in an enormous temple, left her speechless.

As the days passed, adventuring around the peninsula, and the nights were spent in San Francisco's famous restaurants, still managing exceptional meals despite rationing, Ed watched spontaneous enjoyment replace fatigue as Leya was able to relax from the grip of the single-minded determination to do her best that had earned the respect of all who had worked with her.

Ed wanted to take Leya on the overnight stern wheeler

from San Francisco to Sacramento, but passenger service on the pioneer river boat had been suspended. They took the train from the Oakland Mole, stayed overnight at the Senator Hotel in the capital, and picked up the convertible George Roderick had left for them at the agency.

As they drove northeastward toward the Sierra Nevada mountains, Ed entertained her with stories of the Forty Niners. He told her of Sam Brannan, who had galloped up Market Street, shouting, "Gold! Gold! Gold in the Sierras!" to bring San Francisco the first news of Marshall's strike at Coloma; and of Johann August Sutter, in whose mill race the carpenter, John Marshall, had first seen the gleaming nuggets.

As the highway—treacherously narrow and steep—climbed to Donner Pass, Leya recalled reading the tragic story of the Donner Party. Two hours later, she gasped when the spectacle of Lake Tahoe burst upon them as they emerged from the pine forest to look down into the serrated granite bowl that held the seven-thousand-foot-high lake like a shimmering sapphire.

She was still enraptured by the beauty of the surroundings when they arrived at the Rodericks' hillside home on the northwest shore.

George and Ellie Roderick were successful, attractive, plain-as-old-shoe people. Leya might have been an old friend, a frequent visitor who was expected to make herself at home.

"We hoped you'd get here for lunch," Ellie said, "but George predicted you'd stop to rubberneck along the way. Have you eaten?"

"We have," Ed replied. "And drunk our fill of the beauty of this place, too!"

Leya looked around in wonderment. "I don't know what to say! All this leaves me speechless! I can't tell you how grateful I am to be included."

After an hour to herself, Leya came upstairs to the large rustic living room that let out onto a deck running the full length of the house front. When she peered gingerly over the rail to the trees and boulders below and on down to the shore, George Roderick was amused.

"That's how I felt the first time I looked over the rail at

the Empire State Building. You'll get used to it. The water's so clear in the lake that you can see a hundred feet down."

They had drinks and dined early on the deck. Leya could never remember such a luminous night. Later, when it cooled, they moved inside to sit and talk around the granite fireplace.

Leya found she was seeing Ed through new eyes. It was difficult now to relate the strong, pleasant-appearing, relaxed man whose legs were stretched luxuriously toward the fire to the sharply focused, smooth-operating achiever who managed her affairs. She was grateful to that Ed Matson. She liked this Ed Matson much better, had been liking him all day as he surprised her continually with his knowledge of the state. She did not know that with customary thoroughness he had ordered his secretary to get abridged histories and excerpt the pertinent information that he would dispense along the route.

By nine-thirty, the first yawn had been stifled and apologized for. By ten, Leya was snuggled beneath two eiderdown quilts in a bed that invited untroubled sleep. A scant eight hours later, she was awakened by a soft tapping on her door, and Ellie called to see if she felt like going fishing with the men.

"Tell them I'd much rather stay here and applaud their catch later," she replied.

"Why don't you doze a little longer?" Ellie said. "When you feel ready, come on up to the kitchen and I'll run up some eggs."

"Thank you, Ellie. I'll be up in a little while."

Minutes later, she dozed off again.

After a good breakfast, Ellie guided Leya down a steep zigzag path that led to the shore two hundred feet below.

Every step was an adventure. Crested mountain blue jays scolded them for invading their domain. Striped chipmunks, their cheeks bulging with pine nuts, scampered atop rocks to watch them with no motion except the comic twitching of their tails.

At the water's edge, Ellie and Leya scrambled up a

succession of smooth boulders until they gained the top of the highest one.

"This is my favorite retreat. Sometimes I come down here and stretch out in the altogether and get a good tan. By the way," she added, "you have a good base, but this mountain sun's a bit treacherous. Do you burn easily?"

"No," Leya replied, "I live at the beach, and thank the Lord, I just turn darker and darker."

Ellie's hazel eyes twinkled. "I remember poor Ed made that speech a few years ago and wound up the color of a Maine lobster. Has he ever told you about that trip? He came up here to get himself together after his wife died."

"I didn't know about his wife," Leya said. "I mean, I knew he had been married—" She shrugged. "He never talks about it."

"No, I suppose not," Ellie replied. "He's quite a man, Ed Matson."

"I know very little about Ed's background," Leya mused. "I've never asked about his personal life, and he's never talked about it."

"In that case, I'll only volunteer one thing," Ellie said, looking at Leya with frank admiration. "I've never seen him as happy as he is now."

Shortly before noon, they puffed up the trail to the house. Minutes later, the outboard spluttered and died alongside the small dock. Ellie leaned on the deck rail and watched.

"I think it's fresh trout for dinner," she said. "George's gunnysack looks promising."

Two three-pound baked trout were more than enough. After dinner, George looked at his guests apologetically. "Would you all mind if I disappear for an hour or so? I promised a neighbor I'd drop by. He wants to buy a car from me—if he can steal it." He grinned. "So I'm going to let him think that's what he's done."

"I do that all the time," Ed said. "That's how Paramount stole Leya."

Ellie, who was arranging morning things on the breakfast

counter, surprised her husband by announcing that she was going with him.

When they heard the car leave, Ed heaved a sigh. "Know something, honey? Even with the best of your friends, you're on just a little."

Leya nodded emphatically. "How well I know! But they are awfully nice people."

Ed grinned. "I'm going outside and do some rail leaning. Care to join me?" Leya slipped on a sweater, and they stood for a time, their shoulders touching, looking out across the water. Over the south slope of Mount Rose, they could see the beginning of a faint lunar halo.

"Think you could get used to this, little friend?"

"That's a silly question," Leya chided in a low voice.

"You know, don't you, that you can have a place like this any time you want one?"

Leya laughed quietly. "I guess I'm not used to that idea yet."

"Accept it, darling. From now on, you can have anything you want."

"If I pay for it," Leya mused. "So all I have to do is figure out what's worth having and how much I'm willing to pay. Right?"

"That," Ed replied, "is not a simple question for me to answer."

"Why not?"

"Because I'm a special pleader."

In the half light, he saw her frown. "What does that mean?"

Ed wondered if she was being purposely oblique. "I mean I want things for you that you may not know you need."

"Everything I've wanted I've got, thanks to you, Ed. I don't know what I'd ever do without you."

"Well," he said with a bit more lightness than he intended, "you don't have to do without me. In fact, if you were to decide that you could, I—" He broke off and groaned. "Oh, for God's sake. Look, Leya. I could grab you like Rudolph Valentino grabbed Agnes Ayres, bend your back over the rail, pant with passion, stare at you wild-eyed, and tell you that I can't live without you! But I'm much older than you are. You'd have to break up. Then, in humiliation, I'd throw myself down there on the rocks. Except, with my luck, I'd probably get hung up by the seat of my pants in a tree."

Reaching out, he took her gently by the shoulders. She turned to face him.

"Leya, the truth is—I love you. It's not the star-sprinkled night or that anemic moon or the stuffed trout or the miserable Virginia Dare wine that George thinks is vintage. It's simply that I love you. I have known that for two years, and for that long I've deserved a Distinguished Service Cross for restraint under extreme temptation. Does any of this surprise you?"

"Not really, Ed," Leya replied.

He tilted her face up. "I'm sorry, little darling, but sooner or later I had to get it said." The pleading, controlled in his voice, was mirrored in his eyes. "I don't know how long a man can hold his breath, Leya, but I'm going to hold mine until you—" He broke off and continued to search her eyes.

"Until I have my say?"

"Yes."

Leya turned back to the rail and gazed off across the dark mirror of the lake to the jagged mountain silhouette to the east. After what seemed to Ed Matson to be an eternity, she turned to him again. "If you're asking if I love you, too, Ed, I'd have to say, 'Yes, I do—for a great many reasons.' If you are asking if I'm in love with you"—she glanced down uncertainly—"then I'd have to say that I do not love you in the same way I loved Arthur." She shook her head sadly. "I'm afraid I don't know very much about love, Ed."

He reached for her hands and brought her closer. "None of us do, darling. We all have to learn. It starts with liking a person, finding them attractive, sharing a mutual interest and a mutual trust. Too often, we confuse infatuation with love. I have—a time or two. It's like one of those photo flash guns that go off in your face. They blind you, and it takes a while before you can see clearly again. And God help you if, when the glare subsides, you recognize something you cannot love and respect." Gently, he reached out to smooth the hair from her cheek. "Believe me, this is no infatuation! I just began to like you and respect you more and more, and I wanted to do more and more for you. Then, one day, I realized that old Edward Leslie Matson had fallen deeply in love for the very first time in his mixed-up life." He extended his arms helplessly. "It's as simple as that!"

For a moment, they gazed at each other in silence. Then Leya moved to him. "Some of those same things have been happening inside me, Ed." Her voice was hardly more than a whisper. "I feel good and secure with you. And I do like you—very, very much." She looked up at him intently. "Would that be enough?"

"That, little darling," he breathed, bringing her close, "is more than enough for us to build on." He kissed her gently but deeply. When he felt her respond, he whispered, "Oh, my darling. The things I will do for you!"

CHAPTER 40

Leya Leslie married Edward L. Matson in Reno, on the last day of July 1943. George and Ellie Roderick were witnesses. At the courthouse, where the couple applied for a license, the clerk, a heavy woman with a salt-and-pepper Dutch-cut bob, darted glances at the beautiful and somehow familiar young woman in dark glasses who signed her legal name, "Leya Marks," and gave her birth place as "Brooklyn, New York, October 3, 1919." When Ed paid the two dollars, the woman struck the license with an official stamp and said without a trace of humor, "Okay, happy couple, when you get 'em here, they stick!"

A half hour later, using two simple gold bands that Ed had bought in a small shop, they were married in the Lilies of the Valley Wedding Chapel.

On the return drive to the lake, over the spectacularly beautiful Mount Rose road, they completed plans to spend a brief honeymoon in the Rodericks' home.

"I can't get over it!" Ellie said. "There's no way I can tell you how happy we are—for both of you. They used to say about George and me that we looked like we belonged together. If that was true about us, it's God's honest truth about you two!"

At the house, Ellie and George hurried their personal

things out of the big corner bedroom while Leya tried to reach her father by phone. When repeated attempts produced no answer, she resorted to a telegram.

"It's no trouble at all," Ellie insisted over Leya's protests. The Rodericks departed shortly after three o'clock with admonitions to Leya and Ed to have a "great old time!"

"There's one little detail I think we ought to get settled right now, Mrs. Matson," Ed said with mock severity. "You're not going to begin married life cooking." He glanced at his watch. "About five o'clock let's wander down to one of the clubs. The casinos always have good beef."

"Anything you say," Leya replied, toying with the unfamiliar gold band. "I don't mind cooking, really, but I think it would be a cruel thing to do to you on your honeymoon. All I know how to do is scramble eggs and make toasted bagels and cream cheese."

"Up here, darling, bagels are harder to find than a gambler without hope!"

Leya was standing by the sliding screen door leading to the deck. He crossed to her, took her hands, and looked down at her. "Little Leya, I may not be the dark, handsome, romantic movie type, but one thing is certain. Nobody will ever love you more, and nobody will ever work harder for you. Nobody!" Leya allowed herself to be gathered in his arms. "I didn't quite believe, after my bumbling speech last night, that you wouldn't laugh at me. But you didn't, darling. And for that you've got yourself a one-man army that can't lose!"

Smiling contentedly, Leya rested her cheek against his shirt front. "I know, Ed. I feel very good with you, and"—she leaned away to look up at him—"I'm very grateful to you for all you've done."

It was a secure feeling, she thought, being held like this. She knew that what she felt for Ed was hardly the same as the flare-bright emotion that Gardner Sutton had awakened in her or the deep and, at the same time, tender longing to lose herself in Arthur's arms that she had felt back then—before.

Leya closed her eyes to blank out an image too painful to endure.

* * *

Several hours later, lying in bed in the room lit only by the crescent of the new moon, Leya listened to the sounds of a man showering vigorously. She was grateful that Ed had pretended to ignore her nervousness. It was impossible that he had not noticed it. She blessed George for the clever way he had smuggled the champagne into the refrigerator and for the impertinent little hint he had left. Freddy Martin's hit recording of "Tonight We Love" had been propped on edge between two books so that neither of them would miss the B side, "Why Don't We Do This More Often?" The laughter it had caused and the two glasses of champagne on the deck had helped.

They had leaned on the railing with their arms linked, watching the luminous silver melon slice of moon reflected in the lake. He had told her again how deeply he loved her—how, for all those long, frustrating months, he had been afraid to admit it to himself, much less confess it to her. When he had kissed her hands, wrists, neck, and forehead—and kissed her playfully on the nose—and then, with more purpose, on the neck and throat, she had found herself responding, not with the same intensity that she had felt with Gardner or Arthur, but she could not deny a feeling of excitement.

Leya, caught in reverie, started when she saw Ed's silhouette, monklike in the long terry-cloth robe, moving noiselessly across the thick wool shag. He stopped at the front of the bed and looked down at her, smiling.

"Any preference as to sides?" he asked.

"I don't know, Ed," she laughed nervously. "I've never shared a bed before."

Ignoring the tightness in her voice, he removed the robe and slipped under the covers. For a moment, they lay face up, a foot or so apart. She heard him place something on the bedstand. Then she felt his left arm move toward her, and the back of his hand touched her hip. Involuntarily, she reached out to fend him off, and his hand closed around hers. For several minutes, they lay still. Then, very slowly, he began to pull her toward him.

Leya felt the pulse pound in her temples. Ed rolled toward her and lifted himself up on one elbow. She could hardly see his face in the faint light, but she felt the warmth of his body. Then his lips were on hers, and his arms gathered her close.

"Darling, darling," he whispered, trailing his lips to the corner of her mouth. "Don't even try to guess how many times I've tormented myself by imagining this moment!"

He slipped the sheer silk nightgown from her shoulders and helped her work the garment free. An instant later, she felt her breasts being crushed against the wiry matting of hair on his chest. His lips were moving against the base of her neck, mouthing breathy endearments as his arms moved slowly down her back, urging her closer. She realized that she was feeling him thick and hard against her and involuntarily moved her hips away. His hand maneuvered quickly to caress her stomach and explore the upper margin of her pubic hair, and his lips were on hers again. Leya expected him to pull her close again, but he rolled onto his back and reached for something. A moment later, he was fumbling with himself beneath the covers. Then he was half atop her, kissing her more insistently and exploring her body more boldly. Feeling trapped but curious and eager, too, Leya moved against the flat of the finger pressing into her, and his movements became more aggressive. His hand moved away, and she felt him beginning to penetrate her.

"Darling–darling–relax," he whispered. "If it hurts, I'll stop!" Leya grimaced with surprise at the quick stab of pain. And then he was in her–all of him–and his body was moist and rigid, trembling with restraint.

"All right, darling? Is it all right?" he whispered hoarsely. He twisted to kiss her neck and her ear. Smothering his face in her hair, he began to move in her, felt her wince, pressed again, more gently, and again–and again–until, almost imperceptibly, he felt her begin to move with him.

For Leya, the seconds were a measureless time of alien pain and strange pleasure, and then she felt his tension mounting. He began to breathe more heavily and thrust more urgently. His anxious, wordless protests excited her. Suddenly, with an open-throated animal sound, he began battering frantically against her as he came to orgasm far sooner than he had intended.

He held her, viselike, for a time. Then, gradually, his body relaxed, and he settled beside her. With labored breath, he whispered, "Oh, Leya, beautiful little darling! I waited so long. I dreamed so much. My God, do I ever love you!"

Leya stroked the hair at his temples. Sometime later, when she felt him reach down, her hand followed his. When her fingers touched the thin collar at the top of the condom, there was a little shock of comprehension, followed by a sense of relief. She smiled to herself as she felt him pinch the device to strip it off safely.

Leya did not know how long they remained together in silence before Ed withdrew his arm and said softly, "Excuse me, darling—for a minute or two."

Leya watched as he slipped on his robe, crossed the room, and was silhouetted briefly in the bathroom doorway. She wasn't sure what she had expected, but at least she had discovered one thing about herself. She was not frigid. The feeling of a muscle-hard naked body against hers had been exquisitely sensuous. Toward the end, when the pain had begun to subside, and his body had dominated hers, she had begun to feel at another, deeper level. It would be better, she thought, the next time.

The days passed quickly. At nine on Monday morning, they left for Sacramento. By the time they reached Auburn, the temperature was close to one hundred degrees.

As the day lengthened, the heat increased. By late afternoon, when the car was returned to the agency, and one of the salesmen had driven them to the Senator Hotel, Leya was feeling ill.

They lingered in the cool of the dining room for an hour, discussing living arrangements. Instead of buying another house at Malibu for investment, they decided to keep hers, and Ed would buy a home in Beverly Hills or Bel Air, depending on Leya's preference. It would give them an in-town base when they were working.

By nine o'clock, they were stretched out atop the sheets

trying to catch what breeze was possible in the corner room. When Ed reached over to caress her, Leya's pleading produced a chuckle.

"All right, darling girl," he said softly, "I know, it's too hot!"

Leya smiled gratefully and turned back to the old issue of *Life* magazine she had found in the drawer of the night table. It was dated October 11, 1942. Ed had reached over just as she had turned to a photo story of a Halifax bomber crew preparing for a night raid on Dusseldorf. One of the crew members, a Royal Canadian Air Force officer, reminded her of Arthur. She read the story's meager details. It had been a six-hundred-plane raid, carrying thousand-pound bombs and incendiaries and two-ton and four-ton blockbusters. Thirty-one planes had been lost. The crew of the *Halifax*, "B for Beer," had returned. They had been out on seven previous missions.

Aware of Ed, naked beside her as she read, Leya found herself thinking still again of Arthur—and of Gardner. She wondered that her thoughts of those two could persist.

The old memories placed an unwelcome burden of guilt on her. She damned herself for wondering why the promise of sex with Arthur and with Gardner had seemed so much more exciting than the consummation had been so far with Ed. Or was she really anticipating too much? Were her expectations exaggerated unrealistically by fantasy?

Even Dulcy, to whom sex was something to be bartered, had admitted to enjoying the experience with Willie Four from time to time. Did love have anything to do with it, really? Or was it just a matter of physical attraction, stimulation to the point of orgasm and relief? Certainly the anticipation of close physical contact with Matt had excited Kuzzy. Was that part of it, too, just the wanting and winning of an attractive object? Leya studied the faces of the bomber crew again, then closed the magazine and set it aside.

Ed lowered his paper and gave her a questioning look. "Going to call it a day, sweetheart?"

"If you don't mind," she replied. "Good night, Ed."

"Good night, little darling. You're wonderful. Be happy!"

CHAPTER 41

George Roderick had predicted that the stringers for the San Francisco papers would pick up the news of the marriage through their routine checks of the license bureau. He had been right. When Leya and Ed arrived in Malibu, they found Ellen beside herself.

"I don't know where they got your private number, Miss Les—Mrs. Matson—but everybody and his brother has called. And did you see the papers? You're in all the columns."

"I'll get the messages in a little while," Leya said. "Just let me get caught up with myself."

"Outside of that, Miss Leya, everything is fine except I didn't know what to do about the bedroom, now that—"

"Mr. Matson is going to stay here until we find another house closer to work," Leya said.

Ellen's face fell. "Does that mean—?"

"That means we're going to have two houses instead of one, and it means that you and Squires are going to be with us as long as you care to stay."

Ellen's relief was obvious.

While Ed drove into town with Squires to move his things from the Sunset Tower apartment, Leya spent time on the telephone. Calls had come from Howard Pryor and Marty Maizlish, from Celine, from Kuzzy and Matt, from Dulcy in

Maryland, and from Heather, who had left a Florida number. She had received no call from her father and Minnie. She would try calling again in a few hours.

One call that relieved her greatly came from Paramount's publicity department, advising her to refer the paper and fan magazine people to them. The new PR head read a release for her approval and asked to schedule press interviews as soon as possible.

Four in-depth interviews, with photos, were disposed of before the end of the week. The following Monday, Jay Sanford hosted a luncheon in the newlyweds' honor on the lot. He used the occasion to brag about some extraordinary box-office figures being racked up by *The Sweetheart of Company B* and to announce a new Leslie picture.

The story, as yet untitled, would be built around a Russian ballet star caught on concert tour in the United States when the collaboration between Stalin and Hitler is revealed.

That evening, Leya finished the outline and handed it back to Ed with a questioning look.

"I don't know," he said. "It may just be unlikely enough to be entertaining. Ballerina asks for asylum, proves her love of freedom by working as aircraft riveter, is rediscovered, and becomes a great star again? One thing is for sure, darling, you'd better do a hell of a lot of dancing!"

The start date was early October. Ed checked the calendar. "That gives us a little over a month to find a house, get settled, and get you back in condition."

On September first, they opened escrow in Ed's name on a two-and-a-half-acre estate on Alpine Drive in Beverly Hills. The twelve-room Tudor house, complete with pool, tennis court, and guest cottage, was within walking distance of the Beverly Hills Hotel. Things were in reasonable order by the time Ed was due to leave for New York to complete some business there.

At the airport, he kissed Leya and assured her again that he would miss her terribly. She stood watching until the plane disappeared into the late-afternoon haze. In the car driving back, she sat in front with Squires and wondered at the strange ambivalence that left her both sorry and relieved to see Ed go. She needed him and, yes, loved him. But his increasing demands on her were growing difficult to meet.

She settled some things in the partially furnished Alpine Drive house and drove back to the beach. A need to talk about new dance routines prompted a call to Kent. She hoped to find him free to share a pickup supper. Instead, Bruce answered and congratulated her on her marriage.

"Kent may not know yet. He's in New York to try and sell his house on Fire Island."

"Thank you, Bruce. I just wanted to make certain you both know that we're going to start on the new picture in a few weeks."

"Yes, we know. We've only seen a treatment so far. I hope we get a first draft in time to come up with some really unusual concepts."

"You will," Leya reassured him. "You never fail me. Let's talk tomorrow on the beach."

Shortly before six o'clock, Coast time, Ed called. He was in the bar at Twenty-One.

"Darling, how are you?"

"Fine, Ed—a little frazzled but okay. How about you?"

"With or without sleep, I'm the happiest man on earth! Did you have to ask?"

"I never take anything for granted," Leya replied lightly.

"Good. There's somebody here who wants to talk to you, darling. Hold on a minute."

Leya let out a delighted cry when she heard her father shouting to make himself heard, as he always did on long-distance calls.

"We're with your husband, our son-in-law. Can I tell you? We like him. He's a good man. He'll take care of you."

"I know, papa—and you'll never know how glad I am that you like him. It's so good to hear your voice! Where on earth have you been? I've called a half-dozen times."

"Seven days I've been working, *bubeleh.* But never mind. So what do I say? My daughter Leya is married already! Everybody talks! Winchell, even, on the radio. 'Hollywood's brightest new dancing star,' he called you. Your name is in the papers. Minnie is cutting out and saving. She's making a book for you."

"Thank you, papa. Thank you, both. Is Minnie with you?"

"Who else?"

"Put her on, papa." Leya heard her father admonishing Minnie to speak loud. She laughed when Ed's voice reached her, countermanding the instructions diplomatically. She could visualize them in the bar at Twenty-One—her father in his good suit and Minnie in her formidable best—seated in alien surroundings, oblivious of it all. She wanted to reach across the miles and gather them into her arms.

The conversation grew difficult after the first few eager questions. Ed came back on the line.

"I love you for doing that for them," Leya said. "It was wonderful of you."

"It was selfish of me, darling. Now I've got three of you to care for. Also, your father has assured me that if any of our automobiles get out of whack, he will fix them properly, not halfway like the young 'smart aleckers' do!"

Leya laughed, and her eyes began to mist. "Tell them how much I love them," she said, "and hurry back, Ed. I feel lost."

He laughed happily. "I told you, you needed me!"

"I didn't argue, did I?" she countered.

The first-draft shooting script arrived by messenger two days later. It bore the working title, *The Golden Steppes.* Attached was a little note saying there was serious consideration for another title, *The Magic Steppes.*

Kent returned from New York gushing congratulations for Leya. So far as she could tell, he was in good spirits. She wanted to ask if he had seen Matt and Kuzzy and decided not to when Kent volunteered that he had seen "all of the theater worth seeing." Something in his manner told her that he had not bothered to see *This Is the Army.*

Leya, soaked with perspiration, was blocking with Kent and Bruce when Ed walked into the studio. Surprised, she stood before him mopping her face and neck and chided him for not letting her know that he was returning. When he reached to gather her in his arms, she pulled away, but he drew her near, anyway.

"Oh, Ed," she said apologetically, "you're a mess now!"

"You're beautiful," he replied. "A little soggy but beautiful. Squires says Ellen will have lunch at one o'clock, darling. That'll give you time to bathe. Then we can get caught up."

September passed in a succession of twelve- and fourteen-hour days—learning sides, learning Russian words and a credible Russian accent, exacting ballet practice, costume fitting, learning how to hold a riveter. There were other hours, too—exciting but in some ways more demanding—with Ed. From time to time, Dulcy would call. The last call had come after ten P.M.—one in the morning, Eastern time.

Gwendolyn was two—an "unbelievable little doll," Dulcy said. They had been to the Vandercort Long Island estate twice. Both times the occasions had been money-raising affairs for war relief. Crashing bores! Willie was moving up in the War Production Board—had received a letter of commendation from FDR himself. He was still traveling a great deal but got home perhaps one week out of the month, now that things were looking better for the Allies in the Mediterranean and the army air force was so well protected it could make daylight bombing raids over the heart of Germany.

The allusion to raids over Germany revived a persistent sadness. At unexpected moments, Leya found herself thinking of Arthur, of the conviction that drove him to volunteer early with the RCAF, of the waste, of the grief and uncertainty Myra and Martin and Shelly had learned to endure. When the memories of her first dates with Arthur grew too painful, Leya drove herself harder still.

Ed had looked at her strangely several times. "Darling! What are you trying to do? Do you know what they're calling you at the studio? 'The Iron Butterfly!' Take it easy. The world isn't going to end tomorrow."

The picture, finally titled *The Magic Steps,* began shooting the second week in October. By mid-November, the principal dance numbers had been completed, and Leya and the cast moved into the dramatic scenes. It was hard to tell from the rushes each morning just what sort of a picture Lew Frederix was getting out of a script that was continually being rewritten. Ed, watching Leya calmly accept the new green revised pages on the set and try her best to commit them to memory on a lunch break, headed off justifiable blowups several times by insisting to Jay that the director shoot around her.

"She works like a machine," he had said, "but she won't wear like one. Can't Frederix decide what he wants, for God's sake?"

Leya, aware that Ed was making things as easy for her as possible, silently blessed him. In the car, being driven to Malibu by Squires after a particularly grueling Friday, she took Ed's hand in both of hers.

"You are an angel, darling. I don't know anybody in the world who would fight for me like you do."

He comforted her. "You're only going to do two pictures next year, sweetheart, and you're going to get thirty-five hundred dollars a week for forty weeks, with an option to renew for three years at five—count 'em—five grand a week!"

The money was meaningless to Leya. There was more than enough to do the things she wanted, to buy the things she needed and a thousand things that she didn't need. It was fun to be able to send her father a five-hundred-dollar set of mechanic's tools, then call and hear him rhapsodize in a half shout. And Minnie—she called herself "Minnie the Mooch" now because she secretly enjoyed the gifts Leya all but forced on her. And it was good to send checks to the home's scholarship fund.

The late start on the film ran the schedule over into the Christmas holidays. When Leya saw that the runover was inevitable, she called her father and Minnie to urge them to come West. But her father was committed to work straight through the holidays to complete repairs on a light cruiser that had taken two hits and needed a new bow and forward turret. Except for the diamond bracelet from Ed and a multitude of gifts and cards, Christmas was little more than a day off.

A few friends from the studio saw the New Year in with

them at the Malibu house. Kent and Bruce were invited, but the antagonism between them had worsened after the final dance sequences had been shot. Kent returned to New York. Bruce went to Palm Springs to be with his family.

The Magic Steps opened in mid-January to generally good reviews. The most perceptive critics did not ignore the story's weaknesses, but neither did they minimize "Leya Leslie's extraordinary performance in some superb modern and classic ballet sequences created by Kent Kendall." Taken whole, it was "satisfying entertainment," they said.

The first production under the new two-picture deal that Ed and I.A.M had negotiated for Leya with Paramount was scheduled to go before the cameras in March. For the first time, the new Leslie picture would bear the credit *An Edward Matson Production.* Ed had secured the rights to a magazine story, a mistaken-identity piece.

"What appeals to me is the chance for comedy, darling," he said. "I can't imagine a safer time to try it. Everything is box office now. That will help cut down the risk of departing from formula music plots."

The story involved a USO dancer who gets stranded in the South Pacific and masquerades as a Red Cross nurse. The first-draft screenplay was less than satisfactory.

"We can't play this anywhere near straight," Ed told the two writers. "Put Miss Leslie in situations not of her own doing that are essentially comic. Have her victimized by characters who are close to farcical. Then we can cast a strong comedian opposite her who will make the broad stuff work."

The final revisions were ready by mid-February, but the negotiations for a suitable lead and a strong cast took much longer than Ed expected. Even with I.A.M.'s help, the leading man and the principal comedy character man were third choices. Production began in mid-March.

The camp show called for several native ritual dances in which Leya, as the USO girl, is persuaded to take part. Reluctantly, Kent agreed that these should be choreographed and staged by Katherine Dunham.

The early word around the lot was good. The only

misgivings the front office had concerned the dancing. There was not as much of it as there had been in Leya's previous pictures, and most of it was a departure in style for Leya. It would be the first time she had been seen publicly in pure ethnic dance, which, to the uninitiated, often seemed lascivious.

"Darling," Ed assured Leya, "we've got ourselves a very funny picture, and you are a surprisingly good little comedienne. I'm going to bet that this one is our largest grosser."

"You always do, Ed. Your faith is unshakable. I wish mine was."

"You can't judge yourself, darling, except maybe for the dancing."

"That's what I'm really talking about, Ed. I think a lot of people will confuse those bumps and grinds with burlesque."

"Not a chance, darling. Everybody knows Dunham now through her dance concerts. The story is fast and funny, and the dancing is absolutely in context. Relax, honey. You're tired. When you see it all put together in the cutting room, you'll feel differently."

The picture, after many suggestions, was titled, *Fall In!* It received mixed reviews from the "trades" and from the New York critics. Elsewhere, it was generally received as a "refreshing change of pace for Leya Leslie, who displays a charming talent for understated comedy and a superb flair for native dance."

"We are not certain," wrote one critic in Chicago, "whether or not Miss Leslie's convincing befuddlement was a clever bit of acting or the result of genuine confusion in her effort to follow the convoluted plot. Whatever the case, *Fall In!* is a very funny and satisfying spoof of traditional military snafus. The only fault this critic finds is the lack of some solid ballet that would have shown the full range of Miss Leslie's formidable talent."

Ed Matson flipped through the sheaf of clips provided by the service. He wore a satisfied smile.

"Our first Edward Matson production is going to work just fine, darling, even though you may be right about the lack of sufficient dancing. But we proved something else about you, didn't we?"

"As far as I'm concerned, we did not, Ed," Leya said flatly. "I don't want to do any more pictures like that. They may make money, but they lack class. Not for thirty seconds did I ever believe that dumb little Dotty Dillingham I played in this one."

Listening with raised eyebrows, Ed tried to assess just how much of Leya's reaction was conviction and how much was fatigue. She had indeed been an iron butterfly—for two years now. Except for the brief honeymoon at Tahoe, there had been almost no time off.

"Tell you what," he said. "The best part of the season at Malibu is now. Let's take a month off and enjoy it. Then we'll look at the box-office sheets and see what the public thinks."

CHAPTER 42

By the end of the second week at Malibu, Leya was restless. Ed was pleased and ascribed her mood to a desire to get back to work. Ellen Squires knew better. Watching Ed and Leya walking along the beach tossing bread to the gulls on a mild November afternoon, she said, "I feel so sorry for that beautiful child, Squires. She needs to belong to herself for a while. Why don't somebody tell Matson that poontangin' may be relaxin' for a man, but it ain't necessarily for a woman, at least not almost every night!"

Squires' gray eyes twinkled. "Well," he replied with a sly smile, "seems like you got a pretty short memory, woman. I kinda remember that when we was first married, we was pretty busy for a time."

"You kept me busy all right, Squires," Ellen admitted, "but I wasn't a movie star working sixteen hours a day. And you wasn't an older man trying to make up for lost time."

Her husband chortled. "Oh, yes, I was! Besides, Mr. Matson's not old. He's only forty-five."

Ellen Squires sniffed. "That makes him old enough to be her father!"

"I s'pose he could be all right—on a careless Saturday night," Squires admitted.

If she had been able to confide, Leya would have admitted

that sex with Ed was pleasant. There were some skillful things he did that excited her, and he managed them well. In the beginning, they had made love with only the ambient light from the hall shedding a soft glow on the far side of the bedroom. Later, when it was obvious that Ed's enjoyment was heightened when he could see her body and watch her reactions, they made love with the room half illuminated by a rose shaded lamp in the dressing area.

Ed's body was mature—"comfortably padded but not porcine," he admitted—and his muscle line was still good. Since their marriage, he had been working at keeping in shape. When he was erect and over her during their foreplay, Leya enjoyed reciprocating with deliberate little touchings and strokings that she knew pleased him. At times, she took a perverse pleasure in tormenting him until his staying power was tried beyond reason. He would call her his "little cock teaser" then and accuse her of deliberately overtraining him in the preliminaries so she could score a quick knockout in the "main event." Her innocent denials were not convincing.

On November 18, when the American Third Army crossed the German border, a resurgence of optimism swept the country. Ed Matson found himself thinking ahead to the next two years and the possible consequences of peace on the film industry. The studio front office and New York foresaw no negative change. People had grown used to going to the movies; the habit would persist. Radio would keep its share of audience, but television, after the studio's first experiments with it, did not seem to hold much promise.

Howard Pryor adopted a "wait and see" attitude. "Keep her working," he advised. "Get that second picture in production as soon as she's rested enough. And let's get that new contract signed. Remember what happened after the first war. People had a mania for entertainment. Human nature doesn't change that much."

Ed Matson, studying the dollar grosses of pictures with war themes, found little evidence that musicals would be replaced as dependable box-office money grabbers, even though William Wyler's *Mrs. Miniver* with Greer Garson, Walter

Pidgeon, and Peter Lawford had grossed five million dollars with its hard look at the effects of war on an English family. But musicals were still a draw. *Music for Millions, Step Lively, Up in Arms, Bathing Beauty,* and his own production, *Fall In!* were proving that.

Ed suggested a New York trip for Christmas. Much as she wanted to see her family, the ordeal of traveling, with priorities almost impossible to get during the holidays, was too much. Leya chose to relax at the beach house. The Alpine Drive house had become an auxiliary home, more of an office for Ed. He had closed his office on the Strip and administered her personal-manager duties and his new duties as a motion-picture producer from there.

Christmas, never a major event for Leya, was a much-needed quiet time, made even more quiet because Ed, in his new capacity, had less time to spend at Malibu. Kent had closed the beach house again and gone East, presumably to spend the holidays with his family.

Shortly after the start of the New Year, a new executive in the studio's front office became preoccupied with the possibility of making the George Du Maurier classic, *Trilby,* into a musical. The evil Hungarian, Svengali, would be changed to a dance entrepreneur instead of a singing coach. When he dies of a heart seizure, Trilby will suddenly find her talent has gone. Instead of dying soon afterward, she would go back to Little Billy, her first love, where her talent would be reborn, and she would become the toast of the Paris ballet.

Ed was forced to bring the project home. Leya listened in disbelief. "That story is a classic. They can't ask us to change it like that."

"They can ask," Ed said unhappily, "and they are. And they're putting a hell of a lot of pressure on, too, like not participating in the financing of our next venture if you don't do it."

Leya's eyes blazed. "Why this crap all of a sudden, Ed? All you have to do is tell them I don't believe it, and I won't do it!"

"I don't think we can be that blunt about it, darling, but I'll find a way to make your point. I've talked to Howard in

New York. He's going to have a quiet luncheon with Barney and Paul and see what he can do to get the pressure off."

Later, bundled and walking alone on the beach, Leya thought back. Up to now there had never been any trouble about the scenarios. "The right stories for you always seem to fall into our laps," Ed had commented when *Twinkle Toes* had come along. This was the first time there had been any contention. What troubled Leya more was that Ed had not been able to handle the problem without her help. Always before, he had presented her with solutions.

One of the stories he would be fighting for was really a switch on a classic short, short story. A temperamental prima ballerina, working hard to get in condition for an important concert, looks up and sees a young girl watching from the doorway. Annoyed, the ballerina orders her away. When the girl obeys, the ballerina sees that she is crippled. Filled with remorse, she runs to the child, discovers she is orphaned, and becomes the girl's guardian. After a series of operations, the girl is able to start studying. In time, when the ballerina herself is too old to dance, she finds fulfillment in seeing her *protégé* reach stardom.

The story brought tears to Leya's eyes even as she moaned, "Oh, God, it's corny!"

"It'll work, darling," Ed assured her.

Howard Pryor had a different opinion. "You're crazy if you fight for it, Ed. Let Vera Zorina do it. If you get a kid good enough to play the part of the cripple, she'll steal the picture right out from under Leya. You should know that. Kids and dogs are dynamite! Ask Chaplin. The only picture that ever got stolen from him was *The Kid* with Jackie Coogan. Don't let Leya do it."

The uncertainty about the next production and the growing urgency to get it on the schedule troubled Leya. Ed, too, grew increasingly irritable. They had their first real squabble at dinner when Leya said, "We never had this trouble when you were just my manager instead of my producer. You could tell them then. Now it looks like we're always having to ask them."

"That's a damned lie, little friend," he exploded. "I still tell them what you want to do!"

"And they're telling you what I'd better do—or we don't get financing!" Leya retorted.

A compromise was worked out during the last week in February. The next picture would be another GI musical, tentatively titled, *About Face!*

"When do we start?" Leya asked.

"April first, darling."

"April Fool's Day," Leya murmured. "I hope that isn't prophetic."

Ed regarded her sorrowfully. "Look, little friend, we both know the trouble was new top management. That's been solved."

"How much did we pay for this screenplay?"

"Thirty-five thousand for the treatment and the shooting script."

Leya nodded. "That's a hell of a lot for a rubber stamp!"

Concealing his annoyance, Ed came over and put his arms around her. After a few seconds, he backed away with a puzzled look. "I've hugged wooden Indians who were looser, darling. Now look, Leya, take a deep breath. Relax. Everything's going to be okay. All of the kids are coming back. Our lucky team will be together again. It's all going to be fine."

The British and the Canadians reached the Rhine River on February ninth. The Americans met with still more vicious resistance. Elements of the One Hundred and First Airborne and the Eighty-Second Airborne units had taken dreadful losses in their efforts to probe the sector leading directly to Cologne.

The first week in March, just prior to the start of dance rehearsals, the Allies, in a combined assault, took Cologne.

In spite of her misgivings that *About Face!* would be just another war-theme dance musical, now perhaps badly timed, Leya found herself interested in the final version of the screenplay. But Kent's continued absence worried her.

"Try to reach him, Ed," Leya demanded. "I want to know what I'm going to be doing. Tell Kent to get out here, or let's give Peter his chance."

It was one of the few times Leya had delivered an edict.

Ed Matson nodded agreeably. "I'll take care of it, honey. Don't worry."

"Don't worry?" Leya's tone was derisive. "Good God, man, *you* can say that. You don't have to dance!"

During the two days it took to locate Kent, Leya's tension increased. Finally, by calling Captain Fred Stein, who operated the Cherry Grove ferry from Sayville, Long Island, they learned that Kent Kendall and three others had hired the *Sea Horse*, a large work boat that could push through the skim ice on Great South Bay. Most of the houses on Fire Island were closed for the winter season, but a message was gotten through. Kent returned the call late Monday from the Sayville ferry terminal.

"Leya, darling, I'm sorry you had to go to such trouble," he apologized. "I finally found a buyer for my cottage at the Grove. Isn't that marvelous? No, it isn't! I'm in tears, really." He covered the mouthpiece and glanced at Matt, who was standing nearby. "My little star's upset with me!" he said in a loud whisper.

Turning back, he listened, nodding. "Of course I've looked at the script. There are at least four places for great numbers. I'll be back day after tomorrow. We'll go right to work. And please, Leya dear, forgive me. These personal matters are much, much more difficult than I thought." He glanced again at Matt, who was deliberately ignoring the innuendo. "So, dear, I'll see you soon."

Leya replaced the receiver and gave Ed a worried look.

"He sounds on the verge of hysteria."

Ed's smile was less than reassuring. "He's probably excited about selling his place. I think it's a good sign that he's thinking California permanently now."

"Ever since Kuzzy trapped Matt, I'm not sure of anything with Kent," Leya said, and left to tell Ellen to make time to open Kent's house.

A freezing rain was falling over Long Island when Kent Kendall pulled his 1934 MG right-hand drive Tigress into the parking area alongside the Red Barn Restaurant on Route 27.

"I'm frozen stiff," he said, shivering and clutching himself. "I need another drink."

"You need a coffee," Matt grumbled. "You've had enough booze. You can't hit the ground with your hat as it is."

"Dear boy," Kent replied archly, "the implication that I cannot hold my spirits is offensive in the extreme." He regarded Matt down the length of his nose, then pretending an indignant "Humph!" opened the door.

"Jesus!" he shrieked as the sleet struck him. "Hurry up!"

Matt, wrapped in his army greatcoat, was comfortable, but Kent, who had worn only a wool fisherman's turtleneck and a tweed sport coat, had been chilled for most of the afternoon.

When they were shown to a booth, Kent ordered a double Scotch, the fourth or fifth of the afternoon, then fixed Matt with an accusing look.

"You really haven't been the most exciting company this weekend, you know. I can't imagine why you bothered to come along at all."

"I came along because you pestered me to."

"You said you wanted to!" Kent charged. He dismissed the matter with a wave. "Be that—et cetera. Things haven't had much meaning this past year. I wanted you to be with me when I sold the cottage—for sentimental reasons, if you must know—and I want to know how much longer you're going to play in that patriotic GI monstrosity. There are ways out of it, you know. We could pick up on your professional career."

"There is no way out of it for me. I was drafted. I'm in for the duration."

Kent threw back his head and laughed. "Enlisted for the run of the play! That's a scream!"

"It's a hell of a lot better than squatting in a foxhole shitting my pants every time a bomb drops."

Kent sniffed. "But it's not a hell of a lot better than being honest about what you really want, getting a medical discharge and coming back with me." He leaned forward. "Oh, Matt, I can't imagine what you were thinking of, getting into that one-sided thing with Kuzzy. Wedded bliss? That's not your style!"

"There's nothing wrong with it," Matt replied. His tone

was defensive. "Kuzzy takes care of me. She mothers me."

Kent stifled a laugh. "*She* mothers? Preposterous! *I'm* the mother—of the world! From the very beginning, all I have ever done is think of you, worry about you, plan for your career—"

Matt laughed unpleasantly. "Sure, while Bruce Cydney's stroking your poor little head. Come on, mother! We've been chewing this for two days now. Knock it off!"

Kent gazed at him over the top of the glass as he emptied it and signaled for another.

"No more," Matt said as the waitress approached. "We need something to eat."

"I don't need anything to eat," Kent pouted.

"Just bring two coffees," Matt said to the girl.

He finished off two cups, sweetened with sugar packets fished from his overcoat pocket. Kent left his untouched.

When Matt tried to pay, Kent pushed his hand aside and gave the girl a five-dollar bill. "Just keep the change for your trouble, dear," he said thickly.

When Kent ran to the right-hand door of the little British roadster, Matt caught him by the arm.

"Let me drive, Kent."

"Let go of me! You're keeping me out here freezing!" He pulled free and wormed his way behind the wheel. Matt went around to the left side, bundled his coat beneath him, and backed in.

"Look, Kent," he pleaded, "please let me drive."

"No, thank you! You've never driven one of these before. I'd be terrified!"

"I can drive anything on wheels, for God's sake! Now come on, Kent, use your head!"

Kent reached for the ignition key and glared at him. "You are asking me to be sensible?" He laughed. "God, boy! You're the one who should have his head examined. I *know* what I am!"

He slammed the car in gear, and it jerked out onto the highway.

By the time they reached the point where the Montauk Highway joined the Sunrise Highway, the frozen rain was sticking faster than the hand-powered windshield wiper could keep it cleared.

Matt, leaning forward to squint for signs across the wheel of the right-hand-drive sports car, bumped Kent's arm. "Why don't you get off at Carleton Avenue like we used to when traffic was heavy? Let's go on up to Jericho Turnpike. It'll be better in this sloppy weather."

"You watch for the sign, then!" Kent ordered petulantly.

"They're on your side," Matt complained. "I can't see through this stuff!"

"Well, try, damn it!"

Matt hunched to his right in a futile attempt to peer through the quadrant of relatively clear glass on the driver's side.

"Slow down, for God's sake. Do you have to do fifty?" he asked.

"I have to get out of this mess before I freeze my balls off! Just look for the sign, Matt. It should be coming up in a mile or so."

Ahead of them, a single tail light appeared, glowing weakly in the icy downfall. "Oh, Jesus!" Kent muttered. "Some damned potato farmer poking along in his Model A."

Several car lengths behind the old sedan, Kent found his view handicapped by the right-hand drive. He swerved the little MG sharply to the left of the two-lane road. Just as his front wheels were even with the rear wheels of the sedan, a pair of oncoming headlights blazed to high beam through the downpour.

"Oh, Christ! Oh, no!" Kent screamed as he down-shifted. The little sports car shot forward, angled right just inches in front of the sedan. For a few feet it fishtailed on the slippery surface as Kent fought to straighten it out. Then, in an attempt to power it out of the skid, Kent floored the throttle. The screech of the tires drowned their outcries as the car leaped and spun out of control. Seconds later, it crashed headlong into the concrete abutment at the intersection.

At nine-thirty P.M., Coast time, Howard Pryor called from New York.

"I don't know how you're going to tell Leya this, Ed, but Kent Kendall and Matt O'Brien were killed tonight on Sunrise Highway. We're not sure how it happened yet." He gave Ed the few details he knew.

Leya saw Ed's face go white. "Thank you, Howard. Let me get my head together. I'll call you in the morning."

"Ed, what is it?" Leya gasped. "Is it papa? Is something wrong?"

"It's not Harry, thank God," he replied. "It's Kent. And Matt."

"What happened, Ed?" Leya cried.

"They were together in Kent's little car. Traveling too fast." He closed his eyes. "They're both dead, darling."

For a moment, Leya stared in mute disbelief. Then, with a wild little cry, she snatched up a sheepskin-lined coat and fled to the beach.

When Ed caught up with her, she struggled.

"Let me alone—please!" she sobbed.

"Darling, listen to me. It's a tragedy! I feel every bit as badly as you do. But you've got to get a hold of yourself. Come back inside, darling. Let's talk it out. It's happened. We can't undo it. Please, darling—"

Leya allowed herself to be led to the house. On the patio, she stopped to look north to Kent's place, opened now and waiting for him.

"Oh, God," she sobbed. "Oh, God, poor Kent—and Matt—"

Ed held her close as a new spasm of grief wracked her. When she seemed to control herself again, he led her indoors and removed her coat.

"Poor Kuzzy—" Leya sobbed. "She was so confident, so sure—"

"Darling," Ed said gently as he led her to the sofa, "please try to be realistic. Grieve for them, of course. I do, too. I'll miss them as you will, but let us both thank God that we can go on, that we can do the things we've planned. Kent's death will make a problem on the picture but not an insurmountable one."

Leya wrenched free. "For God's sake, Ed Matson, don't you ever see anything on a personal basis—except your own selfish feelings and our business deals?" Suddenly, he was a stranger. "How in the name of all that's decent can you tell me to forget them and go back to business as usual? What are you made of?"

"Leya, darling," he protested, "you're misunderstanding me again."

"Misunderstanding you again?" she repeated. "You mean understanding you for the first time!" She covered her face. "Oh, my God!" she cried as she fled to the bedroom and slammed the door.

Production on *About Face!* started the second week in April. The studio wanted Bruce Cydney to take over as choreographer, but Leya was adamant. Peter Genova, who knew her as well as Kent had, and who was already working out the tap routines for her, assumed the head choreographer's position. Bruce Cydney, with practical good grace, consented to remain as assistant.

The first days of work on the dances were emotionally difficult for Leya. Letters came from friends who had attended the rites. Kuzzy had been a stoic. Heather had blubbered out of control. Both caskets were kept closed. Only the immediate families attended the simple graveside services that followed. Leya wanted to be with Kuzzy and Heather, but the studio had been unable to get an air priority in time. The train was out of the question. Ed asked Kuzzy to come West to stay with them until she felt like resuming her career. She thanked them and asked for more time to make up her mind.

Two weeks after production began, the news came that Mussolini had been murdered with his mistress, Clara Petacci, near Lake Como. The bodies had been brought to Milan and hung upside down, to be vilified by a mob whose members had so recently apotheosized him. Both were buried in unmarked graves. "*La guerra è finita!*" Peter Genova murmured, paraphrasing *Il Duce* at the moment of his pyrrhic victory in Ethiopia.

Two days later, the news flashed over the wires that Hitler and his mistress, Eva Braun, had apparently committed suicide in the command bunker in Berlin.

In Florida, Heather O'Brien looked at her bloated face in the ornate Venetian mirror and laughed bitterly. "It's been a hard week on mistresses, baby!"

On the second day of location shooting at an air base in Kansas, a sudden fever of excitement was evident. In the middle of a sound take, the public-address speakers blared the news of the Allied victory in Europe. The emotional blowoff lasted for hours, but nobody forgot that the Imperial Japanese Army and Navy were still fighting with suicidal determination.

Not until several days later did the West hear the details of the fall of Hitler's Germany. Newspapers on the base told of the liberation of the Jews at Dachau and Belsen and Buchenwald and of the horror their rescuers found. Subsequent dispatches told of the discovery of a number of Stalags—short for Stammlager—the Nazi prison camps in which surviving Allied fliers and ground troops had been interned.

Follow-up dispatches on the atrocities added up to a hideous record of paranoid behavior. Leya remembered Abraham and Ruth Lowenstein and the stories they had told Arthur and his family, stories that ignited the rage that had led to Arthur's early enlistment and, ironically, to his end. As she worked, surrounded by enlisted men and bomber crews learning to man the huge B-29 Flying Fortresses, Leya wondered how many of those sharp, clean faces—white, black, brown, red, and yellow—would contort in terror as they incinerated in blazing aircraft falling into the South Pacific jungles or the sea. She drove the specter from her mind by losing herself in work.

Location shooting was completed shortly after the news came that Okinawa had fallen to United States landing parties, covered from the sea by Task Force Fifty-Eight. Several days later, Leya and millions of other Americans saw the picture of our marines on Iwo Jima raising the colors on Mount Suribachi.

A strange mood prevailed in the *About Face!* company as the final shooting was completed on the lot. Leya sensed that an era was about to end. Peter Genova had great imagination, and his routines reflected more strength and humor than Kent's. Howard Pryor, who had worked out the details of his contract for the picture, immediately set in motion the I.A.M. buildup. Genova needed a hit Broadway musical now, and Jack Beckman had a new one in preparation. Unless Leya Leslie was going immediately into another picture, Genova would be set for the Beckman production.

In the weeks immediately preceding the release of *About Face!* the entire war did an "about face." On August eighth, the B-29, Enola Gay, dropped the first atom bomb on Hiroshima. The act, which destroyed an entire city, shocked the world. Russia declared war on a Japan that was sinking to its knees. The following day, the second atomic bomb dropped on Nagasaki. Five days later, a prostrate Japan agreed to an unconditional surrender.

Alone on the beach at Malibu in the long summer twilight, Leya glanced at Kent's house. It was closed now until his estate went through probate. She stopped, allowed herself to remember the fun and the work they had shared in Kent's rehearsal room and the excited chatter when the routines proved out on the screen.

She recalled, too, Kent's changed mood after Matt and Kuzzy were married, and she wondered again why Matt had been with Kent.

The picture was released in mid-September, after a national ad campaign that promised an intimate peek at the training of the men who had dropped the A-bombs and the fun that had kept their fears under control.

"There's not one damned thing in that film about the A-bomb, Ed," Leya said. "It's dishonest advertising. If it does get people into the theater, they'll blame you and me for doublecrossing them!"

"It's the only hook we have, little friend," he had countered. "Don't be so literal. Nobody knows now just what the public is going to go for. I'm sure you know that I do not have a crystal ball."

"Very funny, Mr. Matson!" Leya snapped, turning back to

the copy of *Women's Wear Daily* that carried a speculative roundup of the probable effects of peace on clothing, travel, and entertainment. The piece had used *About Face!* as an example of "the mindless diversion that millions of men facing combat needed but mercifully will need no longer." The piece opined that "Americans would turn to more serious themes now, seeking to analyze the causes and the effects of the second great holocaust to lay waste the world in a half century." The writer cited as evidence the new William Wyler picture *Best Years of Our Lives,* presently shooting with Fredric March, Teresa Wright, Dana Andrews, and Harold Russell, the nonprofessional double-amputee veteran.

Ed rose from the sofa and fixed a second Scotch and water, then turned to study Leya.

"Instead of wasting energy on bitching, little friend, I'd suggest you devote some of your balanced Libra reasoning and your female intuition to the problem of the next picture. We have a contract that guarantees you about two hundred thousand dollars over the next forty weeks and guarantees me—us—twenty percent of the gross, which could run to a half million dollars or more."

"I am thinking—and worrying. Plenty! All I know is dancing and a little something you cheer me up with by calling it 'acting.' You are a personal manager. One of the best in the business. And now you're a producer, too."

"Thanks to you, Leya."

"Thanks to whomever. The fact remains that you can go either way."

"We're together on this trip, sweetheart. Why does that bother you? It should reassure you."

"Well, it doesn't," Leya replied. "And I'll tell you why. As a personal manager, you had one problem—the right situation for me. If it wasn't right, we could walk away from it. Now you have to work both sides of the boulevard. When Jay Sanford was producing, we could hassle things out. Now I have to sit down opposite the producer and do that, and part of you is thinking about what's best for me and the other part is saying, 'It may not be the best thing for her, but it will play, and we'll still walk away with a quarter of a million, or a half, or whatever."

"That," Ed said deliberately, "is not the way it works at all!"

"The fact that you have to say that to me is proof that it does."

Ed's eyes hardened, and he set the glass down hard on the end table. "Bullshit! Pure, unadulterated bullshit, little friend! If every star in Hollywood waited for the perfect vehicle, they'd make only one or two pictures in their lives! The whole game is a compromise. You've made six pictures. The earnings of the five that are out are all within a few hundred thousand dollars of one another. You're not going to pretend that the excellent screenplays deserve the credit, are you?" He paused. "You know damned well it was you, Leya Leslie, 'brightest new dancing star in Hollywood's galaxy,' that made the difference."

"Now you're putting a load of that stuff on me, Mr. Matson," Leya snapped. "What was it you said? 'With this wartime box office, they'd line up around Music Hall to watch Baby Leroy wet his pants'? Well, they won't line up from here to the front door to see Leya Leslie fall on her face, and that's exactly what's going to happen if you push me into any more of these B pictures masquerading as epics. I don't have a crystal ball, either, but I'll bet you my half of the gross that *About Face!* is a bigger bomb than the one they dropped on Hiroshima."

Ed raised his glass in a mock salute. "You just made yourself a bet, baby, and please remember you lost the last one!"

CHAPTER 43

The tension between Ed and Leya increased with each succeeding box-office report. A trade review that did much to influence the exhibitors' enthusiasm said, "There is little doubt that *About Face!* will get its bait back, thanks to Leya Leslie's exceptional talent. But it will not do Miss Leslie any good to find her name on the bottom line of a double bill, which is certain to happen in some locations. The Joint Chiefs of Staff could not have helped with the timing. Call that the fortunes of war. But they might have helped plot the story, which, except for the uniforms and the Kansas cornfields, is a direct lineal descendant of those cotton-candy canards that used to be set in the mythical kingdom of Belgravia."

Leya flung the paper across the room and slapped the pages of the press book lying open on Ed's desk. "Will this do it for you? Or shall we wait for the other reviews and next week's grosses?"

Ed Matson swung in his chair and looked through the French windows that gave out onto the backyard and the pool at the Alpine Drive house. He had compromised on the story even though he had sensed that things in Europe might happen faster than people thought. "This is one review out of five important ones," he said, "and this is one picture out of six." Turning back, he struggled to suppress his defensiveness. "Do you know how many stars in Hollywood—or on Broadway—have a batting average like that? You're 'five and one' for the season. We're not going broke on this. What's the matter with you, Leya? Have you forgotten that my name's on it, too—as producer?"

"Big deal!" Leya replied. "You get the blame, and I take the licking!"

" 'Thanks to Leya Leslie's exceptional talent' doesn't sound like much of a licking to me, little lady!" Ed turned back and rested his elbows on the desk. "All right," he said, "let's spell it all out. What's really bugging you?"

"You don't hear very well anymore, Ed," Leya said in a level voice. "I told you that I don't like this business of your working both sides of the boulevard. And I told you why."

He nodded. "So, in effect, what you're doing is issuing an ultimatum, is that it?"

"I am not!" Leya blazed. "I'm simply saying that you're in a better position to defend me—us—when you only have one job to do."

"So I should make up my mind which job is the more important. Is that what it nets out to?"

For several seconds, Leya continued to stand silently in front of his desk, glaring down at him. Then she wheeled abruptly and left the room.

That night, in bed, he rolled his head toward her and studied her silhouetted profile. "Little darling," he said quietly, "if you and I start flailing at one another, we both hit the best friend we've ever had. We'll break even on *About Face!* Breaking even, by studio accounting methods, is making a profit for them—not us. Even so, you and I have assets of nearly two million dollars. Suppose I talk to the studio? I'll tell them that you're too tired to go into production again right now. Doctor's orders. I'll get them to postdate the contract. That will take some pressure off and give us time to figure out where we want to go with stories now. In the meantime, there's no reason why we can't go to

New York and see your family and catch some shows. We can stay through the holidays. Squires and Ellen can look after both places. I've even been thinking that perhaps a couple of months studying drama with Lee Strasberg or Stella Adler would be useful."

Suddenly, Leya was up on one elbow. In a quiet, icy voice, she said, "There's one thing you'd better understand, Ed. I'm still a dancer, albeit an erstwhile ballet dancer who has learned some other dance forms she needed to know. At this rate, that's what I'm going to be until I'm too damned old to dance." She paused. "*After* that, if there's any reason to, I may consider trying to become a character woman. If, in the back of your busy head, you are thinking that maybe Leya Leslie ought to convert to straight roles—do a Rita Hayworth—then take another think. If musical pictures are out, I'm out! But I don't think they are. I just think that musical pictures—any pictures—with asinine stories are out."

A heavy silence fell between them. After several minutes, Leya reached out to find his hand. "I'm sorry, Ed. I guess I'm being awful damned rough on you." When he made no response, she lifted her head slightly. "Are you asleep?"

"No, I'm listening."

"I *am* sorry, but I'm tired, Ed. Tired of working, tired of people, tired of Hollywood. Tired! I don't know who I am anymore. I've been six different kinds of idiots in six pictures. I meet myself in the hall and pass myself like a stranger." She paused, searching for words. "What I'm trying to say is this, Ed. New York sounds like a good idea. But I need some time alone." She paused again. "Do you understand, Ed?"

"I suppose I do. I'd be happier if being alone meant being with me—away from here for a while."

"I mean, being alone, Ed," she said firmly.

"Do you think you can accomplish that in the largest city in the world?"

"Yes."

He laughed softly. "What was the lyric—'Alone in a crowd?' "

"You're a New Yorker, Ed. You know what I mean."

"By adoption, I'm a New Yorker, little friend. And yes, I do know what you mean. There were times in New York when I was more alone there than I've ever been. Do you know when that was?"

"No," Leya replied untruthfully.

"When I knew I was in love with you and couldn't do anything about it."

Leya's hand tightened on his. "You are a bastard, Ed Matson," she said gently.

Wearing dark glasses and bundled against the late-autumn chill, Leya registered in the Sherry-Netherland Hotel as "Leya Marks" and went to the corner suite overlooking the park.

After a bath, she wrapped herself in a terry-cloth robe and stretched out on the bed. She thought about surprising her father and Minnie but decided to call them in the morning—Sunday—enjoy their utter surprise, then take a cab to Brownsville. In the last phone call a week earlier, they had imparted the news that they were considering moving out of the city, to Yonkers. "They've got new houses there, very nice!" papa had said. "Even the nearest neighbor, we couldn't hear! Fifty, maybe even a hundred feet away. Also, there's a basement. I could make a shop—and a garden."

Leya smiled to herself. They would have their house, those two. Leya Leslie might have forgotten who she was, but she could never forget who they were.

The phone call at nine the next morning produced the predictable joyous explosion.

"I'll answer all of your questions in a half hour, papa," she pleaded. "I'm coming out now."

On the bottom step, Harry glanced apprehensively after the departing taxi. "*Bubeleh*, your baggage! You forgot!"

"No, papa, I left everything at the hotel."

"What hotel?" Minnie asked.

"The Sherry-Netherland, darling. I'll explain later. Come on, now. I'm ready to hear all about your plans."

The talk ranged from Harry's prospects at the Navy Yard

with the workload winding down to the problems of commuting from Yonkers. In five years, Minnie would retire on her I.L.G.W.U. pension. With her Social Security and with Harry's pension from the Navy Yard—one hundred twenty-three a month, it would be—and with the money he would make from his own little machine shop in Yonkers, they would have five hundred dollars a month, maybe more. Her father's optimism was infectious. As she sat listening, Leya could feel her spirits rising.

She kept the conversation turned to their doings and their plans. When they asked about hers, Leya was evasive.

"So stay here!" Minnie insisted with an injured look. "Who is an extra bedroom for?"

"I'm sorry, darling," Leya said, reaching over to pat her pink hand. "Please understand. I've got phone calls coming from the Coast, people to see. I needed a place where those things could be taken care of—room service and everything."

"Room service we don't have," Minnie conceded, "but the other things we've got. Also, it doesn't look good for the neighbors."

Leya glanced at her father and read his tacit concurrence. "I've been waiting to be invited to stay over tonight," she said, pretending some pique.

Minnie's pout turned into a grudging smile. "So why not? Your room is ready."

Monday at the hotel, Leya found a call from Ed asking that she return it at nine o'clock his time. She bought the morning papers, picked up the December issue of *Movieland* magazine, and went up to the suite. She felt like a visitor in her own city.

For a time she scanned the entertainment pages. There was a follow-up note that Aaron Copland, who had been awarded the Pulitzer Prize the previous May for his ballet, "Appalachian Spring," was at work on another composition and that Martha Graham, who had introduced it in Washington, D.C., in October of 1944, was hoping to introduce the new work at Carnegie Hall early in the coming year.

Martha Graham's innovative posturing had interested her but never really excited her. Kent had borrowed from Graham in "Oneida," particularly on his depiction of the role of the righteous founder. The recollection turned her thoughts to the Kendall Dance Group—and Kuzzy. The only address she had for Kuzzy was the Royalton Hotel. She called and found no forwarding number had been left. A call to Chorus Equity produced an address and number in Queens. It turned out to be the Kuznetsov apartment. In seconds, Kuzzy was on the phone, laughing and crying.

"Oh, God, *padrooga!* You'll never know how happy I am to hear your voice! Where are you staying? When can I see you?"

"Have lunch with me here at the Sherry-Netherland, Kuzzy, and we'll get caught up."

At twelve o'clock sharp, Tanya Kuznetsov was in Leya's arms, trying to speak through her tears.

"I don't know what's the matter with me," she said as Leya led her to one of the big chairs in the sitting room. "I've been very good. Through it all, I held onto myself." Her blue saucer eyes appealed for understanding.

"Do you want to talk about it, Kuzzy?"

Tanya Kuznetsov closed her eyes and drew in a deep breath. "Remember," she said, "how I promised you I'd change Matt to strictly DC—direct current to me only? I did for a while. And then, right after *Twinkle Toes,* Kent came to New York. He never did see the show. But he managed to run into Matt, and I guess they had drinks together.

"We saw Kent again when the show was on the road. He turned up with some sort of an excuse, one of those 'just happened to be in town' things. We both saw him then and got caught up on you and the other kids. But the last time, when he finished his work in *Fall In!,* he came back and chased the show all over the place. He was in a crazy mood, drinking, camping like the Queen of Sheba." Kuzzy frowned. "That was August, two years ago, I think. Then he'd show up at odd moments on all sorts of pretexts until finally the talk got around and I laid it on Matt—straight out."

Leya watched the pain return to Kuzzy's eyes, and

suddenly her friend's cherubic face seemed older and drawn. "He didn't give me any crap. He admitted that they'd been together—every time Kent was in town."

"What did you do about that?" Leya asked.

Kuzzy shrugged. "What could I do? I made my bed. So I tried to make my peace with Matt's bisexual hanky-panky, too. What the hell else was there to do, really?" She laughed bitterly. "No, *padrooga*. I did what I could. I used every trick in the book to make him feel that there was no possible kick like making it with me. I turned into an effing machine—or a machine, effing. I never thought of sex with Matt as dirty. I did things to him I never thought I could do. I loved everything about him—his looks, his really fine talent, his quiet pixie sense of humor, every beautiful muscle in his body, that sassy little ass of his." She flopped her arms helplessly. "Go figure it out. I was just nuts about him. I knew I'd never have to worry about another woman, and as long as Kent was around, I'd never have to worry about another fella, either. So there we were—the three of us—about the coziest little part-time *ménage à trois* you could imagine." Kuzzy lapsed into a reflective silence.

Leya frowned and searched for words briefly. "Do you feel like telling me what happened? I mean the day—they—?"

"—were killed? There must have been some sort of fight or something. Anyway, the autopsy report on Kent showed enough alcohol in his blood to make a Cossack drunk."

"What about Matt?"

"Nothing. He never did drink." Kuzzy lowered her head for a moment and toyed with her napkin. "I could wish for a lot of things, Leya, like Matt had had sense enough to insist on driving, like I'd had sense enough to know that something had been screwing up Kent's head for a couple of years." She looked up with a helpless smile. "What can I say? I asked for everything I got." She paused and looked away thoughtfully. "And I guess that's the way it was for all of us—Kent, Matt, me."

"What happens next with you?" Leya asked.

"The first of the year I go into *Carousel.* If it goes on the road, I'll probably go with it. I'm twenty-seven, honey. I don't know how much longer my bones will hold up. If you're asking what I'd like to do—" She smiled wistfully. "I'd like to turn the clock back, go back to Hollywood and share a Laurel Canyon house with you and make fun musicals and pretend that someday I'd be discovered and become a star, and then I could ask you over to my big house, too! Now how's that for a kooky answer?" Suddenly, her eyes filled, and she got up and came over to Leya. "Oh, honey, they didn't last very long, but those days with you in that crazy canyon with the raccoons and the skunks drinking out of the swimming pool at night, and the deer eating the flowers, and the gypsies eating us out of house and home—" She sighed. "Those were the happiest months of my misspent youth." Kuzzy looked intently at Leya as she rose. "Can I ask what happens next with you?"

Leya looked away. "You can ask, darling, but I don't have an answer yet."

An hour more and Leya saw her friend downstairs. In the suite, the little message memo reminded Leya that she had not called Ed at nine, his time. She glanced at her watch. It was one-fifteen on the Coast. Ed would still be at lunch. She would call later and tell him that time got away.

After bathing and changing, she took a cab to Brownsville. At dinner, she persuaded her father and Minnie to accept a gift that would make it possible for them to get the larger house in Yonkers. Her father tried not to look pleased.

"So, *bubeleh*," he said giving in finally, "the difference between a gift and a loan is you inherit the house someday! And believe me, a shack it isn't't!"

It was odd, Leya thought, but by eight o'clock—after only two evenings—they were talked out. She had told them everything she could and even managed guarded answers to Minnie's perceptive questions about Ed and their relationship. She sensed that Minnie was holding back other questions, and she was grateful that she didn't press.

On Tuesday morning, Leya called Dulcy in Silver Spring. "Where are you, dear heart?"

"In Manhattan, at the Sherry-Netherland."

"But the apartment's still there, sweetie. I told you—anytime."

"I know, Dulcy, and thank you. But I needed a place where I can press buttons and things will happen for me!"

"I understand. Believe me! How long are you going to be there?"

"A week, maybe two. I don't know."

"Is Ed with you?"

"No. He's on the Coast. This is my get-away-from-it-all trip, dear."

"Does that mean—and you can level with me—that you'd just like to touch bases by phone this time?" Dulcy asked.

"Of course not! I want to see you. I need to see you."

"Oh—?"

"I mean, I need to see an old friend who knew me *when.* I need to find Leya Marks again." She sighed heavily. "I'm so damned beat, going from one golden turkey into another, I had to get away. I've seen the family and my friend Tanya Kuznetsov. So far that's all."

"You haven't seen Jon Wales, then?"

"No."

"You should," Dulcy replied, "if only to collect a royalty on the business he's been getting as the discoverer of 'Leya Leslie.' "

"Oh, let him!" Leya laughed. "And *mazel-tov!* In a way, he's right."

"Better give that bow to your stepmother," she cautioned. "Anyway, when am I going to see you? How about coming down here?"

"How about coming up here?"

When Dulcy didn't respond immediately, Leya frowned. "Not possible now?"

"No, sweetie, it isn't. I am playing a game called devoted little housewife, and because I'm playing for about ten million dollars worth of Vandercort gelt, I'm playing very, very close to the chest, which on me is not difficult! If you're going to be there, I'll be up in a week or so and fill you in. How are things with you and Ed?"

"That may make interesting listening, too," Leya countered. "I'm not sure, but I think he's out to become Hollywood's leading film producer."

They talked for a time about Gwendolyn, about to be four, and agreed to get together in a week or so if Leya was still in New York.

Shortly before eleven, Leya called Ed at the Alpine Drive home. He was annoyed.

"What happened yesterday? I had important things to talk about, like did you arrive safely, and are you well?, and I've found a great story for us, a few little details like that."

"I'm safe, Ed," she replied, "and I'm well—not rested. And the last thing I want to hear about for a while is another 'great story for us.' I thought we understood that."

Ed laughed humorlessly. "You'll have to excuse me, kiddo. As I get older—among other things—my memory fails me, I guess. Also, I wanted to tell you that I have to go to Las Vegas. Forget I mentioned it, but the new story has a Las Vegas show setting. I want to talk to some of the people over there about the possibility of shooting on location in a casino."

"How long will you be gone?"

"As long as it takes to make a deal. Also, because I know you don't want to hear about business, I will refrain from telling you that *About Face!* will have its negative cost back by the first of the year."

"Which means I was wrong again?"

"At the risk of being misunderstood, I certainly hope so, and so should you."

"I'll hope," Leya said. "Call me when you get back."

It was strange, she thought when she hung up, how detached she felt. It was as though the three thousand miles that separated them had severed a bond and they were acquaintances again. Nothing more.

For a few minutes, Leya stood looking down on the geometry of walkways and the ranks of Central Park's deciduous trees, with their stark tracery of leafless limbs, dark gray against the asphalt walks, black in the distance, against the gray winter overcast. Across Fifth Avenue, the fountain in front of the Plaza Hotel had been turned off. Waiting on Fifty-ninth Street were only two hacks. The drivers, their shabby stovepipe hats angled forward, sat huddled in mufflers and greatcoats against the east wind while their blanketed nags munched apathetically from nose bags.

On an impulse, she went to the phone to call Jon Wales and remembered that she had never properly answered Dorothy Simpson's Christmas note.

Once again, there was the squeal of surprise and the cascade of questions until the photographer picked up the phone in the darkroom.

"My *protégé!*" Jon cried. "How are you, darling? And where are you?"

Leya offered a minimal explanation.

"Do you know what I want you to do?" Jon said. "I want you to tell me that the famous movie star, Leya Leslie, just happens to have a lunch free and can join me someplace where we can get caught up." He paused. "You know about Arthur, don't you?"

The unexpected questions shocked Leya. "No," she said, half afraid to go on. "That is, nothing except—"

"Darling Leya," Jon Wales cut in, "they found Arthur in a prison camp just outside of Stuttgart. He was half starved, he had pneumonia, he was more dead than alive, but they got him to an RAF hospital in England. Martin and Myra are over there with him. They hope to have him home by Thanksgiving." He paused expectantly. "So—what do you think of that?"

For a time, Leya could not bring herself to answer. "Jon," she managed finally, "I can't have lunch, but I'll call you back—later."

For over an hour, Leya sat alone. Her thoughts, following no pattern, meandered like the first trickle from a breaking dam, seeking emotional paths of least resistance until, at last, the tributaries converged in a flood of reality.

She rose from the sofa and went to the window. The gathering overcast had darkened the city prematurely. Random rectangles of light were beginning to appear in Radio City off to her left and in the apartments across Columbus Circle on Central Park West. Below her, store windows were illuminated. Downtown, on Thirty-fourth Street, the beacon atop the Empire State Building had been turned on. They had taken to turning it on in poor weather ever since the early morning of the previous August first when an army B-25 bomber, flying from New Bedford, Massachusetts, to Newark, New Jersey, had crashed into the one-hundred-and-two-story building. All three crewmen and ten persons in the building and on the street below had been killed. The bomber had been piloted by a veteran combat flyer, home on leave, who was unfamiliar with the New York area.

Leya laughed bitterly. Arthur had been shot down on his first mission. The hapless veteran flyer had survived all of his missions against the Nazis only to have his life taken by one of the world's most spectacular symbols of free enterprise! It could only have been more ironic if he had collided with the torch on the Statue of Liberty!

Suddenly, she did not want to be alone. Her father and stepmother were both at work. She remembered now Minnie's reticence the previous night and reluctantly conceded that in the same circumstances she would probably have been just as hesitant to bring up Arthur's name.

The address book, lying open on the telephone stand, caught her eyes. She walked to it and found it open to the Cs. She had intended to call Carnegie Hall to get a number for the rehearsal studio in case she felt like trying to maintain a semblance of condition. At the bottom of the page, she saw *Cervier, Celine.* It had been two years—except for the Christmas cards. She dialed and found the number was no longer in service. Billy Brenner's office would know, and so would Jack Beckman. She tried the Brenner office first.

After several minutes, Billy came on the line. "Leya?"

"Yes, Billy. How are you?"

"Super! Couldn't be better. Where are you? In California?"

"It's not for publication, Billy, but I'm in the city—at the Sherry-Netherland."

"With Ed? Are you two in town on business?"

"I'm in by myself to visit family and friends and have a little rest away from the aggravation and hassle. I'd love to see Celine, but the number I have for her is no good now. Do you know where she is?"

"Of course!" Billy said with a surprised little laugh. "You mean, you don't know?"

"Know what?"

"That Celine Cervier is Mrs. William Brenner now."

"Oh, wonderful, Billy!" Leya gasped. "When?"

"About a month. It took the girl a long time to make up her mind!"

"Oh, I couldn't be happier, Billy! When can I see you?" Leya paused uncertainly. "Or should I ask if Celine wants to see me?"

"Of course she wants to see you, and so do I! All those old misunderstandings have been long forgotten, Leya. By any chance, could you have dinner with us tonight?"

"I'll move heaven and earth, Billy. Where—and when?"

"What about your hotel? Celine's coming here at six."

"I can't imagine anything I'd rather do!"

The reunion was warm and happy. Celine appeared more chic than Leya remembered her. She asked to be forgiven for being "very French" when her eyes filled with tears. Billy Brenner had changed, too. He was more mature. More poised. It was clear that in the past three years Billy—or was it 'William' now?—had done a lot of growing up.

Celine explained that she had left the long-running show after Chicago and had returned to New York. Jack Beckman had been talking to Kent about doing his next show. No property had been settled on, but it was a foregone conclusion that Celine would have a principal part if she wanted to play it. Celine was not so sanguine.

"It may be, Leya," she said, "that I'm not cut out to be a gypsy. Being 'on the road' is fun—once. But I would not want to go through that again. For one thing, it's almost impossible to keep in condition. I love serious dancing—classical ballet—but not the 'show-biz' variation." She sighed wistfully.

"If only ballet could be a popular art form, then I could find the dedication to stick to it. But all that sweat and liniment and no money or real appreciation—except from a few balletomanes—was just too much for me!"

She paused and reached out to Billy. "The truth is, I really love being Mrs. William Brenner, *former* Broadway dancing star."

As they approached the entrance to the dining room, Billy nodded to the maître d'hôtel. "Miss Leslie's table please, Charles." Leya interrupted quickly. "I'm sorry, Billy, the reservation is under Marks."

When they were seated, Billy glanced at her sheepishly. "*Dummkopf*, Brenner!" he muttered to himself. "So now that you know I can't keep a secret, what do you and Ed plan next?"

Leya laughed helplessly. "Heaven only knows with Matson. The truth is, I'm not anxious to work for a while." She shrugged. "I came back here to try to get a new perspective on Leya Marks, Leslie, or whoever the hell she is!"

Billy Brenner smiled sympathetically and took her hand. "Who you are, Leya, is one of the most beautiful and talented and sensitive women on the screen—or anywhere else. Don't ever doubt that. I've been following your grosses. Your box-office records are fabulous."

"Except for *About Face!*" Leya said.

"That will do all right, too. If you had made it eighteen months earlier, it would have earned four times its negative cost—like the others."

"I know," she replied. "That's what worries me. I think the war thing is dead now."

"One aspect of it, perhaps," Billy agreed. "The country may start some soul searching now. It took nine or ten years for Hollywood to get around to making *The Big Parade* and *All Quiet on the Western Front.* Even then, the decision gave them the 'butterflies'—bad pun, I guess. The only thing I know for sure is—fine talent well used will always find its audience. The consensus around the business is that Ed Matson's turned into a smart producer. I'm sure he must be thinking ahead of the problem."

"That makes two of us," Leya replied flatly. "Let's put it this way. I don't like the material I've been seeing lately. But on the other hand, maybe I'm not capable of judging the best story for me."

Billy Brenner smiled innocently. "That's what managers are for."

The conversation turned to the current shows on Broadway.

"It's very good right now," Billy observed. "*On the Town, Bloomer Girl, The Red Mill* revival, *Are You With It?, Billion Dollar Baby*— But *Carousel* is something else! Have you seen it?"

"Not yet."

"Then go with us. Celine wants to see it again. I've got house seats. I have two kids in it."

"I'd love to. When?"

"Can you make it tomorrow night?"

"I will," Leya replied.

"Good. Have dinner with us at Sardi's. We'll pick you up at quarter of seven."

Billy's slip with the maître d'hôtel was sufficient to lift the thin mask of anonymity. The dinner at Sardi's was interrupted several times by legmen for the columnists. It also produced some speculation as to the reason Leya Leslie was seen in the company of a rising young personal manager.

Carousel, with John Raitt, Jan Clayton, Jean Castro, and Jean Darling, all relatively unknown on Broadway until the enormously successful opening, was everything that Billy and Celine had promised. Leya watched, transfixed, seeing herself in the various parts. The only role in *Carousel* in which she could really see herself was that of Louise, played and danced by Bambi Linn, who had scored such a hit in *Oklahoma!.*

It would be wonderful to play before live audiences again, Leya thought, and to star in a show with such a solid book and score. Frederick Loewe had told Dwight Deere Wyman several years earlier that he felt the future stars of the musical theater would come from the ranks of the ballet. He had been right, certainly. Proof of that were Sono Osato, Allyn

Ann McLerie, and Jerome Robbins in *On the Town* and Joan McCracken in *Oklahoma!* and in *Billion Dollar Baby,* which was coming to the Alvin. None of those dancers had great voices, but the composers had recognized their limitations and had not written material beyond their vocal capabilities.

At Lindy's, after the performance, Leya splurged on cherry cheesecake with Celine after promising herself 'in the presence of witnesses' that she would start classes again soon. As she entered the suite, she found herself humming a few bars from "You'll Never Walk Alone!"

It was really a hymn, she thought, one of the most beautiful songs that she had ever heard in a musical score. As she was preparing for bed, she whispered the lyrics to herself. By the time she had turned out the lights, she harbored little doubt that Leya Leslie, lately of Hollywood, would find a way to come home, to walk on and on—with hope in her heart!

She went to sleep thinking of Arthur, trying to imagine what he had endured at the hands of the Nazis, wondering what those years had done to him, recalling the remorse that he had conveyed to her from the training base by way of Myra, wondering whether the ordeal had altered his feelings, whether a man could feel at all after what he had been through.

"If you ever get the chance," he had said to his mother, "tell Leya that I'll try to get over being a bullheaded idealist."

Leya turned her head to smooth her cheek against the pillowcase. "You were the idealist, all right, my darling Arthur," she whispered, "and I was the bullheaded one!" Tears brimmed as she remembered the feel of his arms around her. "Come back, Arthur darling," she whispered, "and if it will help undo any of the hell you've been through, I'll gladly confess my own bullheadedness to you!"

The phone, ringing only inches from her ear, startled her. It was Ed, calling from Las Vegas.

"I tried earlier but didn't leave a message. I figured you were out with friends."

"I went to the theater with Celine—"

"And Billy? I heard they're married now."

"Yes. They took me to *Carousel.* It's one of the best things I've ever seen."

"I hope you feel the same way about the new story I have for us, honey. I've got everything cleared here in Vegas. We can shoot in the new show room at the Golden Palm Club right after the first of the year. By the way, Carlo and Heather are here, and so are some of the kids. Marc and Luanna are working in the chorus, and Sheri's here, too, working at the Sands. They all send their love."

"Sheri, too?" Leya asked, and regretted it instantly.

"Especially Sheri," Ed replied with an edge of sarcasm. "Anyway, I just wanted to call and touch base. I know you don't want to talk about working again for a while. But when you're ready, I've got us a wonderful show-business comedy about a young minister who falls in love with a dancer in Vegas. The title's *Heavenly Trouble,* and I went through hell to get it!"

"Sounds like another 'money grabber,'" Leya said, matching his sarcasm. "We'll talk about it when I get back."

"Unless I come into New York first. It gets lonesome on Alpine Drive."

"I believe it," Leya replied, "but you can make up for it in Vegas. Give Heather my love, Ed, and my gratitude to Sheri. Okay?"

His harsh laugh grated through the receiver. "If you insist, darling. Call me when you feel in the mood. I'll be home again tomorrow night."

CHAPTER 44

Leya found excuses to linger in New York well into November. The longer she delayed her return to the Coast, the more difficult she found it to resist the temptation to call the Lieberman apartment. She could not bring herself to think about the encounter, what she would say to Arthur, if indeed he was able to see anybody but the family. Somehow that would take care of itself. At the very worst, it would mean talking to Martin and Myra and asking them to convey— To convey what? Her congratulations, surely! Her love? And if she were free to tell him of that, would it still have any meaning for him?

Late in the afternoon, Leya found the courage to call. The maid answered. "No, Miss Leslie, the Liebermans are not here now. They brought Mr. Arthur in for one night and then took him straight down to Florida."

Unable to resist, Leya asked, "How does he look? How is he?" Before the woman could answer, she added hopefully, "If he can travel, he must be feeling better."

"Mr. Arthur's very thin and weak, and he looks older, Miss Leslie. But he's going to be all right in a few weeks, they said."

For a moment, Leya considered asking for the Florida number, then thought better of it. To attempt to reach

Arthur now could do nothing but complicate matters. "Would you tell Mrs. Lieberman that I called?" she asked. "If they want to reach me, I'm at the Sherry-Netherland. I'll be here for a week or so."

"I'll tell them, Miss Leslie."

"Thank you." A moment later, Leya sank into the nearest chair. "Thank God, he's going to be all right!" she whispered. She prayed for patience.

Thanksgiving with her family was a welcome respite from worry. No table in New England could have been set with more attention to tradition.

Harry's blessing, in English, at the start of the meal brought Leya close to tears when he added, "—and dear Lord, even if I didn't do all I could sometimes, you spared my daughter Leya, whose love for her papa and Minnie make blessings on this house. You'll remember that, please, and make blessings on her because money is not always good—even if not having money is worse yet—but happiness is what I wish for her. You would not forget to see that she has it? Amen."

The blessing told Leya that her father and Minnie had perceived much more than she had suspected.

In the living room, after dinner, she spoke of Arthur. "Jon Wales told me," she said, hoping that her attempt at casualness would be convincing.

"So?" Minnie responded. "Prayers were answered. Thank God for that!"

"Why didn't you two tell me?" she asked.

Harry directed a guilty look at Minnie and shrugged. "Yesterday is yesterday, *bubeleh.*"

"But you knew I'd be—interested."

Minnie flopped her hands in her lap. "He's not home. He's in a hospital?—in Europe somewhere."

"He's in Miami."

Minnie looked up. "So thank God for that. You'll call Miami."

Leya found herself at the edge of anger. She understood that her father and stepmother had hoped to cope with a problem they did not understand by ignoring it. She had loved Arthur Lieberman. Now she was married to Ed Matson. Her career was assured. Outwardly, things were going well. You don't meddle with good luck. She forced herself to smile and changed the subject.

Ed's calls became less frequent. In mid-December, he delivered an ultimatum. "I don't know what you're up to, Leya—a one-sided trial separation? Whatever it is, you and I are business partners. We've got to go over things. The studio wants new color portraits. I've engaged David Kovar for the first week in January. I'm catching hell from the front office because no properties are pinned down, and there's no start date on the new picture. You're going to be facing a suspension in a few weeks. Now get yourself on a plane and come home so we can make some decisions. Either that, or I'll come in. Which will it be?"

"I want to spend the holiday season with papa and Minnie. I told you that, Ed."

"No problem. I'll be in. And I'm bringing the treatment of *Heavenly Trouble* with me. When you see it, you're going to perk up like a fire horse. There's not a GI within miles of it, and it will give you a chance to play some great understated comedy again."

Leya met Ed at LaGuardia Field late in the evening of December twenty-third. He looked well and tan, but she was shocked at how much weight he had put on.

After he had registered and joined her in the suite, he ordered an elaborate dinner sent to the room, complete with champagne. Later, in his dressing gown, showered and shaved, he sat studying Leya across the table.

"You look wonderful, honey, just great! I hate to confess it, but you were right to get away. I didn't realize how hard I've been working you."

"You've worked pretty hard yourself, Ed."

"What I've been doing, sweet little one, is reading one damned treatment after another. *Heavenly Trouble* is number fifty-two. But it was worth waiting for." He patted his stomach. "I'll tell you one thing, though. Sitting around the house reading ten hours a day didn't do much for my physique. It'll come off when we start production."

He raised a finger to indicate something remembered. "Incidentally, speaking of weight, Heather and Carlo send their love. I saw them again in Vegas. His new club there is going great. He'll still pay you a Ginger Rogers fee for eight weeks!"

"You know how I feel about that, Ed! How is Heather?"

"She's not the same doll we once knew. I'd say she's in imminent danger of becoming a bar-bellied broad. Her face is still good—if you don't look too close—and her legs are still okay, but she's potty in the middle now. She'll call you on the way back to Florida."

Leya initiated little of the conversation. The burden, falling on Ed, drove him to a half-hour nonstop recital. "So," he concluded, "the principal thing we've got to do is make a decision about the next project so the studio will take some of the heat off. I don't want to influence you," he said, refilling his champagne glass for the fourth time, "but they like *Heavenly Trouble.* Jay Sanford said if we didn't make it, he'd take it off our hands. The first thing Mitch Leisen said when I told him the story of *Trouble* was, 'What a perfect vehicle that would have made for Carole.' His eyes filled, and he couldn't look at me."

As Ed sipped his champagne, Leya saw the alcohol and travel weariness taking effect. To keep him talking and drinking, she asked about the houses and about Ellen and Squires.

Distressed, he put the glass down. "That's another thing. I'm not sure we can keep either of them if you stay away much longer. Ellen's very unhappy. She doesn't have enough to do."

"Aren't you eating at home?" Leya asked.

"Some of the time." He aimed a finger at her. "Look! It gets damned lonesome around that barn without you there. So I go to Chasen's or to Romanoff's and have a few at the bar. I usually find somebody to eat with. But it's not good."

They talked for a while longer before Leya excused herself. When she got up, Ed's bleary-eyed leer left no doubt that he would be expecting to make love. In the hope that the rigors of the trip and the champagne—he had drunk nearly a whole bottle himself—would catch up with him soon, she lingered in her bath. When she came out, a few minutes after one in the morning, he was asleep, in his robe, atop one of the twin beds. Moving quietly, she turned off the lights, pulled a spare blanket over him, and slipped into her own bed, praying that he would not awaken.

At nine-thirty, Ed found a note from Leya propped against the dresser mirror. "Having breakfast downstairs, dear. Didn't want to disturb your rest. Join me if you care to. Leya, 8:45."

"Great!" he grunted as he made his way unsteadily to the shower. "You played that real smart, Matson. Just the way she wanted you to, probably."

When Leya returned to the suite, Ed was picking at a bowl of cereal. He scarcely looked up.

"We're having a late lunch with Howard," he said thickly. "Toots Shor's. One o'clock."

Howard Pryor had been on an extended trip to reappraise I.A.M.'s band department. He was certain that what he had discovered would bear directly on the sort of entertainment the country would be in the mood for now.

He expressed concern over the way the big name bands would be received by returning servicemen, who had been their teen-age fans back in the mid-Thirties and early Forties when the leaders had been at the peak of their popularity. With the exception of Glenn Miller, most of the big leaders were still around. But many of the band singers had gone on to stardom in their own right: Sinatra, Como, Haymes, Peggy Lee, Dinah Shore—

The agencies that booked bands were faced with difficult decisions. Hollywood contracts were not being renewed. Band singers were being released. There were things to think about in other areas, too—how the public would re-relate to the big male stars who had gone off to war. Leslie Howard would not return, but Clark Gable had. So had James Stewart, Alan Ladd, Ronald Reagan, Vic Mature, and a handful of others—and how would those stars themselves relate to the old material on which their popularity had been built? Would the country want new themes? If so, could the old names with established images play in them successfully?

Nothing she heard during the luncheon reassured Leya. Certainly, if the country's taste in entertainment was changing, if, as Howard suspected, moviegoers would be in a more thoughtful mood, then the piece of fluff that Ed was proposing would be a waste of time.

The luncheon ran on until midafternoon. Later, with no real enthusiasm, Leya agreed to see *Anchors Aweigh*, starring Frank Sinatra, Kathryn Grayson, and Gene Kelly. "The grosses on this one will tell us something about musicals with war themes," Ed said. "I'm not sure Howard's right."

"The man's the most knowledgeable agent in the business. I think we should listen to him very carefully," she replied.

"I intend to, honey. But let's not forget that he's glad he listened to me when I made him come and see you and Kent and the others."

"You were a personal manager then, Ed, not a producer."

"What's that mean?" he challenged.

"Your point of view may have been different."

Ed looked at her through narrowed eyes, then smiled humorlessly. "It's a pretty damned safe bet yours has changed, little friend!"

Leya stood in the airline terminal watching Ed have his tickets validated. Somehow they had gotten through Christmas. She and Ed had taken Harry and Minnie to see the New Year in at the Roosevelt Grill.

As they walked together to the boarding area, Leya linked her arm through his. He glanced at her in surprise but said nothing.

"Ed," she began, "I know this has been a difficult time for you—"

He smiled dryly. "The understatement of the century!"

"I know," Leya continued, "and I'm sorry. But I want you to know that I appreciate more than I can say the way you helped me make the holidays enjoyable for papa and Minnie." She smiled at the recollection. "I don't think they ever had such a good time as they did at the Grill on New Year's Eve listening to Guy Lombardo."

"I got the Purple Heart for less than dancing with Minnie, little friend. But if it made you happy, it was worth every wince! If she runs his house like she leads on the dance floor, Harry deserves a medal, too!"

"I know!" Leya laughed. "But they understand each other. Minnie's a *balabusta*—God love her!"

"So," Ed said, stopping to face her. "You're going to stay on here for a while. I'm going back and try to explain to Paramount why my wife does not want to do *Heavenly Trouble.*"

"Because," Leya interrupted, "I honestly believe the young minister's role is the stronger of the two, and I'm no comedienne."

"Okay," he said as they resumed walking, "I'll do what I can."

He slowed for a moment, and his brow furrowed. "There's just one thing, and let me spell it out in plain English. You and I are still business partners, right?"

"Of course."

"But as to the rest of it, the personal aspects, that's sort of hanging on the hook for now. So"—he managed a crooked smile as he slipped his ticket from the envelope to show to the gate attendant—"you'll be here, looking for something you think you want, and I'll be out there, thinking about the things I know I want—and—?" He shrugged.

Leya pulled his arm, turned him to her, and went up on her toes to give him a quick kiss. "Have a good trip, Ed, and call me, please?"

"I'll call you, little friend, when I find a way to tell you how much I wish I were able to give you all of the things you think you want! G'by now." He moved quickly through the door and across the blacktop apron to the boarding ramp.

CHAPTER 45

A message to call a number in Florida was waiting for Leya at the hotel. She returned it immediately and, with Myra and Martin Lieberman on extensions, began picking up threads lost in the tangle when the world turned upside down.

"I can't tell you how good it is to hear your voice, dear," Myra said.

"Only good?" Martin cut it. "It's great!"

"Leya, Martin and I have talked for hours since we got your message. And we've talked to the doctor, too. I know you'd be shocked to see Arthur. He is skin and bones, dear, and still very, very weak. Right now he's stretched out in the sun on the patio."

"He can't get enough sun," Martin said. "For five years those bastard animals moved him around from one dungeon to another. Geneva conference? What a laugh! Anyway, go ahead, Myra."

"So," Myra continued, "we haven't even told him that you're in New York again. The first thing he did when we got him to the hospital was ask about you."

"Did you tell him I was married?"

"No. Frankly, I didn't."

"We told him you were making moving pictures and doing

very well," Martin said. "That made him happy. But he was so weak—one hundred and thirty pounds, would you believe it? All we did was sit with him and hold his hand and tell him that it was all over now. He still doesn't know it's all over for millions of our people, too. We can't tell him. We won't let anybody even talk about it yet."

"So, Leya," Myra said with a trace of impatience, "we'll call frequently to keep you posted. And if you feel like it, please call us here. The number is Lincoln four, two two seven oh. It's the same address as before. We bought the place so the Lowensteins could stay here. The old man died three years ago, dear."

"From a broken heart!" Martin interjected.

"I'm so sorry," Leya murmured.

"If you want to write to Arthur, I think you should," Myra continued, "but please wait until we tell you."

"I will, of course," Leya replied.

"When are you going back to California?" Martin asked.

"I really don't know."

"But you must have a picture to do?"

"I'm not sure I want to do any more pictures for a while, Myra."

"What about your husband? Where is he?"

"He left for California this morning. Things are very uncertain right now."

After a long pause, Martin cleared his throat. "Does that mean personally or business-wise or both, if you don't mind my asking?"

"I would have to say both. I'm not at all sure that Ed and I are going to stay together. I have a lot of thinking to do—" She broke off with an apologetic little laugh. "Forgive me, please! Everything will be fine, really."

"We'll pray!" Martin said softly.

In midweek, Leya lunched with Howard Pryor. "Frankly, I'm on a brain-picking expedition," she confessed.

"The crop may be a bit thin now," he laughed. "Everybody's trying to figure out what happens next. But go ahead. Shoot."

"Two things. I need a new personal manager, and should I do a Broadway musical? It's as simple as that."

Howard Pryor's expression betrayed nothing. "It might be time for a change," he said matter-of-factly. "Who are you thinking about—if you are?"

"For a manager? Billy Brenner would like to handle me, but he's too much of a gentleman to say so."

The head of I.A.M. smiled. "That he is. He's also become one of the best personal managers in the business, and he's just thirty." He paused to light a cigarette. "Who talked to you about a musical? Beckman?"

"He's been hinting about that for three years now."

"How do you feel about doing one?"

"I didn't, until I saw *Carousel.* I know I'm no great singer, but it might be interesting to try a musical that had real substance to it."

"They don't come in bunches like bananas, you know."

"Neither do decent screenplays," Leya replied. "I'm in no hurry."

"How old are you now?"

"Twenty-five. Why?"

"Nothing. Make it twenty-four. How did your voice lessons go at the studio?"

"Not well enough to let them take a chance. All my songs were dubbed. But I've been working. It seems to get better as I get older."

"Like some wine—" Pryor said.

"And some cheese?" Leya asked, smiling.

"There are some excellent voice teachers here now," he said, ignoring her self-putdown. "Certainly you will be able to sing as well as any of the dancers who are playing leads." He paused. "But what about that contract with Paramount that we have?"

"That's the third thing I want to ask you about. Do I have to honor it right away?"

"I don't know, Leya. Let me check it out with our legal department. Ed wants you to go into a picture soon, I know."

"And I will not go into that picture, Howard. It's amusing, but it's not for me. If you read the treatment, you'll see that the real star role is the male one. Ed's got a blind spot about that."

"I've seen the treatment, Leya. I agree with you."

Leya sagged with relief. "Thank God! I was beginning to wonder if I was just being a stubborn, temperamental little no-talent dame."

Howard Pryor held up his hands. "That's the last thing you are, darling!" Serious again, he said, "Talk to Brenner. You have no signed paper with Ed now, and from what I deduce, that relationship is changing. Right?"

"Yes."

"Then be realistic, Leya. Talk with Billy. Tell him I told you to. And set up a meeting with you and Billy and Beckman soon. I'll give you my best judgment along the way if you want it. Then let's see where Leya Leslie goes from here. Remember, if we can keep things sweet at the studio, you can always go back and make up your contract. If you do well on Broadway, we just might make them renegotiate a little—if all the right people are still running the place."

As soon as Leya got back to the hotel, she called Billy Brenner. "I've had lunch with Howard Pryor," she said. "He suggested I talk with you about some things that are on my mind."

"If they're the same things that are on my mind, Leya, the conversation will be short and the answer is yes! When would you like us to get together?"

"When it's convenient for you."

"Would yesterday be too soon?" he joked. "How about a sip of something around five?"

"Good. Would you like to talk here in the suite?"

"Fine. Five o'clock."

"Bring Celine, Billy."

"Not possible dear—but thanks for thinking about it."

Billy Brenner had not exaggerated when he said the meeting would be short and the answer would be positive.

"As far as your aspirations for Broadway are concerned," he said, "the only question I have is why it took you so long?"

He grinned and nodded to himself. "Of course, I know the answer to that—a contract, loyalty to Ed, and a three-thousand-a-week guarantee." He leaned back and smiled. "I don't think you'll have to give away too many dollars, Leya."

"Is Jack Beckman the sort of producer I should be thinking of, Billy?"

"Possibly. Any producer would love to announce a Leya Leslie musical. You are box office. That means you are a bankable property. But none of them would be as eager as Jack. He's wanted to build a show around you ever since the Kendall Trio subbed for Celine. You know that."

"I do," Leya said with a rueful smile. "That's the only reservation I have about this conversation, Billy."

"Have no reservations. The only thing Celine really ever wanted to be was a prima ballerina. She knows now—or she believes—that she does not have the dedication to go that route." He laughed softly. "I guess I *want* to believe that all she really *wants* to be is Mrs. William Brenner, French hausfrau!"

Leya was relieved. No need now to confess to those earlier misgivings. "When can we talk with Jack Beckman?"

"I'll call him tonight at the theater and set something up for tomorrow."

Leya saw Bill Brenner to the door, then walked across the room and stood looking down on the park. She had come to think of the big corner windows as her "staring place," a high place from which her thoughts could soar, unfettered. The nagging guilt over what amounted to a summary dismissal of Ed as both manager and husband troubled her. She thought back over a comment Howard Pryor had made. "Ed needed you to get where he wanted to go, and you needed him for the same reason. Fair exchange!" He had added, "Matson has survived before. As to your business deals with him, please remember that I.A.M. also has a stake in those. He won't get hurt. I'll see that all those arrangements remain just what they always have been—strictly business." Leya wished she could be so confident.

An hour later, Leya was met at the top of the stairs by her

father and Minnie. Harry was holding a copy of the *New York Post.*

"You know, don't you?" he asked, waggling the paper in excitement.

"Know what, papa?"

"About your friend, Mrs. Gottrocks, the Fourth—from the Vandercort money."

Leya felt herself turning pale. "What about Dulcy?" Her voice was shrill as she reached for the paper.

"You'll come inside and read. What a business!"

Leya pushed past them and spread the paper on the dining-room table. In the lower right-hand corner of the front page, she read, "LINGERIE MODEL WINS MULTI-MILLION-DOLLAR SETTLEMENT FROM WILLIAM VANDERCORT, IV." The two-column story spelled out the details: a tax-paid settlement, two thousand-dollars-a-month child support, sole title to a collection of antiques valued at a quarter of a million, title to the home in Silver Spring, Maryland, and title to various other real properties. The grounds were mental cruelty. The annual income from the settlement, to be administered by the Vandercort family bank, was estimated to be around three hundred thousand dollars a year. The real value of the settlement was estimated at eight million dollars.

"What do you think, *bubeleh?*" Harry asked, hovering at her side.

"I think," Leya said with intentional deliberateness, "that Dulcy Devine is a girl who always thought she knew what she wanted—and exactly how to get it."

Leya met with Jack Beckman the following afternoon. The producer surprised her by pulling a file of bound outlines for stories from his desk drawer.

"Every one of these was tucked away against the day when I might be able to tempt you with a Broadway show. Want to know when the first one is dated? June, nineteen forty-one! Four and a half years ago, when you took over the dance spot in *Riddle Me This.*" He shot an apologetic glance at Billy, who grinned.

"Nobody's bleeding, Jack."

"Good! It just so happens that last week I acquired all theatrical rights to a new best seller that's not published yet. How do I know it will be a best seller? I have a cousin—a very bright young lady with a degree in literature from Brandeis—who's in a position to know things."

He reached for a set of galley proofs. "Take this and read it, Leya. Think about it as a basic story, that's all. Don't think about how it can be adapted. Just tell me if you think the theme is solid. After that, we can talk more. The most important thing for me is that Leya Leslie be one thousand percent sold on the property"—he cocked his head uncertainly—"and maybe nine hundred percent sold on the producer."

"I'm sold one thousand percent on half of the deal already, Jack."

Leya dined with Billy and Celine, and, with Jack, they went to see *Up in Central Park,* Michael Todd's musical hit about the Boss Tweed era, which was coming to the end of its New York run. Helen Tamiris's Currier and Ives ice skating ballet in Central Park charmed them. Sigmund Romberg's score was "pure period Romberg," as Billy put it. But the book seemed somehow stilted.

"You can get trapped in a theme sometimes," Beckman observed during the intermission. "You may find you don't have enough room to move emotionally. I'm not knocking traditional shows. I would just like to move the theater another step ahead, if possible."

After a late bite at Reuben's, Leya settled into bed and began to read. At four o'clock she was still reading. At four-thirty, she finally put the galley aside and turned out the light. She picked it up again over breakfast. That afternoon, she called Billy Brenner.

"Tell Jack that I think the book is wonderful—as a book. I'll be anxious to know who is going to do the adaptation and the music. Also tell him that if everything works, I'd like very much to have him consider Peter Genova as choreographer, and I'd like as many of the original Kendall kids with me as we can get."

Billy had started chuckling before she finished. "By the most outrageous coincidence, Miss Leslie, I'm way ahead of you!"

CHAPTER 46

The new Beckman musical, *Lola,* starring Leya Leslie, was announced for late spring. It was adapted from *She Danced for the Devil,* the biography of the dancer, Lola Montez. Born in Ireland in 1818 and christened Marie Dolores Elizabeth Rosanna Gilbert, she assumes the name Lola Montez, claims Spanish descent, marries an army officer, is caught *in flagrante,* goes through a scandalous divorce, becomes a dancer, and after a sensational success in Europe, installs herself as the mistress of Ludwig I of Bavaria. The emperor confers the title of Countess of Lansfeld on her, and she is, in fact, the ruler of Bavaria until she is banished a year later.

Undaunted, the beautiful dancer returns to England, marries again, and goes to the United States in 1851 on a phenomenally successful tour that takes her to California's mining camps. Her husband dies, and she marries S. S. Hull, a San Francisco journalist.

During the height of her success as the toast of the Forty-Niners, she adopts, as her protégé, a child actress named Lotta Crabtree. When Lola goes to Australia on tour, the child becomes the toast of the mining camps. Meanwhile, Lola, ill and deserted, returns to San Francisco. The child, now the darling of the New York stage in Charles Dickens' *Old Curiosity Shop*, hears of her plight and sends money to relieve her once-glamorous benefactress. It arrives too late. Lola dies in poverty in 1861. Some years later, her grateful protégé gifts San Francisco with a fountain that indirectly commemorates the glamorous adventuress.

Jack Beckman was so certain of the property that he had commissioned a young writer to do the stage adaptation some months earlier. In a matter of hours after he received Billy Brenner's call, a meeting was set up for Leya to hear the reading and listen to the music that had been done so far.

"I like it," Leya replied, "up to the point where it gets sticky sentimental. We all get old and die. There's always somebody to take our places. Why not end the story on Lola's triumph in San Francisco and her marriage to Hull? Montez relied on a lot of fortunetellers. The suspense can come when the old gypsy accosts her on the *Embarcadero* when she arrives on the ship. You have a great song and a ballet there, anyway. The child is too important now. The spirit of Lola would not live on through an actress. She was a dancer."

After a long silence, the playwright rose and leaned against the upright piano in Jack Beckman's office.

"I think Miss Leslie's right about it—for a musical. I confess that I've always been uncomfortable with the child—unless, of course, we take some liberties and make little Lotta a dancer."

"Let's make little Lotta disappear," Leya said firmly. "We don't need her. The way it is now, she's being dragged in by the heels, and I'm being dragged in by the shroud."

Jack Beckman's eyebrows lifted. "That's a hell of a line! We should find a way to keep it in the show."

"Let's just find a way to keep it out of the reviews," Billy interjected.

They agreed to rework the ending. The finale would be Lola's wedding and her tour of San Francisco's famous Champagne Route, a ritual reserved for gentlemen only and an occasional colorful lady of their liking. Underlying the gaiety of the occasion would be the ominous soothsayer's theme, first heard upon Lola's arrival in San Francisco.

Howard Pryor frowned as he listened on the extension in his office while Leya talked with Ed Matson. His friend was not giving up easily. The studio liked *Heavenly Trouble* but had misgivings about okaying it for production without Leya Leslie.

"Listen to me, Ed," Leya was saying, "I am not going to make that picture. I don't give a damn if the studio sues me for everything we've got. If I have to, I'll make one more picture for them after I do *Lola,* but I'm going to have final say on the story."

"Listen, Ed," Pryor cut in. "I'm sorry to be privy to all of this, but Leya's right. I've read the libretto of the new musical. Nobody knows for certain 'til it's on its feet, but it feels like gold. We'll work out a deferral on her contract."

"Make that a deferral for me, too, Howard. I'm a producer as long as I can produce Leya Leslie."

In spite of her annoyance, Leya felt sorry for her husband. "Ed," she said softly, "I've never broken a promise to you. I'll do everything I can to see that you get a chance to produce this show for pictures—if Jack has no Hollywood aspiration. Failing that, I'll help you find a story that will be acceptable to me and to the studio. In the meantime, you are not exactly on the bread line. Why not tell the studio that you have at least one, maybe two pictures with me, but they must be deferred? I may be happy to be back on camera again. *Lola* may be a bomb. Who knows?"

"*Lola* won't bomb, little friend. I know you, and I know the quality of the brains you're picking!"

Columnists and gossip magazines were having a field day following up on the Vandercort divorce settlement. Leya, saddened a bit for her friend, had not talked to Dulcy since before the holidays. After the decision was made to go ahead with *Lola,* she called and found her in.

"It's going to take a while to get all of this sorted out,"

Dulcy said, "because the Vandercorts only move fast when they are taking money, not when they are giving. In the meantime, I have enough to get by on if I eat an occasional meal at the Automat!"

"Are you coming up to New York soon?" Leya asked. "I've got a pack of things to tell you about, including my new musical show."

"Congratulations," Dulcy replied. "I'll do an extra lap around my beads for you." She laughed. "Hang on to something and listen to this, dear heart. Gordon Revelsky's ad agency called me last week. Guess what? They offered Mrs. William Vandercort the Fourth a cool fifty grand to endorse their new facial cream, Angel Poo, or whatever. How do you like them apples?"

"Oh, Lord," Leya laughed. "That's divine justice, if you don't mind the pun. Did you take it?"

"Not for fifty. I told my lawyers to ask for a hundred grand and settle for seventy-five."

Leya enjoyed the talk. Dulcy was more like her old bright self. She put the phone back on the end table, kicked off her shoes, and rested her legs on the divan. They were good legs, she thought, but she wished they were a trifle longer from the knees down. Tula Finkles, who had become Cyd Charisse, had the perfect legs—and the perfect looks, too!

She thought about Dulcy for a time and smiled as she remembered her friend's disappointment when she had lost out as the blonde on the Revel billboard campaign. What irony! Yes, and what irony there was in the possibility that she herself, "little friend" Leya, could be the one who would make the decision to save Ed Matson's career! "Life can be funny," she said aloud, "if you're not fussy about what you laugh at!"

She resisted calling the Liebermans, and there was no word from them for several weeks. Then a note arrived from Myra saying that Arthur had gone into the hospital for a series of tests. He was regaining his strength more slowly than they had hoped, and pneumonia had left lesions on his lungs that needed watching. The doctors wanted to try a new variant of the sulfa drugs. The treatment had been ongoing for two weeks, and he was due home by Washington's birthday.

Poor Arthur, Leya thought. *Poor, darling Arthur. If I could just hold you and tell you how much I've loved you all these years! I know! It would be a corny scene. I wouldn't play it in a picture, but I could make you believe it in real life, Arthur dear!*

Suddenly, she could no longer support the frustration. It was ten after five. Billy would still be at the office. She dialed on the private line, and he came on immediately.

"Billy, we've talked about doing something to change this world I'm living in. Right?"

"You mean married? Not married?"

"Of course! Let me ask you something. Do you think your lawyer– What's his name, Harold Bornstein? Could he advise me about a divorce?"

"Certainly."

"All right. Do you think there would be time for me to get it over with before Jack has his production money?"

Billy Brenner laughed. "Leya, if the financing process runs to form, you could have enough time to get married and divorced three times!"

"Then I can go ahead and terminate this travesty?"

"Six weeks in Nevada will do it, Leya, or six weeks in Florida."

"Will you set up an appointment for me—soon?"

The meeting with Bornstein went easily. A comfortable man in his early fifties who knew show business and its vagaries, he led Leya through the intricacies of the proposed settlement in an afternoon.

Later, in Brenner's office, she laughed. "I must tell you, Billy, he's so smooth that if he'd been a surgeon about to amputate my leg, he would have made me feel lucky that I still had one left!"

"I know. He's also handling your contract with Jack. I'm glad you like him. Did you decide anything?"

"He thinks Florida. But there's a personal problem I want to check out first."

"Something I should know about?"

"Not yet. But you will when it's not a problem anymore."

"Okay," Billy said. "I thrive on problems that are not problems anymore. *Mazel-tov!*"

Leya sat for a time with the address book open to the Liebermans' number; then she placed a person-to-person call. After what seemed an eternity, Myra came on the line.

"I'm sorry, dear. We were out on the patio with Arthur. He came home today. I'm so glad you called."

"You may not be, Myra," Leya said. "I want you to be absolutely candid with me. I've decided to divorce Ed and end this never-never land I'm in. I must do it quickly because I'm going into a new Broadway musical. The simplest thing for me is to establish residence in Florida. But I will not even give it a second thought if that might complicate things for you all."

"Complicate?" Myra all but shouted. "Simplify would be the word! It would mean that we could tell Arthur the best news he could hear!" She broke off, and Leya heard a little whisper of remorse. "Oh, how selfish I'm being, Leya! Assuming! Assuming—"

"Assuming that I still love him?"

"Yes, dear. Forgive my eagerness, but—"

"Myra," Leya interrupted, "that I love Arthur is not an assumption. It's a solid fact. He's the only man I have ever loved. You can tell him that now."

Leya hung up with Myra Lieberman's unrestrained joy still echoing in her ears. Excited and impatient now, she wandered to the window and looked out over Central Park. Was she wrong to have steered Bornstein into suggesting Florida? Being with Arthur for any appreciable time during the six weeks would be dangerous, and the temptation would be all but irresistible.

There were Las Vegas and Reno, of course, but she would be too close to Ed and—God forbid!—Carlo Romano, who was there watching over his new interests. Florida's proximity was not the real reason, and Leya knew it. She would go to Miami—not St. Petersburg or Tampa or Sarasota—but to Miami, and somehow she and Arthur would see each other without jeopardizing the divorce action. "That's the truth, Marks!" she said half aloud as she left the window and prepared to dress.

CHAPTER 47

Martin and Myra Lieberman found an apartment on the beach for Leya. The clothing and other personal effects that Harold Bornstein had counseled her to send, to create a plausible impression of permanent residence, were forwarded; and the Lieberman maids settled the closets and drawers under Myra's supervision.

At LaGuardia Field, shortly before her plane for Miami was to take off, Billy and Celine and Harold Bornstein formed a protective cordon.

"We have to go through this charade, Leya," the attorney said, "and it should be a convincing performance. Tell your friends that you've established residence. You will come to New York when you have to—on business. Don't get yourself involved publicly with anybody until after the final papers are handed down. I don't expect any trouble, but you are a public person. You'll have to be more circumspect than most."

Billy agreed. "And remember, next week Peter and Jean will be down so you can start blocking numbers. There'll be plenty to do. Those six weeks will pass quickly."

"Will Jack have his financing completed by then?" Leya asked.

"The first one hundred thousand is his own money. I think we should be set to start rehearsals by then."

Leya turned and linked her arm through Celine's. "Will you come out of retirement and do this one with me?"

"We'll see," Celine hedged. "I really like the role I'm playing now. For once I feel perfectly cast!"

As they walked to the departure gate, Billy leaned closer. "We are hoping that Celine will be a little too large to dance by the time the show opens. But don't say anything yet. I just wanted to explain her reticence."

When the plane started its descent to Miami airport, Leya felt like a battleground of clashing emotions. By now Arthur had been told. She wondered how he reacted. More than that, she wondered how she would react when she saw him. Both Myra and Martin had warned her not to be shocked by his appearance. "He's no longer in a wheelchair," Myra had said. "He's walking—a little bit more each day—on the beach. But he's not permitted to swim yet."

Leya's pulse began to pound, audibly she thought, when the DC-3 taxied to the gate. She could see Myra and Martin craning in the crowd. Minutes later, she found herself enveloped in their embraces.

At first, nothing was said. The Liebermans just beamed mutely, Myra through unashamed tears. Martin retrieved her bags and ordered them carried to the car.

"We're going to take you to your place first, dear," Myra said. "Then would you like to come and see Arthur and stay the evening with us?"

"Thank you," Leya replied, "For sparing me the embarrassment of inviting myself."

The apartment on Indian River Drive near Thirty-sixth Street was more than adequate.

"We've ordered the phone in, dear," Myra said. "They promised it tomorrow. An unlisted number."

"And we did not tell your friends at the club that you were coming in. We weren't sure that you'd like that."

"I'm very happy you didn't," Leya replied. "I'm out of touch with the world now. I'd just as soon remain that way."

Myra showed Leya around and told her about nearby markets, drugstores, and other shops.

"We'll let you get settled now, dear. Will six be too soon to pick you up?"

Leya felt her middle tightening. "I'll be ready."

In the hour and a half she had to herself, Leya did a minimum of unpacking, bathed, and put on one of her California summer dresses. Sitting before the mirror, she studied her image, trying to remember what she must have looked like to Arthur the last time—the last happy time—they had seen each other. That would have been here on the beach, the night he flew in to inspect the house, the night he had come to the club, the night of Carlo's grotesque party, the awful night—morning, really—of their stupid ultimatums.

The happy part had been the afternoon. She remembered Arthur swimming north just outside the surf line while she scampered barefooted around the scallops of opalescent foam, her skirt pulled up, peasant style, between her legs. She touched her cheeks. The uptilted, smoky topaz eyes were the same—wiser, perhaps—the copper hair was the same, and the mouth. The teeth were better now since two of the gold inlays that had shown when she smiled had been capped. She smoothed a palm over her shoulder and down over the side of her bosom—fuller than most dancers—and down to the waist, which was still comfortable in a twenty-two-inch belt. Outwardly, Arthur would see much the same girl. As she stood up for a last inspection, Leya wondered what else he might see. "So much has happened inside!" she whispered.

"If Arthur's half as nervous as I am, he'll have a relapse!" Leya moaned as Martin pulled the convertible into the driveway. She remembered the beach house in detail. But now there were no vacant lots to the north.

"He's out on the patio, dear," Martin said, pointing through the opened door. "He spends most of his time out there, reading and watching the water. He's said a thousand times, 'I never want to be trapped in four walls again!' "

Myra took Leya's arm. "We'll stay here, dear. We have things to do."

Arthur was seated in a wicker lounge chair. As Leya moved quietly through the living room, she saw his head turn slightly as though listening. She paused. When he turned back to the water, she moved closer, close enough to see the gaunt planes in his cheek. A few more halting steps and she could see the gray at his temples. The pulse that she had felt in her temples had become an audible throbbing now. Her chest seemed to be caught in a vise. At the big glass doors leading to the patio, she paused again.

"Arthur—?"

She saw his body tense and his hands move to the arms of the chaise. He pushed himself up and turned a little. For an instant, Leya saw only the familiar strong profile. Then he twisted a bit more and turned to her. In a flicker, Leya read in his face the suffering of an entire race. Her voice caught when she tried to call out again. Suddenly, with a cry, she ran to him, sank down beside the lounge, and buried her face against his chest.

"Oh, Arthur—Arthur—Arthur—" she sobbed.

His hands moved, uncertainly at first, to explore her cheek and her hair. She felt him draw in a great breath and expel it slowly as his body relaxed. "Leya, my Leya"—his voice was a husky whisper—"God forgive me. I never thought this day would come."

During the days before Peter and Jean arrived, Leya and Arthur spent every afternoon and evening together. It was a time of quiet being, a time of remembering, a time of profound gratitude for the inexplicable quirk of fate that had made strangers of friends, only to rejoin them after what seemed an eternity of remorse.

Myra and Martin Lieberman and Ruth Lowenstein, who was frequently at the beach house, Shelly, no longer the jealous little sister demanding attention, and Bert all watched Leya with Arthur and thanked God in their separate ways.

Dr. Levine, who attended Arthur, searched with a beam of light in the interior of his eyes and smiled.

"I prescribe for Arthur," he said, "that he continue for the rest of his life to take the remedy that comes in a one-hundred-and-twelve-pound package of loveliness labeled Miss Leslie!"

In those hours when Leya was forced to be away, Arthur soaked up the sun—a lifetime would be too little to make up for the dungeonlike cells of the Stalags—and wondered at the events of the past several years. He wasted no time in self-recrimination. There had been endless days and nights of that in the POW camps. Now, with dispassion, he recalled the past misunderstandings and the words that had been evoked by them and realized that his demands where Leya's career was concerned had been motivated as much by insecurity as by concern for her well-being. Now he could say with absolute honesty that no love could be complete so long as one required that the other give up some essential part of self.

Leya's anonymity came to an end several days after Peter and Jean found a suitable place to rehearse, an empty loft across the river in Miami proper. The landlord mentioned to somebody that the rental was charged to Beckman Productions on West Fifty-seventh Street in New York City, and a day later the *Miami Herald* carried a story on the entertainment page that Leya Leslie had deserted California for Florida, where she had established permanent residence.

Would she stay the year around? Did that mean she had given up pictures and concerts? What about her marriage to Ed Matson? Was there anybody else?

"Yes. This is my home now. No, I have not given up pictures permanently, just until I meet my commitment to Mr. Beckman. I don't know about concerts. Nobody's asked me. My marriage to Mr. Matson has ended, but we are still friends and business partners. No! Definitely there is nobody new. My entire time is occupied with my first Broadway musical! *Positively,* I have no *new* love interest!"

Almost immediately, a call came to the Liebermans from Heather.

"Oh, bloody hell! I knew this would happen!" Leya murmured, feeling somewhat guilty. She had wanted to get in touch with Heather, but that meant seeing Carlo, too, and he had made it all but impossible to maintain the friendship.

After a few minutes of catching up on superficials, Heather said, "When can I see you, Leya? My God, I'm dying to!"

"I want to see you, too, Heather, but it's going to have to wait for a little while because I'm right in the middle of blocking some dances for the musical."

Leya could almost see Heather's wistful little smile. "If I weren't a pro—or a former one—I'd ask to come sit and watch." She laughed harshly then. "What a dreamer! Spacco and Parroco watch me like I'm a mental defective. About the only way I can have any privacy is when I let them take me out fishing on Carlo's boat." She brightened. "Hey! That's it! We'll spend a day out on the stream. Those two torpedoes would rather fish than rub out somebody—almost."

Leya agreed with some reluctance, and Heather promised to call.

Several times during the next two weeks, special-delivery envelopes arrived from Jack Beckman's office with revised pages. The blocking went on six days a week, with Jean working as her husband's assistant. It was hot, humid work, and they agreed that Hollywood's facilities and California's climate had spoiled them.

The first few hours of barre were torture for Leya. By the end of the second week, muscles too long undisciplined were responding. Peter Genova, a hard taskmaster, was no harder on her than on himself and Jean.

"You may not sing like Lily Pons," he said, "but you're going to dance like a cross between Salome and Pavlova!"

Sundays, Leya spent walking with Arthur along the beach. To comply with attorney's advice, they kept their public behavior very circumspect. Hubert Schlosberg, Harold Bornstein's associate in Miami, had been very specific in his warning. "The press knows you're here now, Miss Leslie. Please don't get careless. Your permanent residence in Florida leaves quite a bit to be desired from a legal point of view!"

Billy Brenner and Celine flew down for a long weekend. Leya met them at the Roney Plaza for dinner.

"I could have done this by phone," he said, "but a legit deductible excuse is irresistible. Besides, Celine wanted to see your face when she told you that you're going to be an unofficial 'auntie'!"

"I think it's wonderful!" Leya exclaimed. "What do you want?"

Billy fixed her with a comic stare. "A baby, what else?"

"A boy that looks like Billy—round chubby cheeks, innocent blue eyes, beguiling smile and all," Celine added.

"If he looks like that, I'll make him a partner! Incidentally," Billy continued, serious again, "speaking of partners—which is what you will be with Jack in this show since you're taking a percentage in lieu of your usual salary—the money isn't coming in as fast as Bornstein thought it would. It's not to worry, but you should know."

"How much do we have—above the hundred thousand that Jack put in?" Leya asked.

"Unless something happened this morning, about forty thousand—eight units. We need sixty more to make it two hundred—plus the overcall. The units don't have to get up the overcall in front, though. And we may not need it."

Leya toyed with the handle of the cup. "If it comes in too slowly, Billy, I could pick up a unit or two."

Brenner held up a staying hand. "No way! I've thought of that, too. Talked to Jack about it. He said, 'Thank Leya for me—if you've spoken to her—and tell her that I'll never produce a show in which the star is a backer. That's the quickest way I know for a producer to become a yes man!' He's right, you know."

"I understand, Billy. In a way, Ed got caught in that same trap when he let Paramount participate in our financing." She smiled brightly. "So—I'll just own a piece of the action, as Ed puts it, and that will make me work harder with an open mind and a closed mouth. How's that?"

"Phenomenal!" Billy exclaimed. "May be the first time that speech has ever been made by a star."

"Are we going to be able to start rehearsals by the middle of next month?"

"I don't see why not," Billy said. "A lot of risk money that was easy to get during the war is playing it safe now. But Jack will be all right. There's a big liquor distributor in New Jersey who's talking with Harold now. A man named Silbert. And Howard Pryor's got somebody on the string. We'll make our opening date."

They finished dinner and talked until nearly midnight, catching up on news of the theater. As Leya was getting into the taxi, she remembered that she had not asked about the other dancers from the Kendall group.

"I thought Kuzzy was going to bawl when I told her you wanted her with you," Billy said. "She'll be ready when we need her. And so will Marc and Luanna. They're in Vegas now and dying to come home."

Heather called several times during the following week. Each time, Leya had a valid excuse for not getting together. Finally, with a weekend coming up, she agreed to go out on the boat for a Sunday if Peter and Jean could be included.

When she told Arthur about the invitation and the continuing problem it posed, he agreed.

"By all means get it over with, darling, while Carlo's still away. If Peter and Jean are along, I can't see how you can have any complications. If Heather drinks too much, put her below and let her sleep it off. You might enjoy fishing. If you latch onto a sailfish and bring it in yourself, I'll get you a solid gold one to start a charm bracelet."

"If she catches a sailfish and brings it in all by herself," Martin warned, "her arms will be six inches longer. Get help, Leya. I'll buy you the charm, anyway!"

The *Buona Fortuna* picked up Leya and the Genovas at the public landing in the Indian River. When Heather introduced Peter to Mike Parroco and Tony Spacco, the dancer grinned and responded in the dialect of his parents. Both men's usually impassive faces warmed with surprise, and they shook hands. When Peter introduced Jean as his wife, they became almost deferential.

Tony Spacco took the forty-foot fishing craft through the overhaul and out to the blue water of the Gulf Stream. The day was perfect. Leya, watching Peter's face as he helped the gray-haired, solidly built Parroco trim the outriggers for trolling, was glad that she could give her friends a special outing.

Peter's skill at removing the backbone from the mullet and baiting the sailfish hooks brought a nod of approval from Parroco.

"You kids fish," Heather said, indicating the two fighting chairs in the stern. "I'll keep the drinks coming." After considerable urging, Leya took the left-hand chair. She would have much preferred to sit in one of the deck chairs and enjoy the lapis-blue water and the Miami Beach shoreline. With the *Buona Fortuna* running north along the edge of the stream, Leya searched the line of low residences in an effort to pick out the Lieberman house.

She had almost forgotten how restful it was to be on the water. There was almost no swell. The sky was at its winter best with a scattering of cotton puff clouds. Off to the southeast, low on the horizon, she could see billows of cumulus clouds that old-time mariners said always marked distant islands.

They trolled for over an hour without a strike. Several times, boats passed flying sailfish pennants. "They're hitting for some people," Mike said. He called up to Tony. "Go more north—off Hallandale. That's where those guys are coming from."

"They went early," Spacco replied.

Peter Genova, with a born fisherman's optimism, turned and grinned up at the bridge. "What's the matter with you guys? Why don't you call them in Italian?" He turned back and leaned over the transom. "Hey *pesca, pesca, pesca! Viene qui, pesca! Viene qui, per favore!*"

He was about to repeat the chant when he heard Tony shout. An instant later, the line snapped from the clothespin on Leya's outrigger. Peter let out a whoop and reeled in his line to clear Leya's. "Not too fast!" he yelled. "Let him take it!"

Mike Parroco hovered behind Leya, ready to help. "Set it now!" Peter shouted as Mike reached over Leya's shoulders to grasp the rod and give it a sharp heave. A gleaming blue-black shape exploded from the water in a burst of rainbow spray, and Leya saw her first live sailfish.

While Mike and Peter coached her, she horsed back on the rod and reeled down until she was soaked with perspiration.

"Oh, my gosh," she wailed. "Please, Peter—somebody—take this thing! My arms are about to fall off!"

"Do what Mike says!" Peter ordered. "You're going to join the club, *ragazza!*"

Leya tugged and reeled and moaned for ten minutes before Peter, handling the gaff, hooked the beautiful fish in the gill and pulled him up enough for Mike to grasp the bill with a gloved hand and pull the struggling body aboard.

"Oh, *mama mia!* You got yourself a beauty," Peter said in an awed voice. "It'll go seventy pounds."

Heather, who had been coaching from the bridge ladder, immediately went below to fix another round of drinks. Mike glanced around, then stuck his head through the companionway.

"You better ask if they want drinks, huh?"

"Of course they do! It's Leya's first sailfish!"

"Hey, never mind the drinks, Heather," Peter called. "Let's rig up again and go for two. If I have a stuffed sailfish, maybe someday I'll get a fireplace to put it over!"

Mike Parroco put his head inside the cabin again. "They don't want drinks. Understand?"

"Okay, no drinks—for them! So I'll celebrate Leya's big catch!" Heather called up as she poured herself rum and coke.

They trolled north for another hour without a strike. Once, Tony called their attention to a school of dolphin moving across their bow. "They're so beautiful," Leya said. "It's a shame to kill them"

"Unless you want to eat them," Peter added. "When they're out of water, all of that color fades."

Jean, who had been content to nurse a beer and let Peter enjoy himself, roused herself. "Most of us do when we're out of our element," she said dryly.

Off Fort Lauderdale, Tony turned the boat south again. It was nearly four-thirty.

"You do the fishing, Peter," Leya said. "I'm going to relax."

"Come on," Heather said. "Let's go up forward and talk."

Mike Parroco watched as Heather led the way unsteadily along the narrow deck to the bow. Safely forward, Heather took two cushions from the seat locker and propped them against it.

"This is my favorite place," she said a bit thickly. "This is where I like to drink and dream. Have you any idea how thrilling it is for me to come out here alone with just those two torpedoes?" she asked.

Leya turned an alarmed glance toward the flying bridge. In the dusk, she could make out the silhouette of Tony Spacco's head and shoulders above them. "He can hear you," she said in a half whisper.

"Not up there. Anyway, screw him! I want to tell you something."

"What?"

"You know Carlo's always been taking credit for your success, don't you?"

"Of course. I don't mind. In a way, it's true."

"Sure. You'd say that because you're decent. What are you going to say when I tell you that he's going to put money in your new show? A big piece."

"He's going to what?"

"He's backing your musical. Not directly, but through one of his connections."

"How do you know?" Leya demanded, leaning closer in an effort to keep Heather's voice down.

"Remember the old guy at the party that night? Carlo's father?"

"Yes."

"He owns the Midland Distributing Company. They distribute most of the liquor to hotels and clubs in New Jersey. A fellow by the name of Jake Silbert fronts it. He's the one who's covering for the old man."

"But why doesn't Carlo do it himself?"

"Because he never comes out front himself. Neither does dear papa."

"Why does he want to put money in my show?"

"Because he thinks you're lucky for him. He'll put money in the pictures Ed does with you, too. The one Ed's going to do in Vegas is half Romano family money."

"But why are you telling me this, Heather? I don't understand."

"I'm warning you because everything those sons of bitches touch turns to shit! If they put money into Jack Beckman's show, pretty soon Carlo will be telling him what to produce. When these slimy bastards put money into anything, sweetheart, they not only own the money, but they own the people who take it." Heather took Leya's hand. "I'm your friend, Leya. I always have been. That's why I've been pestering you to come out here. Lately, when Carlo thinks I'm in the bag, he and those creeps talk where I can hear."

Thoroughly upset, Leya asked to rejoin the others. In the fading light, as they picked their way aft, neither Leya nor Heather saw Mike Parroco ease the forward cabin swing-out window back into place. Some minutes later, he reappeared on the afterdeck, smiling affably.

"I just talked to the house on the radio, Heather. Carlo's home. He says you must be dying to see him." He laughed roughly.

Something in the older man's remark made Leya shudder.

Mike gave her a concerned look. "You cold? I'll get a sweater."

"I'm fine, thank you, Mike."

"Hey!" he said, suddenly pleased again, "I told Carlo about the fish. He says bring it to him. He's going to have it stuffed and mounted for you. Pretty good, huh?"

Heather's little laugh was bitter. "That's his favorite pasttime, honey—stuffing and mounting poor fish!"

A half hour later, Heather stood in the cockpit saluting Leya and Peter and Jean Genova with her refilled glass as the *Buona Fortuna* pulled away from the public landing and headed up the Indian River to Romano's private dock.

When he saw the three guests get into Genova's little car and drive away, Mike Parroco turned to Heather. "You gotta damn big mouth!"

Heather caught her breath. "Just what does that mean?" she demanded with an unconvincing show of defiance.

"It means you shot off about the money for the kid's show." He smiled when he saw her blanch. "Also, baby, it means you're not gonna shoot off anymore, right?"

"I didn't mean anything, Mike," Heather protested, thoroughly frightened now. "All I did was tell Leya—she's my best friend and Carlo's, too—that he's going to help her with the show. Carlo wants her to know."

"When Carlo wants people to know, he tells them himself! This time, *piccola pesca,* you got big trouble." He measured with his hands to indicate size.

Heather continued to stare at Parroco. She had seen such smiles before—on both Mike and Tony. The last thing reflected in them was humor.

Fear and the enormity of her transgression washed over Heather. She had defied Carlo before—in little things. Lately, her defiance had been more open. A time or two it had become reckless. Later, bruised and hung over, she had understood dimly that she had been driven to rebellion by an urge to precipitate an incident that would free her. Just how she would be freed she was not able to fathom. All but disowned by her family, without Matt now, and without the remotest chance to resume a dance career even as a chorus girl, she refused to think of the consequences.

Liquor helped. If she drank enough, the pain of Carlo's beatings was more bearable. Twice he had knocked her around so viciously that a doctor had been called. The last time, six months earlier, the servants swore that she had fallen down the marble stairs to the foyer. Acting on Carlo's orders, they had carried her down and left her sprawled there. "Afraid to move her until you got here," Carlo had explained to the physician who took care of the family.

"I don't know why you have to say anything to Carlo," Heather said, trying to keep from pleading. "It was only between friends—"

"I tell him everything because he told me to. That's enough!"

Heather stood rigid and trembling. Suddenly, she looked at both men wildly and shrieked, "You dirty fucking spies!" A second later, her glass bounced off his shoulder and shattered on the deck. Parroco's open-handed blow caught her on the side of the head and sent her reeling against the after bulkhead.

Dazed but still on her feet, Heather held her cheek and sucked in short, panicky breaths. When Parroco moved toward her, she cried out and scrambled up on the gunn'l, intending to retreat to the bow. Several uncoordinated steps forward her sandal strap caught in the horn of a large chromed cleat. She cursed and tried to kick it loose. Unable to free it, she jerked her body forward to pull at it, and her temple struck the cabin top handrail. For an instant, she stood dazed with both hands to her head. On the flying bridge, Tony Spacco, reacting to Mike's shout, deliberately spun the helm hard over. An instant later, Heather lost her balance and tumbled backward into the dark water.

The *Buona Fortuna* shuddered as Spacco yanked the twin clutches into reverse and pushed the throttles wide open. Caught off balance, Mike Parroco landed in a sitting position on the cockpit deck as the heavy stern swung through the maelstrom churned up by the flying propellers and passed over the struggling form in the water. Both men heard a muffled scream, and then the engines died and the *Buona Fortuna* lay dead in the water.

"Call the coast guard," Mike Parroco ordered. "I'll call Carlo on the radio phone. He's going to be all busted up about the terrible accident."

* * *

At eight o'clock the following morning, Myra Lieberman called Leya at the apartment.

"Did you hear the radio this morning?" Something in the older woman's voice alerted Leya.

"No. I haven't turned it on. Why?"

"Leya, I hate to be the one to tell you this, but your friend, Heather O'Brien, was drowned last night in the Indian River. It was worse than that. She fell overboard, and apparently she was badly cut up by the propellers." Leya sensed her shudder. "The account was horrible!"

"Oh, my God, Myra!" Leya cried. "Are you sure?"

"I'm positive, my dear."

"But how? She was all right when they let us off at the dock. That's only a few hundred yards from Carlo's place."

"The news didn't give that much detail, Leya. Apparently, she slipped and went overboard in the dark. The medical examiner said there was a gash on her temple that might have come from a fall. He said it could have knocked her unconscious. But she was badly slashed—her legs—and—" Myra broke off, unable to say more.

"Oh, Myra—Myra—she didn't fall!" Leya moaned. "I know she didn't."

"But how could you know?" Myra asked sharply. "If you know anything at all—or if the others do—you had better come over here right away and discuss it with Martin and Arthur."

"The others don't know anything, Myra, and maybe I don't, either, really. Oh, please God, I hope I don't!"

CHAPTER 48

Leya gazed down at the ribbons of light moving along the parkway as her plane prepared to land at LaGuardia. The revulsion that had gripped her through the travesty of a coroner's inquest and Carlo Romano's tears had turned to cold anger. When Carlo had embraced her and made a bid for sympathy after the findings, it had taken all of her self-control to keep from shouting, "Murderer!"

On the stand, she had followed Hubert Schlosberg's advice and answered with minimum honesty. So had Peter and Jean, who had corroborated the testimony that they had been returned to shore some minutes before the accident.

The newspapers made the most of the story. It had all of the ingredients—a well-known underworld figure, his mistress, the mistress's glamorous movie-star "best friend." It was all there, with pictures and facts dredged up from the morgue, including shots of Ed and Leya "in happier days."

Sickened, Leya had called Billy and Harold Bornstein and announced her intention to come in, whatever the risk of her residence requirement. A supporting telegram had been sent to "call her back on business."

When she came through the arrival gate, Leya saw that Billy had brought along Howard Pryor.

In the taxi on the way to Jack Beckman's office, both men

analyzed the situation for her. They found the recent publicity both good and bad. For a time, she listened patiently.

"All right?" she said finally. "You've told me how you feel about things. The whole crappy mess will seem glamorous to the 'fan mag set,' and my reputation won't be hurt as long as my nose is clean! I know all that. I thank you for trying to make me feel better. But you two and Jack and Harold are going to hear how I feel when we get to his office. And you may not like it!"

A half hour later, in Jack Beckman's office, facing Billy, Howard, and Harold Bornstein, Leya exploded her booby trap. Turning to Jack, she said, "Do you know a man named Jake Silbert?"

"I do. Why?"

"How do you know him?"

The producer looked mystified. "I got to him through normal money-raising channels."

"Don't you mean, he got to you?"

There was a trace of annoyance on Beckman's face. "He called me. That's right. A mutual friend asked him to."

"Do you know who he is?"

"Of course. He's president of Midland Distributing, one of the most successful liquor dealerships in New Jersey."

"Do you know who owns Midland?"

Beckman's annoyance increased. "Look Leya, I don't know why we're playing Twenty Questions. Suppose you tell me who runs Midland if Silbert doesn't!"

"Carlo Romano and his father *own* it! Silbert's a front. Carlo's using him to buy into this show. Has he—yet?"

A charged silence followed before Jack Beckman answered. "No, he hasn't—yet. But I want to know how you know all of this?"

"Leya," Harold Bornstein cautioned, "we know how you feel, honey, but the implications are—"

"They're not implications!" Leya shot back. "They are facts. Carlo also owns a piece of the picture Ed wants me to do in Vegas, the one I refused to do. Heather told me he thinks I'm a lucky property."

Jack Beckman wandered over to look down on the Fifty-seventh Street traffic. "So," he said, "what this adds up to is an edict that I cannot take the sixty thousand dollars—twelve units—that Silbert has said he'd buy. Right?"

"No, you can take it, Jack," Leya replied, "if Mr. Silbert wants to back the show with somebody else in the lead."

"Leya," Billy cut in, "we have a contract with Jack. There's nothing in it that gives us the right to dictate where his backing comes from."

"I know that. And there's nothing in it, either, that says I can't break a leg." She looked at each in turn. "I have never broken a contract. But I will not set foot in rehearsal hall or theater if one penny of that murdering bastard's money is in the production. None of you has ever heard an ultimatum from me before. But you're hearing one now."

Billy walked over to Leya's chair. "Heather told you this—on the boat. Right?"

"Yes. She spelled it all out because she has always wanted to be my friend . . ." Leya lowered her head. "That friendship—and, God forgive me, lately it was one-sided, really—cost her her life."

"That's only an assumption, Leya," Bornstein said gently.

"It is a fact!"

"But not a provable one?"

"Not in court, probably, but God knows it's true!"

A heavy silence again settled over the room. All four men knew that it was not unusual for money of doubtful origin to end up in shows. In a practical sense, it was none of the star's business so long as the terms of the contract were fulfilled. But Leya clearly felt the present circumstances were different.

Jack Beckman went around to his desk and pulled a sheaf of papers from a pile. He studied them briefly, then looked up.

"If we're going to meet our theater commitments in Philadelphia and here—and we've got air-cooled theaters in both places—we have to be in rehearsal in three weeks. That means that I've got exactly one week to get the rest of the money in—after I lie to Silbert and tell him he's too late." He gave them all a grave look. "And if Leya is right, that may not be the easiest thing I've ever had to do."

"What are the figures now, Jack?" Pryor asked.

"What they were yesterday. We have sixty thousand to go—twelve units—not counting the overcall."

"Was Silbert your only possibility?"

"He was my best one."

Howard Pryor rose and massaged his neck. "There are some days," he said, "when I should be examined for mental incompetence. But there are other days when it may be wise for I.A.M. to invest in its own business." He grinned at a recollection. "I was nearly fired ten years ago for suggesting that we help finance a couple of bands. The two band singers alone have made us a million dollars in commissions since then. So—" He drew in a breath. "I.A.M. will pick up the last four units—twenty thousand dollars—if you can come up with the rest."

The producer beamed. Billy Brenner and Harold Bornstein tried not to look too pleased.

"Thank you, Howard," Leya said, "for *two* votes of confidence."

A call came while Leya was having breakfast in her room at the Gotham. It was Dulcy.

"Good God, dear heart," she shrilled, "I've called all over creation to find you. How long are you going to be in town?"

"I'm going back tomorrow. Where are you?"

"Here. In New York. In my new apartment. I bought a co-op on East Seventy-second Street and the river. Wait 'til you see it! How about lunch? I'm dying to hear about all that *magillah* in Miami." Leya heard her gasp. "I'm sorry, sweetie. That was an unfortunate way to put it. Anyway, can you? Say yes!"

The "new apartment" occupied the entire top floor of the building, with terraces overlooking Seventy-second Street on the south and the river on the east.

"A mere bag of shells," Dulcy joked as she led Leya through eight lavishly furnished rooms. Here and there she recognized familiar works of art—early gifts from Willie Four.

"I may get used to being confined like this after a while," Dulcy said with comic hauteur, "that is, if my two maids stay out from under foot. Oh, yes—and the governess, too. Cawn't stand gov'nesses. Only governors!" She broke into laughter and hugged Leya.

"God, it's good to see you! I've got to gab with you every once in a while just to keep in touch with reality."

Over lunch, Leya recounted everything she could safely confide about her relationship with Ed and the mess in Florida.

"So," Dulcy summed up, "because you're a little picky about how filthy the lucre is, you may get hung up?"

"So it seems. But I'm sure, with Howard putting up the last third, they'll come up with the rest of the money. Anyway, we're going ahead with the rehearsal."

Dulcy studied Leya. "Are you really high on the book?"

"I think it's solid." She blinked thoughtfully. "Certainly the composers have done a fine job."

"Well, sweetie," Dulcy said, "if you're sure, give it all you've got, and on opening night I'll buy out the first ten rows and give the tickets to friends. How's that?"

Leya laughed. "Just make sure they have big hands!"

"They'll all be flamenco dancers. They can clap like hell!" Dulcy saw the little frown return, and her eyes grew serious.

"One thing you and I have never done is crap each other, dear heart. I'm going to ask you once more. Is getting back to the stage the thing you really want to do?"

Leya's frown deepened. "I've missed contact with live audiences. They give me something—as a performer."

"I understand that. Are you going to have to torture yourself to get in shape again? What about your knee?"

Leya inclined her head. "It's okay. I've never really stopped taking class. It should be all right." She laughed lightly.

"To be perfectly honest, I think I may be looking forward to the rehearsals—that whole scene—even more than I am to the actual performances." She shrugged. "I guess that'll change when we get the thing on its feet."

The two friends chatted until the Dutch governess, a

scrubbed, efficient-appearing woman in her early fifties, came in with Gwendolyn.

Leya was enchanted by the four-year-old. Her hair was darker than Dulcy's, but she had the same heart-shaped face, the same incredibly blue kitten eyes, and a perfectly proportioned little body.

"For the first time," Leya exclaimed, "I know what they mean by a living doll. She's beautiful!"

Gwendolyn went to her "Aunt Leya" and offered herself for an embrace. It was the first time Leya had ever held a child. She wondered at the pleasure of it and understood something of the joy her father and Minnie must have known when she had come running to their arms.

"You really are her 'aunt' you know," Dulcy said.

"I'm flattered! It's a wonderful feeling." Leya looked down to meet Gwendolyn's curious gaze, then gave her an impulsive kiss. "I'll try to be a good aunt, but I haven't had much practice."

Dulcy laughed. "Look at her expression. You're doing just fine."

Leya spent a half hour playing with Gwendolyn. The child insisted on presenting for her approval most of the dolls and toys in her closet. There were more of them for one child, Leya thought, than there had been in the entire orphan's home.

When the nurse came to put Gwendolyn down for her nap, Leya lingered talking in the hall for a few minutes. In the doorway, Dulcy gave her an impulsive hug. "You should try for one of those little dolls sometime, sweetie. They're fun!"

That night Leya dined with the Brenners. Celine was beginning to show.

"She's been hanging around Lane Bryant lately," Billy joked.

"You mean Omar the Tent Maker!" Celine retorted.

Much of the conversation with Celine centered on their early ballet days and the demands it made. Toward the end of the meal, Billy laughed. "You two remind me of two combat veterans trying to convince each other that war wasn't really hell."

When they parted later at the hotel, Billy detained Leya. "Relax about the money. Jack and I are the most incurable optimists you'll ever meet. I'll call you tomorrow."

At eleven-thirty the next morning, when Leya returned from shopping, there were two messages—one from Jack Beckman and a later one from Billy Brenner. She called the producer first.

"We've sold four more units," Jack said, "but I want to make certain you have no objection to the new source."

"What is it?"

"Originally, it came from gun-running, hijacking Cornwallis's payroll, a little slaving, and a few other perfectly acceptable pursuits."

Leya was annoyed. "Come on, Jack. Be serious. Who's offering to put up the money?"

"No offering—Has put it up—with your approval, of course,"

"Well, tell me, damn it!"

Jack Beckman laughed. "We received a promise this morning from a very well-to-do *nouveau riche* lady named Vandercort. Mrs. William, the Fourth."

"Dulcy?" Leya half shouted the name. "Did she offer to put up the money?"

"She did, and that's just about the most respectable money you can get these days."

"Oh, my God!" Leya moaned. In the midst of the obvious evidence of Dulcy's new affluence, it had not occurred to her, even remotely, to ask for help. Her explanation of the situation must have seemed like a hint to her friend!

"You sound troubled, Leya. What's the matter?"

"Nothing. Listen, Jack, I'm sorry but I've got to make an important call. Talk to you later, okay?"

Dulcy answered her private number immediately. "Will you stop trying to cop out, dear heart? You're going to have a hit. My tax people tell me I'm crazy to bet on a sure thing.

Losses are much more profitable for me now. But you know me, the kid who could never do things right! God bless, Leya! I mean it."

Leya kept trying to interrupt. Finally, she managed to blurt, "Dulcy, I don't know what to say."

"Don't say anything. If you feel you have to thank somebody, thank God that Willie had reasonable lawyers!"

Arthur met Leya at the airport in Miami It was the first time he had driven alone. When she saw him standing by the arrival gate, she broke into a run and threw herself into his arms. Unmindful of the smiles of recognition and the risk, she continued to kiss him until he drew away laughing.

"You're going to send me into a relapse," he chided. "Besides, I really shouldn't be so delighted to see you after what you've done to the Liebermans. You know you've got trouble, don't you?"

Leya leaned away, frowning. "What sort of trouble?"

"Serious trouble—because you never once hinted that the show was coming up short of money."

"Of course not. That's the producer's worry, not mine."

"Sweetheart, one of the cardinal principles of survival is that family helps family. While it may be a touch premature, you are regarded as such—with benevolent prejudice and without the right of appeal."

On the day the divorce was final, Peter and Jean Genova joined Leya at the Liebermans' beach-front home.

After dinner, the six of them retired to the patio for coffee. Martin produced a large Manila envelope and placed it on Leya's lap.

"I thought this might interest you," he said.

Puzzled, Leya opened the flap and removed a sheaf of legal papers. A moment later, she gasped and let the papers fall atop the envelope.

"How did you manage this?" she asked.

"Influence, darling," Martin said. "You didn't think we wouldn't have at least a rooting interest, did you?" His look was reproachful. "You should have a spanking for not telling us."

Leya picked up the papers again. Half aloud she read, "One unit for Mr. and Mrs. Martin Lieberman, two units for Mr. Arthur Lieberman, one unit for Mr. and Mrs. Bert Farber—"

"Oh, my Lord," she whispered.

Myra Lieberman laughed softly. "Spare us the 'you shouldn't have done its,' dear. We wouldn't have it any other way!"

Later, after the Genovas had gone, and Martin and Myra had retired to leave them alone, Arthur and Leya walked along the beach.

"I really should be out there swimming like a madman," Arthur said, "and you should be wading along with your skirt pulled up and tucked into your belt trying to keep up."

"I'll never keep up with you Liebermans!" Leya replied, laughing. Some yards farther along the tidal pack, she stopped, turned Arthur to her, and gazed up at him with a pensive smile. "Can I tell you something that's been happening to me the last few days?"

Arthur reached out and held her gently. "By all means, as long as it doesn't have anything negative to do with you and me."

Leya glanced down. "It does have something to do with us, Arthur. But I don't think it's negative."

"Well then say it, sweetheart."

"It's just this. For some damned silly reason that I really don't understand, I'm not all that keen on doing Jack's musical."

The confession took Arthur by surprise. "Well, that is a bit of a shock, darling. Any idea why you have cooled all of a sudden?"

"I think so." She looked at him intently. "It's not because I dislike any of the people, or the book or anything. I think the show could be a winner. It's just that—that—"

Arthur pulled her closer. "That you're still suffering from the ballet bug bite?"

Leya lowered her head. "Yes. That's it. I'm afraid I'm never really going to be satisfied until I find out what my chances are on the classical concert stage. I've never ever gotten that notion out of my stupid head, not even in Hollywood." She looked up, appealing. "I know my timing stinks, dearest, but I'm sure that I'll never know any peace if I don't do everything I can to find out about me."

"In short, you want to go back and prove something that Madame Baronova knew years ago. That you have it in you to be a prima ballerina?" He shook his head. "Leya, in God's name, you don't have to prove that. What do you think you've been doing, fancy skating?"

"I've been dancing, Arthur. But it's been a mixed bag—ballet, character, ethnic, romantic, modern—not true classical ballet."

"Maybe not, but your dancing was serious enough to make you a star in pictures. How much more reassurance do you need?"

"Look, Arthur—" Leya was more certain now. "From the time I took those first dance lessons, with Mrs. Zuckerman counting out her 'one—two—three—fours,' I have dreamed of being a ballerina. I thought I'd found another way to go in concert—with Kent and the rest of the kids. When Paramount picked up my option, I thought I'd found still another way to go.

"Then, when I was blocking the new show with Peter and Jean, we 'clowned' a little on the break. We put on some recordings—'The Blue Danube,' Schumann's score for *Le Carnival,* Stravinsky's *Fire Bird,* and Weber's score for *Le Spectre de la Rose.* We tried to remember some of the choreography. Somehow, as rusty as we were, we all sensed the depth and the quality that make the difference between classical dancing and"—she shrugged—"the stuff we've been doing. Suddenly, the rest of it seemed thin and too easy, I guess. We all felt it. But it stayed with me. It was dim for a while, but it's always been in here." She indicated her middle.

In the half light, she could read Arthur's concern, and his confusion, too.

"Are you saying you want to cop out on this musical and go back to ballet school to see if you can still make it to the top?" he asked.

"Yes. That's it. And I know what everybody will say. That I'm throwing away a great chance. I'm too old, I've been away too long, I'm a fool even to consider it."

Arthur brought her close again and rested his chin atop her head. "Do you think you're too old, or that you've been away too long, or that you'd be a fool to try?"

"No, I don't think so. I've never really stopped taking class. When Kent was alive, we worked every day. Tamara Toumanova, Irina Baranova, Maria Tallchief, Vera Zorina—" She broke off. "My God! Martha Graham, too! They're all older than I am, and they're at their peaks. There's still time. I'm sure of it. I have the energy, and now I have the money for the hardest part of it, the private tutoring that I'll need to get up on the proper roles."

Leya sighed. "Yes, Arthur. I want to try. If the show is a hit, and I have a run-of-the-play contract, too much time will have gone by."

He held her quietly before he moved away. "There are some problems for Beckman, you know. Money's been committed."

"How well I know! That's why I haven't been able to make myself spell out the truth. But the money's not really the problem, darling. The backers' money hasn't been spent yet."

"Jack Beckman's spent a lot of dollars developing the property. He has signed commitments."

"Jack's only got about twenty thousand dollars out of pocket—all told. I'll be more than happy to pay him back."

Arthur looked at her closely. "Are you concerned about what Jack and Billy will think?"

"Yes. But I'm really a lot more worried about what you will think and what I'll think of myself."

Arthur's smile was reassuring. "Nothing could change what I think of you. And to be brutal about it, darling, the others don't count."

"I'm being selfish, aren't I?" Leya asked.

"No more than I am," Arthur replied. "You see, darling, I don't want to go through life with a wife who never stops wondering what would have happened if she had found the courage to do what she had always really wanted to do."

Leya snuggled her cheek against his chest. "Thank you, Arthur, but there is someone else, too."

"Who?"

"Ed."

"What about him?"

"I promised I'd do everything possible to see that he produced the picture version of *Lola,* with me in the leading role, if Jack Beckman didn't want to do it in films himself. I owe him a picture."

"You owe Paramount a picture, Leya. You don't owe Ed Matson one damned thing. Realistically, if you decide to go back to ballet, Paramount may be very happy to forget about that contract."

"What if they're not?"

"Billy Brenner is better qualified to answer that. But if they want you, they'll have to take you as a ballerina. There's precedent enough for that. Mia Slawenska and Moira Shearer, for instance." He cradled her cheek in his palm. "Let's take one thing at a time, darling. Remember, from here on out, if there's any trouble, to get at you they've got to get by me first."

Leya studied Arthur. How she loved that face! All the more, if possible, because she read no censure in it.

In New York, the following week, Leya told Dulcy first. The news was accepted with her friend's usual humor.

"Good!" Dulcy said. "I'll set the money aside to send condolence cards to Zorina and the others. If you have enough guts to give up what's waiting for you on Broadway, they're going to need all the sympathy they can get. Good luck, dear heart, and keep me posted."

Jack Beckman paced his office, trying hard to contain his anger. Billy Brenner sat glumly at the end of the desk, ready to take Leya's part if necessary. In the end, Jack dismissed Leya's offer to reimburse him for expenses already incurred. He stopped pacing long enough to gesture impatiently. "You're not the only kid in town who can use a tax writeoff, you know!"

Leya's greatest concern was for Peter and Jean. She persuaded Billy to represent them as both performers and choreographers, and Beckman indicated his continuing interest in Peter. Leya felt certain that he would use Genova in his next production, which quite probably would be *Lola* with a new female lead. Despite their protests, she insisted on paying the couple generously for the time they had spent with her in Miami.

"I wish I had your guts, Leya," Peter said. "I know damned well that in the end I'll wish I'd stayed with the classics. Trouble is, both Jean and I have gotten into the habit of eating regularly. But you know you've got our blessing. Who's going to understand better than a gypsy?"

Their reassurances were comforting. Even so, Leya suffered second thoughts, uncertainties, questions about the odds she was accepting in place of a sure thing, how she would react if she did make it into Mikail Khazar's new National Ballet, only to be badly reviewed—an obstacle that might make a successful comeback impossible.

She missed Kent Kendall. His counsel about a tutor would have been valuable now. Finally, it was Celine who pointed to the obvious.

"Call Madame Baronova. I'm certain she will be delighted to make a suggestion."

From time to time, when Leya had thought of Alexandra Baronova, it was only as a part of her own yesterdays.

"I wonder if she is living in the same place?" she asked.

"Probably," Celine replied, "and still deploring the lack of 'old-fashioned hard work' and discipline in young American dancers."

"Oh, God," Leya groaned. "I wonder if I can face that again."

Celine laughed. "When you and I are her age; we'll be

deploring the sloppiness of the new generation of dancers, too. *C'est la vie—toujours!* Call her."

Leya smiled as the deep, heavily accented voice—a bit more raspish now—came over the line with such force that she was obliged to hold the receiver away. When she explained she needed some advice, the old ballet mistress invited her down to tea.

Alexandra Baronova, more dependent than ever on her cane, surprised Leya with an eager one-arm embrace. The little apartment was an orderly clutter of memorabilia from sixty years of ballet. Photos lined the walls and stood in ranks on the tables. Leya recognized autographed portraits of Serge Lifar, Frederick Ashton, George Balanchine, Leonid Massine, Max Ree, Leon Bakst, Alicia Markova, Anton Dolin, and a huge, gold-framed signed photograph of Anna Pavlova.

"Sit down, Leya," the ballet mistress ordered, "and try to ignore my infirmities." She pointed to the cane resting beside her on the sofa. "I used to use this to rap ankles. Now I use it to keep my own ankles in order."

When Leya settled in the worn brocade chair at the end of the sofa, Madame Baronova reached for the eyeglasses dangling on her bosom, pulled down the little chain reel, and held them to the bridge of her nose.

"You're how old? Midtwenties now?" Before Leya could respond, she nodded. "You still look like a baby! Now, then, what do you want to talk about?"

For several minutes, Leya reviewed her own activities. The old ballet mistress dismissed her recital with an impatient wave. "I've seen those pictures. Trifling stories. But you danced well. Kent Kendall was an exceptional talent. He might have been a great choreographer, like our young Jerome Robbins, had he stayed where he belonged—in classic dance. Instant fame. Instant money. I think of the O'Brien girl, too. Tragic! That is always the trouble. Instant everything!"

"I'm sure you still believe that is what made me leave class, too," Leya said. "Perhaps when I tell you why I'm here, you'll believe me—at last."

"Tell me!" Madame Baronova gestured impatiently.

"I want to know two things. Is it too late for me to return to the ballet in important roles, and if it is not, can you recommend a coach who will work with me, ten hours a day if necessary, to get me up on some of the roles I'll need?"

Leya expected the old ballet mistress to be surprised. Instead, her expression scarcely changed. "I will tell you one thing at the outset, young lady. It is probably too late for you to aspire to be a *danseuse étoile.* Antole Chujoy put it very well when he described Pavlova as 'the sum total of a divine talent, an active mind, a perfect body, a highly developed technique, and superb craftsmanship.' " She cocked her head and regarded Leya critically. "You have a near-perfect body, you have the mind and the talent, but you no longer have the time to refine and refine your dancing until you become a superb craftsman."

She smiled when she saw Leya's crestfallen expression. Gently, she added, "A prima ballerina—very likely. But I cannot say for certain until I see you dance."

Leya brightened. "If I hired a studio and an accompanist and came by for you myself and brought you home, could you possibly watch me and let me have your opinion?"

Madame Baronova seemed about to refuse. Then she straightened and lifted her head almost regally. "Of course I can. Age may make my bones brittle, but it has not impaired my judgment. Make the arrangements." She leaned forward to pull the tea glasses closer. "Now, while we have tea, tell me about that altogether unlikely place, Southern California. I am opposed to it"—her eyes twinkled—"with an open mind, of course."

Leya could find no free studio time at Carnegie Hall. Billy Brenner's office found her an accompanist and an acceptable rehearsal studio on Eighth Avenue near Fifty-third Street.

When the limousine driver helped Madame Baronova from the car and up the stairs to the second floor, the old lady wrinkled her nose. "This place smells of African contortions and the tap dancing!"

In spite of herself, Leya laughed. "It's the floor and the piano I'm worried about."

Her worries were unfounded. The accompanist had been rehearsal pianist for a number of Broadway shows, the upright piano was old but in tune, and the floor, the barre, and the mirrors were excellent. There was even a relatively clean, comfortable chair, provided by the manager at Leya's suggestion.

During the fifteen minutes of barre, Madame Baronova sat with both hands resting atop her cane, concealing her reactions. Leya Marks had indeed been doing her work. Little things in classical styling would need work. Her "line" in the *grande quatrième effacé,* on point, with her pulled-down shoulder, erect spine, and well-arched foot would have been perfect had she managed more roundness in the curve of her arm and if her hip had not been raised ever so slightly in the *arabesque allongée*—but all in all, extraordinarily good.

For an hour, Madame Baronova, calling sharply from her chair, ordered Leya to do progressively more difficult combinations. Finally, when Leya puffed her cheeks, expelled a long breath, and collapsed with an apologetic laugh, the ballet mistress rapped her cane on the floor. "All right! Stop now."

Responding to her signal to come closer, Leya knelt down in front of her, blotting at her forehead, cheeks, and neck. Her practice clothes were soaked.

"You have not lost as much as I expected, Leya. There are things that need work, particularly on point. You will need many weeks of hard work—in class. You should have a partner—perhaps two."

"That's no problem, madame. I'm sure I can get Peter Genova and his wife, Jean Baxter, to work with me."

"I remember them. They'll do very well—for the time being."

Leya rose and picked the soggy black wool away from her chest. "I suppose I would be dreaming to think that I might be lucky enough to have you keep an eye on us."

The old ballet mistress let her gaze wander around the studio. She loved the spartan surroundings—the polished floors, the expanses of mirror, the barres, the hardwood rails, polished to a gleaming patina by the perspiration of ten thousand palms—and the smell of sweat and resin and the muted protests as students twisted and stretched muscles to positions the Good Lord had never intended to demand of any—except a special breed! How very much she had missed it!

"I am retired. I've done no coaching for three years."

"I know, madame. I'm selfish to ask."

"I'm grateful that you did, child. At any age, but especially at mine, nothing is more reassuring than to be needed. Petipa was still coaching at eighty something—a year before he died in nineteen ten. So—I shall try. But I shall ask two things."

"Anything—of course," Leya replied eagerly.

"My poor old bones will have to be hauled back and forth each day, and after we have had some time together, you must tell me as honestly as I promise to tell you, whether or not you think we are working together usefully."

Leya dropped to her knees again and caught the old ballet mistress in an impulsive hug. "Thank you, madame!"

Alexandra Baronova held up a warning finger. "Do not thank me yet, Leya! If you think I worked you unmercifully when you were in my Balanchine classes, wait until you see what I will require of you if you are to get up in three or four solos and *pas de deux*. You may hate me again!"

CHAPTER 49

Leya and Arthur returned to New York with Martin and Myra Lieberman during the first week in May. Peter and Jean Genova, grateful to be a part of Leya's new plans, preceded them by a week and took an apartment at London Terrace. As tactfully as she could, Leya sidestepped her family's repeated suggestions that she live with them until Arthur had recovered completely and a time could be set for the wedding. To ensure her privacy, she took a furnished sublet on Sixty-third Street just off Fifth Avenue.

The news of Leya's decision to abandon her movie career at its apex for an uncertain future as a classical and modern ballet dancer had leaked despite Jack Beckman's efforts to keep it under wraps until he could assess his own alternatives. That he would do a show he did not question. Beckman knew that the right vehicle can make a star, and he did not question the star-making potential of *Lola.* He accepted the inevitable and began looking.

Billy Brenner kept his disappointment to himself. Celine was frankly delighted that Leya was going back to her "first true love."

"I'm not making a bad pun, darling," she said. Only a few hours later, her water broke, and Billy rushed her to New

York Lying-In Hospital. There, six hours later, she was delivered of William Reese Brenner, Junior, seven pounds, fourteen ounces.

Ed Matson was less than philosophical when he called New York to have the rumor of Leya's decision confirmed by Howard Pryor.

"Breach of contract is actionable, Howard!" he shouted over the long-distance line. "Leya has a contract with Paramount."

"Has any money been paid under the contract, Ed?"

"You know it hasn't, Howard. But that's beside the point. The picture is penciled in for this fall."

"And pencils have erasers," Pryor replied mildly. "I've known you for a good many years, Ed. We've made money together, and we will again. So I know that you have been aware for some time that no dancing star on any lot—with two possible exceptions—is really an asset now."

"I'm not debating that, Howard. But I've been bringing Leya along as a versatile dancer who can sing, too. The Beckman show could have established her as a major Broadway star. That would have put a different complexion on things out here. Don't you agree?"

"Possibly," Pryor said thoughtfully. "But don't ever underestimate a girl with as much drive as Leya has. She doesn't make much fuss about it, but she knows where she wants to go now."

"You're dreaming, Howard. She's too old. She'll never make it to the top in classical ballet."

"One thing I've learned, Ed. Clichés get to be clichés because they have a solid core of truth in them. That's why I never say 'never.' "

"Well I say 'never' because I know how long she laid off between pictures."

"But you don't know how hard she's working now. She's hired her old ballet mistress and Peter and Jean Genova. The old lady is telling her she can make it."

"The old lady is conning a meal ticket!"

"That may be, Ed. But I'm going to bet that by now Leya Leslie knows a con job when she hears one."

"And just what the hell does that mean, my friend?" Ed Matson snapped.

"Nothing personal," Howard Pryor laughed. "Just one of those clichés. In any case, my advice to you is not to do anything drastic yet. I still say the studio may be relieved not to have to meet that commitment now. And if she does get where she wants to go as a ballerina, it just might be that you've got a better property after all, one that can move in new directions. I'll smooth things out contract-wise at the Paramount Building and keep you as the producer if she works out as a prima ballerina with picture possibilities. I think she'd want that, anyway, for reasons of conscience."

"She goddamned well should be having some trouble with her conscience!" Matson snapped.

Howard Pryor laughed easily again. "You've just set yourself up for another cliché—the one about glass houses and stones."

By early summer, Jack Beckman, with I.A.M.'s help, had found his new star, a talented young red-headed singer from Wenatchee, Washington, who was a more competent vocalist than dancer. The score was revised and the staging modified to strengthen the vocal solos for the *Lola* character and "trick" the choreography around her to minimize her need to dance.

When Howard Pryor came to Leya to say that he could set Peter Genova and his wife as choreographer and assistant in the Beckman show, Leya released them, happy that their good fortune was also her own. Madame Baronova had said that the time had come to find an older male partner who was well up on principal roles.

In mid-September, *Lola* went out of town for its tryouts in New Haven and Philadelphia. The first reviews were encouraging. Only one paper commented on Leya Leslie's absence:

> While it is unlikely that in her lifetime Lola Montez danced any better—indeed, as well as the talented young singer from the Apple State—one cannot help but

speculate on the added excitement a Leya Leslie would have imparted to the role despite a lesser voice, especially when one recalls her sensuous performances as the temptress in "Oneida" when she was prima ballerina of the old Kendall group.

Lola opened in New York the week before Thanksgiving. Arthur and Leya took the Lieberman family, Harry and Minnie, Madame Baronova, and Billy and Celine as their guests. By intermission, it was clear that Jack Beckman had reinforced his reputation as a successful producer.

Peter Genova had worked a small miracle with Martha White, the twenty-year-old soprano whose prior experience had been some civic light opera in Seattle and San Francisco. Jean danced in the company with Marc Bright, Luanna Parker, and Tanya Kuznetsov. The other seven boys and six girls were among the most competent new gypsies Leya had ever seen. Peter's reputation on Broadway would be firmly established now.

On the way out after the final curtain, Leya saw Howard Pryor and Ed Matson standing at the end of the lobby talking with Jack Beckman. She released Arthur's arm. "Do you mind, darling? I want to just say hello."

"Of course not. We'll wait for you outside," Arthur replied.

Pryor saw Leya edging her way through the first-nighters, many of whom turned to stare in recognition. He came to meet her and linked her arm. *Sotto voce,* he said, "I don't think Ed's going to be hocking you about that Paramount contract! Keep it to yourself, but he and Jack are working out a co-production deal on the show."

"Thank God!" Leya breathed.

The encounter was strained. It was difficult to shake hands and attempt platitudes with a man you had slept with, a man to whom you owed one career and now the freedom to pursue still another.

Jack Beckman slipped an arm around her and smiled a bit smugly. "Aren't you just a little sorry that you're not up there in that title role?"

Leya returned his smile and patted his cheek. "No—if you're not, Jack dear."

Amiable laughter made the parting easier.

The following afternoon, in the rehearsal hall, Madame Baronova drew Leya aside. "The show is excellent, dear. But there is no question that Lola would have been much stronger if you had played her. I did not sleep well last night wondering whether you might be having regrets about your decision." Her eyes searched Leya's. "Tell me the truth, child."

Leya was amused. "Madame, every aching joint, every aching muscle, every 'Good! Good!' confirms the rightness of my decision! That show with its out-of-town tryouts? The run on Broadway? Eight performances a week, possibly for two hundred weeks? And then the road again?" She shook her head violently. "No, thank you! I'm precisely where I want to be, and I mean to hold you to your promise to set up an audition for me with Mikail Khazar for a place in his National Ballet Company—if he's still interested, and you think I'm ready."

"I shall, Leya." But Alexandra Baronova continued to question Leya with her eyes.

"What is it, madame? Why do you look at me so?"

"Leya, you are one of the most talented dancers and one of the most beautiful young women I have known. But you are a woman in love."

When Leya did not respond immediately, a knowing smile softened the old ballet mistress's angular, time-seamed face. "Does it surprise you that once I was a young woman who knew love? I did, you know. And like your Arthur, my loved one was not a dancer, not of my world. So—I know this temptation, Leya, and the price of resisting it."

"You are thinking of Celine, too, aren't you, madame?"

The older woman inclined her head. "And of the O'Brien girl. And dozens of other talented girls through the years who thought they had made the right choice, only to discover that they had not."

"I made a wrong choice—remember?" Leya replied softly. "And so did Arthur. But we understand ourselves now, and we understand each other. There has been more than enough time to think through to the truth."

"And enough love and courage to speak the complete truth to one another?" Madame Baronova asked.

"Yes. That too."

"You realize that because you attained your stardom on the screen, not on the classical concert stage, the critics will not be as generous to you as they were to Vera Zorina or to Mia Slawenska?"

"I'm prepared for that."

Madame Baronova smiled sadly. "I wonder if an artist really is—ever?" she gestured impatiently. "Well, never mind that for now."

"I'm sure," Leya said, "they'll discount the fact that for seventeen years I have trained and trained and trained, that even during the pictures I never really stopped ballet class—or modern or jazz. The Ballet Russe dancers are just beginning to study modern and jazz now. I've had five years of such discipline."

"I'm not so certain, my little Leya, that those dance forms have helped you with the classic disciplines. That remains to be seen!"

"But you and Eddie Caton and Maracci gave me my foundation. It is in my blood now, madame! I might never have gone to pictures if there had been an opportunity in classic ballet when I was ready to try. The world turned upside down then. I did what I *had* to do! And I'm determined, once again, to do what I have to. Only this time I will not compromise. And when the time comes, I will accept your verdict. You believe that, don't you, madame?"

Alexandra Baronova did not answer immediately, for now she was reassessing her own position. Age had overtaken her body, but her mind, her perception of talent, the excitement of helping it develop and flower, all that remained undiminished. And why should she not try one last time?

This Marks girl, with her talent and her training, quite

possibly could command the perquisites of stardom again—this time on the concert stage. And she, Alexandra Baronova, could share in the acclamation and in the satisfaction of having been right.

Leya's hopeful expression gave way to concern when she saw the older woman's lips compress into a familiar line. Suddenly, Madame Baronova's knobby fingers tightened around the golden head of the Malacca staff, and she rapped it sharply on the polished hardwood practice floor.

"So, Miss Marks," she said, in the commanding tone that echoed decades of authority, "if you are ready, let us go to work."

An hour later, in her apartment, Leya reached Arthur.

"Darling," she said, "Madame Baronova apparently does not think I'm hopeless. A bit nutty, perhaps, but not too far gone."

"She's agreed to coach you, then?"

"Until I need other help to get up in certain roles that she'll recommend."

Leya heard his satisfied chuckle. "I'm as happy as you are, darling! Go after it, sweetheart! Give it your best try! We can afford the liniment and the masseurs, and nobody in this world will be prouder of you than I when—not *if*—but *when*—you make it!"

After promising to be ready to go to his family's for dinner by seven-thirty, Leya hung up. Suddenly, she laughed her happiest laugh. Moving to the center of the room, she did an uninhibited triple pirouette on demi-point.

Standing on a trestle table against the wall, she saw the music-box ballerina, which would always be her most treasured possession. Frowning severely, she wound it carefully and returned it to its place.

"I'm not so certain, my little Leya, that those dance forms have helped you with the classic disciplines," she said in a voice approximating Madame Baronova's. "That remains to be seen!" She reached over then, started the dancing doll, and rapped the table top sharply. "So, Miss Marks," she repeated. "If you are ready, let us go to work!"